A JOHN CATT PUBLICATION

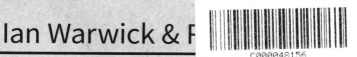

Ian Warwick & P

Learning with Leonardo
Unfinished Perfection

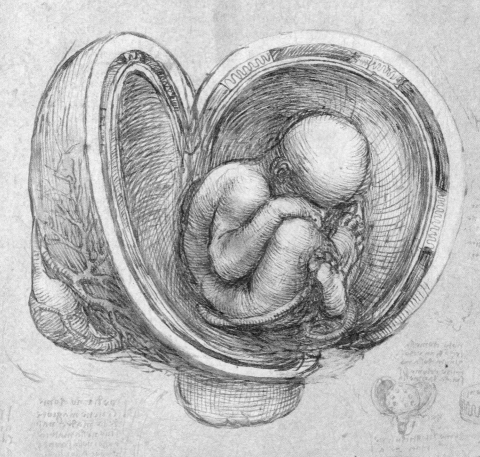

First published 2019

by John Catt Educational Ltd,
15 Riduna Park, Station Road,
Melton, Woodbridge IP12 1QT

Tel: +44 (0) 1394 389850 Fax: +44 (0) 1394 386893
Email: enquiries@johncatt.com
Website: www.johncatt.com

ISBN: 978 1 911382 97 3

Set and designed by John Catt Educational Limited

With heartfelt thanks to our ever-supportive families and to all those colleagues and students we have learned from over the years.

CONTENTS

CHAPTER INTRODUCTIONS

CHAPTER 1

CONSCIOUS IGNORANCE

Developing a beginner's mind

'You shall no longer take things at third or second hand, not look through the eyes of the dead, nor feed on the spectres in books. You shall not look through my eyes either, nor take things from me, you shall listen to all sides and filter them from yourself.'

These words from Walt Whitman launch an exchange of ideas with Leonardo in a way that he would have wanted, predicated on a commitment to adopt, as he did, 'a beginner's mind', to break up our familiarities and to question what we think we know and believe. This first chapter is not only an introduction to Leonardo and his long-ago lifetime, it is also a prelude to the way we think about the present, lifetimes to come and our own learning.

CHAPTER 2

REGAINING WONDER

Developing the fuel of enthusiasm

'There arose in me two contrary emotions, fear and desire.' Using Leonardo's words about standing at the threshold of a cavern – and his subsequent painting *Virgin of the Rocks* – as an anchor, this chapter explores the way curiosity might lead the way to wonder.

We explore Montaigne's description of diversive curiosity as 'learning scatteringly' and trace how such foraging for knowledge and experience might evolve into encounters with unexpected meanings. Knowledge fuels understanding, wonder fuels curiosity, and as Montaigne said: 'Wonder is the foundation of all philosophy, inquiry its progress.'

CHAPTER 3
PERFECTING ATTENTION

Developing a sensory approach

This chapter focuses on Leonardo's obsessive noticing: 'If you wish to have a sound knowledge of the forms of objects, begin with the details.' It's about how he came to be, in Nicholl's words, 'a writer–down of things, a recorder of observations, a pursuer of data, an explorer of thoughts, an inscriber of lists and memoranda' – and then there were the hundreds of drawings, plans and maps.

As well as noticing and recording, Leonardo analysed and imagined. He was interrogating reality through his senses, marrying the concrete and the abstract, the intuitive and the cognitive, pursuing what Simone Weil calls 'the formation of attention'. It's a chapter about the importance of real experience.

CHAPTER 4
UNNECESSARY BEAUTY

Developing the dialogue across disciplines

The Scottish physician William Hunter believed that Leonardo was 'by far the best anatomist and physiologist of his time … the very first who raised a spirit of anatomical study and gave it credit'. Nicholl recognises in Leonardo's drawings of the human body not only a precision and accuracy but also a 'modulation' or a dialogue between the visionary and the practical. An ability to uncover an 'unnecessary beauty'.

Leonardo's knowledge of science, geography, mathematics, architecture, optics, music and so on illustrates perfectly his drive to find the microcosm in the macrocosm, learning to become a matchmaker across fields of study – and to open the gates between the conscious and the unconscious. And of course, he urges us by implication to do the same.

CHAPTER 5
THINKING ASIDE

Developing a metaphoric perspective

'Everything proceeds from everything, and everything becomes everything...' Leonardo believed in the laws of continuity. Modern scientists make a similar point about flashes of insight and explosions of likeness: 'There are no such things as separate parts in reality, but instead only intimately related phenomena so bound up with each other as to be inseparable.' Thinking in this way leads to the possibility of approaching and understanding 'here' in terms of 'elsewhere' – looking for patterns and finding connections in a world that is tantalisingly open to interpretation.

All of this invites metaphors into the conversation, with their potential to simultaneously clarify and make strange, the way they allow us to explore 'associative networks of understanding and embrace the shifts and detours of unfolding knowledge and open the doors to hidden analogies'.

CHAPTER 6
NEGATIVE CAPABILITY

Developing productive frustration

The title of this chapter comes from a letter from John Keats to his brother in which he urges an acceptance of life's 'uncertainties, mysteries and doubts' because they are of far more use than 'fact and reason'. We should beware, Keats says, not to 'unweave the rainbow'. Clive James adds to this with his comment that 'distractions are the stuff of life'.

Leonardo's take on these ideas is bound up in his 'sfumato' technique – his blurred boundaries and elusive edges. This is a technique that carries with it the idea of constructive ambiguity – the power of the undefined limit. Life can be difficult and frustrating, but confusion and uncertainty can also offer a fresh perspective.

CHAPTER 7
UNFINISHED PERFECTION

Developing sustained irresolution

The last word in Leonardo's final notebook is 'etcetera'. He had more to say and do. The word tells us that he was less concerned with endings than he was with beginnings. We argue that Leonardo's life is dominated by the word 'torsion' – a twisting, re-examining and constant rethinking of experience that rarely reaches a last-page conclusion. It's about adapting, adjusting and continuing the search.

Leonardo's life and work is an illustration of how we learn about the world, how it is a process rather than a project with a preordained ending. That process never stops. The former National Theatre director Nicholas Hytner said of his work in the theatre that 'you start with a vision and deliver a compromise'. Throughout his life, Leonardo resisted succumbing to such a compromise – hence the several beginnings but the very few ends.

CHAPTER 1
CONSCIOUS IGNORANCE

Portrait of a Man in Red Chalk (believed to be a self-portrait);
Biblioteca Reale, Turin

Look at that face. What does that intense stare aimed somewhere over your shoulder say to you? We are not confronting Leonardo with queries about his achievements; he is confronting us about ours. Engaging with that 500-year-old face that hovers just behind the faces in his paintings reminds us that the constantly questing Leonardo asks us to probe our opinions more thoroughly and test our preconceptions more surely.

What did Leonardo mean by...?

I am fully aware that my not being a man of letters may cause certain presumptuous people to think that they may with reason blame me, alleging that I am a man without learning.[1]

ASSERTIVE AMBIGUITY

In May 2008, a small group of art experts met secretly in the conservation studio at London's National Gallery to view a 'lost' Leonardo da Vinci painting, *Salvator Mundi*. Rediscovered and renovated by Dianne Dwyer Modestini in 2006 it caused, and continues to cause, much excitement and controversy. Martin Kemp, the emeritus professor of the history of art at Oxford University, was one of this select National Gallery group. He was cautious, but in the end, made a series of comments that provide us with our starting point[2] for this extended encounter with Leonardo and what we might learn from him about learning itself. As he entered the studio where Salvator Mundi was displayed, Kemp felt that 'the painting was asserting its presence ... even before I approached it, the image was confronting me before I could confront it'. This goes some way to describing our relationship with Leonardo: a feeling that he has confronted us in the 21st century rather than that we have set out to question him. In Kemp's first moments with the painting he felt 'a vibration' which confirmed almost immediately for him that the 'signs of Leonardo's magic (had) asserted themselves'. At the heart of that magic is the 'teasing ambiguity' of Christ's facial features – a gaze that is 'assertively direct but removed from explicitness'.[3]

While Leonardo's *Mona Lisa* is the most famous painting in the world, and *The Last Supper* perhaps the second most famous, *Salvator Mundi* has turned out to be by far the most expensive. Charles Nicholl says that Leonardo's *Mona Lisa* is more than a visual phenomenon: it provokes a mental atmosphere; it is more than a depiction of light and shade; it is a mood, an 'autumnal suffusion of transience and regret'.[4] The art historian Sydney Freedberg calls the painting 'an image in which a breathing instant and a composure for all time are held in suspension'.[5] This feeling of a 'breathing instant' is echoed in Matthew Landrus's

1. Da Vinci: Codex Atlanticus 119v: *Notebooks* J. P. Richter Dover 1970
2. Martin Kemp: *Living with Leonardo: Fifty Years of Sanity and Insanity in the Art World and Beyond*; Thames and Hudson, 2018
3. Ibid Kemp
4. Charles Nicholl: *Leonardo Da Vinci: The Flights of the Mind*; Penguin 2004
5. Sidney J Freedberg: *Painting in Italy 1500–1600*; Pelican Classics 1971

description of *The Last Supper* as having 'a sense of proportional commotion and orchestrated noise'.[6]

When *Salvator Mundi*, or the *Mona Lisa* – or any of Leonardo's paintings – confront us, we encounter not just the unknowability of those faces; we also catch a glimpse of the face that we sense lies behind those faces – Leonardo himself. The riddle and spiritual depth implied by the gaze of *Salvator Mundi*, or the elusiveness of *Mona Lisa's* half smile, or the wave-like gestures and undercurrents of *The Last Supper* somehow combine to suggest – and at the same time hide – the face of Leonardo. A face like the drawing that begins this introduction – that is, 'assertively direct' and at the same time 'teasingly ambiguous'.

THE DIALOGUE BETWEEN EXPERIMENT AND THEORY

We began with what Leonardo is probably best known for – his paintings. More and more, however, he is thought of as the first true scientist. Unlike a contemporary scientist, however, he didn't share his observations and discoveries. He was not a collaborator. Nor did he get round to publishing his findings. There were no patents to apply for in his time; consequently he needed to keep his knowledge to himself to protect his marketability, not only as a creative artist, but also as an engineer, architect, anatomist – and scientist. In the 21st century, openness is a key feature of the way science thrives and develops. Leonardo's secrecy has led to later scientists underestimating his importance – minimising the role he played in the history of science:

> Before Copernicus or Galileo, before Bacon, Newton or Harvey, he uttered fundamental truths the discovery of which is associated with their names. The sun does not move. Without experience there can be no certainty. A weight seeks to fall to the centre of the Earth in the most direct way. The blood which returns when the heart opens again is not the same as that which closes the valve.[7]

More than a century before Galileo, Leonardo began 'the dialogue between experiment and theory that would lead to the modern Scientific Revolution'.[8] Centuries before Darwin set sail, Leonardo was studying geology and fossils in the belief that, as he himself put it, 'necessity is the mistress and the teacher of nature ... it is the

---

6. Matthew Landrus: *Leonardo da Vinci: 500 Years On: a Portrait of the Artist, Scientist and Innovator*; Andre Deutsch 2018

7. Edward MacCurdy: *The Mind Of Leonardo da Vinci*, Dover 2008

8. Walter Isaacson: *Leonardo da Vinci: The Biography*; Simon and Schuster 2017

theme and the inspiration of nature, its curb and eternal regulator. The necessity is the need to stay alive – it is the catalyst for the evolutionary process.'[9]

Clearly he was close to seeing the principles of evolution. He also understood and articulated the principles that would in later centuries come to be called inductive reasoning, and the role of experimentation in elucidating the general laws of nature.

> He was among the first to deconstruct complex mechanisms and make separate drawings of each element. Likewise, in his anatomy drawings, he drew muscles, nerves, bones, organs, and blood vessels from different angles, and he pioneered the method of depicting them as multiple layers, like the transparencies of body layers found in encyclopedias centuries later.[10]

ECLECTIC BRILLIANCE

It's probably an understatement to say that Leonardo's mind was overstocked. He immersed himself in every specialised discipline and direction that he could find, often all at once. He took up an extraordinary range of interests and then abandoned almost as many. His was an eclectic brilliance; he dipped his mental brush into a whole range of subjects. His 'personality combined perfectionism with a love of experimentation and an enthusiasm for perhaps too many things'.[11] He was restless; he delayed; he rejected the idea of a default solution, or a standardised notion of excellence – of the sort that might have been expected by patrons and fellow artists alike. He was guided by the belief that: 'Iron rusts when not used, and water gets foul from standing or turns to ice when exposed to cold, so the intellect degenerates without exercise.'[12]

He didn't hang about. He was very hard to keep up with. It is not simply that he assembled scrapbooks or notebooks full of ideas or that he used these as working archives or initial proofs for works in progress.[13] His notebooks – his secretive filing system – went much further. He

9. Leonardo, quoted by Dan Burstein; *Secrets of the Code*; Hachette, 2010
10. Ibid Isaacson
11. Rowland and Charney: *The Collector of Lives; Giorgio Vasari and the Invention of Art*; Norton 2017
12. *Leonardo da Vinci: Thoughts on Art and Life*; from the notebooks translated by Maurice Baring; Dover 1906
13. This idea on how scrapbooks (or notebooks) are used by artists is half-suggested by the *Eric Ravilious Scrapbooks* edited by Peyton Skipworth and Brain Webb; Lund Humphries, 2018

interrogated the beliefs and conventions of his time, the pervasive frames of reference that governed the way his contemporaries thought and lived. He blurred the boundaries between art, engineering, anatomy, maths and science – between reality and fantasy, experience and mystery, between objects and their surroundings.

The notebooks suggest some answers; but more than that, they overflow with questions. Leonardo constantly embraced *uncertainty*. He was a perfect example of Bill Watterson's assertion: 'The truth is, most of us discover where we are headed when we arrive.'[14] Or Montaigne's assertion that 'only fools make up their minds and are certain'[15] – which is why, perhaps, he left so much of his work unfinished.

THE TEMPTATION OF THE HORIZON

Hayek[16] makes the point that in broad terms there are two sorts of intellectual: those who are seen as the master or the authority on a particular subject, and those who toy with problems – 'puzzlers'. Leonardo was as much, if not more, the latter rather than the former, but his breadth of interest was anything but superficial. When his notebooks were eventually understood and read (as late as the 19th century) he emerged as a groundbreaking anatomist, architect, artist, botanist, designer, engineer, geologist, musician and scientist who had made discoveries that were not fully appreciated for centuries. He became the very definition of a Renaissance man and – as Kenneth Clark famously described him, 'the most relentlessly curious man in history'.[17] Even the way that his questions are framed in his notebooks suggests an open – even innocent – mind at work. There is a terse clarity and practical precision to their diversity. 'The moon is dense; anything dense is heavy: what is the nature of the moon?' Or this beautiful expression: 'Between the sun and us is darkness, and yet the air seems blue.' Nicholl comments insightfully on this entry: 'The words are pared back to the quick; it is a statement of lucid simplicity into which lucid scientific questions are folded.'

---

14. Bill Watterson: US cartoonist – commencement address at Kenyon College, Ohio; quoted by Todd Rose and Ogi Ogas in *Dark Horse: Achieving Success Through the Pursuit of Fulfilment*: Harper One, 2018
15. Montaigne: *Complete Essays*; translated by M.A. Screech; Penguin 1991
16. Economist and philosopher Friedrich Hayek: 'The Use of Knowledge in Society'; *American Economic Review* Vol 35; 1945
17. Kenneth Clark, *Civilisation* John Murray 1969

If we can sense, like Martin Kemp when he first encountered *Salvator Mundi*, the 'temptation of the horizon'[18] in the smoky ambiguity of Leonardo's paintings, then we can feel it even more in those notebooks – his working archives. They are a complex map not so much of his feelings – he kept those to himself even when writing in code – but of his observations and questions. He kept what he *felt*, as opposed to what he *thought*, in its 'own cupboard'.[19]

Leonardo wanted to know about everything that could be known, and he gave this self-imposed quest his full brilliance. It is that brilliance that confronts us *now* through his paintings and notebooks. Leonardo's *assertive gaze* – half concealed behind 'the nebulous smoke'[20] of his paintings and the mirror-writing of his notebooks – serves to challenge our own curiosity about his life and to appreciate fully the magnitude of his perceptions and talents; his abiding ability to marry the passionate and the dispassionate – his inner life with the life around him; what his society required and what he was personally driven to do.

In the end Leonardo refused to 'seize and freeze'[21] on a final approach or conclusion – in his paintings or in any other discipline. He knew what the world thought and expected of him, but he chose his own path.

Our efforts and endeavours in this book to hear what Leonardo has to say to us about learning will inevitably abbreviate and reduce his lateral learning legacy. Synthesis is pretty tricky. Interestingly, although he did express scorn for those who try to take shortcuts – 'the abbreviators of works do injury to knowledge and to love'[22] – he himself also tried to simplify and unravel complex principles throughout his life, relentlessly taking notes on what he observed, striving to appreciate reasons, causes and principles. It can be seen in all of his investigations, observations and notebook records: a profound feel for nature's patterns and crosscurrents, and a striving to find a deep connected unity. His notebooks are not simply a

---

18. Alberto Manguel: Curiosity; Yale 2015: *The temptation of the horizon is always present, even if, as the ancients believed, after the world's end a traveller would fall into the abyss*
19. A phrase from the poet, Claudia Rankin: *Citizen: An American Lyric*; Greystone Books 2014
20. 'Nebulous smoke' is a phrase from Cennino Cennini – 'un fummo bene sfumate'. He was writing some time before Leonardo in *Il Libro dell 'Arte*, 1400
21. A phrase from Adam Grant's Originals: *How Non-Conformists Change the World*; W.H. Allen, 2016
22. Leonardo *Notebooks*: Windsor Castle Royal Library

representation of the world he saw, but an attempt to manipulate it. He inspected in order to invent.[23] He wanted to *flood* his and our 'dark chambers with light'.[24]

As we said earlier, Leonardo never seemed particularly interested in sharing his insights. His instincts were certainly not those of a teacher, at least not in the sense that he wanted to add to our database of knowledge. He left many of his attempts to codify his thinking and organise his discoveries unfinished, as if the rushed pursuit of the next big thing took him away from his last passion. He seemed to be far more interested in finding his voice, in becoming Leonardo, to bother with any explanations to others. As far as he was concerned, 'they do not know that my subjects require experience rather than the words of others'. He was a disciple of empiricism rather than of any predecessor or contemporary. But he was not an academic. Nor did he want to be. What he teaches us is to do with how he – and, by implication, we – need to find a space for mental freedom, curiosity and imagination. As Isaacson points out:

> The trove of treatises that he left unpublished testifies to the unusual nature of what motivated him. He wanted to accumulate knowledge for its own sake, and for his own personal joy, rather than out of a desire to make a public name for himself as a scholar or to be part of the progress of history.[25]

EARNED GENIUS

We are drawn into the melting light and shade of Leonardo's paintings and the way he layers half-suggested meanings together with the expectation of illumination in much the same way as he layers his paint. So too does he prompt us to recreate his thoughts into meanings for ourselves in the 21st century. Through him we create the past and then recreate it for the future. Leonardo's gift to our modern world is not just the paintings and the notebooks – miraculous as they are – but rather those questions that he continues to ask. What we hear from this is not some foggy, semi-mystical idea of *inspiration*, but something far more immediate, useful and urgent. As we said at the start of this introduction, we are not confronting Leonardo with queries about his achievements;

---

23. This contrast between inspection and invention comes from a review by Alex Clark of Zadie Smith's essay, 'Feel Free', *The Guardian* February 2018
24. Fernando de Rojas: *Celestina* (1499); Penguin 2009
25. Ibid Isaacson

he is confronting *us* about ours. Engaging with that 500-year-old face that hovers just behind the faces in his paintings reminds us to take on board, and act upon, the certainty 'that the constantly questing Leonardo asks us to probe our opinions more thoroughly and test our preconceptions more surely'.[26]

It's too easy to think of Leonardo as a man touched by some divine lightning. It is too easy, and just not that helpful to us. Our interest is more pragmatic and down to earth. How did he go about actually earning his genius? How did he steer his will towards greatness using, for the most part, a dogmatic (and discreet) focus on the very human and recognisable skills of observation, pattern seeking and imagination? How did a man who made many simple mistakes in mathematical calculations and was not overly blessed with diligence manage to devote hundreds of pages in his notebooks to questions of quadrature and anticipate the current interest in chaos and fractals? How did a man born into a world of such traditional, religious and restricted thinking manage to wander through the world asking profound insightful questions across many disciplines with such a free-range mind? How did a man of such astonishing artistic brilliance who never wanted to waste a second of his life get so distracted by the future that he only left behind a dozen or so finished works?

Isaacson reassures us that 'being relentlessly and randomly curious about everything around us is something that each of us can push ourselves to do, every waking hour, just as he did'.[27] Leonardo would rather sternly encourage us with: 'He is a poor pupil who does not go beyond his master.'[28] Perhaps something like Walt Whitman's more recent instruction would almost certainly find favour with Leonardo: 'You shall no longer take things at second or third hand, not look through the eyes of the dead, nor feed on the spectres in books. You shall not look through my eyes either, nor take things from me, you shall listen to all sides and filter them for yourself.'[29]

All this leads us to declare that we are setting out on what we hope will be an extended discussion between the *here* of 21st-century learning and the *elsewhere* of Leonardo's work 500 years ago. Look at that face on the first page of this introduction. What does that intense stare

26. Rachel Campbell Johnston: 'Salvator Mundi: the critic's verdict': *The Times* – November 2018
27. Ibid Isaacson
28. *Forster Codices*; Victoria and Albert museum
29. Walt Whitman: 'Song of Myself': Create Space Publishing 2013

aimed somewhere over your shoulder say to you? Perhaps something like this, again from Whitman:

> Not I, nor anyone else can travel that road for you.
> You must travel it for yourself.
> It is not far, it is within reach.
> Perhaps you have been on it since you were born and did not know.[30]

Our whole project is not simply to receive ideas from Leonardo, but to exchange ideas with him. Ideas that might lead us to rethink and reshape the way we approach our own world view, our own processes of learning and working and living.

Consequently, we would hope that meeting Leonardo and understanding his approaches to learning and life in these pages will prove, in the end, to be equally as much about all of us as about him, an investment for our future – 'a storing up of information and emotional understanding for tomorrow and … lifetimes to come'.[31]

---

30. Ibid Walt Whitman: 'Song of Myself'
31. Hilde Ostby and Ylva Ostby; *Adventures in Memory: The Science and Secrets of Remembering and Forgetting*; Greystone Books 2018

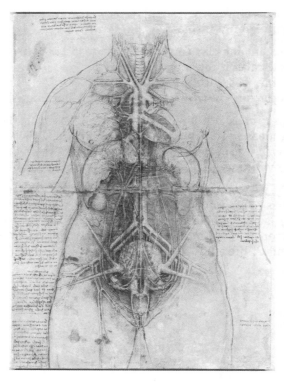

The cardiovascular system and principal organs of a woman; Royal
Collection, Windsor Castle

Breaking up familiarities is at the very core of the Leonardo
approach. He would use his notebooks, filled with scientific
sketches, as an immediate and direct method of exploring his world.
Foraging for new knowledge then testing and owning it, questioning
assumptions, generating and developing his ideas through these
drawings ... He was never addicted to, or even interested in,
consensus, but instead was attentive to the irregular, the odd.

What can we still learn from Leonardo about...?

The real voyage of discovery consists not in seeking new landscapes, but in having new eyes[32]

DOGMA, CLOSED MINDS AND FROZEN THINKING

Gaining expertise means acquiring great breadth and depth of knowledge, but it can also make it more difficult to process new information with an open mind. We make a number of assumptions about anything new we encounter based on a wealth of previous experiences, which constrains the possibilities that we are prepared to consider. We make sense of our world through cognitive filters, which are effectively lenses that we have developed on the basis of what has worked well for us in the past. These become honed and refined over time, resulting in a brain well adapted to its environment. However, relying on the habitual modes of thinking that experts often develop as part of their expertise development can create a fixed orientation, or mental ruts that limit how we act in, and react to, the world around us. We therefore tend to experience things in autopilot mode, in the way we always have – the way we've come to expect. These thinking habits can become highly limiting and impede our abilities to create or accept ideas that conflict with our assumptions or conventional wisdom. Psychologists refer to this as dogmatic cognition. The political theorist Hannah Arendt rather more poetically referred to 'frozen thinking'[33] whereby we adhere to deeply held ideas and principles that we have developed and no longer question.

There is a cost to thinking, to sowing doubt when faced with inherited concepts. Arendt says:

> Thinking has a destructive, undermining effect on all established criteria, values, measurements of good and evil, in short, on those customs and trials of conduct we treat in morals and ethics. These frozen thoughts, Socrates seems to say, come so handily that you can use them in your sleep; but if the wind of thinking, which I shall now stir in you, has shaken you from your sleep and made you fully awake and alive, then you will see that you have nothing in your grasp but perplexities, and the best we can do with them is share them with each other.[34]

32. Marcel Proust, quoted by Lewis, Amini and Lannon in *A General Theory of Love*; Random House 2000
33. Hannah Arendt: 'Thinking and Moral Considerations' in *Social Research* Autumn 1971
34. *Socrates Against Athens: Philosophy on Trial*, James A. Colaiaco Routledge, 2013

To stop and think can be terrifying. The call to think is a call to wonder and wander beyond the safe limits of what we know and what we think we know. The thoughtful person feels the full gravity of facing and bringing under scrutiny those things that are usually the backdrop to our lives. The courage to try to understand. In a further step downwards, according to the 'earned dogmatism hypothesis'[35] it has been shown as socially accepted for the people accredited as experts to adopt more close-minded views. Because experts have already given extensive thought to issues within a domain, they have 'earned the privilege' of harbouring more dogmatic opinions and beliefs. Consequently, situations that engender self-perceptions of high expertise often elicit a more closed-minded cognitive style.

THE BENEFITS OF DESIRABLE IGNORANCE

When we talk about the known universe it is surely in itself an admission of how little is actually perceived, discovered and known. Scientists search for certainty. But there is no certainty. Facts, too, are debatable and vacillate. As Jacalyn Duffin has commented, 'for postmodern scholars, progress, like facts, may no longer exist'.[36] In fact doubt is at the very core of any science. When we ask questions, doubt is a requirement. The physicist James Clerk Maxwell made the point that a thoroughly 'conscious ignorance'[37] is the prelude to every real advance in science. He is not using 'ignorance' in a pejorative sense. He is talking about gaps in our knowledge that we can't make predictions from.

The eminent physicist Enrico Fermi told his students that 'an experiment that successfully proves a hypothesis is a measurement; one that doesn't is a discovery. A discovery, an uncovering – of new ignorance.'[38] Good learning enables understanding, but more importantly, it evinces what we do not know. 'Desirable ignorance' might seem to be a paradoxical idea but ignorance, says Firestein, is 'a communal gap in knowledge ... where the existing data don't make sense, don't add up to a coherent explanation, cannot be used to make a prediction or statement about some-thing or event. This is knowledgeable ignorance, perceptive

35. *Journal of Experimental Social Psychology* Volume 61, November 2015, Pages 131–138

36. Duffin, J. *History of Medicine: A Scandalously Short Introduction*, University of Toronto Press, Toronto; 1999: 374

37. Maxwell, James Clerk (1877): 'Review of H. W. Watson, *A Treatise on the Kinetic Theory of Gases*', Nature 16, 242–246

38. Firestein, S. Ignorance, *How it Drives Science*, Oxford University Press, Oxford; 2012

ignorance, insightful ignorance.'[39] And this leads to the framing of better questions, identification of what should be done, deciding what the next steps might be and, thereby, concentrating energies on achieving better answers.

Richard Feynman adds that in order to make progress, one must 'leave the door to the unknown ajar'.[40] He asserts that we should be informed and shaped by life, free of the despotism of opinion and open to varying degrees of certainty. He argues that in order to progress we must recognise the ignorance and leave room for doubt. In fact he believes that the whole point of facts and knowledge is to make better ignorance, to come up with higher-quality ignorance. The evolutionary biologist Mark Pagel wisely stated that 'the elusive nature of knowledge should remind us to be humble when interpreting it and acting on it, and this should grant us both a tolerance and skepticism toward others and their interpretations. Knowledge should always be treated as a hypothesis.'[41]

BREAKING UP FAMILIARITIES

Our search for knowledge and understanding evokes concern: 'it evokes the care one takes for what exists and could exist; a readiness to find strange and singular what surrounds us; a certain readiness to break up our familiarities and to regard otherwise the same things; a fervour to grasp what is happening and what passes; a casualness in regard to the traditional hierarchies of the important and essential.'[42] We intend to argue that Foucault's phrase about breaking up familiarities is at the very core of the Leonardo approach. He would use his notebooks, filled with spontaneous sketches, as an immediate and direct method of exploring his world. Foraging for new knowledge then testing and owning it, questioning assumptions, generating and developing his ideas through these drawings, 'many of which, cannot be connected with a particular project: he used drawing to develop his eye and hand'.[43] He was never addicted to, or even interested in, consensus,

39. Firestein, S. Ignorance, *How it Drives Science*, Oxford University Press, Oxford; 2012

40. Richard P Feynman; *The pleasure of finding things out*. Cambridge, Mass.: Perseus Books; 1999

41. Pagel, M. Knowledge as a hypothesis in: J. Brockman (Ed) *This Will Make You Smarter*, HarperCollins, New York; 2012

42. Michel Foucault quoted by James S Ackerman in 'Leonardo da Vinci: Art in Science'; *Daedalus* 1998

43. P(L) : Pedretti, C., *The Drawings and Misc Papers of Leonardo da Vinci* in the Collection of HM The Queen at Windsor Castle, Vol. I (1982)

but instead was attentive to the irregular, the odd. Isaacson says Leonardo's 'facility for combining observation with fantasy allowed him, like other creative geniuses, to make unexpected leaps that related things seen to things unseen'.[44]

James Webb Young has his own pragmatic take:

> Every really good creative person ... has always had two noticeable characteristics. First, there was no subject under the sun in which [they] could not easily get interested in – from, say, Egyptian burial customs to modern art. Every facet of life has a fascination for [them]. Second, [they were] an extensive browser in all fields of information...an idea results from a new combination of specific knowledge...with general information about life and events.[45]

Innovative ideas emerge through a process of gathering experiences and working them over – what Ian Leslie calls 'building the database as a prelude to fresh thinking'.[46] Organisations who learn to be fascinated – even obsessed – by what they don't know are the ones that are least likely to be caught unaware by change. Indeed, as a civilisation, our ability to thrive has been seen to rely on analysis, the step-by-step progression of logical and analytical reasoning that Leonard Mlodinow refers to as a 'low-level god'.[47] He argues that we need to be more flexible in the way we frame and generate new concepts and paradigms, questions and issues, using more diverse strategies – such as non-algorithmic, pattern-recognising, idea-generating, divergent thinking – which help to shuffle and reconcile diverse or novel ideas and form new associations. We need to find more innovative ways of integrating complex and unusual information and far-flung ideas. Ray Bradbury comes up with a slightly more extreme strategy when he comments that creative people need to take 'the long march from the rim of the cave to the edge of the cliff where we [fling] ourselves off and [build] our wings on the way down'.[48]

ADOPTING A BEGINNER'S MIND

'The wise person', said Mencius in the fourth century BC, 'is one who doesn't lose the child's heart and mind'. When we are young

---

44. Ibid Isaacson
45. James Webb Young: *A Technique for Producing Ideas*; CreateSpace 2012
46. Ian Leslie: *Curiosity: The Desire to Know and Why Your Future Depends on It*; Curious Quercus 2014
47. Leonard Mlodinow; *Elastic: Flexible Thinking in a Changing World*; Allen Lane, 2018
48. 1979 November 18, *Los Angeles Times*, Section: The Book Review, 'Hymn to humanity from the cathedral of high technology' by Ray Bradbury

we tend not to recognise nonconforming ideas and therefore do not resist accepting them. We possess what Zen Buddhism calls 'shoshin' (初心) – a 'beginner's mind'. Leonardo approached his life and his work without assumptions and preconceptions, driven by the curiosity to know more, rather than an urge to be right, or to come up with the answer he was expected to give. Throughout his life his perceptions and connections to everything around him suggest the attitude of openness and eagerness of a beginner.

For the beginner, it is much easier to approach a task consciously, with an intention of finding the best possible solutions. Maintaining the open mind of a beginner is essential if you are trying to innovate, but also if you want to become an expert in any field. This is because moving to the next level of skill or knowledge often demands the letting go of beliefs and attitudes acquired at earlier stages of learning. In other words, mastering any skill or field of expertise requires you to constantly revise what you assume you already know. Mere competence is often only a process of imitation:

> For there are moments when something new has entered into us, something unknown; our feelings grow mute in shy perplexity, everything in us withdraws, a stillness comes, and the new, which no one knows, stands in the midst of it and is silent.[49]

SIDESTEPPING ANSWERS

Galileo believed (probably like Leonardo) that 'those truths which we know are very few in comparison with those which we do not know.'[50] Alice, in the Lewis Carroll novel, is drawn to follow a white rabbit into a dark hole in the ground because she had never before seen a rabbit with a waistcoat pocket, or a watch to take out of it. Like Leonardo, Alice is intrigued by the unknown, by something she is absolutely sure no one has ever seen. Shortly after a bewildering fall into the spinning darkness of the rabbit hole, Alice asks questions about who she really is. She imagines the world outside coming to her rescue, but insists that any rescue will be on her own terms – she will not be who she does not want to be:

> It'll be no use their putting their heads down and saying, 'Come up again, dear!' I shall only look up and say, 'Who am I then? Tell me

---

49. Rilke, *Letter to a Young Poet*, Translation by M.D. Herter Norton (1934) W.W. Norton and Company
50. Quote from Galileo, various sources

that first, and then, if I like being that person, I'll come up: if not, I'll stay down here till I'm somebody else.'

In other words, Alice wants to make sure that whatever meaning the world around her possesses, it will be her meaning, not someone else's. When it comes to who she is, she insists that she is 'I' with her own individual identity which does not depend on what others think but on what she thinks. What Lewis Carroll seems to be telling his readers during Alice's encounters is that life and the world in which we live are open questions. The answers are down to us, not given to us and we find those answers through two-way, not one-way, conversations. Alice's endless and often absurd question-and-answer encounters with strange creatures leave us feeling that we are on the verge of some marvellous revelation, before the 'answers' are sidestepped in favour of more open questions – the dialogue. This is perhaps why Leonardo found it so difficult to finish many of his paintings: everything he did prompted open rather than closed questions, beginnings not endings, conversations not conclusions.

If Alice's key question is 'Who am I?' then it is Leonardo's key question too. In reaching towards any sort of understanding, both strive to take hold of their own narratives; they resist being defined and led by anyone else's story.

INSUBORDINATION IN ITS PUREST FORM

Talking of resisting other people's stories, we should not dismiss Alice's reluctance to conform to the expectations of her time as a long-gone 19th-century phenomenon. Or Leonardo's challenges to received ideas as just another Renaissance example of that long-ago questioning of the orthodoxy that dominated the world around him. Leonardo and (especially) Alice would certainly have rebelled against a culture that expected them to be what they did not want to be, where the spotlight was constantly pointed at them and where appearance was the all-purpose measure of self-esteem. Alice's insistence is that if she likes who the world wants her to be, she will join in with it – if she does not, then she will stay in the dark. It is in the ambiguities of the darkness that Leonardo, Alice and countless modern students will find some marvellous thing – who they are and what they might achieve.

That is what this book is about: how we might give ourselves the confidence to embrace doubt; and if we do feel that we have woken up and are stuck in the darkness, access to the light switch is in our own hands, not someone else's. Leonardo and Lewis Carroll lived in times where it was steadily emerging that truth in its totality was at the disposition of the individual.

Where there was less and less need for a hypothesis that explained everything in terms of the existence of a divinity; where churches used this hypothesis to make the question 'Why?' either redundant or evil.

The hidden part is the part that wants to question, and challenge, and fight change with change. Clark Kent keeps his super-self hidden[51] – just as we imagine Leonardo did by using codified notebooks. Like Leonardo, Clark Kent's questions fuelled the actions of his other superhero self; but unlike Leonardo, he kept quiet about much of what he thought and imagined. The superhero Leonardo painted *Mona Lisa* and *The Last Supper*; the Clark Kent version of himself hid behind his notebooks and his codes. Manguel,[52] on the other hand, tells us that Lewis Carroll's Alice was completely the opposite. All her questions came out loudly and in public and were an open and supreme act of civil disobedience – rather like those words of Nabokov's about curiosity being insubordination in its purest form. It is Alice's courage in asking her questions that in the end allows her to wake from her dream – not with answers but with open questions about who she really is or who she might become. It is her questions that take her from where she is to where she wants to be. Leonardo, we might argue, never woke up from his dream, ending his life with those numerous drawings of the deluge which have what Nicholl calls an almost hallucinogenic quality.[53] Leonardo was clearly more of a Clark Kent than an Alice. He needed the work, after all, so must have found it difficult to appear loyal and compliant in the eyes of the Church and those with power, and at the same time to ask questions that might be seen to challenge the beliefs and certainties of those around him.

We have to ask: exactly what are his questions questioning? Who or what is being explored or challenged? Are those questions simply responses to his observations in preparation for a painting, or are they, as many of Leonardo's contemporaries almost certainly thought (or suspected), the incontinent outpourings of a meddler and nuisance?

Leonardo's world, dominated by Church and state, was a default system.[54] Jost et al. have developed what they call a theory of system

51. This image – Clark Kent and Superman – is derived from Kevin Ashton's thoughts on the problems of being inventive and conformist at the same time. In *How to Fly a Horse*; Heinemann 2015

52. Alberto Manguel: *Curiosity*; Yale; 2015

53. Ibid Nicholl

54. Jost, Pelham, Sheldon and Sullivan: '*Social Inequality and the Reduction of Ideological Dissonance on Behalf of the System: Evidence of Enhance System Justification Among the Disadvantaged*': European Journal of Social Psychology 33, 2003

justification which argues that people tend to adopt a default response to the world they live in. People rationalise and accept the status quo even if it goes against their own interests:

> Justifying the default system serves a soothing function. It's an emotional painkiller. If the world is supposed to be this way, we don't need to be dissatisfied with it. But acquiescence also robs us of the moral outrage to stand against injustice and the creative will to consider alternative ways that the world could work.[55]

Leonardo's default position would have been to live a private and a public life that fitted the stereotype of how an artist and citizen should operate. Yet in reality, his curiosity and his constant questioning did just the opposite. He was on a constant quest for new options – vuja de rather than déjà vu. The latter is when we come across something new but feel we have met it before, whereas vuja de is when we come across something familiar but see it in a completely different way – a way to gain new insights into old problems.[56]

Encountering these insights will encourage us to look critically at the sort of systems–hardening and dearth of innovation we might meet in the world around us. Leonardo would encourage us to adopt a day-to-day approach that the American sociologist Annette Lareau[57] describes as an environment built on questions, and what she calls 'concerted cultivation'. She describes how parents are able to maximise a child's abilities, through lots of verbal interaction. British researchers Tizard and Hughes[58] also found that the more questions a parent asked of their children, the more the children asked questions back. Question asking and question making not only generate talk and a rich relationship, they also are the basis of change and development. That is what this book is about: concerted cultivation – between Leonardo, the reader and us.

RESISTING A CONCLUSION

The phrase 'As I myself have seen' crops up regularly in Leonardo's notebooks. He is not relying on what he has been told or read. He is relying on his own experience. Interestingly, Nicholl[59] points out that Leonardo's notebooks are more philosophical than scientific, but

55. Adam Grant: *Originals: How Non-Conformists Change the World*; WH Allen 2016
56. Ibid Adam Grant
57. Annette Lareau: *Unequal Childhood, Class, Race and Family Life*; University of California Press 2011
58. B Tizard and M Hughes: *Young Children Learning*; Fontana 1984
59. Ibid Nicholl

the philosophy is under constant scrutiny in the form of a dialogue between the practical and the visionary. His thought processes were serene and accurate[60] but much of what he started was, like many of his other various projects, unfinished. His notebooks feel provisional with a procrastinated quality.[61] This isn't as amateurish an approach as it might first appear. In modern times it is probably accurate to say that we have come to see that scientific ideas evolve as part of a gradual process with no goal or endpoint at which we hope to arrive at a perfect truth. It is a story of unending rethinking.[62] Leonardo knew all about the importance of resisting a conclusion.

Nevertheless, he placed considerable stress on the importance of his notebooks – that little book he had always hanging at his belt[63] – and on the experiences which they record – or the 'experiments', as he sometimes called them (the two words were apparently synonymous in the Renaissance). The overarching purpose of his observations was to identify underlying causes in nature – although nature begins with the cause and ends with the experience, we must follow the opposite course: namely, begin with the experience, and by means of it investigate the cause.[64] His intention was always to achieve more than skillful and accurate representation. He was after pinning down the forces at play. Each painting is, in a sense, proof of Leonardo's understanding.[65] Proof, we might conclude, of this inner dialogue between what he experienced and what he imagined – or deduced. Of the conversation between Leonardo the practical man and Leonardo the visionary.

THINKING FROM THE EDGE

Leonardo would have known about Plato's cave analogy. We talk later of Leonardo's use of the same image to explain the way he was driven by both fear and expectation. Plato's cave contained a group of prisoners chained to a low wall. On the other side of this wall the life of the world went on. A large fire cast shadows of this life onto the wall opposite the prisoners; the prisoners could see the shadows, but

---

60. Georgia Nicodemi: '*Life and Works of Leonardo*' in Michael White: Leonardo da Vinci, the First Scientist, London
61. Ibid Nicholl
62. See Thomas Kuhn in *The Structure of Scientific Revolutions* (1963) Chicago 2013, and Steven Poole: *Rethink: The Surprising History of New Ideas*; Random House 2016
63. Giambattista Giraldo Canzio: *Discorsi* (Venice 1554) – where he cites the reminiscences of his father, Cristoforo Giraldo, a Ferrarese diplomat in Milan
64. I.A. Richter: *Leonardo da Vinci*: Notebooks; OUP 2008
65. Martin Kemp: *Leonardo da Vinci: The Marvellous Works of Nature and Man*; OUP 2006

not the life they reflected, and they believed that the shadows were in fact real life. What we think we see and what is really there are not necessarily the same thing. Reality is outside the cave, not in its shadows. Plato sought that reality through philosophy; others might seek it through religion. Leonardo found his reality through painting, experiments, drawing, science and observations.

The shadows for Leonardo were cast by the Church and the state that ruled his life. The rulers of our times are those who deal with us in ways that are centripetal – ways that pull us back into the cavern of our own minds, into the loneliness of rules, conventions, learned ideas and allegedly objective ways of measuring progress. These things are not reality. Those is charge try to convince us that they are and that they make our existence knowable. They don't. Of course, those leaders will say that there is no time for those they work with to find their own versions of reality; we need to accept that we work in a ruthless world. All available time is used for the organisation's core purposes. We are 'a team, not a family'.[66] However, in a team, your place is measured by your performance (i.e. output and profit), whereas in a family it is well-being, multi-dimensional thinking and individuality that count most.

What we have talked about so far in this conversation with Leonardo is very much about finding reality through developing a 'beginner's mind' and looking beyond the shadows on our own cave walls, about embracing conscious ignorance and uncertainty. There is more to be achieved than competence, or performance, or short-term gains.

So, will we come to know Leonardo through these pages? Possibly; but more importantly, we will definitely come to learn how to weather the world's uncertainty and to know our own learning lives that much better. Leonardo was not subdued by the elusiveness of how things worked or what they meant. He fought back – as this book sets out to show – with curiosity, opening himself to wonder, allowing his senses free rein, relying on experience rather than received ideas, making unexpected connections, blurring the boundaries between one place and another and thinking from the edge.

---

66. Dan Lyons: *Lab Rats: Why Modern Work Makes People Miserable*; Atlantic 20

CHAPTER 2
REGAINING WONDER

Virgin of the Rocks; Louvre Museum, Paris

We need to retain a childlike sense of wonder, never to cease to stand like curious children before the great mystery into which we were born. We should be careful to never outgrow our wonder years, that have a mercurial quality without which we risk losing the impetus and desire to learn for ourselves.

What did Leonardo mean by...?

Study without desire spoils the memory and it retains nothing it takes in.[1]

THE ROMANCE OF LEARNING

In his notebooks, writing about his travels in 1480, Leonardo recounted a seminal experience in a cave in the Tuscan countryside where he had discovered massive fossil bones 'from a mighty and once-living instrument of nature'. This event has often been cited as an important precursor to innovations in the composition of many of his artworks as well as his subsequent conclusions about the unlikely truth of Genesis and the significance of contradictory evidence: 'But sufficient for us is the testimony of things produced in the salt waters and now found again in the high mountains far from the seas.' Within a few years of the following entry from *Codex Arundel*, he drew and painted a number of images in which a grotto or cavern or sedimentary rock formations, home to a host of fossils, figure prominently. Here is how he described his initial encounter:

> Having wandered some way among the rocks I came to the entrance of a great cavern, in front of which I stood some time, astounded by this place I had not known about before. I stooped down with my back arched, and my left hand resting on one knee; and with my right hand I shaded my lowered and frowning brows; and continually bending this way and that I looked in and tried to make out if there was anything inside, but the deep darkness prevented me from doing so. I had been there for some time, when there suddenly arose in me two contrary emotions, fear and desire – fear of that threatening dark cave; desire to see if there was some marvellous thing within.[2]

Fear and desire; the passion to experience and acquire knowledge overcoming the accompanying dread. In the imaginations of his contemporaries, Leonardo's cavern would have represented the entrance to the underworld, or hell; but for him, that dark unknown is ambiguous. On the one hand it holds fear, doubt and uncertainty; on the other, it stimulates a burning desire to turn the lights on. Entering the cavern will almost certainly lead to an encounter with the unknown or the unidentified, and what that meeting will illuminate might be something wonderful – or equally, something terrible.

1. Leonardo notebooks: *Codex Arundel*; British Library
2. Leonardo notebooks: *Codex Arundel*; British Library

Leonardo, of course, is betting on the wonder. Allowing 'the ambiguity of the unknown'[3] to take him with it, to encourage him to summon the courage to 'see the edge, hesitate and jump out of ... ordinary reality into Wonderland', he entered the cave. This drive is at the very least about individual growth, but for Leonardo it became far more: 'Once you have tasted flight, you will forever walk the earth with your eyes turned skyward, for there you have been, and there you will always return.'[4] Once Leonardo has entered the cavern – along with us – we will all want to return to that magical place of uncertainty and newness again and again. We will want to rekindle the excitement of that first experience. The English mathematician A.N. Whitehead called this 'the romance of learning'.[5] We need to retain a childlike sense of wonder, 'never to cease to stand like curious children before the great mystery into which we were born'.[6] We should be careful to never outgrow our wonder years; they have a mercurial quality without which we risk losing the impetus and desire to learn for ourselves.

A DIVER IN DEEP SEAS[7]

I roamed the countryside searching for answers to things I did not understand ... and my intense desire to learn the nature of what was around me led me always to strive to a point which others would consider unnecessary.[8]

Leonardo's notebooks have been a perpetual source of wonder for writers, his brilliance 'whirls across every page, providing a delightful display of a mind dancing with nature'[9] and these notebooks act as a guide to this person who was also the most relentlessly questioning man in history. The word 'relentless' is important. It suggests that Leonardo's questioning never lessened nor ever reached a conclusion or moment of satisfaction. His journey from an apparently volatile child into an old man filled over 7000 pages of notebooks, 'the most astonishing testament to the powers of human observation and imagination ever set down on paper'.[10] These notebooks show

---

3. Ibid Nicholl
4. *Codex Turin*
5. A.N. Whitehead: *Nature and Life*, 1933; reprinted by Cambridge University Press 2012
6. Einstein, Letter to Otto Juliusburger, September 29, 1942, *The Ultimate Quotable Einstein*, ed Alice Calaprice, Princeton University Press 2013
7. Walter Pater on *Mona Lisa* in the *Fortnightly Review* 1869
8. Ralph Steadman: *I Leonardo*; Jonathan Cape 1981
9. Ibid Isaacson
10. Ibid Isaacson

his rampant diversive curiosity[11] in action, eventually reined in by dogged investigation and experimentation, to a point where it becomes more specific and focused. His writings show that not only was he a recognised artist, he was also an inspired engineer, an innovative architect, a world-class dissector of corpses, an expert on optics and a believer in man's ability to fly.

His work on geology (which we will explore further in this chapter) is simply astounding. Writing more than 3500 words on the topic in the *Codex Leicester*, he describes detailed observations of fossils. This research, he believed, demonstrated that the surface of the earth has changed over time, with land where once there was sea. This in turn led him to question (quietly) how Genesis described the shaping of our planet – thoughts which were a potential death sentence in his time. He did not merely think about these things in the abstract – he did real research.

'What he valued most was the thrill of the new and the act of discovery and re-evaluation.'[12]

UNFOLDING STORIES

These profound scattershot notebooks include 'jokes, doodles, snatches of poetry, drafts of letters, household accounts, recipes, shopping lists, bank statements, names and addresses of models',[13] as well as observational, analytical and exploratory drawings, scientific observations, mathematical constructs – and, most of all, questions: 'Why shells existed on the tops of mountains along with the imprints of coral and plants and seaweed usually found in the sea. Why thunder lasts for a longer time than that which causes it and why immediately on its creation the lightning becomes visible to the eye while thunder requires time to travel.'[14] Underlying Leonardo's obsessive note-taking is his determination to find the hidden forms and the inner unity of nature – and he often appears overwhelmed by the task.

This seeming randomness sprayed across the manuscript pages, over approximately 35 years, is in effect a long series of notes to himself and represents a compendium of the artistic, scientific, and philosophical principles that he lived by alongside conjunctions of

---

11. For definition, see Ian Leslie: *Curious*; Quercus 2015
12. Mike Lankford: *Becoming Leonardo; An Exploded View of the Life of Leonardo da Vinci*; Melville House Publishing 2017
13. Charles Nicholl: *Traces Remain: Essays and Explorations*; Allen Lane 2011
14. Ibid Steadman

facts and musings. These notes are also a complete hotchpotch of ideas and observations in a scrawled pandemonium of philosophy, often accompanied by staggeringly beautiful illustrations. Philip Ball[15] calls the contents of Leonardo's notebook a 'ragbag of issues' as opposed to the way a modern-day scientist would use the observations to create an 'explicatory framework'. Nevertheless, Leonardo's notebooks are special. They are special not only because of the methods he used to investigate the world around him, but also because, in Ball's words, 'he considered these things worth studying in the first place: not that he was obsessive in drawing up his lists, but in the object of his obsession'. On one page alone he creates a to-do list that defies any belief, ranging from examining cannons and crossbows, to studying the sun, ice skating in Flanders, optics, and (seemingly incidentally) drawing Milan.

More than anything that Leonardo actually puts into words, the notebooks provide all the evidence we need of its importance to his life and the way he worked. In many of his paintings, there 'is a beauty wrought out from within upon the flesh little cell by little cell'. Those cell-by-cell layers and subtle changes of tone are the result of all those 'conjunctions'[16] of facts and musings – all that ragbag of trifles and questions recorded in Leonardo's notebooks – of his relentless curiosity. In every painting of his that we know about, we sense 'an unfolding story, an implied before and after, within the depicted moment'.[17] Every painting seems to be filled with what Leonardo calls 'accidenti mentali'[18] – mental events – sometimes crucial psychological conflicts, at other times just hundreds of small details, and what Nicholl calls the 'ephemera' of his life, that he had obsessively assembled and recorded in his notebooks. He even apologises for the way he effectively hordes information: 'Do not blame me, reader,' he says in one of his notebooks,[19] 'because the subjects are many.'

HOLDING WONDER

Much of what Leonardo explored, invented and explained was historically and conceptually ground-breaking. He studied rocks and landscapes not simply to improve the realism of his paintings, but also

15. Philip Ball: *Curiosity; How Science Became Interested in Everything*; Bodley Head 2012
16. This is Martin Kemp's word for the way 'the soul, eyes, lips, balconies, architecture' show how Leonardo uses knowledge to create analogy
17. Ibid Nicholl 2004
18. *Codex Urbinus Latinus* in the Vatican library; selections from various notebooks made by Francesco Melzi 1530
19. *Codex Arundel*, British Library

in an attempt to understand how the earth works. Leonardo realised that the earth 'had a dynamic history in which powerful forces caused it to change and mature over the centuries'. By regarding the earth as a living organism, he was inspired 'to explore the way it aged and evolved: how mountains laced with fossils arose from the sea, how rocks became layers, how rivers cut valleys, and how rugged outcroppings eroded'.[20]

From those various fragments of notebook, we know a little of what Leonardo said about curiosity; but now it might be worth looking at how he *showed* that curiosity in his work. Walter Pater[21] memorably said that Leonardo's curiosity and his attention to myriad detail made him 'a diver in deep seas'. Leonardo was not interested in a single representation of the world and everything he painted was part of a whole collection of often partial and contradictory drafts.

HOW THE UNKNOWN ILLUMINATES THE KNOWN

In the early 1480s he painted the *Virgin of the Rocks* (twice), which features a landscape made up of sedimentary rocks. Leonardo seems to have used his cavern experience in this picture. It shows two infants – Christ and John the Baptist – the Virgin Mary and an angel meeting in a dark and gloomy cave. We see them from inside the cave, daylight glimpsed through the mouth of the cave beyond them. The known world outside is seen through the darkness and ambiguity of the cavern we are in. Critically, the unknown illuminates the known. His contemporaries would have seen this the other way around, the known shedding light on the unknown, the cavern representing an entrance into the underworld; but Leonardo turns that idea on its head: the cavern, with its fearful rocks and darkness, points the way to the light, to some wonderful thing – redemption or understanding perhaps – but we reach that understanding through the darkness. *The Virgin of the Rocks* offers an exit from the darkness. Such a setting was traditional for the representation of St Jerome but unusual for the Virgin and through it he may well have been suggesting that nature was his church.

The *Virgin of the Rocks* (in the Louvre particularly) demonstrates astounding geological accuracy because of the subtlety with which Leonardo represents highly complex geological formations. The two

---

20. Ibid Isaacson
21. Ibid Pater

versions of this picture are set in two different imaginary caverns, each with its own rich earth–scape of stone perforated and sculpted by wind and water. The complete geological authenticity of the Louvre rock formation has been used to suggest that the second version in London was not painted by Leonardo (at least not the background). Hence, precise geology can be seen as an index to authenticity and serves as Leonardo's inimitable trademark. As Isaacson says about the depiction of the cavern: 'It took a deep appreciation of geology to conjure up a vision that was both so imaginative and so real.'[22]

---

22. Ibid Isaacson

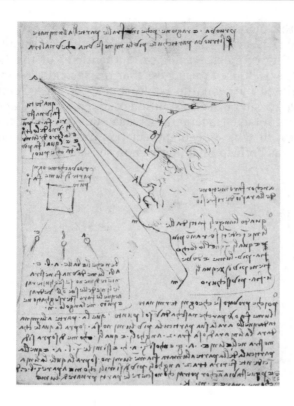

The fall of light on a face; Royal Collection, Windsor Castle Library

The life of the mind, cannot be postponed until you have sharpened it. Whatever interest attaches to your subject-matter must be evoked here and now. You cannot wait until you know all the rules and have taken on board all those things you believe you ought to know before being allowed to participate or have a view. Our need to know needs to be urgent.

What can we still learn from Leonardo about...?

Philosophy begins in wonder. And at the end when philosophic thought has done its best the wonder remains.[23]

FEEDING YOURSELF WITH QUESTIONING

So where does this leave us? Do we dare go into the cave? Or do we stay at the doorway? How might what begins as random curiosity turn into wonder? Understanding and applying Leonardo's ideas is a quest that never ends. One moment we experience curiosity towards what he shows or tells us, then at the next moment we are filled with wonder at what he doesn't tell us. Although the words 'Feed yourself with questioning' come from Hymen in Shakespeare's *The Tempest*, they could easily have appeared in one of Leonardo's copious notebooks.

Tim O'Brien[24] notes that the thing to understand about true stories is that they never end. The same might be said about Leonardo's story – and about our intentions to apply Leonardo's life and thinking to the way we respond to change or challenge. The task we have set ourselves in applying Leonardo's life and work to our own lives and learning is unlikely to reach an ending. As the educational philosopher R.S. Peters says, 'to be educated is not to have arrived at a destination; it is to travel with a different view'.[25] When the poet Antonio Camellia (Leonardo's contemporary) wrote 'Leonardo, why so troubled?', he was not simply addressing that mood of anguish and uncertainty that permeates much of Leonardo's work; he was also foreshadowing the mix of uncertainty, ambiguity and wonder that we too feel in Leonardo's presence. Curiosity engages, leading to the kind of wonder that both inspires and challenges. Go down rabbit holes and enter caves, however scary they might be. There's wonder in the darkness.

LEARNING SCATTERINGLY

Sometimes curiosity is superficial and temporary; sometimes it is more focused and lasting. Like those of Darwin after him, some of Leonardo's passing interests exemplify Montaigne's idea of learning 'scatteringly'. What he observed and what he did with his observations is illuminated, perhaps, by a metaphor from Lorrie Moore.[26] She talks

---

23. Ibid Whitehead
24. Tim O'Brien, *The Things They Carried*; Flamingo 1991
25. R.S. Peters, 'Aims of Education – A conceptual enquiry' in *The Philosophy of Education*, edited R S Peters; Oxford University Press 1973
26. Lorrie Moore: 'On Writing' in: *See What Can Be Done*; Faber and Faber 2018

about the relationship between the cook and the kitchen cupboard: 'What the cook makes from the cupboard is not the same as what's in the cupboard.' In other words, if curiosity is the source or the seed, the fruit and the reward is what we make of our experiences. The cupboard contains a collection of randomly collected ingredients; they are the source. The fruit and the reward come from further exploration of the potential of those ingredients and how they might work together.

Curiosity can work in a circular manner, from the general to the specific, from a fleeting interest to the experience of wonder. Philip Ball[27] writes that 'sometimes scientists would place wonder on the far side of curiosity'. Diversive curiosity has the potential to evolve into specific curiosity – and specific curiosity holds a potential for wonder. In Montaigne's words, learning scatteringly is the start, informed or specific curiosity is the destination, wonder is the reward.

Diversive curiosity is an inquisitiveness that can be quickly sated by finding an answer, touching, playing with, asking – or turning on the computer and interrogating the search engine. It's a characteristic of childhood, and our encounters with Leonardo encourage us to, like him, relive those feelings. Leonardo's contemporaries would have seen his voracious curiosity as an indication of a lack of concentration, or of pride and over-arching ambition – think of Icarus or Doctor Faustus. Hence, he managed to find employment, but over and over again, failed to complete the projects he was being paid to do. Leonardo's notebooks are full of examples of diversive curiosity: endless to-do lists, diversions and speculation – 'a jostling, often cramped, agglomeration of interests'.[28] A.N. Whitehead[29] suggests that this diversive curiosity sets us off on a journey from 'romance' towards what he calls 'precision' – and back again. The process is cyclical. Once we have embraced curiosity and tasted 'the wine of astonishment',[30] we reach towards a point where we can articulate that astonishment.

THE FOUNDATION OF PHILOSOPHY

Much of what Leonardo appears to have felt about absorbing and processing his experiences of the world is echoed in the writings of Montaigne.[31] Leonardo and Montaigne describe most of what they

27. Ibid Philip Ball
28. Charles Nicoll: *Leonardo da Vinci: The Flights of the Mind*: Penguin 2005
29. Isabelle Stengers: *Thinking With Whitehead*: Harvard 2011
30. Title of a novel by Earl Lovelace: *The Wine of Astonishment*; Heinemann 1982
31. *The Essays of Montaigne*; trans John Florio Oxford University Press 1906

found in books as 'dogma', a 'static' experience. Montaigne explains that this lack of vitality happens because 'we are taught to be afraid of professing our ignorance' and feel 'bound to accept everything we cannot refute' – including, by implication, our own capacity to expand our understanding. To build on what we discussed in the first chapter: he articulated what he called a theory of ignorance – which offers some clues as to how diverse curiosity morphs into specific curiosity:

> I like these words, which soften and moderate the rashness of our propositions: 'perhaps', 'to some extent', 'some', 'they say', 'I think' and the like. And if I had to train children, I would have filled their mouths so much with this way of answering, inquiring, not decisive ... Anyone who wants to be cured of ignorance must confess it. Wonder is the foundation of all philosophy, inquiry its progress, ignorance its end.

Whitehead would argue that this implied uncertainty in our encounters with things should encourage us to seek out ways to refresh curiosity and to undertake constant, endless inquiry. The intention is to press against the limits of human knowledge and in doing so to force us, as Bacon later said, to 'find forms' to include new knowledge. Montaigne found these new forms through his reading because books encouraged him to reflect on the human condition. Montaigne coined the word 'essay'. For him, the French word 'essai' means 'attempt'. Instead of learning having an end point, there is always more to say, a better way of putting it, ways to improve. Leonardo also read books, of course, but he preferred to attribute his new understanding to observation. They would both probably agree that from reading and observation, 'wisdom is won scatteringly, eclectically, almost incidentally, not systematically or ploddingly'.[32] We might disagree with his conclusion, but Montaigne has a point when he argues that 'the profit from learning does not have to be worked for: it comes as a free gift along with the pleasure'.[33] The truth is that in our own lives, most of the knowledge we are offered is 'provisional and complicated'.[34] It cries out for dialogue, not only as an aid to understanding but to rethink and recreate what we learn. When Alice Roberts says that the archaeology she is reporting on in *Digging for Britain*[35] is not just about uncovering the past but about

---

32. Jonathan Bate: *Soul of the Age: the life, mind and world of William Shakespeare*; Penguin Viking 2008
33. Jonathan Bate's words ibid
34. William Deresiewicz: *Excellent Sheep: The Miseducation of the American Elite*; Free press 2014
35. *Digging for Britain*: BBC series reporting on archaeological excavations since 2010

rewriting the past, she is saying exactly what Leonardo and Montaigne were saying about their own imaginative encounters and conversations with received or experienced knowledge. Such encounters can never be static. Conversations with information ensure a continuance of the excitement, the inspiration, and the fascination of learning.

RELENTLESS SEARCHING

After the notebooks and the lists – and the overwhelming diversive curiosity – specific curiosity comes closer to what we eventually see in Leonardo and his work. This sort of curiosity happened when a particular problem or issue (or painting) is investigated and reworked by Leonardo over an extended period of time – over 15 years in the case of the *Mona Lisa*. As well as the mechanics and meaning of painting, Leonardo was fascinated by science, by water, optics and anatomy and he returned to them again and again – but they weren't temporary or diversive fascinations. This is the sort of sustained attention and exploration which is the precursor to informed wonder. The 17th-century philosopher Bernard de Fontenelle[36] said that 'nature is never so wondrous, nor so wondered at, as when she is known'. Mihaly Csikszentmihalyi,[37] describes this focus, this informed wonder, as a 'flow' or absorption state where the individual has identified distinct and urgent goals and maintains deep concentration. William Carlos Williams[38] urges us to keep that gap and interaction between what we have learned scatteringly and what we have chosen to become obsessed with in these terms: 'Catch an eyeful, catch an earful, and don't drop what you've caught.'

Our curiosity is dependent upon a 'receding horizon'.[39] Specific (obsessive, persistent, sustained) curiosity both is and leads to wonder. Leonardo was reaching for the fruit and the reward of wonder, not just initial gratification. His curiosity is not a passing fancy, a return to childhood innocence, a diversion or an assemblage of disconnected facts. It is a relentless search. He uses those gathered facts in his work, not just to mimic what he sees, but to find the meaning beyond the superficial and to apply it. For Leonardo, copying what he sees in nature can never be the end of the story. He is attempting to 'mimic

---

36. Bernard de Fontenelle: *Conversations on the plurality of words*: University of California Press 1660 translated 1990
37. See his TED Talk: '*Flow and the search for happiness*' 2004
38. Quoted by Lorrie Moore
39. Adam Phillips: *The Beast in the Nursery: Curiosity and Other Appetites*, Faber and Faber 1999

her [Nature's] inventiveness'[40] – not simply her appearance – just as in his painting he is not simply presenting us with the *outside* of his subjects, he is showing us the *inside* – the skull beneath the skin, the mind behind the smile.

THE WONDERLAND OF SHIFTING SCALES

Plato and Aristotle, and Whitehead after them, urge us to use the processes inherent in a curiosity-driven approach to life in order to dismantle familiar ideas and explore the strange and the new. If the world is presented to us as completely known, then we remove the mystery and the motivation necessary for the beginnings of engagement. A diet of questions is the impetus. Once engaged, the appetite gathers enthusiasm. Curiosity is like a thread in a piece of cloth which, as we tease it out, unravels more threads, all of them leading to deeper or different meanings:[41] 'But we hold several threads in our hands, and the odds are that one or other of them guides us to the truth. We may waste time following the wrong one, but sooner or later we must come upon the right.'[42]

Unravelling the thread is a process of exploration, and following those threads stands every chance of being a voyage into the wonder of the unknown. As Charlotte Higgins[43] says about labyrinths:

> The centre may not be where you think it is or where you want it to be. But humans desire pattern and shape and design. They spin thread, they tell stories, they build structure. There is meaning to be made, meaning to be excavated.

The importance and potential of curiosity for learning has, in recent times, come to be seen as 'the third pillar of academic achievement'.[44]

Leonardo exemplifies all of this, a process that the physicist and novelist Alan Lightman calls an excursion into 'a wonderland of shifting scales' where one set of absolutes is repeatedly replaced by another set of absolutes[45] so that our lives are not just about absorbing more

40. Ibid Philip Ball
41. This idea comes from Tim O'Brien writing about Vietnam in *The Things They Carried*; Flamingo, 1991
42. Sir Arthur Conan Doyle: *The Hound of the Baskervilles* Penguin edition 2012
43. Charlotte Higgins: *Red Thread: On Mazes and Labyrinths*; Cape 2018
44. Sophie von Stumme et al: 'The Hungry Mind: Intellectual Curiosity is the Third Pillar of Academic Performance'; *Perspectives on Psychological Science, Vol 6*, 2012
45. Alan Lightman: *Searching for Stars on the Island of Maine*; Corsair 2018

past ideas but about revealing possibilities, facing up to uncertainties and delving into mysteries. Leonardo would have understood this. He would say, like the modern playwright James Graham, that his work is not making one point, it is making 1000 points and invites us to just pick one – and you don't know which one to pick until you've picked it.

The blurred edges, the sfumato technique, in Leonardo's portraits invite the viewer into that unknown. Daniel Dennett develops these thoughts when he describes[46] our mind in terms of a storyteller who deceives us into believing that the sketchy and incompatible impressions we take in add up to a narrative that is somehow unified. Lightman says that part of him desires to be a scientist wanting to name things, but there is another part of him that leans towards being the artist who wants to *avoid* naming things.[47] Perhaps we all want our understanding to have a final chapter, but then we also want the quest for understanding to go on forever. It's like 'the deep darkness' of the cavern he describes in his notebooks. It conveys uncertainty, ambiguity but more than anything, fills him and us with the possibility of experiencing *wonder*.

THE ANAESTHETIC OF FAMILIARITY

Plato suggests that for wonder to effect its magic, it needs to be linked with courage. We need to do more than look open-mouthed at what takes our attention: we need to embrace the unknown; we need to realise that we can make something new out of the results of our curiosity – out of the ingredients in the kitchen cupboard. Without wonder, Whitehead says, learning about things is inert. Curiosity is not enough on its own and is unlikely to lead to initiative; unless we can approach new ideas and experiences with courage we will fail to embrace and acquire new knowledge.

In A.N. Whitehead's assertion that 'philosophy begins in wonder – and at the end when philosophic thought has done its best the wonder remains'[48], he suggests that learning is a circular and an endless process, kicked off by curiosity and sustained by wonder. It begins with what Lewis Carroll's Alice calls 'burning curiosity' about a world with few given answers and a fair amount of rabbit-hole-like darkness but where that darkness offers endless opportunities to ask lots of open questions and engage in dialogue – as Alice does on every page. The questions and the dialogue take us towards the experience of wonder.

---

46. Daniel Dennett *Consciousness Explained*; Penguin 1993
47. Alan Lightman: *'The physicist as novelist'*: youtu.be/OBfRAaE2n6I
48. Ibid Whitehead

They lead us to challenge an everyday life that is for much of the time not 'lived consciously' – a place where 'nothing makes an impression [and] the world seems bland, muffled and vague'. Curiosity and encounters with wonder promise 'exceptional moments, moments of response to shocks of awareness'.[49] Finding ways as individuals to fuel wonder, as Leonardo repeatedly shows, provides us with alternatives to what Richard Dawkins calls 'the anaesthetic of familiarity'.[50]

Leonardo's challenge to received ideas is, of course, an example of Renaissance questioning of orthodoxy. He was resisting a culture that saw asking questions as an indication of evil and that wanted and expected him to be what he did not want to be. Through his work (and more particularly in his notebooks) he is saying (like Alice) that if he likes who the world wants him to be, he will join in with it; if he does not, then he will stay in the dark – but of course would much prefer to speak out. Nevertheless, these thoughts remained a secret for his notebooks – a visionary and a pragmatist to the last.

That is what this book is about: how we too might find the confidence to question, to doubt, discover and 'shake off the surly bonds of earth and touch the face of God'.[51] Leonardo could have said this. He might have added Heidegger's observation that 'truth in its totality was at the disposition of the individual'.[52] Like Leonardo, we have to seek it out – even if we don't, like him, really know what or where that truth really is. Wonder is most definitely to be found somewhere on the far side of curiosity. Or as Higgins says, 'the act of excavation and the act of creation are not so different'.[53]

REREADING REALITY

> Curiously enough, one cannot read a book: one can only reread it. A good reader, a major reader, an active and creative reader is a re-reader.[54]

This idea of experiencing wonder by reacting to the world in an active and creative way would not have been what was expected of Leonardo

49. Maxine Greene, *Landscapes of Learning*; Teachers College Press 1978
50. Richard Dawkins: *Unweaving the Rainbow: Science, Delusion and the Appetite for Wonder*; Teachers College Press 1998
51. Ronald Reagan's words from 1986 about space exploration
52. Martin Heidegger, German philosopher 1889–1976
53. Ibid Charlotte Higgins
54. Vladimir Nabokov: 'Good Readers and Good Writers' in *Lectures on Literature*; Harvest Books 2002

in late 15th-century Italy. The Church would have demanded, in line with its medieval outlook, 'ignorant gaping wonder'[55] – the sort of wonder, says Mary Baine Campbell, that 'is a form of perception mostly associated with innocence: with children, the uneducated (that is, the poor) women, lunatics and non-Western cultures. And of course, artists.'[56] Since the Enlightenment, according to Daston and Park,[57] wonder has become 'a disreputable passion in workday science, redolent of the popular, the amateurish and the childish'. The medieval mind would have seen the wonders and mysteries of nature as entirely the work of God and as such it was our role to be simply struck with awe and not ask questions or seek to know more. In the 19th century, Keats replaced this religious notion of wonder that leads us to experience awe with something similar: 'poetic wonder'. Keats argued vehemently against any desire we might have to 'unweave the rainbow'.[58] Accept the noun; don't try to employ the verb.

This brings us back to those two takes on the meaning of the word 'wonder': *uninformed* or *informed* – ignorant gaping wonder or the cold stare of what we imagine on the face of the modern scientist. The medieval view was that we should simply delight in the world God shows to us – and we can't help thinking that this is the approach some would have us take to learning. Keats appears to agree with this 'eat what you're given' approach, arguing that asking too many questions will spoil the magic. Leonardo's endless and almost random to-do lists might suggest that he too looked at the world around him and felt regular moments of awe and wonder – before moving on to the next thing in ways that some people might describe as self-indulgent.

The truth is, of course, that Leonardo didn't stop rereading. He hardly considered anything he undertook as complete; he kept returning. His gaze wasn't fleeting; it was fixed. If the medieval mind experienced wonder in a passive, accepting way, or if we simply see ourselves as consumers of wonder, then it becomes a temporary thing, a passing diversion. If, on the other hand, we are able to combine the passion that wonder can ignite with a desire to look more closely, then there is a good chance we can fuel further understanding and achievement. As Nabokov said about reading, don't just encourage *readers*, develop

55. Philip Ball: *Curiosity: How Science Became Interested in Everything*; Bodley Head 2012
56. Mary Baine Campbell: *Wonder and Science*; Cornell University Press 1999
57. L Daston and E Park: *Wonders and the Order of Nature*; Zone Books 1998
58. John Keats, 'Lamia' in *John Keats: The Complete Poems*, edited by John Barnard; Penguin Classics 1977

re-readers. Find ways to help wonder shape-shift from a noun to a verb in the workplace, the classroom, the home and in life generally.

WISE UNKNOWINGNESS

After reading Virginia Woolf's *To the Lighthouse*, Eudora Welty wrote how it 'dissolved all the sediment of my dull days into a perfect stream of motion and intensity'. The novel, she said, offered the reader a 'light under a door'. That light was perhaps an enticement to open the door, or perhaps a warning to stay out – just like the entrance to Leonardo's cave. If we engage, explore, embrace chance and welcome serendipity, we will bring a kind of innocence to our eavesdropping on the world. When the poet David Morley[59] calls a collection of his poems *The Magic of What's There*, he is suggesting that if we add minute observation and focus to our innocence (if we apply what we know already) we will begin to see how 'evocation and awe can combine to create powerful possibilities for the expansion of meaning'.[60] When we listen in on the world, or when we apply what Moore calls a 'wise unknowingness' – by which she means a combination of innocence and experience – we will discover the meaning of that light under the door and what it might lead us to. We will experience wonder – and when we use the word 'wonder' we are talking about what Ormrod[61] calls 'emotionally charged' curiosity which leads us to 'pay attention ... continue to think ... and repeatedly elaborate'. A way of living that we allow to be punctuated by 'shocks of awareness'.[62] This is the challenge implicit in cognitive conflict and the 'shock of awareness', in seeking out magic – and, of course, allowing the 'light under the door' to draw us in.

THE COMPONENTS OF AWARENESS

Descartes defines all the above as allowing for 'a sudden surprise of the soul'.[63] In practical terms, this means using the notion of 'wonder' to 'constantly ... keep the world and experience interesting'. Wonder, he says, 'is the great enemy of taking things for granted ... It can be used in ... focusing students' attention on unexpected dimensions of

59. David Morley: *The Magic of What's There*; Carcanet 2018

60. Dave Trotman: *'Wow! What if? So What?'* in Egan et al: *Wonder-full Education*; Routledge 2014

61. J. Ormrod: *Human Learning*; Merrill 1999

62. Maxine Greene: *Landscapes of Learning*; Teachers' College Press 1978

63. Quoted by M.F. Deckard in 'A sudden surprise of the soul: the passion of wonder in Hobbes and Descartes'; *The Heythrop Journal* XLIX 2008

reality and the human qualities connected with anything'.[64] There's a sort of innocence about the whole idea of diversive curiosity, the way it engages and enthuses, whereas specific curiosity (or wonder) implies an element of what Hadzigeorgiou[65] calls 'a component of awareness'. Raymond Loewy[66] talks about the importance of finding occasions to provoke 'an aesthetic aha' – that moment when we meet something new, or challenging or surprising, that leads us to feel an 'expectation of meaning'. This is exactly what people feel very often when they step into a cathedral, or an ancient monument, or a sports stadium or concert hall or theatre.

The possibility of the light under a door – the possibility of encountering wonder, imagination, and magic – will inevitably mean that we will collide with its opposite, what Balarin and Lauder[67] call 'a state theory of learning' (a preoccupation with measurable outcomes and inflexible definitions of 'best practice'). This is a world where, as Eisner[68] observed, 'imagination is not on anyone's list of basics', where retention and understanding are seen as the same thing, a world where Whitehead's 'romance of learning'[69] is seen as missing the whole point. It's when the 'peril and promise of novelty and change'[70] turns, simply, into fear – another way of expressing what Leonardo was facing – and resisting – at the entrance to the cavern.

THE FAR SIDE OF CURIOSITY

When it was launched in 1977, *Voyager 1* was setting out on a mission to investigate the outer planets. It completed its tour in 1980 and then in 2012 left the solar system. It has become an icon of modern science, 'an exemplar of human curiosity that represents the joy of exploring what is beyond the horizon and beneath the surface of things'.[71] In *The*

---

64. Kieran Egan: *The Future of Education: Reimagining Our Schools from the Ground Up*; Yale 2008
65. Yannis Hadzigeorgiou: 'Reclaiming the Value of Wonder in Science Education'; *Wonder-full Education*; Egan et al; Routledge 2014
66. Raymond Loewy; *Never Leave Well Enough Alone* (1951); John Hopkins University Press 2002
67. Balarin and Lauder 'The governance, administration and control of primary education' in *The Cambridge Primary Research Surveys*; Routledge 2010
68. Elliot Eisner: *Reimagining Schools; The Selected Works of Elliot Eisner*; Routledge 2005
69. Alfred North Whitehead; 'The Rhythm of Education' in, *The Aims of Education and Other Essays*: The Free Press 1929 reprinted 1967
70. Ibid Eisner
71. Manjit Kumar: 'The truths that are out there – and how to find them'; *The Observer* August 2018

Consolations of Physics, Tim Radford[72] makes the point that the story of the Voyager mission offers him consolation when he feels desolate about the behaviour of the world in the 21st century. He finds solace in the fact 'that humans are also capable of selfless co-operation in pursuit of unearthly satisfactions'.

What propels us on from what Ball[73] called Leonardo's 'ragbag' curiosity? What do we need to take us from our personal solar system and towards our own individual versions of interstellar space? A.N. Whitehead[74] says that the 'the life of the mind' cannot be postponed 'until you have sharpened it. Whatever interest attaches to your subject–matter must be evoked here and now.' You cannot wait until you know all the rules and have taken on board all those things you believe you ought to know before being allowed to participate or have a view. Our need to know needs to be urgent.

Burns and Gentry[75] say something similar in their tension-to-learn theory. It's about matching manageable knowledge gaps with the learner's natural curiosity. This can happen when we encounter 'complexity that invites inquiry ... interesting materials, seductive details, and desirable difficulty' as opposed to 'material that has been made as straightforward and digested as possible'. When we 'encounter objects, texts, environments, and ideas that draw [us] in and pique [our] curiosity', our understanding will grow. Burns and Gentry also talk about the difference between 'retrieval strength', which is when we acquire and learn something quickly (for a test, say), and 'storage strength', which is the slower acquisition of knowledge. Making the learning easy and accessible can improve retrieval strength and enhance performance but it is at least as important that we find ways to enhance storage strength – or long-term retention – rather than emphasising short-term performance. In a study called 'The Wick in the Candle of Learning',[76] the authors conclude that when an individual's interest is at its height, so too is their capacity to learn and remember. When learning is satisfying, it tends to be long lasting.

---

72. Tim Radford: *The Consolations of Physics*; Sceptre 2018
73. Ibid Phillip Ball
74. A.N. Whitehead: *The Art of Education* 1916
75. Burns and Gentry: 'Motivating students to engage in experiential learning: a tension to learn theory' 1998 (available online)
76. Research article by Min Jeng Kang *et al*: *The Association for Psychological Science* 2000 (available on line)

Unsurprisingly, Leonardo also has something to say about this too: 'Study without desire spoils the memory and it retains nothing it takes in.' We need to ensure that we expose ourselves to our own ignorance. Only then will we find the desire to properly investigate further. When a researcher chases a problem through to its most fitting conclusion, their thinking *converges*; but then once that point is reached, the conclusion has to be tested through the application of a series of hypotheses – *other possibilities*. The possibilities need to be located. This requires *divergent* thinking. Or even insubordination. Which brings us to David Storey's assertion that it's people who are liabilities – rather than the reliable – who win the prizes.

NOTES TOWARDS SOMETHING

Bernard MacLaverty sums up this tension between what we are told to think and what we are driven to create for ourselves in this description of an admired teacher: 'He was a great teacher and he liked to give students enough self-confidence to create, yet instil in them enough knowledge to self-doubt.'[77] This is a version of what Leonardo means by 'fear and desire': the balancing of one with the other. 'What we want to know and what we can imagine are two sides of the same magical page.'[78] Curiosity opens the door to knowledge; wonder tests and deepens that knowledge.

Like Leonardo, the writer Bernard MacLaverty kept copious notebooks. When asked what he puts in the notebooks he answered, 'notes towards something'. Leonardo would have given the same answer. He kept notes towards *something* because he believed that 'everything proceeds from everything, everything becomes everything, and everything can be turned into everything else' – or learning scatteringly as a way of bumping into wonder and launching those 'flights of the mind'. Like MacLaverty, Leonardo no doubt felt that his notes were liable at any minute to lead him towards uncovering *something* – some vital revelation, some small detail which would cause one of those 'unearthly satisfactions'[79] and cause everything to become clear. He is not simply using his notebooks to record but to identify the forces at play in whatever those somethings are that he is looking at. He reminds us that surface skimming will not do – not all the time, anyway. If he wanted to paint an old man's body, he would not just view the surface of that body:

---

77. Bernard MacLaverty: *Midwinter Break*, Jonathan Cape,2017
78. Alberto Manguel: *Curiosity*; Yale 2015
79. Ibid Tim Radford

he would seek out opportunities to slip into the morgue in the dead of night and dissect an old man's body. Looking at surfaces is a sort of empiricism minus interpretation and can be a waste of time. Leonardo looks for meaning and underlying causes, 'a reason for everything in this unreasonable universe'[80] – and if he experiences a moment like that moment of hesitation at the cave's mouth, or if the world seems to be telling him to be someone he doesn't want to be, he refuses to abandon the desire to illuminate the darkness. When Leonardo wrote in his notebooks that 'the sun does not move', he was almost inviting a death sentence in his time; but it didn't stop him. This is what Nicholl calls 'the edginess that accompanies the great Renaissance quest for knowledge'[81] – a reminder that the route to effective learning isn't predictable; it's provisional.

The emotional dynamics of much (if not all) of Leonardo's work reminds us why curiosity and wonder are now seen as the 'knowledge emotions'. The urgent desire to find a piece of information, make use of it and connect it to our broader understanding makes us feel good about ourselves – and as a result, we are motivated to go on finding out and processing more information. If the gaps in our knowledge are filled for us, or if we are so sure we know everything (like when we stereotype people or repeat untested opinions) then the motivation to learn similarly disengages. As Erik Stronstrom puts it: 'Curiosity is inherently dynamic and propulsive, not sedentary and passive. Most traditional instruction depends on the latter state and seeks to control the former.'[82]

THE SERVICE OF DELIGHT

Of course, knowledge fuels understanding, but it is wonder that fuels curiosity. Wonder challenges certainty and leads us into discursive adventures and creative conversations with others – or even within ourselves. When we say that learning, and making connections, is dependent on having fuel in the tank, we don't just mean the fuel provided by stored up knowledge; we also mean the fuel of emotional commitment, outward-looking enthralment, fascination. Enthusiasm, that beautiful word derived from the God within, is key. It is the beauty that Blake called 'exuberance' and 'the service of delight'.[83]

---

80. Ibid Manguel
81. Ibid Nicholl
82. Erik Stronstrom: *Education Week* 3.6.14
83. William Blake: *The Marriage of Heaven and Hell*, Dover Facsimile Edition 2000

Curiosity is therefore far more than what we mentioned earlier, 'the third pillar of academic achievement'. Emotions like the urgent desire, the need, to find a piece of information – then actually finding it ourselves and (when we have found it) using it to make connections to our broader understanding – make us feel good about our abilities. They also encourage us to start all over again, to travel from curiosity to wonder and back again. Without constant learning we are standing in the entrance to whatever caves we might meet in our own lives and denying ourselves the chance to feel either fear or desire, or to step forward into the unknown or step back into what we know.

Some facts might well be fixed but how we interpret those facts, how we assemble further knowledge and new thinking is a mystery that we shall be investigating later. The truth is that there are no finite solutions. What we hope we have shown here is that true engagement with the world is the key – 'as opposed, say, to obsessive pedantry, acquisitiveness or problem-solving'.[84] The pleasures of interest and research are not always easy to sustain, but they are the best things that we have going for us. In no small measure, they make our lives liveable. Leonardo was addicted to and driven by what he didn't know, prying into everything, committed to unravelling the mysteries and urgencies that surrounded him. For him, curiosity and wonder were tools, like scalpels and searchlights, that helped him to explore dark recesses, to engage in his rapturous research.

Perhaps that mystery, that reason we hope to experience wonder, is here in Emily Dickinson's definition:[85]

> Wonder – is not precisely Knowing
> And not precisely Knowing not –
> A beautiful but bleak condition...

Leonardo's beautiful and bleak condition is expressed here by Ralph Steadman, when he adopts Leonardo's voice in *I, Leonardo*: 'disappointment and self-doubt [existed] alongside exuberant achievement'. It was a life where 'miraculous vision' and 'apocalyptic nightmares' coincided and collided. On a slightly more positive note, as Montaigne previously pointed out, 'wonder is the foundation of all philosophy – inquiry its progress'.[86] And it is to inquiry that we now turn.

---

84. Ibid Philip Ball
85. Emily Dickinson: *Collected Poems*: Wordsworth Poetry Library, 1994
86. Montaigne: *The Complete Essays*, Translated by D. Frame, Stanford University Press, 1958

CHAPTER 3
PERFECTING ATTENTION

Salvator Mundi; Louvre Abu Dhabi

Leonardo was interested in more than scientific accuracy. He was at least as much, if not more, concerned with 'atti e moti mentali' – 'psychological expositions' – the intentions of the mind. Depicting both motion and emotion, the psychological portrait.

What did Leonardo mean by...?

All of our knowledge has its origin in our perceptions.[1]

SCIENTIFIC PRECISION

The news story[2] about the authenticity of a painting called *Salvator Mundi* ('saviour of the world') and its sale for a world record-annihilating figure of $459m in 2017 – and all the arguments about authenticity that accompanied this event – exposes a key question for us when we engage with Leonardo's work. Are we looking at his paintings with our senses or with our emotions? The tipping point along the way to establishing the authenticity of *Salvator Mundi* was the recognition – and assertion – that this 'lost' painting 'offers the viewer shifting emotional interactions'.[3] Martin Kemp says very much the same when he talks about feeling Leonardo's magic on his first encounter with the painting.[4] The painting is felt as much as it is seen.

The doubters on the other hand – led by Matthew Landrus, a former pupil and academic associate of Kemp at Oxford – believe that most of the painting is the work of Leonardo's studio assistant, Bernardino Luini. As well as questioning the exact extent of the painting's restoration, the doubters focus most particularly on what they call 'an unusual lapse by Leonardo'.[5] The crystal orb in the painting has 'up to a point, been rendered with beautiful scientific precision', but if it *is* Leonardo's painting, he has not shown the optical distortions in the orb that we know from his notebooks he would have both observed and understood – the reflections in the orb would have been inverted. Precise and accurate observation is what many art historians expect and anticipate in Leonardo's work. For Landrus et al., questions of attribution depend on hard evidence, not feelings; technical features typical of Leonardo, not instinct.

This is not to say that those convinced of the authenticity of the painting were relying entirely upon instinct. This is Philip Mould, one of the small group of National Gallery verifiers:

> This is a very secular image of Christ. There's no cross, there's no halo, and also there's something sexily quite ambiguous about his

---

1. Da Vinci: *Notebooks* Richter (1888) Dover 1970
2. *'Puzzling anomaly at the heart of £75 million artwork'*; Dalya Alberge The Guardian 19.10.17
3. Ibid Isaacson
4. Martin Kemp: *Living with Leonardo: Fifty Years of Sanity and Insanity in the Art World and Beyond*; Thames and Hudson 2018
5. Ibid Isaacson

appearance, a slightly gender-fluid aspect to it that makes it very zeitgeisty ... It is the face of today.[6]

That phrase – 'the face of today' – echoes throughout this book. Scientific inaccuracies or imperfections may occupy the doubters[7] but it is difficult to escape the shadow of Leonardo's face behind the face of *Salvator Mundi* – reassuring and unsettling us with its extraordinary beauty – or to turn away from Martin Kemp's perception that the painting resonates 'deeply with Leonardo's science of art'.[8]

Just as with almost everything else we meet in these conversations with Leonardo's work and life, our response goes beyond artistic scrutiny. We repeatedly meet what Kemp meets in *Salvator Mundi*, what he calls the painting's loud 'Mona-Lisa-ish echoes'. These echoes are what many have described as 'the Leonardo effect' and they go some way towards helping us to understand why there has been this long dispute about the painting's authenticity:

> His skill of observation was so acute that even an obscure anomaly in his paintings, such as an uneven dilation of pupils, causes us to wrestle, perhaps too much, with what he might have noticed and thought. If so, it is a good thing. By being around him, viewers are stimulated to observe the little details of nature, like the cause of a dilated pupil, and to regain our sense of wonder about them. Inspired by his desire to notice every detail, we try to do the same.[9]

And so the argument goes on. Do we look with our eyes or our hearts? Do we see Leonardo, or do we sense him? Are we interacting with the painting emotionally or cognitively? As we write, the painting, which apparently had been bought on behalf of the Louvre Abu Dhabi, has disappeared from view. Lost again. Unanswered again.

OBSESSIVE NOTICING

When Leonardo's near-contemporary Galileo Galilei[10] (1564–1642) wrote that 'the grandest of all books, I mean the Universe, stands open

---

6. Philip Mould: see *The Guardian* November 2017: *How did 'male Mona Lisa' earn a price tag of $450m?*

7. And the search for inconsistencies goes on at time of writing: see Jonathan Jones: *The Da Vinci Mystery*, in *The Guardian* October 2018. The questions about the orb have been replaced by questions about the restoration process – what it reveals and what it conceals

8. Martin Kemp: *Living with Leonardo: Fifty Years of Sanity and Insanity in the Art World and Beyond*; Thames and Hudson 2018

9. Ibid Isaacson

10. Stephen Hawking compares Leonardo and Galileo in 'Of course da Vinci was an artistic scientist, but Galileo and Copernicus too?' www.birdiechamp.com

before our eyes', he appears to be arguing that truth works in exactly the same way. It is tangible, within reach, and as Leonardo argues, all we have to do is look: 'those sciences are vain and full of error which are not born of experience, mother of certainty, first-hand experience which in its origins, or means, or end has passed through one of the five senses'.[11] First-hand experience means stimulating and refining the five traditional senses: taste, sight, smell, hearing and touch. He commented that he gave 'the degrees of things seen by the eye as the musician does of the sounds heard by the ear'. Understanding the harmony and patterns in nature is the basis of all of our knowledge and has its origins in our perceptions. What he wrote about seeing might well apply to the other senses: 'The eye, which is said to be the window of the soul, is the principal means by which the brain's sensory receptor may fully and magnificently contemplate the infinite works of nature.'[12]

Art historians see the accuracy and precision of Leonardo's observation as proof of his paintings' authenticity. He gazed at everything: 'As you go about town, constantly observe, note, and consider the circumstances and behaviour of men as they talk and quarrel, or laugh, or come to blows.'[13]

For Leonardo, observation is pragmatism: 'If you wish to have a sound knowledge of the forms of objects, begin with the details of them, and do not go on to the second step until you have the first well fixed in memory.'[14] For instance, when he observes the dragonfly, he writes, 'the dragonfly flies with four wings, and when those in front are raised those behind are lowered'.[15] This before the invention of ultra slow-motion cameras – or indeed, of any cameras at all. When he turned his attention to birds and flight, he asked whether a bird moves its wings faster on the upstroke or on the downstroke. Was this – along with all the other observations and questions (and attempts to quantify and analyse) – about an artist diligently researching for the benefit of his paintings, or was he as much drawn to science as he was to art? Whatever his motivation, Leonardo's notebooks indicate pure joy just seeing in order to understand things. In these notebooks he is 'a writer-down of things: a recorder of observations,

---

11. Leonardo da Vinci: *Treatise on Painting*; ed Maggie Mack; Create Space Independent Publishing 2012
12. Ibid Isaacson
13. Codex Ashburnham, l'Institute de France, Paris
14. Ibid Codex Ashburnham
15. Ibid Codex Ashburnham

a pursuer of data, an explorer of thoughts, an inscriber of lists and memoranda [and] the overall tone of his writing is terse, colloquial, practical, laconic'.[16]

That small notebook which many of his contemporaries noticed hanging from his belt was just the tip of the iceberg. It contains just a few of the many pages of working archives, lists of questions and observations all hidden away in his studio. In fact Isaacson calls them 'the most astonishing testament to the powers of human observation and imagination ever set down on paper'.[17]

THE UNIVERSAL MEASURE OF MAN

Observation for Leonardo is about much more than recording: '[He] observed natural phenomena, conducted experiments in physics, mixed pigments and varnishes, dissected animals, analysed construction techniques, built models – and, above all, never stopped asking questions.'[18] It's about understanding and, in the end, about reshaping a future built on looking and thinking. He seeks underlying causes. Whatever theory he comes to believe must be based on experience:

> All the branches of a tree at every stage of its height when put together are equal in thickness to the trunk below them ... All the branches of a river at every stage of its course, if they are of equal rapidity, are equal to the body of the main stream.[19]

In the same way, as an acute observer of all things geological (whether in fossils or rock formations) he pieced together evidence about the age of the earth. Individual perceptions in the *Codex Leicester* – such as 'one sees the strata on one side of the river corresponding with those on the other'[20] – led him to think about the forces of time and geological change. His observations about sea animals – 'Why are there bones of great fishes and oysters and corals and other various shells and sea-snails found on the tops of mountains?' – opened up wider thoughts with regard to questioning the likelihood of the Biblical version of world history. Leonardo's reliance on empiricism in relation to the study of rocks leads the science historian Fritjof

16. Charles Nicholl: 'Sneezing ... Yawning ... Failing: The Notebooks of Leonardo da Vinci' in *Traces Remain: Essays and Explorations*; Penguin 2012
17. Ibid Isaacson
18. Toby Lester: *Da Vinci's Ghost*; Free Press 2012
19. Paris Manuscripts in *l'Institute de France*, Paris; translated J. Venerella ed Ravaison-Mollien 1999
20. Codex Leicester (1508–1512) now owned by Bill Gates, at his home in Seattle, Washington

Capra to assert that 'The superposition of rock strata would not be recognized and studied in similar detail until the second half of the seventeenth century.'[21] In fact, Leonardo also doesn't seem far from pre-empting by several centuries Darwin's theory of evolution when he says, 'Nature, being inconstant and taking pleasure in creating and continually producing new forms, because she knows that her terrestrial materials are thereby augmented, is more ready and more swift in her creating than is time in his destruction.'[22] That word 'augmented' seems to suggest he realised the existence of the natural selection process in nature. As well as this, he jotted down in his notebooks (long before Galileo was accused of heresy) that 'Il sole no si muove'[23] – 'The sun does not move.' Isaacson asks: 'Is this statement a brilliant leap decades ahead of Copernicus, Galileo, and the realization that the sun does not revolve around the earth?'[24] Whatever the truth may be, it is certain that his capacity to see clearly and without fear launched him far beyond either his contemporaries or indeed the intellectual understandings of his time.

As he uncovered the structure of the human body, Leonardo became fascinated by the 'figura istrumentale dell' omo' – 'man's instrumental figure' – and he sought to comprehend its physical working as a creation of nature. He did practical work in anatomy on the dissection table in Milan, then at hospitals in Florence and Rome, and in Pavia, where he worked closely with the physician-anatomist Marcantonio della Torre. By his own count Leonardo dissected 30 corpses in his lifetime and his anatomical drawings take measurement and investigation several stages further:

> Every part will be drawn, using all means of demonstrations, from three different points of view; for when you have seen a limb from the front, with any muscles, sinews, or veins which take their rise from the opposite side, the same limb will be shown to you in a side view or from behind, exactly as if you had that same limb in your hand and were turning it from side to side until you had acquired a full comprehension of all you wished to know.[25]

---

21. Fritos Capra: *Learning from Leonardo: Decoding the Notebooks of a Genius*; Berrett-Koehler Publishing 2013
22. Ibid Codex Leicester
23. Windsor – The Royal Collection, Windsor Castle
24. Ibid Isaacson
25. Ibid J.P Richter

'The painter,' he says, 'should aim at universality.'[26] His intention was nothing less than knowing how man fits into the cosmos, 'to fathom what he called "universale misura del huomo" – the universal measure of man'.[27]

THE EDGES OF SHADOWS

Isaacson explains that Leonardo 'instructed himself to learn about the placenta of a calf, the jaw of a crocodile, the tongue of a woodpecker, the muscles of a face, the light of the moon, and the edges of shadows.'[28] That last phrase stands out. The 'edges of shadows'. His concern was with modelling reality and the part light and shade plays in this process – how it was achieved and its emblematic significance in his life – as well as ours: 'Relief is the soul of painting ... Shadow is of greater power than light, in that it can entirely impede and entirely deprive bodies of light and the light can never chase away all the shadows of bodies.'[29] Kemp talks about 'Leonardo's remorselessly systematic quality of radiant forms emerging from obscure darkness'.[30] In terms of our concern with what Leonardo might tell us about learning, it is this juxtaposition of light and shadow that offers us a paradigm for how learning (and maybe life) works. Kemp repeatedly makes the point that the meeting of light and shade is both an optical *and* a psychological phenomenon and that defining what we see in any precise way is difficult: 'our discernment of edges was never absolutely certain'[31] – or as Ernst Gombrich put it, 'the blurred outline and mellowed colours ... allow one form to merge with another and always leave something to our imagination'.[32] Dr Francis Follen highlights this interaction between what we see and our imaginations when she writes of a painting by Bridget Riley: 'Neither the movement nor the colour exists on the canvas, but that is not the same as saying that they are not there. They are in your head, in the complex eye-brain system that gives you the experience of light.'[33]

Leonardo knew that the achievement of a three-dimensional painting is not just about representing reality, it's about interacting with reality

26. Ibid Paris Manuscripts

27. Notebooks/J.P. Richter: *The Notebooks of Leonardo da Vinci* Dover 1970

28. Ibid Isaacson

29. Ibid Paris Manuscripts

30. Martin Kemp: *Leonardo da Vinci: The Marvellous Works of Nature and Man*: Oxford 2006

31. Ibid Kemp and Pallanti referring to *Codex Urbinus Latinus* in the Vatican library

32. Ernst Gombrich *The Story of Art*; Phaidon 1950

33. Dr Francis Follen, 'An Optical View of History' in: *Seurat to Riley: The Art of Perception*; Sexton and Follen; Compton Verney Art Gallery 2017

in ways that invite a dialogue – in much the same way as we hope the learning process encourages. Painting, ideas, understanding, invention '[arise] from light and shade';[34] 'shadow is the means by which bodies display their form. The forms of bodies could not be understood in detail but for shadow.'[35] There was no rigidity in his techniques because 'between light and darkness there is infinite variation, because their quantity is continuous'.[36]

He became a master of infinite variation, legitimate and manoeuvred. As Isaacson astutely says, 'Once he knew the rules, he became a master at fudging and distorting them.'[37] He saw that every painting was about research – rather than creating a finished work of art.[38] In Martin Kemp's words, 'Every act of looking and drawing was, for Leonardo, an act of analysis.'[39]

OBSERVATION, INVENTIVENESS AND IMAGINATION

Leonardo wrote in his *Treatise on Painting* that 'the painter must not seek to improve on nature, nor show only the beautiful in nature. Rather, he should record nature's full variety, not merely copying nature slavishly, but exploiting his inventiveness (invenzione).'[40] Leonardo's skills of observation did not conflict with his imaginative skills. When it came to geometric transformation of volumes, he looked at how to understand what he was seeing, but also as it applied to the human body. He was obsessed by motion, be it curved reflections, the movement of water, shapes and transformations of volumes – 'of everything that moves, the space which it acquires is as great as that which it leaves'.[41] When he is drawing the human body his concern seems to be with 'moti corporali' – 'the motions and workings of the body'. It was essential to him that he got the anatomy right (as his numerous dissections of dead bodies show); but following on from that he wanted to know how the body itself changes through movement – how 'one geometric shape morphed into another'.[42]

---

34. Ibid Isaacson
35. Ibid Notebooks J.P. Richter
36. Ibid Notebooks J.P. Richter
37. Ibid Isaacson
38. Picasso said something similar: he saw he painting as a constant search
39. Martin Kemp: Leonardo: *Inside the Mind of a Renaissance Genius*; Oxford University Press 2004
40. Ibid Trattato della pittura
41. Leonardo: *Codex Atlanticus*
42. Ibid Isaacson

MOTION AND EMOTION

Which brings us back to those arguments about *Salvator Mundi* and its attribution. Clearly Leonardo was interested in more than scientific accuracy. He was at least as concerned with 'atti e moti mentali' – 'psychological expositions' – or what Gombrich[43] describes as 'motions of the mind'.[44] In addition to portraying the movements of the body that are contained in a moment, Leonardo focused on conveying 'molti dell'anima', 'the motions of the soul'. He writes that 'a picture of human figures ought to be done in such a way as that the viewer may easily recognise, by means of their attitudes, the intentions of their minds'.[45]

Leonardo's enigmatic and beautiful *Lady with an Ermine* illustrates his anatomical precision and at the same time his understanding of the dynamic effects of movement. Cecilia Gallerani's right hand is depicted with painstaking accuracy. She is caught in the act of moving to her left – in an example of the classical ideal of 'contrapposto'. There is the hint of a smile on her lips as she seems to shift her attention away from the painter (and of course us) towards something outside our view. It suggests that 'from varied viewpoints, each human action is displayed as infinite in itself'.[46] This is more than a static portrait, a record of what Cecilia looked like; it's a moment in a conversation – a moment of listening as well as telling. As Leonardo put it, a 'figure is most praiseworthy when it expresses the passion of its mind'[47]. John Pope-Hennessy[48] writes that the *Lady with an Ermine* is the first portrait in European art to show that a painting could express the sitter's thoughts and soul simply through a combination of posture and gesture; a painting that shows the sitter's personality and mind, not only her beauty. As a result, she talks to us too. Those motions of the mind that Leonardo was trying to capture in his subjects spill over to capture our minds too.

---

43. Ernst Gombrich: "Tobias and the Angel" in *Symbolic Images: Studies in the Art of the Renaissance*; Phaidon 1972
44. Ibid Isaacson
45. Leonardo: *Codex Atlanticus*, 137a,415a; Notebooks/J.P.Richter, 593; Marani. movements of the soul, 233
46. Ibid *Trattato della pittura* (Treatise on Painting)
47. Leonardo on Painting: *Treatise on Painting*, edited Kemp, Yale 1989
48. John Pope-Hennessy: *The Portrait in the Renaissance*; Pantheon 1963

When Leonardo said that 'he who can go to the fountain does not go to the water jar', he was pressing the point that the real world could offer far more directly to us than any second-hand experience. Embracing Leonardo's ideas on attentiveness and precision sharpens the intellect.

Leonardo was determined that observation and empiricism should not overshadow his drive to be inventive. We can learn from that.

Lady with an Ermine; Czartoryski Museum in Kraków, Poland

Meaning is in everything – learning to see in the broadest way possible will release multitudes of unexpected and brightly lit moments. Leonardo wasn't simply trying to find the way a dragonfly's wings worked, or how a bird flies, or how the human body moves, or how light and shade interact – he was striving to capture and charge the whole cosmos with emotion, imagination and meaning.

What can we still learn from Leonardo about...?

Meaning comes from the physical embeddedness of all human experience.[49]

THE FORMATION OF ATTENTION

Tireless observation, empathy, an openness to experience and the constant questioning of the world are all part of what we can learn from Leonardo. The mid-20th century German philosopher Simone Weil calls the process of marrying prolonged effort and imagination 'the formation of attention'.[50] This is perhaps the neatest phrase to encapsulate what we have been describing in relation to Leonardo's obsessive and precise attention to detail *and* the learning processes that we would hope to experience and to replicate in our own lives. It encapsulates that development from curiosity, to discovery, to discipline and independence that we hope to experience. It is not about certainties but possibilities; neither is it about preconceptions but is rather about doubt. Leonardo's whole approach tells us that much of what is worth thinking about, or studying, does not have ready-made answers and as a result we need to respond to the world with observation, reflection, contemplation and thought – to the point of letting go, or at least questioning, existing knowledge. In the poem 'Thought', D.H. Lawrence writes that 'Thought is not a trick, or an exercise, or a set of dodges / Thought is a man in his wholeness, wholly attending.'[51] Whitehead describes learning where the 'vividness of novelty' is a first step towards a 'precision' stage where learners develop 'an exactness of formulation'.[52]

Leonardo's notebooks contain pages and pages of questions arising from his desire to scrutinise and explain. His questions foster attention; his attention leads to understanding. He undertook this quest for precision all of his life, and his notebooks document his journey. Even when he didn't feel he was getting any closer to answers, he kept going. Weil believed that 'even if our efforts of attention seem for years to be producing no result, one day a light that is in exact proportion to them will flood the soul. Every effort adds a little gold to a treasure no power on earth can take away.'[53]

---

49. A paraphrase of Martin Heidegger
50. Simone Weil: 'Reflections on the Right Use of School Studies' in *Waiting for God*; Harper Perennial 2009
51. D.H. Lawrence, *Thought*
52. Alfred North Whitehead: *The Aims of Education and other essays*; Macmillan 1929
53. Ibid Simone Weil

Anyone who saw the writer Dennis Potter being interviewed just three months before his death will remember what he said about seeing: 'The fact is, if you see in the present tense, boy do you see. And boy can you celebrate it.' Leonardo's paintings, just like so many poems, carry with them brightly lit moments in our earth and time–bound lives. Leonardo's constant project to understand how everything connects and helps interpret everything else shows us the way down from what might become theoretical ivory towers so that we can join in with the wider world. The scientist Steven Weinberg[54] makes a plea for interdisciplinary and real–world interaction with a reference to one particular poem: 'Event Horizon' by Clive James:[55]

> You get to see the cosmos blaze
> And feel its grandeur, even against your will,
> As it reminds you, just by being there,
> That it is here we live or else nowhere.

He seems to be saying that the meaning of his life is to be found in that refraction that occurs between his own gaze and the enormity of the world and the universe around and beyond him. Meaning is in everything – learning to see in the broadest way possible, as Leonardo says, will release multitudes of unexpected and brightly lit moments. He wasn't simply trying to find the way a dragonfly's wings worked, or how a bird flies, or how the human body moves, or how light and shade interact; he was striving to capture and charge the whole cosmos with emotion, imagination and meaning.

EMOTIONALLY CHARGED LEARNING AND THE SENSES

Gautreaux has a useful way of leading us into this next section: 'We can only learn that which we love, and eyes are useless to a blind brain.'[56] Without prolonged effort and imagination – without attention – there is no learning. When Simon Baron–Cohen[57] categorises autistic children as either 'extreme systematisers' that look for patterns or 'empathisers' that look for feelings and motivations, he is identifying how each of us respond to our senses. Like those art historians shouting at each other about *Salvator Mundi*, we all tend to respond either emotionally or cognitively to the stimulation of each of our senses.

54. Steven Weinberg: *Third Thoughts*; Belknap Press 2018
55. 'Event Horizon' is in Clive James, *Sentenced to Life* 2017
56. Rosalba Gautreaux in her speech in the 1st Conference on Neuroeducation, 26th May 2018
57. Simon Baron–Cohen, R. Knickmeyer and M. Belmonte: *Sex differences in the brain – Implications form explaining autism*, Science 2005

Yet, taste, sight, smell, hearing and touch all have the capacity to elicit emotions and thinking at the same time. They also engage the surprise instinct[58] and, as a result, promote learning with all its unexpected delights. The potential of the senses is to link the distant with the immediate, the abstract with the concrete, and it pushes us towards new thoughts and experiences rather than simply pulling us into our comfort zones. All of which is a way of saying that exploring our senses has the potential to be analytical. Our senses lead us towards interrogating reality. What we see in a painting by Leonardo, or in a new piece of learning, is created twice: first by whoever provided that experience – the artist or the teacher – and second by whatever we bring and apply to the experience.

In *The Marriage of Heaven and Hell*, William Blake[59] mentions each of the five traditional senses of perception, profoundly believing that 'if the doors of perception were cleansed every thing would appear to man as it is, Infinite. For man has closed himself up, till he sees all things thro' narrow chinks of his cavern.' That Leonardo moment again – the cavern – fear coupled with excitement. The five senses are the way into, or a way out of, that cavern of self in order to 'abundantly appreciate the infinite works of nature'.

INTERROGATING REALITY

Other writers and artists have focused their attention on the workings of the individual senses in order to better interrogate reality. When the narrator of Marcel Proust's *Remembrance of Things Past*[60] dipped a small cake – a 'petite Madeleine' – into his cup of tea, the resultant **taste** led him into an intricate and detailed journey into his memories of the past. This sudden recollection is often called the 'Proustian moment' or the 'Madeleine moment'. The novel constantly and repeatedly links that moment of perception to his memory. Through the unexpected taste of tea and cake, the narrator opens a door into an understanding of reality and relationships and as a result his perceptions of himself and the world are altered. Taste also works to '[propel] us far from our roots – not just geographically, but also existentially'.[61]

---

58. A phrase from Steven Johnson in *Wonderland: How Play Made the Modern World*; Macmillan 2016, and Pan 2017
59. William Blake: *The Complete Poems* edited by W. H. Stevenson; Longman 1971
60. Marcel Proust: Remembrance of Things Past Penguin Classics 2016
61. Steven Johnson: *Wonderland: How Play Made the Modern World*; Macmillan 2016

Leonardo would most probably have put **sight** first in his hierarchy of his 'ministers of the soul' – the five senses – emphasising the importance of 'saper vedere', 'knowing how to see'. As an artist he is noted for his extraordinary accuracy, seemingly seeing with greater clarity than the rest of us could hope to. When, for instance, he shows birds in flight, he is clearly conscious of the structure of feathers – so much so that in Baron–Cohen's terms, he is not only an 'empathiser' revelling in the beauty of flight but also a 'systematiser' concerned with the science of the process. John Lubbock makes the point with: 'What we see depends mainly on what we look for ... In the same field the farmer will notice the crop, the geologist the fossils, botanists the flowers, artist the colouring.'[62] And in Leonardo's case, all of the above – and probably more.

In 'Smells like Old Times'[63] Maria Konnikova opts for **smell** as the most important sense. She argues that visual perception has its limitations whereas a sense of smell evokes deep memory and understanding. As the many and various products of the perfume industry would suggest, smells and their associations are also highly emotive. There's a wonderfully evocative passage in *The Picture of Dorian Gray* where Wilde talks about the metaphorical nature of several different scents and uses them to evoke a variety of experiences:

> He felt keenly conscious of how barren all intellectual speculation is when separated from action and experiment. He knew that the senses, no less than the soul, have their spiritual mysteries to reveal ... He saw that there was no mood of the mind that had not its counterpart in the sensuous life and set himself to discover their true relations.[64]

Alfred A. Tomatis[65] stresses the vital importance of **hearing** in learning and understanding: 'We read with our ears ... the ear is the organ of language, the pathway to language assimilation, the key that controls it, the receptor regulating its flow.' Or, if it's music we are thinking about, there's Nietzsche's emphatic phrase: 'without music, life would be a mistake'. As an artist, Leonardo may have favoured sight, but he was an accomplished musician, aware of the extent to which sound enriched the human mind. We use music to create or stimulate a state

62. John Lubbock: *The Beauties of Nature and the Wonders of the World We Live In*; 1892
63. Maria Konnikova: 'Smells Like Old Times'; *Scientific American* 2012
64. Oscar Wilde: *The Picture of Dorian Gray* Wordsworth Classics 1992
65. Alfred A Tomatis: *The Conscious Ear: My Life of Transformation Through Listening* 1992; Station Hill Press

of mind – anticipation, excitement, energy, concentration, reflection, calmness, stillness – or to evoke a place, or a time, providing a fairly uncluttered, emotive and suggestive 'pathway to language' and learning. Steven Johnson[66] argues that 'music sends us out on a quest for new experiences; more of the same, but different'. He goes on to argue that music is the most abstract of the arts and that what sounds like music is closer to 'the abstracted symmetries of maths' than any other sensual experience. Or, as Ralph Steadman says in his imagined Leonardo diary, music more than anything taxed Leonardo's imagination and encouraged him to find ways to 'shape the invisible'.[67]

In *The World at Our Fingertips*[68] Cabrera and Colossi argue that **touch** helps children group abstract ideas into concrete experiences: 'By helping children build mental constructs of the complex web of relationships among objects, ideas and people, the sense of touch prepares them to approach any problem – even the most challenging and sophisticated ones.' Using a line from John Keats as the first line and the title of their song, Clive James, with Pete Atkin, wrote the following in a song about touch:

> Touch has a memory, better than the other senses
> Hearing and sight fight free, touching has no defences
> Textures come back to you real as can be
> Touch has a memory.

James and Atkin are talking about a sense experience that Ormrod[69] calls 'emotionally charged' learning which in turn leads us to 'pay attention ... continue to think ... and repeatedly elaborate' – a learning experience that is punctuated by 'shocks of awareness'.[70]

CONFOUNDING EXPECTATIONS

Steven Johnson argues that in addition to our senses igniting in us an instinct which draws us towards novel experiences – tastes, textures, sounds – illusions (and visual art in general) take our perceptions of objects in the world and confound expectations in startling ways. He claims that through our senses, we become more alert and engaged; from those encounters we receive 'a novelty bonus' which helps us to learn from new experiences. He goes on to say that 'humans

---

66. Ibid Johnson
67. Ibid Steadman
68. www.scientificamerican.com/article/the-world-at-our-fingertips
69. J. Ormrod: *Human Learning*; Merrill 1999
70. Maxine Greene: *Landscapes of Learning*; Teachers' College Press 1978

[have] evolved neural mechanisms that promote learning when they have experiences that confound their expectations. When the world surprises us with something, our brains are wired to pay attention.'

When an individual's interest is at its height, so too is their capacity to learn and remember, and when learning is satisfying, it tends to be long lasting. Johnson might have added that if our ways of learning are centripetal then we miss a trick. Engagement through the senses separates delight from demand; it pushes us towards exploration, it propels us to seek out new twists.

THE MIND AND THE BODY

Have you ever looked at someone and wondered what is going on inside their head?[71] What is going on in the brain? What is in there, how did it get in and what are we doing with it? What *should* be going in the brain, how do we stimulate and enhance what's in there and how should we encourage it to be used?

We want to explore our culture's apparent assumptions that the mind and the body are separate entities. We want to talk about the senses – how seeing, touching, smelling, hearing and tasting work in relation to our understanding. We want to know what thought is made of, how it got there and what we can do to produce more of it.

Leonardo had similar ideas. He was hoping he would find a degree of certainty, even some inkling of universal truth. He believed that it ought to be possible to work out a mathematical formula to explain the workings of the brain, as if there were static truths hidden somewhere inside the mind. Discovering the secrets of the mind, how it is developed and modified, is in Leonardo's terms the key task. There is (or should be), he thought, a formula to describe the perfect mind – if he could but find it.

This question of who is directing us and what is inside the cave of our own isolated minds[72] is raised in the source of our opening quotation to this section. It comes from the Pixar animation Inside Out. Most of the narrative takes place inside the psyche of a teenage girl called Riley; the characters who live in her mind are her feelings and they operate as a sort of mission control for the whole of her life. The film seems to work on the Cartesian premise that 'nothing can be in me,

71. This question is asked by a character called Joy in the animation *Inside Out* written and directed by Pete Docter and Ronaldo del Carmen 2015
72. Siri Hustvedt: *A Woman Looking at Men Looking at Women*; Sceptre 2017

that is, in my mind, of which I am not conscious'.[73] Aristotle argued that our very soul is to be found in a proposed region of the brain that coordinates and makes sense of experience and information, the 'sensus communis'. Our environment provides the grain of sand, the experiences, then the pearl is made by those cognitive processes which in the end shape who we are.[74]

But is the essence of who we are entirely inside our heads? It is suspected that Leonardo was bothered by the simple structure described by Mundinus[75] and many who followed him. Despite his pursuit of mathematical certainties and universal truths, Leonardo was not predicting Descartes; he clearly did not accept that there was a clear divide between the psychological and the physiological – between the mind and the body. Our bodies, as Guy Claxton says,[76] tend to be seen in the Cartesian view merely as 'an irritatingly fallible form of transport' where how we feel and perceive comes a very poor second to how we think and reason.

Leonardo and his emphasis on the importance of the senses and genuine experience clearly did not go along with this. He may have seemed to be searching for mathematical certainty about the workings of the physical location of the soul (and place where the senses are processed) but in his day-to-day life he embraced and promoted doubt and uncertainty. Although he appeared to want to uncover a static and unchanging analysis of how the mind worked, in many other ways he behaved as though he was sure that questions were more useful than answers. Put in our terms as learners, if the answers are out there just waiting to be uncovered, then what does that do to our attempts to ignite curiosity and develop understanding? Where does that leave the imagination? Or creativity? According to a later scholar, Vico,[77] if we are putting all our eggs into the basket of teaching reasoning and number, we will produce unresponsive children with stunted language skills and a limited capacity to adapt to change.

ACTS OF VISUAL SPECULATION
If he were asked whether ambiguity and uncertainty were dangerous or liberating, Leonardo would have answered, 'Liberating, of course.' So,

73. Rene Descartes: *Meditations*
74. This image comes from William Deresiewicz
75. Mundinus: the Italian anatomist 1275–1384
76. Guy Claxton: *Intelligence in the flesh*; Yale 2015
77. Giambattista Vico (1687–1744) author of *The New Science*

Leonardo did not do as Aristotle and others over the centuries told him. He happily followed Mundinus's other recommendation (about cutting up bodies to see for yourself) and located a corpse, probably left after an execution, and opened the skull. He was surprised by what he found. No three ventricles; no obvious centre of understanding; no organ that might be the soul. But he nevertheless went ahead and produced pages and pages of meticulous anatomical drawings and still, despite the evidence of his eyes, concluded that 'the soul seems to reside in the judgement; and the judgement would seem to be seated in that part where all the senses meet; and this is called the sensus communis'.[78] Toby Lester excuses all this by pointing out that what Leonardo was doing following his observations was not telling us what he actually found, but rather making a metaphysical point – 'an act of visual speculation' pointing the way towards 'boundless investigative possibility'.

What Leonardo is saying to us is that the soul is not an ethereal thing forever turning its gaze skywards, nor is it an abstract concept which might be passed on to us through other people. It is rooted in our earthly lives. This implies that our souls are made and grow through direct or primary experiences rather than those which are derivative. The German philosopher Martin Heidegger[79] said much the same thing when he talked about 'the physical embeddedness of all human experience'. A similar point is made by Martin Kemp:

> For Leonardo the greatest function of man's soul was to understand the operation of the natural world, not to indulge in the kind of abstract speculation so popular among certain Florentine philosophers of his day.[80]

It matters to us, probably, because we have tended to accept without question the Cartesian dualities of mind and body rather than Leonardo's understanding that the mind consists of a three-way mutually dependent process involving the senses, thought and memory. Descartes's 'I think therefore I am' has led us to believe that the thinking part of our existence is the more important part – followed closely by memory. Even if we believed and accepted the 'three ventricles' version of how our brains work – receiving, processing and memorising information – we have nevertheless often

---

78. Quoted by Toby Lester in *Da Vinci's Ghost*; Simon and Schuster 2012
79. Martin Heidegger 1889–1976
80. Martin Kemp: *Leonardo Da Vinci: The Marvellous Works of Nature and Man*; Oxford University Press 2006

behaved in ways that laid most of the stress on the second and third aspects of learning and growing. We seem to believe that knowledge and received ways of seeing and thinking are more important than experience, that cognitive skills are superior to sensory skills – hence our exploration of how the senses inform understanding.

SHAPING THE INVISIBLE

The truth is less clear, fussier. Heisenberg's uncertainty principle[81] might be applied to this discussion about mind and body, reminding us that it is impossible to separate human existence into distinct aspects – thinking and experiencing, the cognitive and the sensory. In the play *Heisenberg*,[82] a character says:

> It's not about where you go in life, is it? It's not about how fast you move. It's about trying your very hardest to keep your eyes open while you are moving. Even if you know it's not possible. Really trying.

So, when we talk about shaping the invisible and the soul we are saying that these things come into being through the experiences we have. It's not so much about testing as it is about working 'to keep your eyes open while you are moving'. Not offering experiences on a plate – to learn off by heart – but combining sensory and cognitive experiences. Keats[83] called the world around him 'the vale of soul-making', by which he meant a place where we embrace a variety of experiences and participate in a process of thinking that leads towards finding out who we are – our soul. Looking for questions at least as much as we look for answers.

A play about the mid-20th-century German impressionist Emil Nolde gives us another way of foregrounding the importance of sensory perception. At a post-1945 hearing, Nolde defends himself against accusations that he had not used his art to articulate opposition to Nazi policies. He responds to the criticism by saying, 'I leave my thinking mind aside and simply allow my hand to work uncluttered and unfiltered by thought so that what results can only be a pure expression of feeling.'[84]

In recent times scholars have begun to question Descartes's concept that 'there is nothing in the mind that belongs to the body and

---

81. Werner Heisenberg; German physicist 1901–1976
82. Simon Stephens: *Heisenberg* Bloomsbury 2015
83. Ibid Deresiewicz
84. Roy Mitchell: *Degenerate* 2017 (as yet unpublished)

nothing in the body that belongs to the mind'. The 2017 Nobel Prize for medicine was awarded to three scientists whose research has been about circadian rhythms and how they affect our lives, how they dictate energy, health, fertility and how our bodies react in relation to time. In short, how our biological makeup influences who we are and how we live. The clear belief is that we are not only cognitive beings; we are physical beings too, and to divide is dangerous to both. Leonard Mlodinow[85] makes the case for the power and significance of association cortexes with regard to our senses. We have an association cortex for each of our five traditional sensory systems and for each motor region:

> Neural networks that represent ideas can activate one another, creating associations. The association cortices are where those connections are made. Associations help to confer meaning on what you are seeing, hearing, tasting, smelling, and touching ... In humans, however, about three-quarters of our cerebral neurons reside in the association cortices.

As we have seen, Leonardo did not find physical evidence for the location of the soul. Modern scientists, similarly, have not opened the brain and found the modern equivalent – the neural correlates of consciousness (the NCC) – what we now might call the soul, perhaps. Our point here is that in the past we have almost certainly put more emphasis on mind than on body, on thought rather than the senses, as though the two were entirely separate. Freud said that 'psychoanalysis was psychology rooted in biology'[86] and Stanley Cobb[87] added that 'I solve the mind–body problem by declaring there is no such problem ... [such imagined binaries] are not only wrong but lead to bad habits of thinking because they lead to static and obsolete ideas and do not allow for modern and pluralistic ideas.'

Learning is as much about direct observation as it is about encountering fresh experiences alongside the conclusions of others. The given as well as the found; the concrete as well as the abstract. We mention elsewhere that as learners we are intrigued by difficulty; our curiosity is aroused by subtlety and complexity. We are drawn by the uncertainty. What we learn from Leonardo is that the uncertainty is not just to be found in abstract ideas or in books; it is to be found

---

85. Ibid Mlodinow
86. Sigmund Freud: *New Introductory Letters in Psychology* 1933; Hogarth Press 1964
87. Stanley Cobb: *Borderlands of Psychiatry* Harvard University Press 1943

in our physical environment. This way of thinking about learning is articulated by Jarvis, writing in praise of David Kolb's theory of experiential learning[88] – 'learning from primary experience, that is, learning through sense experiences'[89] – or as Borzak[90] put it: 'a direct encounter with the phenomenon being studied rather than merely thinking about the encounter'.

In fact, Kolb could have been describing Leonardo's methodology and concern to develop and refine the five senses when he identified the learning process as a cycle which begins with concrete experience, leads on to observation and reflection, expands into the shaping of abstract ideas and then tests those ideas. This might sound like a linear process, but is not; the starting point for this cycle might be any one of these four elements but only if the whole approach is underwritten by direct sensual experience. Underlying the approach is the premise that, for as long as possible, there should be no right or wrong but only genuine experience – because only with real experience will there be real engagement.

And finally, if we do believe that a focus on the physical environment and the way it is processed through the perceptions – the five senses – is a viable approach, then it is certainly worth thinking about the mileage to be had from *cross wiring* the experience of these senses as a next step. The result might well be a perfect expression of inventiveness, immersion and imagination. It will also lead us on to more of Leonardo's ideas of how learning works.

88. David A Kolb: *Experiential Learning: Experience as the source of learning*; Prentice Hall 1983
89. Peter Jarvis: *Learning from Everyday Life*; HSSRP Vol 1 available online.
90. Borzak, L. (ed.) (1981) *Field Study – A source book for experiential learning*, Beverley Hills: Sage Publications.

CHAPTER 4
UNNECESSARY BEAUTY

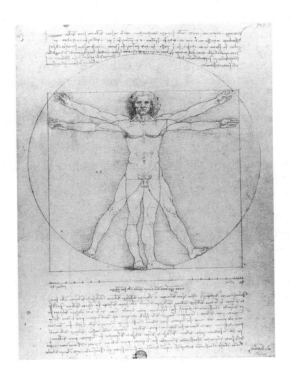

Vitruvian Man; Gallerie dell'Accademia, Venice

Vitruvian Man achieves a modulation – a dialogue – between the visionary and the practical. By setting out to achieve this microcosm-macrocosm connection, Leonardo was aiming not just for useful analogy; he was reaching for something much more spiritual and mystical. A perfect example of how Leonardo takes us from the concrete to the ethereal.

What did Leonardo mean by...?

The art of science and the science of art

WAYS OF SEEING AND THINKING

'Leonardo's anatomical studies belong under the heading "Leonardo the scientist" but are also,' as Nicholl makes plain, 'vitally connected with Leonardo the artist; they bridge the gap between those roles.'[1] Leonardo would have known the word 'scientia', but he would not have known the word 'scientist'. 'Scientia' meant 'knowledge' – of nature and the universe, and the principles behind the way they worked. He looked with his intellect as much as with his eyes. He would have called himself a natural philosopher:

> In the history of science, Leonardo is like a bridge. He stands right between the medieval view of the world and the modern view based on observation and experimentation. He looks back to a time when nature seemed illogical, magical. He looks ahead to a time when nature is viewed as operating by rules and laws that can be discovered.[2]

From his early twenties, Leonardo wanted to be seen as more than an everyday craftsman. By the age of 20 he had joined the painters' guild in Florence and was working in the studio of Andrea del Verrocchio, where he was recognised as an exceptional painter. However, he wanted more – more than craftsmanship, more than self-expression. He wanted each of his paintings to be a 'thing of the mind' – a collection of problems to be turned over and over. For instance, *Annunciation* (1472–73), the first major commission with which he was involved, is described by Landrus as a 'combination of science and sensibility' – the sacred and the miraculous mirrored through the science of perspective, light, shade, texture and colour. Leonardo's approach was driven by endless experimentation. In striving to achieve a three-dimensional representation of nature it must often have seemed, especially to his patrons, that Leonardo was far more interested in the science of his work than he was in the finished product. He knew, for instance, that if he were to achieve what the sculptor Lorenzo Ghiberti[3] called the 'statua virile' (statue of a man), his standing as a painter would be elevated. He

---

1. Ibid Nicholl
2. Kathleen Krull: *Giants of Science: Leonardo da Vinci*; Puffin Books 2005
3. Lorenzo Ghiberti: *First Commentary* (circa 1450): *I commentarii*: Biblioteca rationale centrale di Firenze, II, I, 333 (Biblioteca della scienza italiana) (Italian Edition) Giunti 1998

needed to learn the possibilities of his art, built on an understanding of how the body worked as well as what it looked like.

In about 1483 Leonardo moved from Florence to Milan, where his interests grew to include architecture and engineering. But his main focus was still on putting together a treatise on painting that went further than Cennino's earlier technical manual *Libro dell'Arte* (circa 1400).[4] He wanted to encompass both the technique and the theory of painting – the practicalities and the undertow of meaning that they might lead to. What began as a collection of precise notes and sketches, intended to elevate his standing as an artist rather than jobbing craftsman, became the raw materials for a full-scale treatise on painting: *Trattato della pittura*.[5] The finished work wasn't actually assembled and completed until after his death, but the fact that he hadn't quite finished didn't put him off launching into plans for writing about flight, optics, geology, water and the human body.

What interests us in all this is not so much his drive to understand, theorise about, observe, analyse and catalogue anatomy and physiology – and then to apply this knowledge, this 'scientia' to his art – but that having done all that he still sensed that there was more to discover beyond what might be seen: 'He was concerned not just with appearances but with the underlying causes of those appearances.'[6] Art historians note that once he moved from Florence to Milan, Leonardo spent more and more of his time studying science rather than painting pictures. Certainly, towards the end of his life, from 1508 until 1513, and following what appears to have been a stroke, 'he worked essentially as a scientist who occasionally put his hand to paintings that he had begun in earlier years'.[7]

COLLABORATION AND CROSS-FERTILISATION

'Waking up while everyone else in his world was still asleep in the dark.'[8] It was Freud who said this about Leonardo, also characterising him as a loner, an outsider, secretive with notebooks full of mirror-writing, isolated, uncommunicative and unread by anyone until long

4. Cennino d'Andrea Cennini: *The Craftsman's Handbook: Il Libro dell'Arte* (circa 1400); reprinted in a translation by Daniel V Thompson, 1954 Dover Instructional.
5. Leonardo: *Trattato della pittura* 1651, available as *Leonardo on Painting* edited by Martin Kemp, Yale 1980
6. Martin Clayton and Ron Philo: *Leonardo da Vinci: Anatomist*; Royal Collection Trust 2012
7. Ibid Clayton and Philo
8. Leonardo da Vinci and a Memory of his Childhood 1932

after his death. But this certainly isn't the whole picture. If there was a side to Leonardo that was very private, there was also a side that was quite the opposite – according to contemporary accounts, he was handsome, immaculately well-presented and an enthusiastic partygoer.[9] More than this, he also knew that each book he read opened doors into other books, each topic he studied uncovered further topics, each conversation inevitably led to more conversations. He set about engaging with expertise from many disciplines.

Leonardo's fascination with perspective, for instance, was ignited by Filippo Brunelleschi's[10] writing on the mathematical principles of linear perspective. Also, in Florence, one of his closest friends was Paolo Toscanelli[11] who encouraged and guided Leonardo in his interest in science – particularly by introducing him to Leon Battista Alberti.[12] A prominent intellectual, Alberti promoted the application of geometry, optics, mathematics and anatomy to art. Another close friend, the mathematician Luca Pacioli, said that 'without mathematics there is no art', and as a result explored the idea of ratios in art, anatomy and architecture in his book *De Divina Proportione*.[13] Leonardo was asked to illustrate the book.

Later, in Milan, Leonardo befriended Fazio Cardano,[14] a professor of medicine and mathematics, who had edited a book on optics. For a while Leonardo lodged with Cardano's family, and Cardano helped him gain access to a medical library and, presumably, corpses for dissection. The physician and historian Paolo Giovio[15] collaborated with Leonardo between 1513 and 1516 and had seen the notebooks. He later wrote a brief biography arguing that even if they were written in the 'vulgar tongue' (not in Latin) the notebooks needed to be published for 'the benefit of art'.[16] Leonardo's drawings and investigations in Pavia between 1510 and 1511 suggest that he had access to that city's medical school – its materials and methodology – and almost certainly he met and worked alongside Marcantonio della Torre,[17] a leading authority on the writings of Galen.[18]

---

9. Ibid Krull
10. Filippo Brunelleschi, architect and artist, 1377–1446
11. Paolo Toscanelli: 1397 to 1482; physician, astronomer, mathematician and mapmaker
12. Leon Battista Alberti:1404–1472: the archetypical 'Renaissance man'
13. Luca Pacioli: *De Divina Proportione*, CreateSpace Independent Publishing Platform, 2014 (Illustrated by Leonardo da Vinci)
14. Fazio Cardano: 1444–1524; mathematician.
15. Paolo Giovio: 1483–1559: physician and historian.
16. Quoted by J.P. Richter in *The Literary Works of Leonardo da Vinci*; Oxford 1939
17. Marcantonio della Torre: 1481–1511
18. Galen: Greek physician and anatomist 129AD – 210AD

All of this serves to confirm the fact that Leonardo was not alone in his endeavours. He needed to 'compound diverse concepts and observations to form new ones'[19] through contact with books and other people: 'Genius is often considered the purview of loners who retreat to their garrets and are struck by creative lightning ... [but] *Vitruvian Man* was produced after sharing ideas and sketches with friends.'[20]

In 1498, at quite an early stage in all of this cross-fertilisation between disciplines and experts, Leonardo played a prominent part in a debate that was held at Sforza Castle. The event was called a 'paragone' – the Italian word for 'comparison' – a public debate about the importance and validity of various types of intellectual pursuits. Leonardo's role was to be the champion of the visual arts, and to give a scientific and aesthetic defence of painting, arguing that instead of it being seen as a mechanical art of the hands, it should be regarded as the highest of the liberal arts, transcending poetry in particular, but also music and sculpture.

Painting, argued Leonardo, combined art and science, its visual harmonies created from a combination of the concrete and the ethereal. Paintings do not require translators, whereas literature is disjointed and music is transitory. Painting goes beyond language, however poetic that language might be. Poetry exists in the realm of 'divine emotional idealisation' which deals with the writer's conceptual imagination. When Leonardo paints a portrait of a woman, we may feel that even if the sitter is idealised, she nevertheless has a concrete presence: 'However much he exploits the blurred indefiniteness, she sits in front of us as someone we cannot but relate to as an individual, however strange an individual we may feel her to be. She is at once a real person and a poetic enigma.'[21] The poet lacks that level of reality. Painting is about appearances, of course, but it is as much about the underlying causes of those appearances.[22] Isaacson calls this 'the ability to combine observation with imagination, thereby blurring the border between reality and fantasy'.[23]

Leonardo argued that the painter was a transmitter of visual observation, and as a result plays a significant role in our understanding of the world and the mysteries of creation: 'Thirst will parch your tongue and your body will waste through lack of sleep ere you can

19. Ibid Mlodinow
20. Ibid Isaacson
21. Martin Kemp: *Mona Lisa: The People and the Painting*; Oxford 2017
22. Ibid: Clayton and Philo 2011
23. Ibid Isaacson

describe in words that which painting instantly sets before the eye.'[24] In his *Trattato della pittura*[25] Leonardo is clearly offended by hearing his work (and that of other artists) talked about as the mechanical arts. He insists that it is an intellectual pursuit as much as (if not more than) it is a craft. He saw what he did as a process of expanding the language of painting and what the painting might say, so that paintings like *The Adoration of the Magi* or sketches of Isabella d'Este change our understanding of the past and future and at the same time lead us towards exchanging new meanings for and with the painting – and for the event it describes. His contribution wowed the audience at the Sforza Castle paragone. So much for Leonardo as lonely introvert.

Leonardo's approach to science, alongside his investigations into humanities and technology, served to inform his art. His endless experimentation and his merging of science and sensibility, started with the following approach:

> First, I shall make some experiments before I proceed further, because my intention is to consult experience first and then by means of reasoning show why such experiment is bound to work in such a way. And this is the true rule by which those who analyse natural effects must proceed; and although nature begins with the cause and ends with the experience, we must follow the opposite course, namely (as I said before), begin with the experience and by means of it investigate the cause.[26]

THE SCALPEL AND THE PEN

Nicholl makes the point that 'in terms of what he actually contributed – of the difference he made – (Leonardo's) work as an anatomist is far more significant than his work as an engineer, or inventor, or architect ... His anatomical drawing constituted a new visual language for describing body parts.'[27]

Leonardo invented what is now called the 'exploded view', in which the parts of a joint, such as the shoulder for example, are drawn as though separated from one another, in order to demonstrate their relationships. The Church continued to prohibit dissections and so

---

24. *Leonardo da Vinci: Thoughts on Art and Life*; translated by Maurice Baring (1906) CreateSpace Independent Publishing 2015
25. Martin Kemp and Margaret Walker have translated and edited *Trattato della pittura* in, *Leonardo on Painting*; Yale; 2001
26. Ibid *Thoughts on Art and Life*
27. Ibid Nicholl

European medicine in the Middle Ages relied heavily upon Galen's ancient authority rather than on direct observation for its anatomical knowledge. Leonardo refused to rely on the given, the accepted or the assumed. He calls those who came before him the 'ancient speculators': Galen, Hippocrates, Aristotle, and Plato. Investigation and inquiry were what mattered and what excited him most. His intricate and closely observed drawings of the human body were premised on the certainty that 'this demonstration is as necessary to good draughtsmen as is the origin of words from Latin to good grammarians'.[28]

In 1784, the Scottish anatomist William Hunter said that his own intention, as a teacher of anatomy:

> ...was to introduce into the annals of our art, a genius of the first rate, Leonardo da Vinci, who has been overlooked because he was of another profession, and because he published nothing upon the subject. I believe he was, by far, the best anatomist and physiologist of his time ... the very first who raised a spirit of anatomical study and gave it credit: and Leonardo was certainly the first man we know of who introduced the practice of making anatomical drawings.

Despite the taboos and doctrinal doubts of his time and the 'repulsive procedures' of post-mortem examination, Leonardo produced (with 'dogged courage'[29]) 240 drawings and over 13000 words – science deftly interwoven into art and each informing the other. Isaacson articulates this idea neatly: 'Leonardo's hand was deft with both pen and scalpel.'[30] In many ways, the scalpel cut becomes the pen stroke.

As access to dead bodies for the purposes of dissection was limited, Leonardo turned to animals – supposing that, apart from the proportions, the anatomy of an animal might fill the gap. He dissected and drew monkeys, dogs, pigs, bears, and frogs. Encouraged by a commission to prepare and model a large equestrian monument to Francisco Sforza, Leonardo put together a treatise on the horse's anatomy. Later he was asked to undertake a fresco for a refectory wall in the monastery of Santa Maria Novella: *The Battle of Anghiari* (1503–1504). Two preparatory studies survive: the heads of two soldiers and, most notably, a melee of horses and horseman locked in battle. The rest are lost.

---

28. Royal Library, Windsor
29. Ibid Nicholl
30. Ibid Isaacson

Like so many of Leonardo's closely observed anatomical drawings, his depiction of a five-month foetus in the womb is a thing of divine beauty: 'a miracle of intense presentation'[31] with more than a hint at the similarity to a seed in a shell. It stands as a masterwork of art, and considering the very little that was at the time understood of embryology, a masterwork of scientific perception at the same time. Leonardo's extraordinary ability to dissect, observe, and interpret led him to see that even though there is no direct communication between maternal and foetal placental blood vessels, the embryo was still part of its mother, so much so that 'one and the same soul governs these two bodies, and one and the same soul nourishes both'.[32] It is no wonder, then, that Joseph Needham calls Leonardo 'the father of embryology [being] regarded as an exact science'. Leonardo simply saw art and science as two essential sides of the same coin: 'Those who become enamoured of the art, without having previously applied the diligent study of the science of it, may be compared to mariners who put to sea in a ship without rudder or compass and therefore cannot be certain of arriving at the wished-for port.'[33] That he produced such a work of beauty to illustrate a scientific idea is fascinating and highly indicative of how he felt about the supposed divide between art and science.

THE HUMAN AND THE DIVINE

We began by talking about appearances and what might lie behind those appearances. We went on to look at the part Leonardo played in the Sforza Castle paragone and how he argued that paintings were about concrete detail and at the same time conveyed poetic enigma. Leonardo's drawing *Vitruvian Man* echoes these ideas and has become a sort of emblem or logo for Leonardo and what he has come to mean as a scientist, mathematician and artist.

It was commissioned to be a cover for Giovani Giocondo's folio edition of the works of Vitruvius, published in Venice in 1511. Working with a friend, the mathematician Luca Pacioli, Leonardo was interested in producing a picture chart of the human body, a 'cosmografia del minor mondo' ('cosmography of the microcosm') where he considered the proportional theories of Vitruvius, and by imposing the principles of geometry on the configuration of the human body, aimed to demonstrate that the ideal proportion of the human figure corresponds with the forms of the circle

31. Ibid Martin Kemp
32. Ibid Isaacson
33. Leonardo: *Trattato Delia pittura (Treatise on Painting)*

and the square. The anatomy shown in this drawing is concrete – real and closely observed. The geometry is abstract; it suggests movement – flight, even. The body is drawn with distinct and economical precision, but the face is much more intense, suggestive, shadowy – enigmatic. In an interview, Toby Lester says that for him the *Vitruvian Man* 'embodies a timeless human hope: that we just might have the power of mind to figure out how we fit into the grand scheme of things'.[34] For Isaacson, the drawing uses 'delicate lines and careful shading to create a body of remarkable and unnecessary beauty. With its intense but intimate stare … his masterpiece weaves together the human and the divine.'[35]

In this way, *Vitruvian Man*, like so many of Leonardo's anatomical studies and drawings, achieves a 'modulation' – a dialogue – 'between the visionary and the practical'.[36] By setting out to achieve this microcosm–macrocosm connection, Leonardo was aiming not just for useful analogy; he was reaching for something much more spiritual and mystical. A perfect example of how Leonardo takes us from the concrete to the ethereal.

What Leonardo left behind is not as much to do with 'discoveries' – much of his work remained hidden in his notebooks until the 19th century – but to do with a way of thinking about how things worked. It's about means rather than ends; scientific methods rather than the scientific outcomes; a process as much as a completion. Nevertheless, the medical historian Charles Singer has said of him: 'His anatomical notebooks … have revealed him for what he was: one of the greatest biological investigators of all time. In endless matters he was centuries ahead of his contemporaries.' It is for such thoroughness of so many of his studies that the foremost historian of the field, Joseph Needham, calls Leonardo 'the father of embryology regarded as an exact science'.

---

34. Toby Lester, *Talk of the Nation*, BBC March 8th 2012
35. Ibid Isaacson
36. Ibid Nicholl

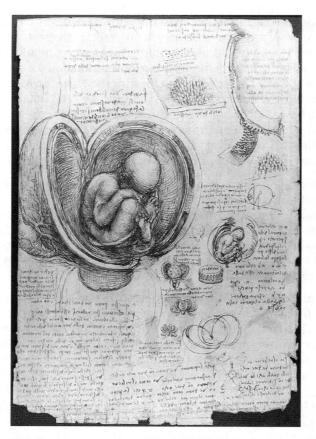

Studies of the Foetus in the womb; Royal Collection, Windsor Castle Library

When we look at Leonardo's anatomical drawing we are of course struck by the beauty and detail of his draughtsmanship; yet, more than that, we are taken aback by how he is constantly pushing his understanding to the edges of what was possible for him and his contemporaries, and for those who followed.

What can we still learn from Leonardo about...?

Everything is to be peered into, worried away at, brought back to first principles[37]

IMAGINED POLARITIES AND FALSE BINARIES

Perhaps it was the very public 1959 argument between C.P. Snow and F.R. Leavis that injected into our bloodstreams an assumption that the arts and the sciences live in separate worlds. For Snow, scientists had 'the future in their bones' while the 'literary intellectuals were natural Luddites'. For Leavis, on the other hand, traditional culture taught us to be more probing and reflective. Between them they helped to build the barriers between art and science which are still there, if expressed in slightly different ways. Fundamentally this choice is about which subject tells the most convincing stories and best answers those questions we might have about how the world works and our place in it.

We made the point earlier that Leonardo would have rejected the idea that art and science are two separate and distinct disciplines. What we see as Leonardo's bridge building was, to him, not bridge building at all. He might have called himself a natural philosopher and that's as far as he would go. Science meant processing and testing knowledge; seeing with the mind. Science and art nourish each other. Keats, like Leavis, felt that science 'would clip an angel's wings'. It dissolves beauty, it sets out to 'unweave a rainbow'. Edgar Allan Poe said something similar. He saw science as a 'vulture' that shrivelled wonder. Richard Dawkins, on the other hand, argues that science does the very opposite of destroying beauty: it reveals it.[38]

Leonardo, like so many of the scientists who followed him, looked for the universal insight or law through a close and first–hand examination of the particular. Just as Darwin spent seven years studying barnacles before putting together any general conclusions, Leonardo spent half a lifetime working and reworking the tendons in the neck and shoulder of *Saint Jerome in the Wilderness* – and dissecting 30 or more corpses along the way to understand how the muscles work.

Writing about the polarities which might be seen to exist between poetry and science, Ruth Padel[39] argues that 'science ... is not about

37. Ibid Nicoll
38. Richard Dawkins: *Unweaving the Rainbow: Science, Delusion and the Appetite for Wonder*; Penguin 2006
39. Ruth Padel: 'The science of poetry, the poetry of science': *The Guardian* December 2011.

facts; it is about thinking about facts ... The deepest thing science and poetry share, perhaps, is the way they can tolerate uncertainty.' The briefest of encounters with Leonardo's notebooks – and their endless lists and questions – would confirm this; and as we will say repeatedly, the implications of uncertainty echo throughout not just his work but ours too. As an artist and as a scientist Leonardo would be the first to say he didn't know. Padel reports a conversation with a biologist during which he made the observation that 'a scientist goes forward towards truth but never gets there'. Perhaps this explains why Leonardo rarely, if ever, finished what he had started. At some point, we have to ask ourselves whether not arriving at the truth is a good thing or not. Or is it once again more about means rather than ends.

We have tried to show that Leonardo existed in a collaborative but careful community where ideas could, in many circumstances, be networked. He recognised – as Louis MacNeice[40] says in his poem 'Snow' – that however hard we work to find answers to everything, the world is 'suddener and ... crazier and more of it than we think, incorrigibly plural'. MacNeice's and Leonardo's solutions to this imperfect world are in this imperfect world. Life's imperfections and limitations are of creative value and the fact that our understanding and our knowledge changes and never reaches a state of perfection is the very thing that gives that quest to find answers value. Padel's poems[41] say something else that we might apply to Leonardo's obsessive and yet unfailing attention to detail: the mundane, she says, often gestures towards the profound, the details lead to the universal, the concrete to the abstract, the known towards the unknown. A reviewer[42] recently described her work as being about 'the microcosm reflecting the macrocosm'. Leonardo's work will carry on doing the same thing for many more centuries to come.

THE ADJACENT POSSIBLE

As we have already implied, Leonardo's network of friends and contacts, particularly those he met in Milan, served not just to keep him emotionally safe but also to open doors between a variety of academic pursuits. The mere presence of other points of view creates 'a spirit that encourages liberation from deeply ingrained

---

40. Louis MacNeice: *Collected Poems*; Faber and Faber 1966
41. We're thinking here of Ruth Padel's 2018 collection, *Emerald*; Chatto and Windus
42. Rory Waterman: *Times Literary Supplement*, December 2018

assumptions and expectations'.[43] This process exposed him to the 'adjacent possible'[44] – a kind of shadow future, hovering on the edges of the present state of things, a map of all the ways in which the present can reinvent itself. He did more than encourage new ideas, he helped set up 'collisions' between ideas: the collisions that happen when different fields of expertise converge in some shared physical or intellectual space.

It's an idea that helps us to comprehend the potential of the world's plurality, to take note of it – and allow ourselves to be led towards and to reframe our understanding. In the 21st century, when the paths we are encouraged to take tend to lead us towards becoming specialists and reductionists, Leonardo's drive to explore the intersections between his art and maths and an entire range of sciences illustrates the potential of the 'adjacent possible', and the benefits of allowing greater serendipity into our work.

As a painter it was important for Leonardo to understand the *structure* of the human body; but, as his notebooks show, he clearly felt the need to appreciate the *function* of what he saw. Painting becomes more than representation: it becomes science. This is particularly evident in his fascination with neuroanatomy. He trawled everything he knew using observation, experience, received knowledge and his own understanding and analysis, and realised that if nothing matched, then he felt he was onto something entirely new – like sound waves or helicopters. As Arthur Conan Doyle has Sherlock Holmes say, after you've eliminated the impossible, whatever else remains – however improbable – is the truth. Just as Leonardo made seemingly serendipitous discoveries across art and science, we are seeking to discover similar adjacent possibilities in these conversations with him across time.

Leonardo began a quest to establish a physical basis to explain the mind's functions, however elusive they might seem to be. He wanted to know, for instance: how the brain received and processed information from the senses; how we sneeze; the function of dreaming; how a mother's mental state influenced the unborn child; and how the senses feed and develop the soul. This is a perfect illustration of how the

43. Moscovici, Elastic, 171
44. Stuart Kaufman: *Investigations*; Oxford University Press, 2000, and, *At Home in the Universe: The Search for the Laws of Self-Organisation and Complexity*; Yale University Press 1995

concept of the 'adjacent possible' operates: he set out as an artist to understand the surface features of human anatomy but along the way explored the physical sources of behaviours and which parts of the brain created and controlled those sources.

He planned to publish descriptions of his methodology and what he had discovered about anatomy (and engineering, etc.) but in the end, apart from his illustrations for a mathematics text mentioned earlier,[45] his anatomical works were not published until the late 19th century. When we look at Leonardo's anatomical drawing we are of course struck by the beauty and detail of his draughtsmanship; yet, more than that, we are taken aback by how he is constantly pushing his understanding to the edges of what was possible for him and his contemporaries, and for those who followed.

FORMS AND PURPOSES

Lara Gilinsky[46] takes this discussion about art and science a step further when she talks about the difference between 'passion' and 'purpose'. Young people, she says, are intimidated by the word 'passion'. They are not sure they know what that should feel like. Alongside this thought she puts William Damon's[47] talk of 'purpose', which is the way, he maintains, that we unite the inner with the outer, the self with the world; what you want to do with what needs to be done. This notion of purpose has the potential to bring together the inner (the potentially passionate) and the outer (the dispassionate) – or, if you like, art and science. It's not about art versus science; it's about both – or as Isaacson says of Leonardo's work, about how maths and science together form 'nature's brushstroke'.[48] They don't just work together: they belong together. For Leonardo, any idea that there is a disconnect between the two – that they are binaries or represent two distinct polarities – would be entirely imaginary.

This chapter is predicated upon Leonardo's urging that we 'study the science of art, and the art of science' and about how we might weave together many forms and disciplines in ways that teach us to be at some times analytical and at other times subjective: how we encourage

---

45. L. Pacioli: *De Divina Proportione*; CreateSpace Independent Publishing produced a facsimile edition of this in 2012

46. Lara Galinsky: *Work on Purpose*; Echoing Green 2

47. William Damon: *The Path to Purpose: How Young People Find Their Calling in Life*, Free Press 2009

48. Kim Williams in Verrocchio's Tombslab for Cosimo de' Medici: *Designing with Mathematical Vocabulary*, Nexus 1 1996

an understanding of facts and knowledge in context; how we engender purpose; and, most of all, how skills and imagination are (as we say elsewhere) two sides of the same magical page and how both have stories to tell and knowledge to share.

In Ralph Steadman's imagined autobiography[49] of Leonardo, he has the latter write this:

> Perspective is the one law that no artist can ignore, because it is the bridle and the rudder of painting and unites art with science. It rationalises our view of the world but in this I sometimes doubt its cold precision for it has no feeling. It can construct but it cannot see inside a man's soul.

Art and science as the bridle and rudder. This is what this discussion is all about: how we learn to see inside the soul without abandoning the simultaneous drive to accumulate and utilise received knowledge; how we find that sense of purpose which encourages action; how we balance the complexity of knowledge against the provisional nature of how we learn to come to terms with that knowledge. Steven Poole[50] makes this process very clear when he says that 'the world of ideas is a moving target' and 'if we are not constantly rethinking ideas, we are not really thinking'.

Are we in some ways still locked into that 1959 Snow/Leavis two cultures debate? Or are we educating ourselves to become the sort of enquirers that Francis Bacon called 'merchants of light', where light is identified with truth? Long before C.P. Snow and all those in our contemporary world who think the free exercise of our imagination is not what learning should be about, Leonardo lived a life that can perhaps be summed up through the words of the Russian poet Olga Sedakova[51] when she noticed how Dante's *Commedia* is 'art that generates art and thought that generates thought and experience that generates experience'. Leonardo is the perfect example of this: he was an artist, scientist, anatomist and mathematician. Everything he learned led to more learning. For him, the answer was always just over the horizon. A constant updating and layering of his pictures as he gained new understandings. No binaries. No polarities.

We need to reach for a balance between science, art, logic, philosophy and the imagination; between what we are taught and what we imagine;

---

49. Ibid Steadman
50. Steven Poole: Rethink: *The Surprising History if New Ideas*; Random House 2016
51. Quoted by Alberto Manguel in *Curiosity*; Yale; 2015

between what we know and what we feel. For Leonardo, learning happens not only through the acquisition of existing knowledge but also because of what the Qur'an calls 'the inquisitive spirit of the searcher'. Leonardo's approach involves learning scatteringly from experience and observation as well as from existing theory and books with the result that 'there is always that typically Leonardian modulation between the visionary and the practical: a dialogue between them'.[52]

RESPONDING TO CHANGE

Serge Moscovici put a positive gloss on the Snow/Leavis binaries when he says that:

> In addition to whatever brilliant ideas individuals might bring with them, the mere presence of those with other points of view creates a spirit that encourages liberation from deeply ingrained assumptions and expectations. It promotes the consideration of more options and leads to better decision-making. It builds an atmosphere in which people can better respond to change.[53]

Arthur Koestler points out that 'all decisive events in the history of scientific thought can be described in terms of mental cross-fertilization between different disciplines'[54] – and it's not hyperbole to suggest that the decisive moments in our own learning probably emerge from moments of cross-fertilisation between that whole cacophony of facts and conversations we meet in all of our environments. Finding ways to stoke that cacophony is essential if we are to prime the pump of our learning.

Alice Roberts[55] argues that the study of science ought to be multidisciplinary, 'weaving together many forms and disciplines: genetics, archaeology, anthropology and history' together with 'personal anecdote, travelogue and little pieces of fiction'. Using all of these disciplines enables, she says, writing which is both 'rigorously scientific and full of empathy'. Helen Czerski[56] says something similar when she talks about 'linking the little things we see every day with the big world we live in ... how playing with things like popcorn, coffee

52. Ibid Nicholl
53. Serge Moscovici, Elizabeth Lage, Margaret Naffrechoux: 'Influence of a Consistent Minority on the Responses of a Majority in a Color Perception Task'; *Sociometry*, 1969
54. Arthur Koestler: *The Act of Creation*; Hutchinson 1969
55. 'You are allowed to be emotional about the way you engage with science'; Alice Roberts interview by Katy Guest; *The Guardian* 28.10.17
56. Helen Czerski: *Storm in a Teacup: The Physics of Everyday Life*; Penguin 2016

stains and refrigerator magnets shed light on Scott's expeditions, medical tests and solving our future energy needs'. Or as Hayley Birch says about chemistry, 'its reactions are responsible for supporting life and everything that depends on it. Its products chart the progress of our modern existence – from beer to Lycra hot pants.'[57] Czerski adds: 'Science is not about "them", it's about "us", and we can all go on this adventure in our own way.' Roberts, Czerski and Birch would argue that art and science coalesce when they are being 'passionate' about the science whilst being 'critically dispassionate' about the rules, understanding and knowledge that underpin that science – or any other subject for that matter. It seems entirely possible that John Donne's 'No man is an island' lies somewhere behind Oldenburg's concept of the importance of a third place[58] – a public, connective space where ideas can be aired and argued about by people with diverse interests. The 18th-century coffee house and the 20th-century Paris cafés were places where ideas collided and, as a result, innovations blossomed. So too was the court in Milan that Leonardo experienced.

COMBINATORY CREATIVITY

Charlie Munger[59] reminds that if we're not exactly standing on the shoulders of giants, at least we're sitting at the feet of quite a few people who knew what they were doing:

> You've got to have models in your head. And you've got to array your experience – both vicarious and direct – on this latticework of models. You may have noticed students who just try to remember and pound back what is remembered. Well, they fail in school and in life. You've got to hang experience on the latticework of models in your head ... [and] you've got to have multiple models – because if you just have one or two that you're using ... you'll torture reality so that it fits your models ... And the models have to come from multiple disciplines – because all the wisdom of the world is not to be found in one little academic department.

Whereas Iain McGilchrist[60] believes that although the two sides of the brain are interdependent, they are in fact unaware that they are actually

57. Hayley Birch: *50 Ideas you Really Need To Know; Chemistry*: Quercus 2015
58. Ray Oldenburg: *The Great Good Place: Cafes, Coffee Shops, Bookstores, Bars, Hair Salons, and Other Hangouts at the Heart of a Community*; Marlowe and Company 1999
59. Charlie Munger, *A Lesson in Elementary, Worldly Wisdom* (USC Business School 1994)
60. Iain McGilchrist: *The Master and his Emissary: The Divided Brain and the Making of the Western World* Yale 2010

dependent: the right is about comprehensiveness, the left about precision – and they compete. He describes the left hemisphere as the 'emissary' of the right side – which he describes as the 'Master'. 'However,' he says, 'it turns out that the emissary has his own will, and secretly believes himself to be superior to the Master. And he means to betray him. What he doesn't realise is that in doing so he will also betray himself.' So, the way we get it wrong, according to this take on the way the brain works, is when we invest too much into one way of learning or the other. McGilchrist points out that there has been a swing away from that drive towards self-expression with an approach where there is an:

> ...encouragement of precise, categorical thinking at the expense of background vision and experience ... [which] has now reached a point where it is seriously distorting both our lives and our thought. Our whole idea of what counts as scientific or professional has shifted towards literal precision – towards elevating quantity over quality and theory over experience.[61]

Leonardo would have thrown up his hands in despair at this.

Clearly McGilchrist is more than a little concerned that the 'uneasy relationship' between the two hemispheres is likely to end in 'the final triumph of the left hemisphere – at the expense of us all'. He would worry about views such as those expressed by Peter Atkins,[62] who argues that the road to understanding is navigated only with the help of science: 'The only faith we need for the journey is the belief that everything can be understood and, ultimately, that there is nothing to explain.' Darwin, on the other hand, believed that human imagination is our most valuable tool for survival. Leonardo probably agreed with both – with the negotiable image that embraces the need for science *and* imagination. It's not about the arts. Or the sciences. It's both. So, when we think about how Leonardo's skills of observation colluded rather than collided with his imaginative skills, we have to admire this combinatory creativity.[63]

THE UNCONSCIOUS AS MATCHMAKER

The question must have arisen by now: how do we travel from intimate detail to broad understanding? From the microcosm to the macrocosm? How did Leonardo do it? Is there any chance we might take a similar approach? Should we be going for 'karaoke' Leonardo, or would we be better thinking for ourselves? Pirsig's *Zen and the Art of Motorcycle*

---

61. Mary Midgley reviewing the McGilchrist book in *The Guardian* January 2010
62. Peter Atkins: *Creation Revisited: The Origin of Space, Time and the Universe*; Penguin 1994
63. Ibid Isaacson

Maintenance[64] – and particularly the way he uses Henri Poincaré's[65] ideas on the power of the 'subliminal self' – gives us some clues.

Pirsig uses Poincaré to describe how, when faced with numerous options, it is virtually impossible to use any set of rules as a guide to action. Rules or laws are at their most effective when they are felt rather than formulated. Decisions are best made by the 'subliminal self' – that self that responds to a sense of beauty or harmony.

The progress of science is neither gradual nor continuous. Each basic advance in the past was affected by a more or less abrupt and dramatic change: the breaking-down of frontiers between related territories; amalgamating previously separate frames of reference or experimental techniques; the sudden falling into a pattern of previously disjointed data. When a situation is blocked, straight thinking has to be superseded by the search for some alternative auxiliary matrix to unblock it: 'The process of idea generation is seated deep within our unconscious mind and is most active when our conscious processes of analytical thought are at rest.'[66]

The ultimate matchmaker between disciplines is the unconscious. There is a greater fluency in the freedom of the unconscious, where there is an indifference towards logical niceties or prejudices consecrated by tradition. And we all possess this non-verbal visionary power – with its tendency towards the irrational, the intuitive and the creative.

Leonardo allowed his mind to wander and spin free. Good combinations unblock, proceed on several planes, and involve conscious and unconscious processes at various levels of depth. Great changes are not made by orderly progression, step by laborious step. It is sometimes necessary to suspend that methodical discipline. The period of innovation is itself a state of receptivity, a readiness of the prepared mind to pounce on unfavourable chance constellations and to profit from any casual hint, for then 'Einstein imagines himself riding a light beam, Kekule formulates the ring structure of benzene in a dream about a snake eating its tail, and Fleming's eye travels past the annoying mould on his glassware to the clear ring surrounding it — a lucid halo in a dish otherwise opaque with bacteria — and penicillin is born'.[67]

64. Robert M Pirsig; *Zen and the Art of Motorcycle Maintenance: An Inquiry into Values* (1974); Bantam 1975
65. Henri Poincaré, mathematician and philosopher of science; 1854-1912: *Science and Method*; translated by George Bruce Halstead, CreateSpace Publishing 2016
66. Ibid Mlodinow
67. Ibid Koestler

As Einstein said (helpfully as far as our thinking about Leonardo is concerned), 'after a certain high level of technical skill is achieved, science and art tend to coalesce in aesthetics, plasticity, and form. The greatest scientists are always artists as well.'[68] By this he means that there is a certain trust needed in more freewheeling insight and intuition. The marshy shore between disciplines is a fertile region. 'Most advances in science come when a person for one reason or another is forced to change fields. Viewing a new field with fresh eyes, and bringing prior knowledge, results in creativity.'[69]

William Carpenter[70] believed 'the action of the brain ... through unconscious cerebration, produces results which might never have been produced by thought'. One thought can arise immediately after another without there having been any apparent associative link between them. Carpenter argues that the unconscious mind can produce logical conclusions 'below the plane of consciousness, either during profound sleep, or while the attention is wholly engrossed by some entirely different train of thought'.[71] Often a question or a conflict will 'settle itself'. Koestler uses the image of an immersed chain in water. Only the beginning and the end of the chain is visible above the surface of consciousness. The diver vanishes at one end of the chain and comes up at the other end guided by the invisible links.

Mlodinow[72] calls all this a conflict between the executive brain – doing what we're told to do and how we are supposed to think – and our capacity for originality:

> When we are at our best, our executive eases up enough that the brain achieves a balance of bottom–up and top–down operation ... That's the beauty of the human mind. We can execute an interplay of top–down and bottom–up processing, and of analytical thought and elastic thought ... The elastic thinking that produces ideas doesn't consist of a linear train of steps, as analytical thought does. Sometimes big, sometimes inconsequential, sometimes in crowds,

68. Albert Einstein, *Remark* (1923) as recalled in Archibald Henderson, Durham Morning Herald (21 Aug 1955) in Einstein Archive 33-257. Quoted in Alice Calaprice, The Quotable Einstein (1996), 171

69. Peter Borden, Quoted in Roger Von Oech, *A Whack on the Side of the Head* (1982)

70. William Benjamin Carpenter: *Principles of Mental Physiology: With their Applications to the Training and Discipline of the Mind, and the Study of its Morbid Conditions (1874)*; Cambridge University Press 2009

71. Ibid Carpenter

72. Ibid Mlodinow

sometimes as loners, our ideas seem to just appear. But ideas don't come from nowhere; they are produced in our unconscious minds.

Ideas – solutions, ways forward – are most likely to appear when we're doing something else. After staring at his *The Last Supper* mural for hours and days, Leonardo would suddenly shoot off to work on another project (a clay horse), and then return in a mad rush to add something to his unfinished painting. Einstein played Mozart on his violin to 'reconnect with the harmonies of the cosmos',[73] whilst Robert Pirsig found the meaning of life through messing about with his motorcycle.

Alice Roberts tells a story about Charles Darwin.[74] In 1868 he and Alfred Russel presented a paper on the theory of evolution to the Linnean Society. In the society's minutes for 1868 year they reported that nothing all that interesting had happened that year. The following year, Darwin published *On the Origin of Species* for a wider public and it made considerable impact. As Alice Roberts says: 'So, it wasn't the academic paper that made the big splash; it was the popular science book that he wrote to go with it.' It's not what you say, it's the way that you say it.

Of course, we are not arguing that we should ditch reason and facts and rely on emotion and instinct. When Poincaré talks about the 'subliminal self', he doesn't mean pure Rousseau-like instinct: he means the way we process and make selections and connections from existing knowledge. The French doctor Gustave Le Bon[75] made the point that you can't substitute feeling for reason – and we should beware the emotions and the instincts of the crowd. When Poincaré, Pirsig, Carpenter and Mlodinow talk about creativity, they don't mean the responses of the senses and instincts to romantic beauty, they mean the sort of harmony we might perceive through 'mathematical beauty' – Poincaré's phrase – or what Leonardo called 'the supreme certainty'[76] of mathematics. Science – maths in this case – offering harmony and beauty and, in the end, reality.

WEAVING TOGETHER DISCIPLINES

Roberts maintains that her raison d'etre is not to make popular or to dumb down science but to provide 'forums for interaction and dialogue

73. Ibid Isaacson p3
74. Ibid Alice Turner interview with Katy Guest
75. Gustave Le Bon: *The Crowd: A Study of the Popular Mind*; (1895); Cosimo Classics 2006
76. Royal Library: *He who does not know the supreme certainty of mathematics in wallowing in uncertainty*

between scientists and the public'. We're back to 'coffee houses, cafes and bookshops', those contemporary versions of Leonardo's paragone event at Sforza Castle in 1498. If we want science and the arts – as well as maths and humanities – to tell their stories in a meaningful and immediate way, then don't we have to take on the weaving-together of many forms and disciplines – all the sciences, with history, travelogue, pieces of fiction – work that is rigorous and at the same time full of empathy?

Leonardo tells us that we need to recognise that all the disciplines are interconnected and together have something to say about the world now – about things like GM crops, climate change, genetics, migration, population, war, terrorism, trade, world hunger, poverty and so on. As Deresiewicz says, work on the premise that so much of what we learn about the world is 'provisional and complicated, and you don't acquire information, you debate it'.[77] Knowledge isn't static, it's a process. Max Planck, the father of quantum theory, wrote in his autobiography that the pioneer scientist must have 'a vivid intuitive imagination for new ideas not generated by deduction, but by an artistically creative imagination'. It is clear even from seemingly ice-cold mathematical logicians that large chunks of irrationality need to be embedded in the creative process, not only for the arts, but also in the immodestly named 'exact' sciences.

---

77. Ibid Deresiewicz

CHAPTER 5
THINKING ASIDE

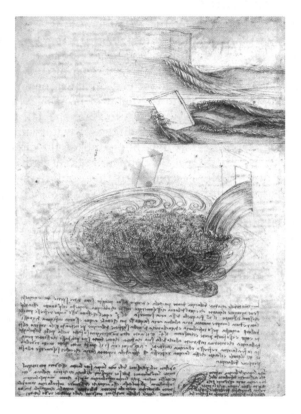

Studies of flowing water, with notes; Windsor Royal Collection

Leonardo's lateral discoveries in terms of water and sound are a perfect example of what has been called 'a solution looking for a problem'. Leonardo called this process of connecting two apparently dissimilar ideas the 'law of continuity'. For him, and for us, it is about the drive to integrate, to find patterns, create analogies and ultimately uncover solutions. He believed that the brain cannot focus on two unconnected subjects without eventually forming some connection between them.

What did Leonardo mean by...?

By thinking about some thing that is not related, different,
unusual patterns are activated[1]

THE LAW OF CONTINUITY

Leonardo was obsessed by water throughout his life; 'it appealed equally to his artistic, scientific and engineering sensibilities'[2] He made hundreds of observations on the movement of water and his notebooks reveal that he was planning a series of 15 books to be called 'The Nature of Water'. In 1500, Leonardo dropped stones into a well and watched the ripples spread from the point of impact. At that moment a church bell began to ring. He began to time the fall of the stones to the chimes of the bell. Just as the circles of water spread and then eventually disappeared so too did the sound of the bell spread and then fade away. By imaginatively connecting the sight of the water and the sound of the bells he concluded that sound travels in waves. What began as a study of water became a study of sound. Similarly, his love of music launched him into the science of percussion, investigating vibrations, waves, and reverberations. The connections that he sensed were for him guides for further inquiries. So later in his life he experimented with holes in walls to investigate and draw what happened when different types of wave hit the openings. This work on diffraction, apertures and wave mechanics effectively prefigured the work that was carried out by Huygens over two centuries later. Leonardo being Leonardo, this in turn led to his work on water eddies and air turbulence and the flight of birds:

> To arrive at knowledge of the motions of birds in the air, it is first necessary to acquire knowledge of the winds, which we will prove by the motions of water. The understanding of the science of water will serve as a ladder to arrive at the knowledge of things flying in the air.[3]

Leonardo's lateral discoveries in terms of water and sound are a perfect example of what has been called 'a solution looking for a problem'.[4]

---

1. See Michael Michalko: *Creative Thinking and Leonardo da Vinci*; available at www.bit.ly/2WgNxJG
2. Philip Ball: *Curiosity: How Science Became Interested in Everything*; Bodley Head 2012
3. Paris Ms:. Notebooks/Richter
4. A phrase used by Taleb in *The Black Swan*, Penguin, 2010, which seems to have its source in common discourse

Leonardo called this process of connecting two apparently dissimilar ideas the 'law of continuity', the process of throwing knowledge into fresh combinations; of connecting, cohering, testing and applying what we learn. 'Everything proceeds from everything, and everything becomes everything, because that which exists in the elements is composed of those elements.'[5]

For him, and for us, it is about the drive to integrate, to find patterns, create analogies and ultimately uncover solutions. He believed that the brain cannot focus on two unconnected subjects without eventually forming some connection between them. Steinberg[6] sees the complexity and potential in this idea in his discussion of *The Last Supper* when he writes:

> I am trying to track in the painting a mode of thought pervasive and all-embracing – an intellectual style that continually weds incompatibles, visualises duration in one seeming flash, opposites in marvellous unison. Again and again, whether in choice of subject or formal arrangement, whether addressed to a part or the whole, Leonardo converts either/or into both.

Inevitably, this response leads us towards thinking about how metaphor might serve in Leonardo's work. His experience at the well which we began with – measuring the spaces between the ripples and then making a connection between the water and the progressive fading waves of sound from the church bell – perfectly illustrates the way his observations of nature often led to mental leaps, providing the raw material for metaphors, analogies, or parables. The etymology of the word metaphor comes from the Greek, 'meta' (meaning 'over and above') and 'pherein' (meaning 'to bear across'). They carry us from the concrete to the abstract, from a single meaning to the possibility of several meanings. Leonardo's intuitive feel for the unity of nature meant that he sensed connections which he then expanded on, letting his mind wander and then theorising through analogies and metaphors.

This constant searching for form and continuity meant that when he looked at the branching pattern he saw in trees and in the arteries of the human body he was dissecting, he offered this thought: 'the water which rises in the mountains is the blood which keeps the mountain

5. Quoted in Maurice Baring' translation of the Notebooks: *Leonardo da Vinci: Thoughts on the Art and Life*; Dover 1906 (CreateSpace Independent Publishing 2012)
6. Leo Steinberg: *Leonardo's Incessant Last Supper*; Zone Books 2001

alive'[7], and he compared the river's flow to the branching human digestive, urinary, and respiratory systems. He found connections everywhere around him, such as between the flow of water and the movements of the air; and whilst 'studying the curls on a beautiful woman's head he thought in terms of the swirling motion of a turbulent flow of water' – 'and sketched alongside it, a seed germinating into shoot'.[8] So this tendency to collate observation with imagination goes on – generating and integrating, associating and recombining.

As Kemp has pointed out, Leonardo's dedication to his art overflowed into his obsessions with how things worked and what those workings meant. That fascination wasn't just about gathering knowledge, it was about experiencing beauty. In his own words, 'from this experiment you will be able to proceed to investigate many beautiful movements which result from one element penetrating into another'.[9]

QUANTUM JUMPS

Leonardo's fascination with the flow of water led him to the human heart. In particular, he was the first to understand completely how the aortic valve works, how the spiral flow of blood through a part of the aorta known as the sinus of Valsalva creates eddies and swirls that serve to close the valve of a beating heart. Leonardo based his studies of the heart on an autopsy he conducted of a 100-year-old man 'to see the cause of so sweet a death'. He came to the conclusion that the ageing process is linked to the degeneration of the blood vessels: 'This coat of vessels acts in the man as in oranges, in which the peel becomes thicker and the pulp diminishes the more they become old.'[10] Another vivid Leonardo metaphor. His understanding of the heart and of the muscles and bones and his drawings 'have a clarity and subtlety not to be seen again until at least the eighteenth century'. But 'his treatise on anatomy was never written, and Leonardo's astonishing investigations were to languish unappreciated for centuries'.[11] It took 450 years or more for anatomists to realise that Leonardo's observations on blood flow were correct. In the 1960s a team of

---

7. *Leonardo da Vinci: Thoughts on Art and Life*; quotations from the Notebooks translated by Maurice Baring 1906; CreateSpace Independent Publishing 2012
8. Adam Gopnik: *Renaissance Man: The Life of Leonardo*; The New Yorker 2005
9. Paris Manuscripts/MacCurdy
10. Quoted by Kenneth Keele (1909 – 1987) in *Leonardo da Vinci; Elements of the Science of Man*; Academic Press 1983
11. Keele, K, & Pedretti, C, *Leonardo da Vinci: corpus of the anatomical drawings* in the Collection of Her Majesty the Queen at Windsor Castle. 4 vols, London 1979

medical researchers led by Brian Bellhouse at Oxford published a series of papers on the aortic valve, detailing experiments which Francis Robicsek[12] showed were almost exactly the same as those undertaken and planned by Leonardo. He came to believe that analogy, metaphor and image combine most effectively and compellingly in painting. Shlain[13] puts it like this: 'Great visual art is authentic, non-logical, and non-discursive. The artist frequently uses visual metaphor to transport us to complex feeling-states ... there are no transitions. It is an all-at-once quantum jump.'

METAPHORIC THINKING

Leonardo's tendency to think in metaphors is illustrated in this passage from one of his notebooks, where he sees a connection between the earth and the human body:

> We may say that the earth has a spirit of growth, and that its flesh is the soil, its bones are the successive strata of rock, its cartilage is the tufa, its blood is the veins of its waters. The lake of blood that lies around the heart is the ocean. Its breathing is the increase and decrease of the blood in its pulses, and even so in the earth is the ebb and flow of the sea.[14]

This is a good example of Leonardo making connections and yet he goes even further with this passage from *Trattato della pittura*[15] where he writes with seeming irritation: 'Merely throwing a sponge soaked in various colours at a wall will leave a stain in which a beautiful landscape can be seen.' This is Leonardo going beyond the concrete and quickening the spirit of invention through contemplating the abstract – and towards the end of his life, in his vision of the end of the world through all those deluge drawings, Leonardo went beyond metaphor. He 'blurred the distinctions between objects and patterns'[16] – presaging 20th-century abstract painters like Jackson Pollock and Wassily Kandinsky by quite a few centuries.

Metaphor is interwoven through much of what Leonardo tells us: the way, for instance, he saw 'reverberations of light' as analogous

12. Francis Robicsek: 'Leonardo da Vinci and the Sinuses of Valsalva'; *Ann Thorg Sunrg* 1991
13. Leonard Shlain: *Leonardo's Brain: Understanding Da Vinci's Creative Genius*; Lyons Press 2014
14. Codex Leicester: Bill Gates Collection, Seattle
15. *Trattato della pittura*, Leonardo's 'Treatise on Painting'; published in Paris in 1651 – after Leonardo's death
16. Ibid Shlai

to the 'bounce of a ball'[17] – leading to him thinking about the light – and suggesting a promise of the light of understanding or lighting the way. Much of his thinking involves this quest to take us from one place to another. To 'bear us across' means having to think of how we might come to see change or new learning as 'a house which magically expands with every door you open'.[18] Understanding Leonardo's use of metaphor and analogy not only helps to refresh and expand how we understand ourselves and to challenge those frameworks that shape and limit us, but it also is a way to transfer meaning across time in two directions, from Leonardo to us, and from us back to him. 'Through metaphors,' says Cynthia Ozick, 'the past has the capacity to imagine us, and we it.'[19]

As a result, Leonardo helps us to grow as 'constructive learners ... who actively build bridges from the known to the new'.[20] This bridge-building process between subject disciplines, observations, facts and existing knowledge shows us that 'the comparative mind is a particular case of the human cognitive condition and an even more particular case of the inquiring mind'.[21]

VISUAL THOUGHT EXPERIMENTS

The world 'is tantalisingly open to interpretation',[22] where patterns will inevitably emerge. If you are Leonardo, in possession of a cognitive condition that demands inquiry and comparison, the search for a taxonomy of vortices and waves inevitably leads to a list of 64 descriptive terms for water in motion – from rotating, to repercussing, to submerging and surging. And from there into speculations about the biblical Deluge. And then on to observations about diffraction and air turbulence. And then from there to all the movements in the universe that are there wherever you look – human limbs, cogs in machines, the blood in our veins and the water in rivers. All, he was absolutely sure, must be operating according to the same laws: 'Man is a machine, a

---

17. Quoted by Martin Kemp in, *Leonardo: The Marvellous Works of Nature and Man*; Oxford University Press 2006
18. Steven Johnson: *Where Good Ideas Come From*; Penguin 2010
19. Cynthia Ozick 'The Moral Necessity of Metaphor': *Harper's Magazine* 1986
20. Pugh, Hicks, Davis and Venstra: *Bridging: A Teacher's Guide to Metaphorical Thinking*; NCTE 1992
21. Ibid Pugh *et al*
22. A phrase from Francis Ames-Lewis in: *The Intellectual Life of the Early Renaissance Artist*; Yale 20

bird is a machine, the whole universe is a machine'[23] – or as Isaacson says: 'These laws are analogous; the motions in one realm can be compared to those in another realm, and patterns emerge.'[24]

Leonardo's notebooks, bursting with drawings and jottings, served him throughout his life as visual thought experiments. They took him 'beyond the existing order', much further than what he and his contemporaries thought they knew. He was learning to let go of unchallenged ideas – what Mlodinow[25] calls 'scripted behaviour' – and learn to relish 'ambiguity and contradiction, to re-frame the questions', and keep on and on generating and integrating a whole universe full of ideas.

23. Marci Cianchi: *Leonardo's Machines*: Becocci Editore 1988
24. Ibid Isaacson
25. Ibid Mlodino

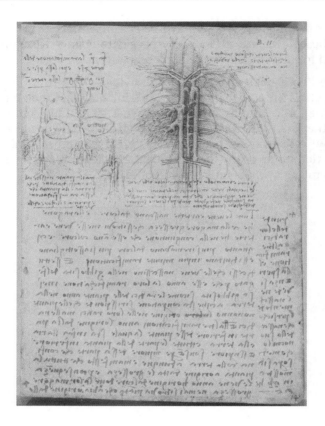

The heart compared to a seed; Royal Collection, Windsor Castle

Metaphors shift the focus from the central to the peripheral. They can disorientate, and as a result inspire imaginative connections; they fuel creativity ... the capacity to conjure up flashes of insight and make cognitive leaps – embracing the capacity and confidence to allow new saliencies to arise.

What can we still learn from Leonardo about...?

What is not surrounded by uncertainty cannot be truth[26]

THE VISIONARY AND THE PRACTICAL

Leonardo teaches us that acquiring knowledge and understanding is a constructive and dynamic (not a static) process. Of course, the practicalities have to be taken on board – he had to know about the mechanics of painting and what artists had done before him, but that was simply the start of what he set out to achieve. 'Knowledge is always constructed, never passively received.'[27] When he bristles at his work being described as 'mechanical' – the work of a craftsman rather than an intellectual – Leonardo is saying that his world expected (directed, even) his paintings to conform to what the state approved in terms of content and method. Leonardo insisted that he had to put what 'the ancients' handed on to him to the test of experience. Writing about the painter Édouard Manet, Pierre Bourdieu[28] said that 'Manet painted in order to learn how to paint a Manet ... He painted in order to know what to paint and how to paint it.' Leonardo shows us that paintings, like knowledge, can show but they can also *lead*. Paintings, like the parables, aren't about illustrating what someone in authority wants us to know, but they are metaphors to 'gain our attention, enhance our understanding, facilitate communication and even persuade us in ways we might not expect'.[29] Just as metaphors take us into and beyond Leonardo's paintings, so too do they take us into and beyond the learning process.[30] Learning is a seed.

UNDERSTANDING 'HERE' IN TERMS OF 'ELSEWHERE'[31]

'I believed in the Church's acres of symbolism ... all the ceremonies layered with meaning ... the flame of a candle in a darkened church ... the cleansing nature of the waters of baptism ... the reverberations of the altar bell ... I grew up knowing things represented other things.'[32]

26. Richard Feynman, *What Do You Care What Other People Think?* 1988

27. Pugh, Hicks, Davis, Venstra: *Bridging: A Teacher's Guide to Metaphorical Thinking*: National Council of Teachers of English; 19

28. Pierre Bourdieu: *Manet: A symbolic revolution*; translated by Collier and Rigaud–Drayton; Polity 2018

29. Ibid Pugh et al *Bridging*, 1992

30. Based on the work of Graham Low in: 'On Teaching Metaphors' in *Applied Linguistics 9*, 1988

31. Samuel Beckett quoted by John Calder in *Texts for Nothing* (1959); Signature Books 1990

32. Bernard MacLaverty Introduction to *Collected Stories* Vintage 2014

MacLaverty's discovery as a boy growing up in Northern Ireland that 'things represented other things' mattered to his learning processes. This realisation encouraged him to look for the links between the known and the unknown. The symbolism of the church, the *metaphors* he grew up with, became ways to expand meaning and language in ways that were not only logical, but also imaginative. This was good for him, he says, as a first step towards becoming a writer.

Writers will often identify the creative act in its entirety with the unearthing of hidden analogy. The discoveries of science and the works of art are explorations – but, more than that, they are 'explosions' of a hidden likeness.[33] Leonardo would probably have agreed with the poet Michael Donaghy when he says: 'I couldn't look myself in the eye unless I used verse as a means of discovery rather than a method of persuading my audience of what I thought I knew'[34] – or perhaps even as a means of challenging what the audience thought they knew. Painting and visualising, like writing, is a significant form of thinking. And using metaphors and analogies can be a powerful process to shake up thinking. They take us further. Towards understanding, as Samuel Beckett says, 'here' through exploring 'elsewhere'.

HOW METAPHORS CLARIFY, THEN MAKE STRANGE

Metaphors can act as a framework for getting to grips with highly abstract or difficult concepts. Parables work like this – simple accessible stories about recognisable people but with underlying implications that take the listener deeper than the surface narrative. 'Quantum theory indicates that there are no such things as separate parts in reality, but instead only intimately related phenomena so bound up with each other as to be inseparable.'[35]

When the scientist Stephen Hawking[36] talks about time as three types of arrow that always shoot in a particular direction – the psychological arrow, the thermodynamic arrow and the cosmological arrow – he is employing a simple metaphor that helps us to address significant issues to do with our understanding of consciousness, recognition and disorder. All of them travel outwards in the direction of the expanding universe and towards entropy. But why

---

33. Bronowski: *Science and Human Values* London Hutchinson 1961
34. Michael Donaghy: 'By any means necessary'; *Poetry News* October 2004
35. Russell Targ: *Limitless Mind: A Guide to Remote Viewing and Transformation of Consciousness*; Novato CA, New World Library; 2004
36. Stephen Hawking: *A Brief History of Time: From the Big Bang to Black Holes*, Bantam 1988

is it that time's arrow has only one direction, from past to future? Is this a universal law or a merely a limitation in our understanding of time? When we talk about how metaphors work – and we also mean similes, allegories, analogies, parables, anecdotes, fables – we are talking about all those ways to 'transfer and translate the abstract into concrete, thus making the abstract more accessible and memorable';[37] but, as we have already suggested, they are more than a simple linear aid to understanding – just as Leonardo's paintings are much more than biblical illustrations.

Metaphors can be used to make connections in order to illuminate whatever is under discussion. Identifying connections between texts or films or practically any difficult phenomenon can help in understanding that phenomenon – or it can point to meanings that the original source did not either make clear or intend. The end result of such a network of connections – of extensive intertextuality – is that the process 'cultivates the mind' and 'prepares furrows for planting ideas'.[38]

Metaphors, consequently, are about a lot more than clarification in order to make the difficult idea more accessible. They can work to extend thought. Seamus Heaney urges us to 'go beyond what is reliable'.[39] He would say that what Leonardo was attempting is very similar to what a poet reaches towards – offering 'the security of what is known' or expected together with 'the challenges and entrancements of what is beyond'. Making the ordinary strange; and at the same time, inviting you beyond – to see with new eyes.[40]

Ruth Padel[41] points out that Heaney maintained a 'double consciousness' in a good deal of his work – that of farm boy and scholar. This is a useful image to unwind some thoughts about Leonardo and, as importantly, some thoughts about how his life and work allow us to *exchange* ideas about how we learn and grow and how these processes might be enriched: how metaphors might play a role in helping us understand the potential of a double consciousness.

---

37. Judith Best: 'Teaching Political Theory: Meaning through Metaphor': *Improving College and University Teaching* 1984
38. Howard Peelle: *Computer Metaphors*: International Council for Computers in Education 1984
39. Seamus Heaney: 'Making Strange' in *Station Island* Faber 1986
40. Seamus Heaney: *Preoccupations: Selected Prose 1968 – 1978*, Faber 1984
41. Ruth Padel: *The Poem and the Journey*; Vintage 2008

The complexities and layers of Leonardo's painting exemplify that Beckett phrase we used earlier about understanding 'here' in terms of 'elsewhere'. He does it all the time. In the relatively recently (1991) rediscovered drawing *Angelo incarnato* ('the Angel made flesh') we encounter 'all the contradictions'[42] between male and female, ecstasy and sadness, the satanic and the angelic, between our own ability to comprehend the coherence of the work, and, quite possibly, the incompatibility of the divine and the human.

Metaphors can also dramatise an idea or a concept. Kenneth Clark said that one cannot look for long at a Leonardo composition without beginning to speak of it as drama and motion. Like Greek theatre, Leonardo's paintings are not simply about illustration or entertainment, nor even a way of representing the teachings of the church back to the church and its followers. They provide 'the smithy' in which the basic concepts of Christianity are forged in the first place – what Tom McCarthy calls 'a quasi-sacred mechanism for placing order and meaning in the world'.[43] A way of 'conquering the resistance of the air'. This idea is implicit in much of Leonardo's work; he doesn't simply *assume* the meaning of a Christian story, he enquires into it. Like other Renaissance artists, he was a great admirer of the 'ancient speculators', such as Aristotle.[44] So, when he undertakes a painting like *Virgin of the Rocks* (which we talk about in chapter 2), the nature of the cave and what it signifies – in terms of looking out or looking in, of fear or desire, of the ambiguity of the unknown – becomes part of the dramatisation that Clark talks about. Like the Romantics or the Impressionists who followed, Leonardo teaches us to read the landscape.

In addition, metaphors can insulate emotionally charged subjects. Alberto Manguel[45] says the use of metaphor in writing or in painting is about 'apprehending the reality of experience not directly but once removed, as Perseus did in order to see the face of the gorgon, or Moses the face of God. Reality, the place in which we stand, cannot be seen as long as we are in it.' As Eliot suggested, 'we cannot take too much reality'. It is the process of once removed that allows us to see where and who we are. 'Metaphor, in the widest sense, is our means of grasping (and sometimes almost understanding) the world and our bewildering selves.'[46]

---

42. Andre Green quoted by Nicoll.
43. Tom McCarthy 'Point of View'; *The Guardian* January 2017
44. Ibid Nicoll 2005
45. Alberto Manguel: *A Reader on Reading*; Yale 2010
46. Ibid Manguel 2010

Manguel's observation about the difficulty of seeing reality when we are in it must remind us of all those 'selves' we have experienced in our own lives, particularly during adolescence. Julian Barnes[47] says that 'nothing can compare to the loneliness of the soul in adolescence'; C.S. Lewis talks about this period in life as being full of 'the inconsolable longing in the heart for we know not what'.[48] It's a time when encounters with metaphors can appeal to 'a point of view which is somehow dislocated, removed'.[49] Appropriately, Lorrie Moore says all this with a memorably startling image: 'Poised between childhood and adulthood, adolescence stands there for a short, vivid time howling like a dog. Eventually it is buried – but buried alive.'[50] In the end, we get through, but the struggle is not forgotten: 'The ball I threw while playing in the park has not yet reached the ground.'[51]

Like Dylan Thomas's evocative analogy of the ball in the park, metaphors provide 'transformations into new meanings that never end'.[52] It's not that they simply make connections between things that are already known and understood, they 'cut between the known and the unknown'[53] and 'open up endless possibilities ... giving words the chance to be more than words'.[54]

Metaphors can evoke insights into what has not yet been understood:

> By shifting the focus from the central to the peripheral limits of language, metaphors can jockey around with established categories ... and allow new saliencies to arise. By dislodging us from fixed conceptual schemes, metaphors are prime for helping us place our impressions into newly fashioned units of meaning.[55]

---

47. Julian Barnes: *Levels of Life*; Jonathan Cape 2013

48. C.S. Lewis: *The Weight of Glory* Macmillan 1966

49. Ian McEwan talking about stories in 'Adolescence and After' an interview with Christopher Ricks, *The Listener*, 1979

50. Lorrie Moore writing about Peter Cameron's novel, *Someday This Pain Will Be Useful To You*, (Picador 2009) in *See What Can Be Done: Essays, Criticism and Commentary*: Faber and Faber 2018

51. Dylan Thomas: 'Should Lanterns Shine'

52. Pugh, Hicks and Davis: *Metaphorical Ways of Knowing: The Imaginative Nature of Thought and Expression*: NCTE, 1997

53. Howard Peelle: *Computer Metaphors*: International Council for Computers in Education 1984

54. Carl E Bain: *The Norton Introduction to Literature*; Norton 1981

55. Paul Muscari: 'The Metaphor in Science and in the Science Classroom'; *Science Education* 1988

In other words, the metaphor is a heuristic device – it leads to discovery, to new understanding and new knowledge. For instance, an exploration of the concept of entropy – the tendency that systems have to degenerate into chaos – is enlivened by Stephen Hawking's metaphor of the jigsaw puzzle.[56] There is only one arrangement of all the pieces of the jigsaw that will produce a complete picture – and there are endless combinations of those pieces that will not. So, the world appears to be hugely in favour of disorder. And once you give the perfect picture, any change at all will simply serve to increase disorder.

Metaphors, as we have seen, take us out on the edge. Paul Muscari has observed that metaphors '[shift] the focus from the central to the peripheral'. Part of us might want to be pulled back to the centre, into a world of safe meanings; but a bigger part will 'want to stay as close to the edge as we can without going over. Out on the edge you see all kinds of things you can't see from the centre.'[57] Metaphors can disorientate, and as a result inspire imaginative connections; they fuel creativity. Sharon Pugh[58] describes creativity as the capacity to conjure up 'flashes of insight and make cognitive leaps' – embracing the capacity and confidence to 'allow new saliencies to arise'.[59] This sort of thinking is not all that easy to measure and grade; the intuitive tends to lose out to the observable, the rational and the processes of problem-solving. Creativity is seen to equal non-conformity and individuality. It is likely to get in the way.

CROSS-CUTS AND TRANSITIONS

We might speculate about what was happening in Leonardo's brain all those years ago if we spend a few moments looking at the concept of 'phase-locking'.[60] This idea comes from brain scientist Robert Thatcher and describes moments when the neurons in the brain pulse in perfect rhythm. Ideas come together and the brain, having learned certain habits or knowledge, acts in tune with expectations. That is when we tend to 'phase-lock'. Our understanding and its future application become fixed. A state of mind that Leonardo clearly avoided.

---

56. Ibid Stephen Hawking
57. Kurt Vonnegut: *Piano Player*;(1952) available from CreateSpace Independent Publishing 2007
58. Ibid Pugh et al: *Bridging* 1992
59. Ibid Paul Muscari 1988
60. Robert Thatcher, D.M. North and C.J. Biver: 'Intelligence and EEG Phase Rest: A Two Compartmental Model of Phase Shift and Lock': *NeuroImage* 42, 2008

Thatcher offers some idea of how we can overcome phase-lock – no mean achievement in the religious and political atmosphere of Leonardo's time. If we are to learn and develop, the synchrony of phase-lock mode needs to be interrupted, fed, even, by what Thatcher calls the 'chaos mode'. By this he means that we need to disrupt certainties, embrace anomalies and contradictions – to recognise the incorrigible plurality of the world. He says that our brains need to experiment with *new* links between neurons, to take in additional information, and more strategies for thinking and working. Writing towards the end of the 19th century and without access to Thatcher's scientific knowledge or methodology, William James[61] said something similar when describing the highest order of minds:

> Instead of thoughts of concrete things patiently following one another, we have the most abrupt cross-cuts and transitions from one idea to another, the most rarefied abstractions and discriminations, the most unheard-of combinations of elements ... a seething caldron of ideas, where everything is fizzing and bobbing about in a state of bewildering activity; where partnerships can be joined or loosened in an instant, treadmill routine is unknown, and the unexpected seems the only law.

Which is why, perhaps, Leonardo did not get around to publishing his investigations or his studies of water and sound and why he so often failed to meet a deadline or complete a project. His mind was 'fizzing and bobbing about' – whilst still managing to make discoveries that have only been fully appreciated in the last hundred years.

Doors that can be opened are important. Mark Stevenson[62] applies the idea of phase-lock to organisations and systems. He calls a broader manifestation of phase-lock 'systems-hardening'. He describes those organisations that point to the past as evidence of their success and impact – education, industry, finance, commerce – when in fact they have passed their sell-by date. What he suggests draws our attention to 'governments and education systems that, rather than rising above the curse of systems-hardening, seem to have embraced it as a virtue'. What began simply as a method of organising a company or a school system becomes a *belief* system which serves itself rather than its core purpose. Testing and examination systems were invented to

61. William James: *Great Men, Great Thoughts, and the Environment*; reprinted by Dodo Press 2002
62. Mark Stevenson: *We Do Things Differently: The Outsiders Rebooting Our World*; Profile Books 2017

measure progress but are now no longer a means to an end, but an end in themselves. William James's thoughts about the 'seething caldron of ideas' and the Leonardo-like minds we should be hoping to develop seem to have fallen by the wayside. Perhaps we should, Luther-like, nail Johann Wolfgang von Goethe's words over the gates of our learning institutions: 'Daring ideas are like chessmen moved forward; they may be defeated, but they are the start of a winning game.'[63]

THINKING ASIDE

Thinking aside is a temporary liberation from the tyranny of over-precise concepts, the axioms ingrained in the very texture of specialised ways of thought. It is a period of incubation which represents an opportunity for a 'reculer pour mieux sauter' ('drawing back in order to leap better'). A time aside from a world that we, like the Confucian scholar Mencius living in the late fourth century BC, might find is fragmented and capricious. Mencius would advise that we should work to set trajectories in motion, embrace the shifts and detours, the chance conversations, experiences, interactions – and use them to nurture an expansive life.

A Mencian approach would allow analogist thinking to escape the straitjacket of habit, to shrug off apparent contradictions and to acquire in exchange a greater fluidity and versatility. This rebellion against constraints which are necessary to maintain the order and discipline of conventional thought is essential for the creative leap. Arthur Koestler describes[64] how scientists often sleepwalk into discoveries without appreciating exactly what those discoveries might mean or where they have come from. Taleb[65] suggests that what we are calling 'thinking aside' also connects with how scientists, inventors and artists capitalise on serendipity and sleepwalking to make discoveries: 'It is hard to look at a computer or a car and consider them the result of an aimless process. Yet they are.'

Progress in apparently rational human pursuits such as mathematics can often be achieved in a highly irrational manner, as Carl Friedrich Gauss[66] admitted: 'I have had my solutions for a long time, but I do not

---

63. Johann Von Goethe, quoted by Stevenson in *We Do Things Differently* (2017) possibly from Goethe's autobiography
64. Arthur Koestler: *The Sleepwalkers; A History of Man's Changing Vision of the Universe*; Penguin 1959
65. Nassim Nicholas Taleb: *The Black Swan*; Penguin 2010
66. Gary Waldo Dunnington: *Carl Friedrich Gauss: Titan of Science*; LLC 2012

yet know how I am to arrive at them.' The German word for 'creating' is 'schöpfen', literally meaning 'to scoop', rather like buckets of water are drawn from a well. The bucket doesn't pick and choose the varieties of water. Leonardo too was seduced by chance, by serendipity, the adjacent possible, chaos mode and also by what evolutionary biologists Stephen Jay Gould and Elisabeth Vrba[67] call 'exaptation' – where we set off with one end in mind but end up pursuing a completely different purpose or project. The classic model of discovery, according to Taleb[68] is that 'you search for what you know (say, a new way to reach India) and you find something you didn't know was there (America)'. If an awareness of the adjacent possible nudges us into noticing that there are other doors to open, then exaptation takes us through those doors. Unsurprisingly, Steven Johnson[69] calls the development of the World Wide Web a 'story of continuous exaptation'. Tim Berners–Lee designed early web protocols as a way for scientific communities to share ideas, but it has led us to a whole plethora of unexpected outcomes.

Montaigne[70] reminds us, even more persuasively, how 'cognitive solutions' can burst out of the big database of received knowledge through exaptation, and transform themselves into 'creative solutions':

> A spirited mind never stops within itself; it is always aspiring and going beyond its strength; it has impulses beyond its powers of achievement. If it does not advance and press forward and stand at bay and clash, it is only half alive. Its pursuits are boundless and without form; its food is wonder, the chase, ambiguity.

A mind that is open to chance discoveries functions on several hierarchic levels at once and often one level does not know what the others are doing. The essence of the creative act is bringing them together. Bridging gaps is about searching for a matrix which might be found by way of analogy or association or by similarity – 'the explosions of likeness'. One of the basic mechanisms of the eureka process is the discovery of a hidden analogy; bringing successive perceptual or conceptual analyser codes to bear on a problem in much the same way as an optician tries out a series of lenses in the frame before the client's eyes.

67. Stephen Jay Gould and Elizabeth Vrba: 'Exaptation – A Missing Term in the Science of Form'; *Paleobiology 8*; January 1982

68. Ibid Taleb

69. Steven Johnson: *Where Good Ideas Come From: The Seven Patterns of Innovation*; Penguin 2011

70. Michel de Montaigne: 'On Experience' in *The Essays of Montaigne*; The Project Guttenberg Volume 19; 2006

Clearly, we are promoting the idea that opening opportunities for exaptation is a good thing, a way to replicate Leonardo's 'law of continuity'. We must add quickly, however, that this is not simply a case of a sort of benign tolerance of lateral thinking, or of the unusual, the idiosyncratic or the original. We need to expect and engage with the sort of creative thinking and learning that may well emerge from collisions rather than going with the flow. We learn more from moments that jar than from moments that gel. Innovation is making new connections and combinations, reinvention and mapping new routes from the present to the future. Some of us are bound not to like the ideas and the words that might emerge but if we are hearing what Leonardo is telling us, then we must make the attempt.

The general idea behind so much of what we have written about innovation and creativity stresses the need to lead people away from the islands they have settled on, either alone or in insular groups that reflect an inward-looking groupthink, and expose them to the widest possible network of other people and ideas. This is true for schools, universities, businesses, political groups – society in general. We need to find a route from phase-lock mode, via chaos mode, and towards greater individuality and originality.

EMBRACING THE CHASE

Like Leonardo, we need never to give up, never to be satisfied, to strive to create a working environment where we learn to 'think like poets and work like a bookkeeper'.[71] Sir Francis Bacon said that the most important discoveries are often the least predictable ones – hence our emphasis on taking on board Mencius's 'shifts and detours' of learning and progress. Bacon[72] puts it like this: crucial advances in understanding are those 'lying out of the path of the imagination'. It's a phrase that appears at first to be a misprint. What at first glance seems to be urging us to use our imaginations is in fact encouraging us to go *beyond* what we can imagine, to embrace the chase.

71. This is E.O. Wilson talking about what makes a good scientist quoted by Susan Engel in *The Hungry Mind*; Harvard 2015
72. Francis Bacon: *The Advancement of Learning and New Atlantis*; edited by Arthur Johnston Oxford University Press 2006

We need to think more about what an individual's database looks like and how that grows. Mihaly Csikszentmihalyi[73] and his work on what he calls 'flow' might begin the conversation. Flow is complete absorption. Success comes about for individuals, he says, out of a complex mix of the individual, their environment and their culture. Mencius said much the same in the fourth century BC. Individuals operate always as 'links in a chain', a part of a process – hence the need for a well-stocked and wide-ranging database of knowledge and this would include – Leonardo would stress with vehemence – 'experience', as well as what is taught or read. We need to accept that, as Newton believed, we stand on the shoulders of giants. We must build 'associative networks of understanding' so that we might widen our 'cognitive bandwidth' – which is Ian Leslie's[74] take on the same idea. To be an original thinker, first you must master traditional thinking; it's difficult to embrace chaos mode if there is no phase-lock to anchor thinking – or as Csikszentmihalyi said, new thought comes in the first place from realignments of old thoughts.

After that, as Tom Butler Bowden[75] points out, deep-thinking people desire 'to create order where there was none before' – just like Leonardo's story of the well and the bell. If you're a Leonardo, thinking and creativity has to happen sometimes when there is no database to build on. So how can this happen? Mikhail Bakhtin[76] says that knowledge is a 'polyphony' of perspectives, voices, worlds and courses, and that narratives do not have a single explanation or interpretation but are 'dialogic'. They invite participation and engagement. This is not just the business of having a conversation but rather a dialogue which has direction and focus. Dialogue is creative because it is about improvising and making connections between ideas and concepts that you have not thought of connecting before.

It is an achievement much closer to the birth of a poetic simile than to a logical production. Lewis Carroll's walrus was also arguing by analogy when he talked 'of shoes and ships and sealing wax, of cabbages and kings'. The essence of the unlikely marriage of cabbages

73. Mihaly Csikszentmihalyi: *Finding Flow: The Psychology of Engagement with Everyday Life*; Basic Books 1998 – a book about how to be happy. Less well known perhaps is his work on creativity and inventiveness, *Flow and the Psychology of Discovery and Invention*; Harper Perennial 2013 reprint

74. Ian Leslie: *Curiosity: The Desire to Know and Why Your Future Depends on It*; Quercus 2014

75. Tom Butler-Bowden: *Never Too Late to Be Great: The Power of Thinking Long*; Viking 2012

76. Alastair Renfrew: *Mikhail Bakhtin (Routledge Critical Thinkers)*; Routledge 2014

and kings is the connection between previously unrelated frames of reference whose union may solve previously unsolvable problems. In the subtitle to his book *We Do Things Differently*,[77] Mark Stevenson implies that it is outsiders (like Leonardo) who change the world. George Bernard Shaw makes a related point when he asserts that, 'the reasonable man adapts himself to the world; the unreasonable one persists in trying to adapt the world to himself. Therefore all progress depends on the unreasonable man.'[78]

In the introduction to his book, Stevenson uses an old Chinese proverb: 'When the winds of change blow, some people build walls, others build windmills.' If this extended conversation with Leonardo leaves us with a final thought, this proverb is it. In order to respond to the world, rather than resist it, we should be teaching ourselves to build windmills.

---

77. Mark Stevenson: *We Do Things Differently; The Outsiders Rebooting Our World*; Profile Books 2017
78. George Bernard Shaw, *Man and Superman*

CHAPTER 6
NEGATIVE CAPABILITY[1]

The Adoration of the Magi; Galleria degli Uffizi, Florence

As we look at a Leonardo painting, contours become ambiguous; figures and landscapes are defined by light and shade, not by outlines. As a result, the paintings are enigmatic, have a spiritual mystery, and allude to something beyond sight, to something ineffably unsettling, to an acknowledgement that there is a dimension to the universe that was not knowable to the human intellect.

---

1. John Keats: *Selected Letters*, edited by John Barnard, Penguin Classics 2010

What did Leonardo mean by...?

Confused things kindle the mind to great inventions[2]

THE PERSPECTIVE OF LOSS

Leonardo's insistence that all boundaries, both in nature and in art, are blurred has tended to lead us to think of 'sfumato'[3] – or 'sfumate', 'sfumose' – as a process that he invented and used as an essential feature of his art. In fact, he didn't invent it. It was used and written about much earlier by Cennino Cennini.[4] He recommended that shadows should be blended, like 'nebulous smoke' ('un fummo bene sfumate'). Martin Kemp cautions us not to inflate the significance of this technique[5] in relation to Leonardo – but in the end has to concede that it is 'a handy shorthand to describe Leonardo's melting effects of light and shade'. It is 'a visually seductive device'[6] and its effect is enigmatic and often deeply mysterious. So, although Leonardo never actually said that sfumato was the secret ingredient for his art, he did advocate its use in a very practical way:

> Paint so that a smoky finish can be seen, rather than contours and profiles that are distinct and crude ... When you paint shadows and their edges, which cannot be perceived except indistinctly, do not make them sharp or clearly defined, otherwise your work will have a wooden appearance.[7]

We know what Leonardo thought about the techniques of painting from his *Treatise on Painting*[8] (which is for the most part a technical guide for painters) and from his notebooks – which he clearly used, like his drawings, as tools for analysis and as a depository for the outpourings of a mind bursting with free associations. What these writings do not have is even a hint of any heartfelt expression of personal 'sentiment'.[9]

---

2. Ibid Nicoll
3. *Trattato della pittura* first published in 1651 and available in Martin Kemp's *Leonardo on Painting*; Yale 1980
4. Cennino L'Andrea Cennini: *The Craftsman's Handbook: Il Libro dell'Arte (circa 1400)*; reprinted in a translation by Daniel V Thompson, 1954 Dover Instructional
5. Martin Kemp: *Living with Leonardo: Fifty Years of Sanity and Insanity in the World of Art and Beyond*; Thames and Hudson 2018
6. Martin Kemp: *Leonardo: Inside the Mind of a Renaissance Genius*: Oxford University Press 2004
7. Codex Ashburnham (now part of the Paris Mss)
8. Ibid *Trattato della pittura*
9. Martin Kemp and Giuseppe Pallanti: *Mona Lisa*; Oxford 2017

Rather like sfumato, his writings invite us to fill in the person behind the words and the pictures.

So in those writings – made public in the *Treatise* and kept hidden in his notebooks – tell us that superficially at least, he promotes sfumato as a means to depict distance,[10] where nearer objects have sharp boundaries, but those further away have, in his words, 'smoky, blurred boundaries'. Clearly the technique comes to mean a great deal more to him than a simple step-by-step guide to making paintings look convincing. His description of sfumato as 'the perspective of loss' ('prospettivo de'perdimenti')[11] suggests that this process is about far more than technique. It is about, as he puts it in his notebooks, how 'confused things kindle the mind to great inventions';[12] it is about an intellectual as much as a visual phenomenon, the psychological as well as the optical. For Leonardo the technique of smoky, blurred boundaries is not simply about depicting increasing distance; it is clearly intended to take us beyond surface meanings. In *Mona Lisa*, for instance, Nicholl[13] observes that the technique 'suggests a mental atmosphere'; it is 'more than a depiction of light and shade – it is a mood or atmosphere, an autumnal suffusion of transience and regret'.[14] A poetic distillation – and like poetry, Leonardo's painting can sometimes clarify, sometimes obfuscate, sometimes confound, sometimes lead us to places we didn't know existed.

The importance of Leonardo's 'smoky boundaries' is nicely illustrated by an episode in 2001 when the Uffizi in Florence announced a plan to clean and restore Leonardo's painting *The Adoration of the Magi*.[15] The restorers at the Uffizi argued that there was a need to make the painting 'legible' to the modern world; they described the work as a 'buried poem' with many of the words missing. The anti-restorers, led by Professor James Beck of Columbia University, argued that this plan was based on a misunderstanding or an ignorance of Leonardo's notion of sfumato. *To clarify* the painting in the way the Uffizi intended would

10. Described in Leonardo's *Treatise on Painting*; edited by Martin Kemp as, *Leonardo on Painting*: Yale 1980

11. Ibid *Treatise/Trattoro*

12. Vatican library, Codex Urbinus Latinus; collected by Francesco Melzi 1530; abbreviated version of these published as *Trattato della pittura* 1651

13. Ibid Nicholl

14. Ibid Nicholl

15. The story of the proposed restoration of the *Adoration* comes from the *Daily Telegraph* June 2001 – which also contains a letter denouncing the plan as 'folly' and signed by forty experts.

destroy what Leonardo deliberately intended to be ambiguous. Beck recognised that the missing words in Leonardo's 'buried poem' are the words we who see the painting will be inspired to find.

The Adoration of the Magi is usually described as Leonardo's first important commission and was intended (had he completed it) to be displayed on the high altar in San Donato a Scopeto. Mary and the infant Jesus sit on a rocky outcrop from which two trees grow, whilst the three kings and their entourages look on alongside Joseph. Most of the figures face the Madonna and Child, but some look up towards the sky and at the star of Bethlehem. In the background there are the ruins of the palace of King David and alongside Mary there are two young trees, their roots reaching towards the infant Jesus. The painting is more than a means of teaching congregations about Bible stories – a sort of 15th-century version of a graphic novel to be painted on the wall of the church to make Christianity more accessible. The images carry a great deal more meaning than that. The palace in the painting, for instance, alludes to the past and the Old Testament, and the two trees might be read as symbols of a new era, a time of peace and plenty that was to follow the birth of Christ. The roots of the tree, pointing towards the infant Jesus, suggest the beginning of new growth. Leonardo makes a sharp division in the painting between the background – the past – and the foreground – a new age of grace.

So, the painting becomes a combination of precise observation, which is what Leonardo professed himself to be primarily interested in, and the sort of mysterious symbolism that his patrons would have been able to show off about to other churches. Yet it doesn't end there: masterful composition, affective gesture, layers of symbolism – these all come together with those smoky boundaries between the seen and the implied to suggest, as we said earlier, 'movements and the motions of the mind'.[16] It is an 'illustration' of the Bible story, certainly – a 'storia'[17] – useful in a church where many of the congregation did not have access to the Latin scriptures; but more than that, it is an invitation to explore the strangeness of the individual images. It is this combination of explanation and storytelling set against a seizing of the viewers' imaginations that takes us much further.

---

16. Codex Urbinus

17. *Storia* – a word used by Leon Battista Alberti to describe a painting that shows a dramatic scene or story. Quoted by Carlo Pedretti in, *Leonardo: I codica* 1995

Isaacson[18] says:

> Sfumato is not merely a technique for modeling reality more accurately in a painting. It is an analogy for the blurry distinction between the known and the mysterious, one of the core themes of Leonardo's life. Just as he blurred the boundaries between art and science, he did so to the boundaries between reality and fantasy, between experience and mystery, between objects and their surroundings.[19]

As we look at a Leonardo painting, contours become ambiguous; figures and landscapes are defined by light and shade, not by outlines. As a result, the paintings are enigmatic, have a spiritual mystery, and allude to something beyond sight, to something ineffably unsettling, to an acknowledgement that there is 'a dimension to the universe that was not knowable to the human intellect'.[20]

ACCEPTING THE ELUSIVE

Like those anti-restorers, Leonardo resisted defining what he saw in terms of outlines. He is drawn towards recognising and accepting the elusive; towards questioning absolute certainty. He is interested in the obscure, and the impact it can have on our creativity:

> Look at any wall marked with various stains, or at a stone with variegated patterns, and you will see therein a resemblance to various landscapes ... or to battles with figures darting about, or strange-looking faces and costumes: an endless variety of things which you can distil into finely rendered forms. And the same thing that happens with walls and stones can happen with the sound of bells, in whose peal too you will find any name or word you care to imagine ... and if you consider them well you will find marvellous new ideas, because the mind is stimulated to new inventions by obscure things.[21]

Sfumato implies that there are gradations of certainty: objects nearer to us have sharp boundaries but those further away have increasingly uncertain edges. The further we move away from the sharp edges of the tangible and the certain, the more ambiguous things become. In

---

18. Ibid Isaacson
19. Codex Ashburnham; also: Codex Urbinus
20. Martin Kemp: *Leonardo*; Oxford 2004
21. See Kenneth Clark: 'A note on the relationship of his science and art'; *History Today* May 1952

the world of international relationships and political oppositions there is a similar recognition that entrenched divisions are often only shifted when the opposing parties accept constructive ambiguity – where red lines are *not* drawn, and where future re–interpretation and adaptation is always a possibility. The way we learn, acquire knowledge and understanding is something of a similar process:

> If all knowledge were explicit, if it consisted of pieces of information immediately present to the mind, and impersonally transferable from one mind to another, then there would be no learning and 'a fortiori' no discovery, which is learning what no one ever knew before.[22]

Or as David Galenson[23] says of artists like Leonardo: 'They consider the production of a painting as a process of searching, in which they aim to discover the image in the course of making it; they typically believe that learning is a more important goal than making finished paintings.'

Modern painters talk about finding 'truth in the material' – the actual process of mixing and applying the paint takes the artist ever closer to a truth not evident, perhaps, at the outset. Hence Leonardo's endless experimentation with his materials and his constant retracting of his work. Kemp and Pallanti, writing about *Mona Lisa*, go to the heart of what sfumato aims to achieve: 'Leonardo's embrace of the analogy between the macrocosm of the world and the microcosm of the human body is not simply an immigration of nature but ... a **remaking** of it, the artist acting as a second nature in the world.'[24] So, in *Mona Lisa* it appears that the landscape seems to flow into her and she in turn becomes a part of it. Isaacson puts it beautifully: 'The winding road coils as if it will connect to her heart. Her dress just below the neckline ripples and flows down her torso like a waterfall. The background and her garments have the same streaked highlights, reinforcing what has progressed from being an analogy into a union.'[25] That last phrase, 'from an analogy into a union', hints at an even wider philosophical position.

Malorie Blackman allows us another take on the implications of sfumato when she talks about how books can be both 'mirrors and

---

22. Marjorie Grene: *The Knower and the Known*; Faber and Faber 1966
23. David W Galenson: *Old Masters and Young Geniuses: The Two Life Cycles of Artistic Creativity*; Princeton University Press 2007
24. Ibid Kemp and Pallanti
25. Ibid Isaacson

windows'.[26] They might reflect things as they are, but they can also reveal possibilities. Books, like Leonardo's sfumato technique, show us who we are, the world we inhabit, and then question those perceptions, those ways of seeing that we previously had thought settled and complete. This image of mirrors and windows also comes up again in a George Herbert poem:[27]

> A man that looks on glass,
> On it may stay his eye;
> Or if he pleaseth, through it pass,
> And then the heav'n espie.

We may see ourselves reflected in a window, or we may look through the glass to what lies on the other side – heaven, understanding, change, new perceptions or innovations. The window may act as a mirror which speaks to the self we are (or could be leaving behind) or to the self we might become on the other side of the glass. It answers to our current values and beliefs and to our vague sense of how those values and beliefs might evolve. In this sense, Leonardo's blurred boundaries could be said to contain a strong element of 'aspiration'.[28] A.N. Whitehead[29] would have said that our 'reflected' image indicates a 'spirit of conservation' whilst the 'view beyond' the glass is 'the spirit of change'; Leonardo would say, more simply and practically, that 'true creativity involves the ability to combine observation with imagination … [and] a great painter depicts both.'[30]

There is an entirely more obvious and direct answer to the question 'What did "sfumato" mean for Leonardo?' It meant that there are and will always be more things to discover and more things to question. When he looks at his world, he reimagines how it looks and questions how he might represent it. When he looks through those smoky boundaries, he is not recording; he is reframing that world.

26. See www.malorieblackman.co.uk Q and A session
27. 'The Elixir' in *The Temple* (1633); Penguin Classics 2017
28. See Agnes Callard: *Aspiration: The agency of becoming*; OUP Press 2018
29. Isabelle Stengers: *Thinking with Whitehead*; Harvard 2014
30. Ibid Isaacson

Mona Lisa; Musée du Louvre

Leonardo's paintings never close. Their smoky boundaries take us to the thresholds and edges of our understanding – to the experimental, to dreams and in-between feelings – about his subjects, his world, his life – and about his art.

What can we still learn from Leonardo about...?

The most beautiful thing we can experience is the mysterious. It is the source of all true art and science[31]

THE IMPORTANCE OF CONSTRUCTIVE AMBIGUITY

Learning is a search – an active not a passive process. As Leonardo discovered, in a world that seems to value prescribed learning, flat-pack opinions, and sameness, it requires the sort of courage that looks on ambiguity as a desirable intention. Taking ambiguity on board is surely a constructive, even essential, element in our own learning processes. There is a connection between Leonardo and the female protagonists in Jim Cartwright's *The Rise and Fall of Little Voice*[32] and Arnold Wesker's *Roots*,[33] both of whom transcend mimicry to find their own voices – a concise metaphor, we think, for the way Leonardo remakes and reframes the world around him. We might also see it as the way we in turn should think about learning as a process of developing: from mimicking received knowledge to rejigging and reinterpreting that knowledge; from accepting the given to looking beyond what we're told to see. Alberto Giacometti[34] hammers the point home when he says: 'The more I work, the more I see things differently; that is, everything gains in grandeur every day, becomes more and more unknown, more and more beautiful. The closer I come, the grander it is, the more remote it is.'

Sfumato is Leonardo's constructive ambiguity. Those blurred boundaries are an invitation to explore the unknown or the untested – to look through the window, not at it. When he speaks of loss in relation to perspective he means a loss of sharp definition, of certainty, and the subsequent haziness allows for the possibility of finding something unexpected and even unlooked for. We might uncover new possibilities within that misty ambiguity. Or, as Louise MacNeice succinctly puts it,[35] we will feel that 'round the corner is – sooner or later – the sea'.

Gregory F. Treverton,[36] a US national security expert, would say that interpreting Leonardo's misty ambiguity – his sfumato – is not a puzzle, it's a mystery. This distinction is useful. Treverton maintains

---

31. Albert Einstein: *The world as I see it*, Citadel Press Inc; 2006
32. Jim Cartwright: *Rise and Fall of Little Voice*; Berg 3PL 1992 edition
33. Arnold Wesker: *Roots*; Bloomsbury Methuen Drama 2015 edition
34. Alberto Giacometti, Swiss sculptor, 1901 –1966
35. Louis MacNeice in his poem, 'Round the Corner' in *Collected Poems* 1966
36. Gregory F Treverton: 'Puzzles and Mysteries': *Smithsonian Magazine* June 2007

that puzzles can be solved, they can be answered. A mystery, on the other hand, 'offers no such comfort. It poses a question that has no definite answer because the answer is contingent; it depends on a future interaction of many factors, known and unknown.' Malcolm Gladwell picks up Treverton's distinction when he says: 'If things go wrong with a puzzle, identifying the culprit is easy: it's the person who withheld information. Mysteries, though, are a lot murkier ... Sometimes the question itself cannot be answered. Puzzles come to satisfying conclusions. Mysteries often don't.'[37]

There is a whole bookcase full of variations on this idea: the English-born physicist Freeman Dyson sees science not as a collection of truths, but as a continuing exploration of mysteries; and Ray Dolby, the audio engineering genius, said that in order to invent, 'you have to be willing to live with a sense of uncertainty, to work in darkness and grope towards an answer, to put up with the anxiety about whether there is an answer'.

SERENDIPITY

In 1754 Horace Walpole[38] read a translation of the 16th-century Italian fairy tale called *The Three Princes of Serendip*. ('Serendip' is what Sri Lanka was called before it was Ceylon.) In this story the characters 'were always making discoveries, by accident and sagacity, of things they were not in quest of'. As a result of his reading, Walpole coined the word 'serendipity'. Scientists would say that the serendipity strand – an openness to the unexpected – is vital in research. We would concur. It is crucial to the learning process.

Alan Baumeister[39] picks up on this idea when he says that the researcher must be 'sagacious', by which he means 'attentive and clever', so that they can respond to whatever chance observation or discovery comes their way. The novelist John Barth[40] says much the same thing: 'You don't reach Serendip by plotting a course for it. You have to set out in good faith for elsewhere and lose your bearings serendipitously.' We say all this to remind ourselves that knowledge is two tiered. Much of it is authentic, of course, and we accept and agree on that authenticity; but

---

37. Malcolm Gladwell: 'Open Secrets: The Mystery of Enron': *The New Yorker* 2007
38. Horace Walpole coined the word *serendipity* in a letter to Horace Mann, dated January 28, 1754 (details online)
39. Alan Baumeister: 'Serendipity and the cerebral localisation of pleasure' in *Journal of the History of Neurosciences*; 2006
40. John Barth: *The Last Voyage of Somebody the Sailor*; Little, Brown; 1991

we have to leave the door open to the belief that much of what we learn is 'inherently provisional'.[41]

Steven Johnson[42] leads us to think about the balance between accepted knowledge and the possibility of reinterpretation:

> Serendipity needs unlikely collisions and discoveries, but it also needs something to anchor those discoveries ... The challenge ... is how to create environments that foster serendipitous connections, on all the appropriate scales; in the private space of your own mind; within larger institutions; and across the information networks of society itself.

We need the anchors but have to open our minds to understand, as scientists have understood, that no sooner are the facts established than we must start to work on how to disprove, improve or generalise them.[43]

Leonardo described himself as a dreamer and a drifter channelling visual fantasy and free associations into productivity. This is exactly why A.N. Whitehead[44] describes the way we learn as a romance which 'begins and ends with research' – it begins with Leonardo's dreaming and drifting and ends, temporarily, with Emily Dickinson's end–of–line dash – that device she uses in most of her poems to invite our continued reaction and participation. We need to be intrigued, have our inquisitiveness and creativity stirred and welcome opportunities to experience Walpole's serendipity.

NEGATIVE CAPABILITY AND ELASTIC THINKING

The phrase 'negative capability' comes from a letter John Keats[45] wrote to his brother in which he describes a state 'when a man is capable of being in uncertainties. Mysteries, doubts, without any irritable reaching after fact and reason.' Many modern artists use a phrase similar to Keats's 'negative capability' – 'negative space'. For a sculptor of abstract forms, solid objects exist within a negative space – the apparently empty space which is around and sometimes passing through a sculpture. Similarly, for a dramatist, the use of pauses in

41. Lynn Hunt: *History, Why it matters*; Polity 2018

42 Steven Johnson: *Where Good Ideas Come From: The Seven Patterns of Innovation*; Penguin 2011

43. This point is made by Tim Radford in, *The Consolations of Physics: Why the Wonders of the Universe Can Make You Happy*; Sceptre 2018

44. Ibid Whitehead: *The Aims of Education*: full text available on line

45. John Keats (edited by John Barnard): *Selected Letters*; Penguin Classics 2010

dialogue can carry uncertainty and the possibility of ambiguity; and film–makers, novelists and poets – with their 'showing–not–telling' approach – regularly use the inherent mystery of silence to stimulate potentially imaginative exchanges between the work and its audience.

Leonardo's smoky boundaries similarly teach us to relish encounters with uncertainties – with complexity and ambiguity – and see them as dynamic processes which lead us to raise new questions, meet unforeseen problems, and to regard old problems from a new angle. Keats, like Leonardo, and like Darwin, realised that understanding and change come about through 'accidents and disruptions which overturn convention'. As a result the status quo is sometimes 'reconfigured through abnormality'. It's about being responsive to flexible thinking. It's about jumping off the cliff knowing or simply hoping that wings will appear on the way down.

Writing about education, A.N. Whitehead observed that 'the most striking phenomenon is that schools of learning, which at one epoch were alive with a ferment of genius, in a succeeding generation exhibit mere pedantry and routine. The reason is that they are overladen with inert ideas.'[46] He might have been writing this now rather than at the beginning of the 20th century. He went on t50 say that 'the broad primrose path leads to a nasty place where students learn by heart all the questions likely to be asked at the next external examination'. He insists that 'as parents and teachers we are dealing with human minds and not with dead matter' and it is our role to encourage our children – and our colleagues at work – not to be passive but rather embrace the 'complicated tangle' and the distractions of learning – and life.

Have we accepted a society where standardisation and conformity – sameness – are the most desirable attributes? Leonard Mlodinow[47] broadens the context of these concerns quite dramatically when he writes about how we need to adapt our *thinking* to take into account a world of accelerating change, globalisation and technological innovation:

> There are certain talents that can help us, qualities of thought that have always been useful but are now becoming essential. For example: the capacity to let go of comfortable ideas and become accustomed to ambiguity and contradiction; the capability to rise above conventional mind–sets and to reframe the questions we ask; the ability to abandon our ingrained assumptions and open ourselves to new paradigms; the propensity to rely on imagination

46. Ibid Whitehead
47. Ibid Mlodinow

as much as logic and to generate and integrate a wide variety of ideas; and the willingness to experience and be tolerant.

It is no wonder that in the late 15th-century world Leonardo found himself in, trying to find his way through a world of too much order created by Church and state and the overwhelming uncertainty – chaos, even – of that dark cavern that haunted his imagination, sfumato – blurred boundaries and ambiguity – became the technique by which he is most often defined.

Leonardo chases ambiguity in his paintings. Like the contemporary artist Giorgio Morandi,[48] he recognised that 'nothing is abstract ... There is nothing more surreal, nothing more abstract than reality.' Nothing is more ambiguous than reality. This echoes something Seamus Heaney said about poetry being 'a model of inclusive consciousness. It should not simplify. Its projections and inventions should be a match for the complex reality which surrounds it and out of which it is generated.'[49] Just like learning. It shouldn't be allowed to solidify into fixed certainties or what Hannah Arendt[50] calls 'frozen thoughts' – thoughtlessness, scripted behaviour. Nor should it be chaotic but rather part of a liquid network where 'the elegance of meaningful complexity'[51] plays a significant role in the learning process.

These encounters with Leonardo, Walpole, Whitehead and the rest encourage us to resist a reductionist view of the world of work, learning and politics. Our lives do not have to have *predetermined* outcomes; they are part of a *process* which, although subject to particular constraints, can offer us the opportunity to experience outcomes which are decidedly *indeterminate*.[52] In other words, we need to take a good look at Leonardo's sfumato technique and try to adopt and to adapt it to our own lives and the world we live in.

PRODUCTIVE FRUSTRATION

This might be an appropriate moment to pause and think about the place of the internet in this discussion. Is our thinking helped or hindered by our easy access to information? Ben Greenman,[53] writing about his young

---

48. Giorgio Morandi quoted by Hustvedt (ibid)
49. Seamus Heaney: *The Redress of Poetry*; Faber and Faber 1995
50. Ibid Arendt
51. Marilynne Robinson: *What Are We Doing Here?* Essays; Virago 2018
52. See Robert E Ulanowicz: *A Third Window: Natural Life beyond Newton and Darwin*; Templeton Foundation Press 2009
53. Ben Greenman: 'Online Curiosity Killer' *New York Times*, September 2010

son, argues that although the internet can answer questions with 'ruthless efficiency', it simultaneously 'cuts off the supply of an even more valuable commodity: productive frustration'. He goes on to say that of course we need effective ways of accessing information, but as importantly we need to find ways to fill ourselves 'with questions that ripen, via deferral, into genuine interests'. Earlier we talked about the two types of curiosity – diversive and specific: learning scatteringly and becoming an expert. The internet facilitates the former, but a good deal of what we have talked about so far leads us to think that the latter is more often than not driven by constructive ambiguity and productive frustration.

The internet is a convenient way to impart ideas, knowledge and learning but it runs the risk of turning mysteries into puzzles – which is why sfumato is so important and why Greenman's wonderful phrase 'productive frustration' is so powerful a description of how our thinking processes should work and grow. Through serendipitous distractions we can start to develop what Simone Weil called 'the formation of attention' – which we talk about elsewhere – and the Louis MacNeice approach to everything that we also mention elsewhere – distractions celebrate 'the drunkenness of things being various'.[54]

This is why those well-meaning conservationists perhaps got it wrong when they wanted to clean up Leonardo's *Adoration* to remove its blurred edges; and why politicians miss the point when they try to draw lines beyond which they swear they will never tread; and how shareholders and managers get it wrong when they use share prices as the only measure of success; and why we – you and me and those we work with – lose direction when we fail to recognise Leonardo's implied assertion that ambiguity should make sense not just to us, but *of* us.[55]

NEOPHILIA[56] AND DESIRABLE DIFFICULTIES[57]

How do we scaffold experiences of learning, working and living so that we encourage the ability to think, engage and revel in ambiguity? How do we create a framework which not only allows but promotes that

---

54. Louis MacNeice; 'Snow' *Collected Poems* Faber 1966

55. This is a paraphrase of William Deresiewicz's point in *Excellent Sheep*; Simon and Schuster 2015

56. This is a word coined by Robert Anton Wilson to describe an intense desire for novelty – a person who seeks what Steven Johnson calls, in *Wonderland* 2016, the 'novelty bonus' – learning experiences that 'confound expectations'-sometimes referred to as the 'Rescorla- Wagner model'

57. This is a phrase from the American psychologist, Robert Bjork who argues that encountering difficulties when learning enhances long term retention

'skein of grace' which Clive James talks about below? L.S. Vygotsky[58] argues that the sort of cognitive development that leads to higher mental functioning has its origins in 'social interaction' – not just in conversation but in dialogue. One participant in the dialogue, the partner in talk, says Vygotsky, needs to be 'the more knowledgeable other' – a person who knows or understands 'the distance between the individual's ability to perform a task under adult [or expert] guidance and/or with peer collaboration and the individual's ability to solve a problem independently'. It is in this space between the teacher and the taught, Vygotsky says, that learning occurs. He calls it the 'zone of proximal development'. Bjork[59] adds his 'desirable difficulties' to this equation. If the material in hand stretches the learner, it not only excites interest but also facilitates long-term retention.

How do we, in whatever sphere we operate, create those 'habits of thought, reading, writing, and speaking which go beneath surface meaning ... to understand deep meaning, root causes, social context, ideology, and personal consequences of any action, event, organisation, experience, text, subject matter, policy, mass media or discourse'?[60]

Leonardo's sfumato invites exactly this: to go beneath surface meaning and help each other move on from accessing knowledge in a *mechanical* way with its emphasis on *decoding* rather than on shades of meaning. How can we usher ourselves into a place where we can not only read the words, but interpret them? David Holbrook: 'The hidden planet we have been searching for is meaning: once we accept that man's primary aim is for meaning, then we can find a better basis for our work.'[61] The truth is that we are all drawn to novelty and change. We all possess the potential to develop a trait called 'neophilia'[62] – an instinctive need for complexity, ambiguity – for sfumato, in fact, and for what Garner, Brown, Sanders and Menke[63] see as a need to encounter more opaque as opposed to transparent language. They conducted an experiment in which they gave one group of children a series of straightforward and simple transparent passages to read, and a second group of children opaque passages to read – ones containing

58. L.S Vygotsky: *Mind in Society*; Harvard 1978
59. Robert Bjork: *Learning and Forgetting Lab*; www.bit.ly/2uw000y
60. I Shor: *What is Critical Literacy?* 1999
61. David Holbrook: *English for Meaning*; NFER Publishing 1979
62. Ibid Mlodinow
63. Garner, Brown, Sanders and Menke: *The Role of Interest in Learning and Development*; Lawrence Erlbaum 1992

ambiguity, subtlety and complexity. The opaque group remembered the complex and the difficult much more completely than the transparent group remembered their simplified material.

Language can be seen as a thought crystalliser, typified by Forster with the question 'How can I know what I think till I see what I say?'[64] However, there are issues. Words are important tools for formulating thoughts. But they are not verbal tags; they are to a great extent artificial constructs, behind which innocent facades 'hide the traces of the logic that went into their making'.[65] The stream of language carries thought, so that the formation of ideas or concepts and verbal formulation become indistinguishable. Time, space, mass, force, weight, wave, sensation, consciousness and divisibility are categories which have embedded within them Greek grammar and self-evident common sense. This can result in the words themselves serving as decoys or straitjackets – or, as Koestler said, 'a great number of the basic convertible concepts of science have turned out at various times to be both tools and traps'. When Aristotle drew up his table of categories which to him represented the grammar of existence, he was really projecting the grammar of the Greek language onto it; and 'that grammar has kept us to this day ensnared in its paradoxes. Every revolution since then has had to make a hole in the established fabric of conceptual thought.'[66]

M.A.K. Halliday[67] makes a crucial point when he says that learning language, learning through language and learning about language all involve learning to 'understand things in more than one way' – which is exactly what sfumato is about. We learn in a *multimodal* way – questions, interactions, finding ways to scaffold understanding, talking about vocabulary, comprehension, developing confidence, fluency, participating in stories, inference and most of all, interpretation. These things are not simply about reading aloud; they are about dialogue. It's not simply about checking for understanding and delivering knowledge; it's about testing and questioning experience. It's laying the foundations for negotiating unfamiliar materials – which is also, crucially, what those who negotiate international agreements on our behalf need to remember.

---

64. E.M.Forster, *Aspects of the Novel* ed. Oliver Stallybrass Harmondsworth: Penguin, 2005
65. Arthur Koestler: *The Act of Creation*, Hutchinson 1969
66. Ibid Koestler
67 M.A.K Halliday: in 'Towards a language-based theory of education', *Linguistics and Education* 1993

THE SKEIN OF GRACE

Like Koestler after him, the British mathematician A.N. Whitehead pictures a world where the way we learn to behave and think too often becomes a straitjacket, where the natural curiosity and creativity is trodden on in favour of 'an unrhythmic collection of distracting scraps'[68] in order to meet the demands of government policies, production targets, the examination system and what we have been told is company culture. In a world like this, we miss the 'possibility that there may be other choices and better ways'.[69] We will miss those other choices and better ways if we fail to give the next generation – for some of the time, at least – the space to improvise, to put away the script.

Improvisation certainly has the potential to inspire but it does, of course, have its limits. It needs that word Steven Johnson used when we quoted his remarks on serendipity: an 'anchor'. So, the question becomes, how and when do we prime the pump with existing knowledge and practice? How do we pay *some* attention to the mechanics of learning new things without sacrificing entirely the desire to participate and understand – or to feel secure and valued? In short, we need to act upon Picasso's belief that 'inspiration does exist, but it needs to find us working when it arrives'.

If you are an employer operating in a challenging marketplace, or a parent with a child about to take a test, or a teacher struggling to prepare your class for an external examination, then any call to reject the system (or existing knowledge and practice) is not going to strike you as particularly practical. Despite his disdain for tests and rote learning, A.N. Whitehead, writing at the beginning of the 20th century, was a bit more realistic. He talks about 'cycles of discipline and freedom' and about how we can 'fly' whilst at the same time using our knowledge and skills as 'an anchor' for those uplifting new ideas and discoveries. The truth is that creativity does not exist in a vacuum. Even Leonardo, just as he rails against the ideas of the past, shows in almost the same breath just how much he knows about the past. It's difficult to *rewrite* the past without first *reading* the past. This is part of what we were saying in the chapter about curiosity: it is not enough to spark interest; we must encourage a long-term commitment to exploration, discovery and learning.

---

68. Ibid Whitehead (in his essay, *'The Aims of Education'* – available online)
69. Ellen. J. Langer: *The Power of Mindful Learning*; De Capo Press 1998

This notion was given perfect expression by Clive James.[70] He had come across a group of street musicians in Cambridge town centre. Marvelling at their 'contrapuntal intimacy', he observed: 'The short, stout clarinettist was a wonder: he had that rare knack of sticking to the melody even as he sailed off into the unknown. It's my favourite quality in any work of art: the framework participates in the skein of grace.'

This then is our challenge. How do we allow for and encourage this 'skein of grace' – this loose thread linking the potential for freedom in our lives and work, to the expediency of everyday demands? How do we satisfy what Leonardo, Whitehead and James so much admire, whilst maintaining that knack of 'keeping to the melody'? Or, for instance, how do we teach the mechanics of reading without abandoning what reading is really for? How do we make sure that 'the framework' – the nuts and bolts of how language works, or the knowledge base and vocabulary of any subject – supports and even inspires a 'skein of grace' – that necessary imaginative and creative participation and understanding which might follow from a comfortable grasp of the conventions and history of the subject?

How do Leonardo's 'smoky blurred boundaries' show us the way towards allowing ourselves to go beyond what we have been told is the way things should be? As Friedrich Hayek[71] says, how do we avoid becoming like those experts who seek objectivity at the expense of other perspectives on the world; or – as William Davies[72] puts it, remember that 'even truths and great triumphs are temporary – as Napoleon discovered'. Hannah Arendt[73] makes the point even more succinctly: 'There are no facts without interpretations.' Apparent facts, events and statistics, she says, are much more 'fragile' than we sometimes think. Cennini's 'nebulous smoke' and Leonardo's 'smoky boundaries' offer us the possibility of a close encounter with the truth – perhaps more so, even, than all that objective data passed off as objective fact.

LIVING FOR THE GREEN LIGHT

We see the world of sfumato as a pathway. Leonardo's 'perspective of loss' thus becomes our perspective of discovery. The film director

---

70. Clive James: 'Reports of my death'; *The Guardian* 2016
71. Friedrich Hayek: 'The use of knowledge in society'; *American Economic Review*, vol 35, 1945
72. William Davies: *Nervous States: How Feeling Took Over the World*; Jonathan Cape 2018
73. Hannah Arendt: 'Understanding and Politics'; *Essays in Understanding 1930-1954*; Harcourt Brace and Co 1994

Baz Luhrmann said that working on the screen adaptation of F. Scott Fitzgerald's novel *The Great Gatsby* taught him that we should 'live not for ourselves but for those ideals that are grander than ourselves'.[74] We should live for the green light, even though it is and will always be just out of reach. He goes on to say, quoting Fitzgerald, that 'the test of a keen intelligence is the ability to hold two opposing ideas in your mind, at the same time, and know that both are true'.

The two ideas that Leonardo held in his mind are evident when we place the ambiguities implicit in the smoky boundaries of sfumato alongside his certainty that determination, endless patience and purpose would, in the end, ignite the green light of understanding and completion.

We need to view the unknown, those 'blurred boundaries', that ambiguity, positively – constructively – with excitement and expectation. We have to believe that understanding is always about to happen, and knowledge is about to connect with other knowledge. For Louis MacNeice, Leonardo's sfumato – his 'perspective of loss – would have been a way to 'answer questions I was not fully aware I had asked'.[75] If those layered and indistinct edges are not quite serendipity, they almost certainly open us to the possibility of serendipity. They can lead us towards elastic thinking, perhaps. MacNeice embraces that elusive understanding (and complexity and ambiguity) precisely because it is 'an answer; on a plane, just a shade above or below our own or just round the corner ... so near and yet so far in fact, [it] lies somewhere that might make sense of our past and our future and so redeem our present'.[76]

So, where once we thought we were listening to *one* voice imparting knowledge, now we hear several. Where once there was moral certainty, now there are multiple interpretations and voices we did not even know were there. When we thought we could hear just one voice in a Leonardo painting, we have come to hear more than one voice – and those voices include our own. The painting is not just about its surface, it's about simultaneity and reciprocity.[77]

---

74. www.bit.ly/2JCRBTi Why The Great Gatsby Remains The Best Reflection Of The American Dream
75. Louis MacNeice: 'Experiences with Images' *Orpheus* magazine 1949
76. Louis MacNeice: 'A Modern Odyssey'; *New Statesman* 1960
77. This idea about the potential for painting to have a psychological impact is from, Merleau-Ponty, *The Primacy of Perception*; ed. James M. Edie, trans. William Cogg *et al*, Northwest University Press 1964

There is no such thing as a final or concluding thought for this chapter, but we can't resist one more observation. In his anthology of prose poems, Jeremy Noel-Tod[78] says that such writing 'drives the reading mind beyond the city limits'. The power, he says, is in the fact that it is 'neither one thing nor another'. In her review of the collection,[79] Kate Kellaway adds that prose poems lend themselves 'to the liminal, experimental, to dreams and in-between feelings – especially about writing itself'. Substitute 'writing' with 'painting', replace 'prose poems' with 'sfumato' and we could just as easily be talking about Leonardo and how his paintings never close.

We might purloin Kellaway's review title – 'The poem that keeps on giving' – and apply it to Leonardo's work: the *paintings* that keep on giving. Their smoky boundaries take us to the thresholds and edges of our understanding – to 'the experimental, to dreams and in-between feelings' – about his subjects, his world, his life – and about his art. The voices that are behind and coming from these paintings don't stop encouraging us to live for what Luhrmann called the 'green light' – even though we have to accept that the green light is always just out of reach.

---

78. Jeremy Noel-Tod: *The Penguin Book of the Prose Poems*; Penguin Classics 2018
79. Kate Kellaway: 'The poem that keeps on giving'; *The Observer*, December 2018

CHAPTER 7
UNFINISHED PERFECTION

The Virgin and Child with St Anne and John the Baptist (cartoon);
Burlington House, London

The layering in this painting is not just about perfectionism, it is
about complexity, paradox, challenge and the realisation that the
questions about what things look like, and more importantly, what
they mean, never come to an end. We would do well to remember
what Leonardo said about reaching conclusions too readily. That the
abbreviators of works do injury to knowledge and to love.

What did Leonardo mean by...?

Observe the light. Blink your eye and look at it again. That which you see was not there at first, and that which was there is no more[1]

BEGINNINGS WITHOUT END

In the Department of Manuscripts at the British Library is an undistinguished-looking page, probably one of Leonardo's last-ever pieces of writing, dating from 1519, the year he died. He was working on the transformation of shape in a geometric visualisation that had frustrated him for many years, when his housekeeper, Mathurine, interrupted his work. Three-quarters of the way down the page the text breaks off with an abrupt 'etcetera'. The whole last sentence that Leonardo wrote in his notebook reads: 'Etcetera, perche la minesstra so fredda.' As Charles Nicholl says, 'it could be mistaken for part of the theorem'. Leonardo stops his work almost literally mid-sentence and puts down his pen, possibly for the final time, 'because the soup is getting cold'. His great enterprise of knowing everything that there is to know about everything, to which he devoted his entire life, tails off with a one-liner about soup. There is also within this domestic scene 'more than a hint of foreboding'.[2] As far as anyone can tell, he never did return to these notes, and so this minor interruption seems to foreshadow the more definitive one soon to come. We might call this episode Leonardo's last theorem. Yet another unfinished project.

Leonardo uses a particular squiggle for the word 'etcetera' that Nicholl[3] calls 'a glyph of non-completion'. A hieroglyphic signifying that there was still much to discover and achieve. We would argue that what Leonardo feared most in 1519, as death approached, was not the unknown mystery of the final judgement but the awfulness of that last word 'etcetera' and the unwritten words behind it:

> He didn't fear hell and damnation at the end of his life, but rather the weight of that last word 'etcetera' and the empty grey paper beneath it. The fact that he left so many incomplete or abandoned projects illustrates his characteristic uncertainty and his life-long belief that declaring a work complete meant that its continued evolution was ended. Any piece of work he undertook could never be completed, only abandoned.[4]

1. Leonardo: *Codex Arundel*, 190v
2. Ibid Nicholl
3. Ibid Nicholl
4. Ibid Nicholl

Vasari says that towards the very end of his life, Leonardo 'protested that he had offended God and mankind by not working harder at his art, as he should have done' – hence that phrase which occurs again and again in his notebooks: 'Dimmi, dimmi se mai fu fatta cosa alcuna' ('Tell me, tell me if anything ever got done'). These words suggest a intensifying despondency over all those projects that were never completed, a level of despair that had led him to write in the days before his death: 'He who has frittered life away leaves no more trace of himself upon the earth than smoke does in the air or the foam on the water.'[5]

There is a kind of philosophical vertigo implicit in all this. Alongside that last 'etcetera' in Leonardo's notebooks, we might place Isaacson's[6] comment that Leonardo's repeated attempts to depict the biblical Deluge, particularly during those last few years in France, are not just about his fascination with water, but they provide a bookend to his life, giving us 'a powerful and dark expression of many of the themes of his life'. For us, too, the key themes of Leonardo's life are powerful, but we hesitate to call them dark. His passionate curiosity is everywhere, but it is filtered through a determination to be critically *dispassionate* about what he saw and was told. Nevertheless it is certainly true that, as Steadman noted, everything he created is suffused with 'disappointment alongside exuberant achievement'.[7]

WHAT'S PAST IS PROLOGUE[8]

Leonardo was obsessed with water flowing, feathers rippling in the wind, emotions swiftly passing. Even the end of the world pictured in the frenzies of his Deluge drawings comes about not through a wrathful act of God, but rather through the turbulence and fury of raw nature at work. He was concerned throughout his life with capturing incidents in nature or in an individual's emotional engagement with the world and yet, at the same time, he was all too aware of the elusiveness and uncertainties of the world he was attempting to describe.

In amongst the almost endless divergent thinking that fills Leonardo's notebooks, there comes this: 'In rivers, the water that you touch is the last of what has passed, and the first of that which comes. So, with time

---

5. Ibid Vasari *Lives*
6. Ibid Isaacson
7. Ibid Steadman
8. Shakespeare: Antonio in *The Tempest*

present.'[9] Time is elusive: 'The instant does not have time; and time is made from the movement of the instant.' In his paintings he wanted to capture all of the intensities of a moment, and for that moment to suggest what had come before and what might come afterwards. 'Things that happened many years ago,' he wrote in one of his notebooks, 'often seem close and nearby to the present.'[10]

The line we have used as the title of this section – about the past acting as a prologue to the present – is from *The Tempest*. It's Antonio trying to persuade Sebastian to forget the past and embrace the future by murdering his brother. The past is a prologue to what happens now and what is to happen in the future. For Leonardo this would be about more than the personal. It is about art, thought and civilisation. What he is learning and achieving now is 'the first of that which comes ... and time is made from the movement of the instant'.

HERETICAL STATES OF MIND

Understanding Leonardo is as much about the political and religious voices that surrounded him as it is about those inner, intensely private voices we might see as driving his perceptions and his purposes as an artist – and scientist. His secretiveness was partly a defence against artistic plagiarism; but more than that, he was engaged in a quiet battle to question those in authority around him, and to undermine the traditions of thought that were part of the intellectual heritage of the time. As he said, 'anyone who in discussion relies upon authority uses not his understanding but his memory'.

Leonardo's life was framed by those two imperatives: his personal history and the times in which he lived. A dominant Church asserted that Christianity had all the answers; questions about life and the meaning of the universe were unnecessary. Couple this with an almost equally ambitious political system and we can see that Leonardo's world was not, for the most part, conducive to thinkers or critics. Alongside the power of the Church and the state there was another unifying principle (or frame) at work to inform 15th- and early 16th-century Italian culture: art, science and learning operated as an emulation of classical antiquity. 'He fought powerfully against the unseen temptations of his intellectual heritage and won far more often than he lost.'[11]

9. Ibid Isaacson
10. Leonardo: *Codex Atlanticus*
11. Ibid Isaacson

Apart from finding ways to deal with political and social issues, he was also coming to terms with his personal history – his illegitimacy, his lack of a formal education, his sexuality. On top of all this, Isaacson[12] suggests that as well as his personal past and oppressive present, 'much of Leonardo's career was consumed by his quest for patrons'. We might explain this search in terms of a constant need for new commissions and an income from the various city states, a quest pursued in a climate of intermittent invasions, wars and changing rulers; but it could also be about something more to do with Leonardo himself. His introspection, perhaps. For Isaacson, the illegitimate Leonardo's patron-search suggests that he was looking for someone who would be 'unconditionally paternalistic, supportive, and indulgent in ways that his own father had only occasionally been'. Until the French king Francis I, all Leonardo's patrons fell short.

Yet even in those last relatively secure years at Château de Cloux in France, he continued to be uncertain, to doubt everything until it was tested. Vasari said of him: 'He had a very heretical state of mind. He could not be content with any kind of religion at all, considering himself in all things much more a philosopher than a Christian.' This sentence comes from the first edition of Vasari's *Lives of the Artists*, published in 1550; for the second edition he deleted the sentence because he thought it sounded too critical of Leonardo – by which we assume he meant in the eyes of those who held the power in the Church and state. Clearly Leonardo knew about and learned from the past – the subjects of most of his painting attest to that; but he treated the past – and indeed most of the things he was told – with a profound conviction that everything must be doubted, and tested, before it was held to be true. He has taught us that the best ways to engage with learning and educate the next generation are far more provisional and complicated than many would like to admit, but it can be done – and he managed it in times far more prescriptive than our own.

Throughout his life Leonardo teaches us to challenge these 'givens' – and, of course, to fret over 'the weight of the empty grey paper' on the table beneath bowls of soup. The key message we take from Leonardo's life is that it doesn't have endings – Zollner[13] calls one of his chapters that deals with Leonardo's early life 'Beginnings without ends'. Just as we purloined this title to begin a previous section, Zollner might well have used this title for a chapter on Leonardo's final years. That word 'etcetera' in the last notebook reminds us

12. Ibid Isaacson
13. Frank Zollner: *Leonardo*; Taschen 2015

all that our attempts to learn from Leonardo also have no finishing point; there is always more to learn and understand.

THE ONLY CERTAINTY IS UNCERTAINTY[14]

It might seem odd that the title of this chapter is an oxymoron. How can perfection be unfinished? Are we talking simply about those paintings that Leonardo believed incomplete? Those works that he could not leave alone or let go? Or, do we mean something more? Something in those paintings *and* our relationship with them that seems incomplete; something that keeps niggling, worrying and challenging us as we look at them?

In Leonardo's paintings 'we sense an unfolding story'.[15] They seem to suggest a story with both a before and an after. They are not paintings that illustrate or confirm – or celebrate – a story we already know. The world has come to see *Mona Lisa*, for instance, as more than a record of a beautiful woman: it is paradoxical, ambiguous and perplexing – like all of Leonardo's paintings. The soft and tender surfaces we see in the face of Lisa del Giocondo at first mute the implicit tragedy of the portrait and then deepen it.[16] Leonardo creates a new frame of understanding for how a portrait might work. He tells a story that his contemporaries (and we) thought was known. He began painting *Mona Lisa* in 1503, yet 16 years later, in the year of his death, he had neither handed it on to the person who commissioned it nor finished it. This suggests he had a significantly more fluid conception of an end point.

All of Leonardo's works – and the obvious struggle he had to complete them – tell us that life is complicated, hard and difficult to describe. When he shows us a portrait or a scene from the Bible the vividness of what we see engages and deepens our attention; but at the same time that scene invites us into an unending conversation with him, with ourselves and with the world.

The phrase 'the only certainty is uncertainty' dovetails nicely with the overall title of this chapter, 'Unfinished perfection'. We could be describing that procrastination of which so many of his contemporaries, as well as modern writers, accuse him. Or we might be using Leonardo's life and work as an illustration of how we learn

---

14. A phrase from Ian Kershaw in *Roller-Coaster: Europe 1950-2015*; Allen Lane, 2018
15. Ibid Nicholl
16. This point is made by Willard Spiegelman in 'Leonardo da Vinci's "The Virgin and Child with St Anne" '; *The Wall Street Journal*, July 2010

about the world, how it is a process rather than a project with a preordained ending. That process never stops. The former National Theatre director Nicholas Hytner[17] said of his work in the theatre that 'you start with a vision and deliver a compromise'. Throughout his life, Leonardo resisted succumbing to such a compromise – hence the several beginnings but the very few ends. Isaacson describes it in the following way, asserting that:

> As frustrating as it is to us today, there was a poignant and inspiring aspect to Leonardo's unwillingness to declare a painting done and relinquish it: he knew that there was always more he might learn, new techniques he might master, and further inspirations that might strike him. And he was right.[18]

EXCUSES, CREATIVE RATIONALISATIONS AND UNFINISHED QUESTIONS

> Men of lofty genius sometimes accomplish the most when they work the least, seeking out inventions with the mind, and forming those perfect ideas which the hands afterwards express and reproduce from the images already conceived in the brain.[19]

These words of Leonardo's, written to Duke Ludovico Sforza and recorded by Vasari, might be called in evidence to show Leonardo as 'a master of many things, including creative rationalisations and excuses'.[20] This comment comes from Rowland and Chaney and refers to the very slow start Leonardo made with a commission to paint *The Last Supper*. Throughout his life that 'tone of impatience is constant'[21] as far as Leonardo's relationships with his various patrons are concerned. Even what must have been a more than prestigious commission from the Pope led this eminent patron to complain: 'Alas, this man will never get anything done, for he is thinking about the end before he begins.'[22] Wordsworth's cryptic advice – 'To begin, begin' – might surely have been useful to Leonardo, who, towards the end of his life, complained that he had failed to complete a single painting. 'He was exaggerating,

17. Nicholas Hytner: *Balancing Acts: Behind the Scenes at the National Theatre*; Vintage 2017
18. Ibid Isaacson
19. Giorgio Vasari: *Lives of the Artists*: various editions
20. Ingrid Rowland and Noah Charney: *The Collector of Lives: Giorgio Vasari and the Invention of Art*; Norton 2017
21. Martin Kemp: *Leonardo*; Oxford 2004
22. GiorgioVasari: *The Lives of the Most Excellent Painters, sculptors and Architects*; now called *Lives of the Artists* in various editions

but not by much.'[23] Would it be too harsh and beside the point to suggest that perhaps Leonardo was living out Mark Twain's words from a few hundred years later: 'Never put off until tomorrow, what you can do the day after tomorrow.'[24]

As a novice monk,[25] the future novelist Matteo Bandello spent a good deal of time watching Leonardo at work at the monastery where he had been commissioned to paint *The Last Supper* on the north wall of the refectory:

> Sometimes he stayed there from dawn to sunset, never once laying down his brush, forgetting to eat and drink, painting without pause. At other times he would go for two, or three or four days without touching his brush, but spending several hours a day in front of the work, his arms folded, examining and criticising the figures to himself.[26]

There is a phrase used by Keats describing what he called 'diligent indolence'; and there's another from his contemporary Wordsworth who speaks of the benefits of 'wise passiveness'. Both phrases suggest an imaginative dreamlike state when an initially calm reception triggers imaginative reaction. Both regard this sort of inactivity as the embryonic state of creativity. Both focus on an active focusing underneath what appears to be a state of passivity.

This was how Leonardo's creative rhythms worked[27] – 'bursts of strenuousness interspersed by those puzzling spells of silent cognition which others – particularly those who were paying him – tended to mistake for dreamy inactivity'. Nicholl concludes that 'every inch [of *The Last Supper*] has been fought for'. It's too easy to think (like some contemporary commentators, particularly scientists) that Leonardo was lazy or unfocused. He rewards our attention too much to be written off as superficial. As Vasari says: 'In his imagination he frequently formed enterprises so difficult and so subtle that they could not be entirely realised and worthily executed by human hands. His concepts were varied to infinity.'[28]

Those words of Leonardo's which we quoted at the beginning of this section – 'forming those perfect ideas and inventions of the mind' –

23. Ibid Rowland and Charney
24. Mark Twain: *Quote Investigator* 2013
25. At the Dominican Monastery of Santa Maria delle Grazie in Milan
26. Matteo Bordello, *Novelle*; in *Opere* ed. F Flora, Milan 1996
27. Ibid Nicholl
28. Ibid Vasari: *Lives*

are worth unpicking a little more. He seems to be suggesting that the imagination required to form perfection is the inevitable first part of his processing; and that the second part, where his hand reproduces these ideas, takes a back seat – for a while at least. Almost as if the conception, for him, is by far the most significant stage. The actual production and expression? Much less so.

The period of incubation that Leonardo offered the duke as a reason for his apparently slow progress with *The Last Supper* is perfectly explained in a more recent French saying about the importance of 'reculer pour mieux sauter' – as we saw earlier, how it is necessary that we 'draw back in order to leap better'. Leonardo's contemporaries, rival artists as well as frustrated patrons, would have seen him as a starter not a finisher. In more recent times writers like Philip Ball have blamed the delays and diversions on Leonardo's wide-ranging curiosity, calling it 'incontinent: an outpouring of questions, apparently listed simply in the order which they popped into his head ... a ledger of phenomena'.[29]

Notwithstanding these critics, we have to recognise that Leonardo clearly had a streak of stubborn refusal to produce anything that he considered to be second best, and when 'faced with challenges other artists would have disregarded but that he could not ... [he] put down his brushes'.[30] Leonardo's 'intelligence of art,' says Vasari, 'made him take on many projects but never finish any of them, since it seemed to him that the hand would never achieve the required perfection.'[31] It was impossible to execute faultlessly, so he stopped.

His unwillingness to declare a painting completely finished means that we now have only 15 paintings that can be attributed to him. Ralph Steadman uses this somewhat limited catalogue of paintings to argue that Leonardo was not a 'company man' (unlike his great rival Michelangelo, who despised Leonardo's seeming lack of drive and direction) to the extent that:

> In a cunning display of subtle contempt he contrived never to finish a single painting to his own satisfaction or else he spent such inordinately long periods of time on work that it was never delivered. The patron either lost interest, lost power, or died.[32]

---

29. Philip Ball: *Curiosity: How Science Became Interested in Everything*; Bodley Head, 2012
30. Ibid Isaacson
31. Ibid Vasari: *Lives*
32. Ibid Steadman

The Virgin and Child with St Anne and St John the Baptist, sometimes called *The Burlington House Cartoon*, takes us some way towards understanding more about why Leonardo's output was so limited and why some saw him as slow (at best) or unreliable (at worst). It is to do with the layers of meaning that Leonardo invested in his work. On the surface the painting shows a gentle family scene with three generations; and yet beneath the surface, 'such tenderness mutes tragedy for a moment and then deepens it'.[33] The hand of St Anne points towards heaven; the Virgin mother understands that her son will soon die and 'must be filled with sorrow', and yet despite this a tenderness and compassion links the three generations which conveys a connected unity alongside the impending separation. It is, in Spiegelman's words, 'a study in support, connection, direction, in separateness and unity'. Despite the picture's unfinished status, he says, 'its conception exceeds its execution, but this hardly matters: the picture takes us in. Its formal elegance and the humane portrayal of its characters are perfection enough.'[34]

In a similar way, the *Adoration of the Magi* remained unfinished, but it became, in the words of Kenneth Clark,[35] 'the most revolutionary and anti-classical picture of the fifteenth century'. Isaacson echoes Clark when he says that this painting has become 'the most influential unfinished painting in the history of art ... that encapsulates Leonardo's frustrating genius: a pathbreaking and astonishing display of brilliance that was abandoned once it was conceptualized'.[36] Isaacson goes on to offer an interesting take on this lack of completion: 'One reason why he was reluctant to relinquish some of his works and declare them completed was that he relished a world in flux.' Perhaps his belief was that we need to sustain the conflict inside us, not try to resolve it.

In his version of Leonardo's life story, Serge Bramley[37] also plays with the perplexing unfinished question in relation to the *Adoration*: 'Leonardo had put a great deal of work into the *Adoration*, which some consider, even as it stands, to be one of the most extraordinary pictures of the century' – so why not finish? Was it, as Toby Lester[38]

---

33. Ibid Spiegelman
34. Spiegelman, the Hughes Professor of English at Southern Methodist University
35. Kenneth Clark: *Civilisation* John Murray 1969
36. Ibid Isaacson
37. Serge Bramley: *Leonardo: The Artist and the Man*; Penguin 1994
38. Toby Lester: *Da Vinci's Ghost*, Free Press 2012

maintains, a simple case of 'trouble with deadlines'? Or was it, as Isaacson suggests, additional layering to perfect his craft over time (as well as his understanding of geology and anatomy)? Or was it more to do with the growing realisation that the world is in flux and that the only certainty is uncertainty?

The layering in this painting is not just about perfectionism, it is about complexity, paradox, challenge and the realisation that the questions about what things look like, and more importantly, what they mean, never come to an end. We would do well to remember what Leonardo said about reaching conclusions too readily: that 'the abbreviators of works do injury to knowledge and to love'. Leonardo wasn't interested in any strategy that accepted the first satisfactory option. He was always looking out for the best possible one. As Mlodinow points out, the way that so-called satisficers differ from maximisers (who always try to choose the best) is that 'those who accept options that are good enough, rather than feeling compelled to find the optimal one, tend to be more satisfied with their choices and, in general, happier and less stressed individuals'.[39]

Nuland[40] takes a wider perspective on Leonardo. After 20–plus years of study and a lifetime obsession with him, Nuland believed that Leonardo had taken his observations and studies so far beyond his era that it was inevitable that he could not finish his work, as he was aware that it could never be verified and was inevitably going to be incomplete because it challenged much of the architecture of thought that had gone before:

> He has been criticised, now and in his own time, for finishing so little of what he started. And yet, how could it have been otherwise, at least in the areas of his scientific work? The probings of his mind had gone well beyond the supporting knowledge and technology of his era ... As his ultimate direction was to question the heritage of earlier ages and seek only the truth of his own experience, he was able to blaze new paths through territories that his contemporaries believed to have been correctly charted long before their time.[41]

This goes some way towards explaining why, when Leonardo died, he had several of his masterpieces still by his bedside, keeping him

39. Ibid Mlodinow
40. Sherwin B Nuland: *Leonardo da Vinci*, Penguin–Random House 2005
41. Ibid Sherwin B Nuland

company. Leonardo's whole approach to his work suggests that he was never intending us to see a single representation of the world. Everything he did is part of a whole stream of often partial and sometimes contradictory drafts. This is particularly true of his 1480 painting *Saint Jerome in the Wilderness*. In this painting he shows the figure of the saint – the fourth-century scholar who translated the Bible into Latin – in the wilderness about to strike himself with a stone in an apparent act of penance. We might assume that, given the date 1480 attached to the painting, he worked on it (or at least started and then left it incomplete) sometime during that year; but there is evidence that he made changes to the depiction of the neck muscles, correcting them as late as 1510. Knowing this, we might think that Leonardo was primarily concerned with 'moti corporali' – 'the motions and workings of the body'. He certainly wanted to make sure he got the anatomy right, and as such each new dissection he completed meant that his understanding continued to evolve. Although the painting is not finished, and the lion's figure particularly is not much more than a sketch, it is that gaping mouth that draws us. It prompts us to feel, to discover or rediscover, uncertainty, to wear our uncertain hearts on our metaphorical sleeves.[42] We see St Jerome through the lion's and Leonardo's eyes. Leonardo has brought us firmly into the painting, to feel his anguish in his act of mortification.

His refusal to relinquish his work wasn't confined to his art. He had started countless highly ambitious projects – such as the flying machines, diving equipment, changing the course of the River Arno, the circular fortress, and the draining of the Piombino swamps – all without completion. After decades of intense observation he planned to take his notes and to embark on the polishing of them to produce various treatises, but never quite managed it – he didn't really seem to be that interested in the practical application once he had nailed the core of whatever it was to his satisfaction. Many of them did happen, of course, albeit long after his death. Some still haven't. 'Innovation,' Isaacson sagely observes, 'requires a reality distortion field.'[43] Steadman would have put the impact of his general approach rather more prosaically: 'The wealth of his activities overpowered those who revered him, so that they were virtually unable to employ him.'[44]

42. Brian Appleyard *Sunday Times*, interview about James Graham's play *Quiz*: Methuen Drama 2018
43. Ibid Isaacson
44. Ibid Steadman

So, where does that leave us? Do we have any clearer understanding of Leonardo's refusal to foreclose on any of his projects?

Perhaps William Pannapacker's thoughts might help us towards an answer:

> [Leonardo's] final achievements in painting depended on ... experiments. Far from being a distraction – like many of his contemporaries thought – they represent a lifetime of productive brainstorming, a private working out of ideas on which his public work depended. If creative procrastination, selectively applied, prevented Leonardo from finishing a few commissions – of minor importance when one is struggling with the inner workings of the cosmos – then only someone who is a complete captive of the modern cult of productive mediocrity could fault him for it. Productive mediocrity requires discipline of an ordinary kind. It is safe and threatens no one. Nothing will be changed by mediocrity ... but genius is uncontrolled and uncontrollable. You cannot produce a work of genius according to a schedule or an outline.[45]

Whilst it is true that Leonardo's interests and learning processes were both recondite and idiosyncratic, perhaps the same in some sense could be said of all of us. Readiness is all.

45. William A. Pannapacker: 'How to Procrastinate like Leonardo da Vinci'; *Chronicle Review* February 2009

Saint Jerome in the Wilderness; Vatican Museums

Leonardo had no finishing point, there is always more to learn and understand – always more subtle refinements made possible by the application of new insights, just as there is, or should be, open questions remaining within any project we undertake in our own work or learning...He would insist that saying our quest is complete, or frozen denies the possibility of going further. What we know of our own lives and work can never reach a conclusion.

What can we still learn from Leonardo about...?

Talent hits a target that no one else can hit.
Genius hits a target no one else can see.[46]

PARADIGM SHIFTS

Thomas Kuhn[47] writes about 'paradigm shifts' in science – alterations that represent more than incremental advances in thought, but are focused on contradicting beliefs that formed the framework of assumptions and concepts that had previously been shared and accepted. Kuhn writes that scientists 'hold institutionalised everyday beliefs, which may, on occasion, be altered by a transformational discovery ... For some, those paradigms never evolve, but for the fortunate they do change.'[48] These Kuhnian leaps into the darkness occur rarely, but they look beyond the existing order to imagine something that completely reframes what has happened before.

It was this kind of mental leap that Leonardo specialised in. If we had written 'this is the first time it was thought about like this' or 'this had never been done before 'on every occasion described in this book where Leonardo had had the mental flexibility to take a Kuhnian jump, it would have become tiresome – or worse, unbelievable. He spent his life surrounded by ingrained assumptions that were not valid, but that had often remained unchallenged because of the authority of those that were committed to them. To challenge was highly dangerous, but to Leonardo, it was almost instinctive. He looked beyond the existing order in almost every aspect of his creativity. He sought perfection when he was offered pictures of the world and of the human body that were ugly or, for him, not to be believed. He seemed to process information from nature in an entirely different manner from any of his contemporaries. He wasn't bound by the rules that others in his world became accustomed to, and his default mode seemed to raise himself imaginatively into an entirely different realm, above the existing doctrines of belief that shaped those around him. But how? Mlodinow would see Leonardo's whole approach to his work as a more than serviceable definition of an 'elastic thinker':

> Elastic thinking is what endows us with the ability to solve novel problems and to overcome the neural and psychological barriers that can impede us from looking beyond the existing order.[49]

46. Schopenhauer, *The World as Will and Representation*, Vol. 1: v. 1 Dover Publications 1960
47. Thomas Kuhn: *The Structure of Scientific Revolutions*, University of Chicago Press 1996
48. Ibid Mlodinow
49. Ibid Mlodinow

Ursula K. Le Guin is often quoted as having said 'the creative adult is the child who has survived'. Perhaps there was a childishness to Leonardo. His natural divergences might suggest this, as might his abandoning of enterprises once he had finished with them – or been tempted away by another more challenging project. Perhaps his drowning in highly original but less productive thinking might be another indicator too. Or perhaps the greatest danger of becoming an adult is that we are supposed to, or pretend to, know the answers.

BREAKING THE FRAME

As an illegitimate child segregated from other better-educated children, Leonardo might well have grown up feeling that although he was a part of the world, he was also detached from it. Zadie Smith believes that the result of such alienation leads a child to feel 'not at home in themselves ... [They] don't experience themselves as "natural" or "inevitable" – as so many other people seem to do.'[50] Smith's sense of segregation came from her birth. Not illegitimacy, like Leonardo, but from being biracial. This caused her to feel 'anger, sadness, despair, confusion'. Her compensation in these circumstances came from a growing awareness of what she calls 'the radical contingency of life'. She learned to break the frame of her early experiences through the other lives in her stories, and through those narratives, to create characters 'who are who they are' rather than representations of some acquired knowledge or an historical, social or idealism-driven frame. Her target in the stories she reads and writes is not aimed at being a cultural critique but rather what she calls 'an ever-present torsion' of experience.

'Torsion' is the twisting, re-examining and rethinking of experience, rather than a hope to achieve a last-page conclusion or clarity – a final word. This reminds us of Leonardo's abiding belief that completion freezes evolution and of his late notebook word, 'etcetera'. That strange word 'torsion' seems an oddly appropriate word to describe the 'radical contingency' – or endless uncertainty and possibility – of adapting and adjusting to experience. The word evokes the prospect of all sorts of interactions or tensions between those entrenched beliefs that resist change and new ways of seeing and thinking and searching.

---

50. Zadie Smith: 'The I Who is Not Me' in *Feel Free: Essays*; Hamish Hamilton 2018

FLIGHTS OF THE MIND

As a result of all the imperatives that surrounded Leonardo, he would of course have taken a carefully measured approach to his questioning, keeping much of it hidden in secret notebooks – and there were hundreds of them. Many of the ways he challenged the dominant frameworks of his time were left to be read by later generations. In fact, it was well into the 19th century before his notebooks were properly unravelled. Whitehead uses a memorable image to challenge the idea of thinking as you are told to think when he writes: 'In the Garden of Eden, Adam saw the animals before he named them; in the traditional system [of education], children named the animals before they saw them.'[51] Leonardo was told what to think before he thought it – like we all are, perhaps. He resisted. As Deresiewicz says,[52] 'being an intellectual begins with thinking your way outside of your assumptions and the system that enforces them'.

In the notebook where Leonardo writes about 'flights of the mind' there is a shadowy red-chalk drawing of his face which is half hidden by the phrase 'suprando la resistentia dellaris' – which means 'conquering the resistance of the air'. Nicholl[53] explores the idea that Leonardo uses his dreams of flight as a metaphor: a flight of escape, of evasion, of irresolution – of fleeing rather than flying. In his obsession with flight, Nicholl concludes, there is a kind of existential restlessness, a desire to float free from his life of tensions and rivalries, from the dictates of warmongers and art-lovers alike. Leonardo yearns for the great escape, and in failing he feels himself more captive. In the same way, the early memory of a bird (the kite that came to him in his cradle) that Freud commented on echoes across the years, intertwined with feelings of maternal love and loss, and combines, for Leonardo, with the vaulting ambition of mechanical flight, the achievement of which might allow him to meet again that half-remembered, half-imagined visitor from the sky. With the dream of flying comes the fear of falling, and we understand him better if we see him also as 'a trader in doubts and questions, and with them self-doubts and self-questionings'.[54]

Leonardo saw his work as a process of expanding the language of painting and what the painting might say so that acknowledged unfinished works like *The Adoration of the Magi* or *The Burlington House Cartoon* change our understanding of the past and future and at the

---

51. A.N. Whitehead: *Science and the Modern World*, (1926th) Pelican edition 1938
52. William Deresiewicz: *What the Ivy League Won't Teach You*, New Word City Inc. 2011
53. Ibid Nicholl
54. Ibid Nicholl

same time lead us towards exchanging new meanings for and with the paintings – and for the event it describes.

Writing about Leonardo we have come to see the difference between what Zadie Smith[55] calls 'inspection' and 'invention' – between what we are told and what we make of what we are told. If, as Isaacson suggests, Leonardo's deluge drawings blur the boundaries between experience and fantasy, then our approach to our own lives might similarly seek to blur the boundaries between what we see and experience in the present, and what we imagine our lives might become in the future. A.N. Whitehead[56] uses a phrase that might shed some light on what we see and what we imagine when we think about Leonardo: our whole project is to try to read Leonardo's history 'forwards and backwards', to meet his ideas 'in their full interplay of emergent values' and in the process, begin to shape how we see ourselves. Whitehead would call the process a 'creative initiative', simultaneously looking *back* to reimagine Leonardo's voice, and *forwards* to reframe and find our own voices 500 years later. As we have said, we are driven, like Whitehead, by two embodiments: 'the spirit of change and the spirit of conservation'. It draws us towards questioning absolute certainty.

Writing about classic books, Italo Calvino[57] said that such books '[haven't] finished saying what they have to say'. Leonardo similarly hasn't finished saying what he has to say to us – so neither should we finish saying what there is to say about him, or in the end, about our own society, work and the lives we lead. If we can be sure that we have found and listened to Leonardo's voice, with all of its doubts and contradictions, then perhaps we might come to find a greater belief and trust in our own voices. This must in turn have radical implications for our beliefs about learning.

This is given some extra purchase though the work of Erving Goffman[58] when he talks about how we all use frameworks to understand the world. We frame our perceptions and those frames determine how we think and behave in the situations we meet in our lives. The scientist Susan Bales[59] uses the term 'strategic frame analysis' to describe being conscious of this filtering of perceptions and beliefs. She argues that

55. Zadie Smith: *Changing My Mind: Occasional essays*; Penguin 2011
56. Ibid A.N. Whitehead's *Science and the Modern World*
57. Italo Calvino: *Why Read the Classics?* Vintage 2001
58. Erving Goffman: *An Essay on the Organisation of Experience*; reprinted 1986 by North Eastern University Press.
59. See: www.bit.ly/2YrhOYu

people tend to harbour deeply held preconceptions which are likely to make them resistant, even blind, to alternative ideas, particularly if those ideas appear to contradict the embedded frames which shape a view of self or the world. Leonardo's purpose was to challenge, if not to break, the frames that surrounded him.

ACCEPTING NON-COMPLETION

That word 'etcetera' in the last notebook reminds us too that our attempts to learn from Leonardo also have no finishing point; there is always more to learn and understand – always more subtle refinements made possible by the application of new insights, just as there is, or should be, open questions remaining within any project we undertake in our own work or learning. What we know and understand of Leonardo can never be settled. He would insist that saying our quest is complete, or frozen, denies the possibility of going further. What we know of our own lives and work can never reach a conclusion. Our mistakes need to incite us into greater curiosity, greater desire in our learning – no matter what obstacles we may then face. Desire is an obstacle course and wanting is a sign of life.

The facts about anything may be fairly well established, of course, but the way we interpret those facts will always be provisional. Or as John Berger[60] puts it: 'The relationship between what we see and what we know is never settled.' We might add: the relationship between what we experience in our workplaces or our domestic lives and how it impacts upon us is never resolved. This is not to say that meaning is dispersed or out of reach, rather that it is *expanded* because our voices – and the voices of various characters who share our lives – join in and play a part. John Berger simply adds: 'Never again will a single story be told as though it's the only one.' And he might have added, never will knowledge and understanding be pursued as though there is only one method of travel. We know that knowledge is a dialogue, not a monologue. And perhaps all learning ends in a dash, not a full stop. Loose ends need to be seen as new beginnings in our search for what is of interest and importance.

It's about patience and dissatisfaction, not relinquishing our inarticulate selves in a pointless quest to find the perfect answer, but also not abandoning that quest. Perhaps the true perfection of mankind is to find out our imperfections, to abandon our aspirations toward the obvious. There are dangers inherent in our passive acceptance of the

---

60. John Berger: *Ways of Seeing*; Penguin 1972

common sense view, our defensive associations, our preference towards safety and accommodation. Too often we seek a false consensual certainty, simply because it is acceptable or reassuring. It's more important to reject this compulsive cramping ideal and to choose to live with complexity, our ability to hold doubt, suspend judgement and accumulate additional information that allows growth. We need to accept that when it looks as though we have the answer, we may well have frozen the evolution of our understanding into a static order, or as Leonardo would argue, abandoned the chance of perfection.

BIBLIOGRAPHY

Select Bibliography (162 referenced)

Frances Ames-Lewis: *Isabella and Leonardo: The Artistic Relationship between Isabella D'Este and Leonardo Da Vinci*; Yale 2012

Frances Ames-Lewis: *The Intellectual Life of the Early Renaissance Artist*; Yale 2000

Hannah Arendt: *Essays in Understanding 1930-34*; Jonathan Cape 2018

Kevin Ashton: *How to Fly a Horse: The Secret History of Creation, Invention and Discovery*; Heinemann 2015

Peter Atkins: *Creation Revisited: The Origin of Space, Time and the Universe*; Penguin 1994

Philip Ball: *Curiosity: How Science Became Interested in Everything*; Bodley Head 2012

Mateo Bandello: *Novelle*: in Opere edited by F Flora, Milan 1996

Maurice Baring (translation): Leonardo Da Vinci: Thoughts on Art and Life; Dover 1906, reprinted CreateSpace Publishing 2012

Julian Barnes: *Levels of Life*; Jonathan Cape 2013

John Berger: *Ways of Seeing*; BBC and Penguin Books 1972

Hayley Birch: *50 Ideas You Really Need to Know*: Chemistry; Quercus 2015

Gustave Le Bon: *The Crowd: A Study of the Popular Mind* (1895); Cosimo Classics 2006

Pierre Bourdieu: *Key Concepts* ed Michael Grenfell; Routledge 2012

Pierre Bourdieu; *Manet: A Symbolic Revolution*; translated by Collier and Rigaud-Drayton; Polity 2018

Serge Bramley: *Leonardo: The Artist and the Man*; Penguin 1994

Jacob Bronowski: Science and Human Values; Hutchinson 1961 (reprinted 2010)

John Calder: *Texts for Nothing* (1959); Signature Books 1980

Agnes Callard: *Aspiration: The Agency of Becoming*; OUP Press 2018

Italo Calvino: *Why Read the Classics?* Vintage 2001

Mary Baine Campbell: *Wonder and Science*; Cornell University Press 1999

Fritos Capra: *Learning from Leonardo: Decoding the Notebooks of a Genius*; Berrett–Koehler Publishing 2013

William Benjamin Carpenter: *Principles of Mental Physiology: With Their Applications to the Training ands Discipline of the Mind, and the Study of Morbid Conditions*; Cambridge University Press 2009

Cennino L'Andrea Cennini: *The Craftsman's Handbook: Ill Libro dell 'Arte* (circa 1400) translated by Daniel V Thompson, Dover Instructional 1954

Marc Cianchi: *Leonardo's Machines*: Becocci Editore; 1988

Kenneth Clark: *Civilisation*; John Murray 1969

Guy Claxton: *Intelligence in the Flesh*; Yale 2015

Martin Clayton and Ron Philo: *Leonardo da Vinci: Anatomist*; Royal Collection Trust 2012

Mihaly Csikszentmihalyi: *Creativity*; Harper Collins 1986

Mihaly Csikszentmihalyi: *Finding Flow: The Psychology of Engagement with Everyday Life*; Basic Books 1998

Helen Czerski: *Storm in a Teacup: The Physics of Everyday Life*; Penguin 2016

William Damon: *The Path to Purpose: How Young People Find Their Calling in Life*: Free Press 2009

Lorraine Daston and Katharine Park: *Wonders and the Order of Nature*; Zone Books 1998

William Davies: *Nervous States: How Feeling Took Over the World*; Jonathan Cape 2018

Leonardo da Vinci, translated by Jean Paul Richter: *The Notebooks of Leonardo Da Vinci*; Create Space Publishing 2010

Leonardo da Vinci: *Leonardo on Painting*; edited by Martin Kemp; Yale 1989

Leonardo da Vinci: *Thoughts on Art and Life*: translated by Maurice Baring 1906

Richard Dawkins: *Unweaving the Rainbow: Science, Delusion and the Appetite for Wonder*; Penguin 2006

Daniel Dennett: *Consciousness Explained*; Penguin 1993

William Deresiewicz: *Excellent Sheep: The Miseducation of the American Elite*; Free press 2014

William Deresiewicz: *What the Ivy League Won't Teach You*; New Word City Inc 2011

Rene Descartes: *Meditations*; Penguin Great Ideas 2010

Emily Dickinson: *The Complete Poems*; Create Space 2010

Angela Duckworth: *Grit: The Power of Passion and Perseverance*; Penguin Random House 2016

Cary Waldo Dunnington: *Carl Friedrich Gauss: Titan of Science*; LLC 2012

Kieran Egan, Annabella Cant and Gillian Judson: *Wonder-full Education: The Centrality of Wonder in Teaching and Learning Across the Curriculum*; Routledge 2014

Kieran Egan: *The Future of Education: Reimagining Schools from the Ground Up*; Yale 2008

Susan Engel: *The Hungry Mind: The Origins of Curiosity in Childhood*; Harvard 2015

Susan Engel: *Your Child's Path: Unlocking the Mysteries of Who Your Child Will Become*; Atria Paperback (Simon and Schuster) 2011

Richard Feynman: *The Pleasure of Finding Things Out*, Perseus Books 1999

Stuart Firestein: *Ignorance and How it Drives Science*, OUP 2012

Sidney Freedberg: *Painting in Italy 1500-1600*, Penguin Classics 1971

David W Galenson: *Old Masters and Young Geniuses: The Two Life Cycles of Artistic Creativity*; Princeton University Press 2007

Lara Galinsky: *Work on Purpose*; Echoing Green 2011.

Garner, Brown, Sanders and Menke: *The Role of Interest in Learning and Development*; Lawrence Erlbaum 1992

Lorenzo Ghiberti: *First Commentary* (circa 1450) Giunti 1998

Ian Gilchrist: *The Master And His Emissary: The Divided Brain and the Making of the Western World*; Yale 2010

Malcolm Gladwell: *Blink: The Power of Thinking Without Thinking*; Penguin 2005

Ernst Gombrich: *The Story of Art*; Phaidon 1950

Adam Grant: *Originals: How Non-Conformists Changed the World*; WH Allen 2016

Maxine Green: *Landscapes of Learning*; Teachers' College press 1978

Marjorie Grene: *The Knower and the Known*; Faber and Faber 1966

Seamus Heaney: *The Redress of Poetry: Oxford Lectures*; Faber and Faber 1995

Seamus Heaney: *Station Island*; Faber 1986

Charlotte Higgins: *Red Thread: On Mazes and Labyrinths*; Cape 2018

E.D. Hirsh: *The Knowledge Deficit*; Houghton Mifflin Harcourt 2007

David Holbrook: *English for Meaning*; NFER Publishing 1979

Lynn Hunt: *History: Why it Matters*; Polity 2018

William Hunter: *Two Introductory Lectures, delivered by Dr William Hunter*; Ulan Press 2012

Siri Hustvedt: *A Woman Looking at Men Looking at Women*: Sceptre 2016

Siri Hustvedt: *Living, Thinking, Looking*; Sceptre 2012

Walter Isaacson: *Leonardo: The Biography*; Simon and Schuster 2017

Clive James: *Play All: A Bingewatcher's Notebook*; Yale 2016

Clive James: *Sentenced to Life*; Picador 2017

William James: *Great Men, Great Thoughts, and the Environment*; Dodo Press 2002

Steven Johnson: *Wonderland: How Play Made the Modern World*; Macmillan 2017

Steven Johnson: *How We Got to Now: Six Innovations that Made the Modern World*; Penguin 2015

Steven Johnson: *Where Good Ideas Come From: The Seven Patterns of Innovation*; Penguin 2010

Stuart A Kaufman: *Investigations*; Oxford 2000

Stuart A Kaufman: *Humanity in a Creative Universe*; Oxford 2016

John Keats: *Selected Letters*; Penguin Classics 2010

Martin Kemp: *Art in History 600 BC-2000 AD*; Profile Books 2014

Martin Kemp: *Leonardo: Inside the Mind of a Renaissance Genius*; Oxford 2004

Martin Kemp: Leonardo da Vinci: *The Marvellous Works of Nature and Man*; Oxford 2006

Martin Kemp: *Living With Leonardo: Fifty Years of Sanity and Insanity in the Art World and Beyond*; Thames and Hudson 2018

Martin Kemp and Giuseppe Pallanti: *Mona Lisa*; Oxford 2017

Arthur Koestler: *The Act of Creation*; Hutchinson 1969

Arthur Koestler: *The Sleepwalkers: A History of Man's Changing Vision of the Universe*; Penguin 1959

David A Kolb: *Experiential Learning: Experience as a Source of Learning*; Prentice Hall 1983

Kathleen Krull: *Giants of Science: Leonardo da Vinci*: Puffin Books 2005

Thomas Kuhn: *The Structure of Scientific Revolutions*; University of Chicago Press 1996

Matthew Landrus: *Leonardo Da Vinci: 500 Years On: A Portrait of the Artist, Scientist and Innovator*; Andrew Deutsch 2018

Mike Lankford: Becoming *Leonardo: An Exploded View of the Life of Leonardo Da Vinci*; Melville House Publishing 2017

Ian Leslie: *Curious: The Desire to Know and Why Your Future Depends on It*; Quercus 2014

Toby Lester; *Da Vinci's Ghost: Genius, Obsession and How Leonardo Created the World in His Own Image*; Free Press 2012

C.S. Lewis: *The Weight of Glory*; Macmillan 1966

Alan Lightman: *Searching for the Stars on an Island in Maine*; Corsair 2018

Dan Lyons: *Why Modern Work Makes People Miserable*, Atlantic 2019

Edward MacCurdy: *The Mind of Leonardo da Vinci (1928)*, Dover 2008

Ian McGilchrist: *The Master and his Emissary: The Divided Brain and the Making of the Western World*, Yale 2010

Bernard MacLaverty: Collected Stories; Vintage 2014

Bernard MacLaverty: *Midwinter Break*; Vintage 2018

Louis MacNeice: *Collected Poems*; Faber and Faber 1966

Alberto Manguel: *Curiosity*; Yale 2015

Alberto Manguel: *A Reader on Reading*; Yale 2010

Alberto Manguel: *The Library at Night*; Yale 2006

Maurice Merleau-Ponty: *The Primacy of Perception* ed Edie, translated Cogg; Northwest University Press 1964

Charlie Munger: *A Lesson in Elementary, Worldly Wisdom*; USC Business School 1994

Sherwin B Nuland: *Leonardo da Vinci*, Penguin-Random House 2010

Luca Pacioli: *De Divine Proportione*: Create Space Publishing Platform 2014

Ruth Padel: *52 Ways of Looking at a Poem*; Chatto and Windus 2002

Michael Pruett and Christine Gross-Loh: *The Path: A New Way to Think About Everything*; Viking 2007

John Pope-Hennessy: *The Portrait in the Renaissance*; Pantheon 1963

Marcel Proust: *A General Theory of Love*, Random House, 2000

Pugh, Hicks and Davis: *Metaphorical Ways of Knowing: The Imaginative Nature of Thought and Expression*; NCTE 1999

Robert E Mittelstaedt: *Will Your Next Mistake Be Fatal? Avoiding the Chain of Mistakes That Can Destroy Your Organisation*; Warton School Publishing 2005

Leonard Mlodinow: *Elastic: Flexible Thinking in a Constantly Changing World*; Allen Lane 2018

Montaigne: *The Essays of Montaigne* translated by John Florio; Oxford University Press 1906

Lorrie Moore: *See What Can Be Done; Essays, Criticism and Commentaries*; Faber and Faber 2018

Robert K Merton and Elinor Barber: *The Travels and Adventures of Serendipity*; Princetown University Press 2004

Vladimir Nabokov: *Lectures in Literature*; Harvest Books 2002

Charles Nicholl: *Leonardo Da Vinci: The Flights of the Mind*; Penguin 2004

Charles Nicholl: *Traces Remain: Essays and Explorations*; Allen Lane 2011

Ray Oldenburg: *The Great Good Place: Cafes, Coffee Shops, Bookstores, Bars, Hair Salons and Other Hangouts at the Heart of a Community*; Marlowe and Company, 1999

Hilde Ostby and Ylva Ostby: *Adventures in Memory: The Science and Secrets of Remembering and Forgetting*; Greystone Books 2018

Ruth Padel: *Emerald*; Chatto and Windus, 2018

Robert M Pirsig: *Zen and the Art of Motor Cycle Maintenance: An Inquiry into Values*; (1974); Bantam 1975

Henri Poincare: *Science and Method*; translated George Bruce Halstead; CreateSpace Publishing, 2016

Sharon L Pugh, Jean Wolph Hicks, Marcia Davis and Tonya Venstra: *Bridging: a Teacher's Guide to Metaphorical Thinking*; NCTE 1992

Steven Poole: *Rethink: The Surprising History of New Ideas*; Random House 2016

Eric Ravilious, *Scrapbooks*, edited by Skipworth and Webb, Lund Humphries 2018

J.P. Richter: *The Notebooks of Leonardo Da Vinci*; Dover 1970

Alice Roberts: *Tamed: 10 Species That Changed Our World*; Hutchinson 2017

Marilynne Robinson: *What Are We Doing Here?* Essays: Virago 2018

Todd Rose: *The End of Average: How to Succeed in a World That Values Sameness*; Penguin 2015

Todd Rose and Ogi Ogas: *Dark Horse: Achieving Success Through the Pursuit of Fulfillment*; Harper 2018

Ingrid Rowland and Noah Charney: *The Collector of Lives: Giorgio Vasari and the Invention of Art*; Norton 2017

Arthur Schopenhauer, *The World as Will and Representation, Vol. 1: v. 1* Dover Publications 1960

George Bernard Shaw: *Man and Superman*; Penguin 2000

Rupert Sheldrake: *The Science Delusion*; Coronet 2012

Leonard Shlain: *Leonardo's Brain: Understanding Da Vinci's Creative Genius*; Lyons Press 2014

Zadie Smith: *Changing My Mind: Occasional Essays*; Penguin 2009

Zadie Smith: *Feel Free: Essays*; Hamish Hamilton 2018

Ralph Steadman: *I, Leonardo*; Jonathan Cape 1983

Isabelle Stengers: *Thinking with Whitehead: A Free and Wild Creation of Concepts*; Harvard 2014

Mark Stevenson: *We Do Things Differently: The Outsiders Rebooting Our World*; Profile Books 2018

Nicholas Taleb: *The Black Swan*; Penguin 2010

Dylan Thomas (ed Paul Muldoon): *Collected Poems* New Directions, 2010

Derek Thompson: *Hit Makers: How Things Become Popular*; Penguin 2017

Alfred A Tomatis: *The Conscious Ear: My Life of Transformation Through Listening*; Station Hill Press 1992

Paul Tough: *How Children Succeed*; Random House 2012

Robert E Ulanowicz: *A Third Window: Natural Life Beyond Newton and Darwin*; Templeton Foundation Press 2009

Kurt Vonnegut: *Piano Player* (1952); CreateSpace Independent Publishing 2007

Roger Von Oech: *A Whack on the Side of the Head*; 1982

Simone Weil: *Waiting for God*; Harper perennial 2009

Steven Weinberg: *Third Thoughts*; Belknap Press 2018

Alfred North Whitehead: *Science and the Modern World*; Pelican 1926

Alfred North Whitehead: *Adventures of Ideas;(1933)* Free Press 1967

Alfred North Whitehead: *The Aims of Education and Other Essays*; Macmillan 1929 (and online)

Walt Whitman: *Song of Myself*: Create Space publishing 2013

James Webb Young (1886–1973): *A Technique For Producing Ideas*; Stellar Editions 2012

Frank Zollner: *Leonardo 1452-1519: Artist and Scientist*; Taschen 2015

V P Zubov: *Leonardo da Vinci*, Metro Books 2002

Leonardo's manuscripts/ notebooks (10 referenced)

More than half are lost. Those that survived are mostly to be found as follows:

Codex Arundel: 238 manuscripts bought by Lord Arundel for King Charles 1 with notes on architecture, geometry, weights, sound and light. For a detailed look go to Turning the Pages at The British Library: http://www.bl.uk/collections/treasures/digitisation.html#leo

Codex Atlanticus: assembled by 16th–century sculptor Pompeo Leoni; contains 1119 pages on astronomy, botany, zoology, geometry and military engineering. Pompeo called his collection *Drawings of Machines, the Secret Arts and Other Things by Leonardo Da Vinci collected by Pompeo Leoni*. It's now called the Atlanticus and is housed at the Biblioteca Ambrosiana in Milan. (Pompeo was more interested in collected Leonardo's scientic notes, so the artistic elements of the collection were separated – and have ended in in the Royal Windsor collection.)

Codex Trivulzianus: mostly concerned with Leonardo's programme of self–education in books and architecture among other things. Stored in the Biblioteca Trivulziana at the Castle Sforzesco in Milan. Originally 62 sheets; seven now missing.

Codex 'On The Flight of Birds'; written by Leonardo in 1505, now kept by the Biblioteca Reale in Turin; 17 sheets of 18 have survived. It's about birds, the mechanics of flight, air resistance, winds and currents.

Codex Ashburnham: a wide variety of drawings put together by Napoleon Bonaparte, it covers the period of Leonardo's life from 1489 to 1492. Now housed in the Institut de France in Paris.

Codices of the Institut de France: a further 12 manuscripts are kept here, each labelled with letters from A to M: the flight of birds, hydraulics, optics, geometry and military issues.

Codex Forster: geometry and hydraulic machines; kept in the Victoria and Albert Museum in London.

Codex Leicester: lost until 1690, found in a sculptor's truck, bought by the Earl of Leicester. Purchased in 1995 by Bill Gates of Microsoft for $30 million. It contains 72 linen sheets about water and its movement.

Royal Windsor Folios: housed at the Royal Collection at Windsor Castle, it contains the drawing gathered together by Pompeo Leoni: 600 studies of human anatomy, horse anatomy, the 'deluge drawings' and geography among other things.

The Madrid Codices: created by Leonardo sometime between 1503 and 1505, they were for a time in the possession of Pompeo Leoni, but then lost. In 1966 they were rediscovered in the National Library of Madrid, where they have remained. There are two manuscripts: *Madrid I* (on mechanics for the most part) and *Madrid II* (on geometry).

Illustrations (14 referenced)

Cover:

Studies of the Foetus in the womb (edited); Royal Collection, Windsor Castle Library

Chapter 1:

Portrait of a Man in Red Chalk (believed to be a self-portrait); Biblioteca Reale, Turin

The cardiovascular system and principal organs of a woman, Royal Collection, Windsor Castle Library

Chapter 2:

Virgin of the Rocks; Louvre Museum, Paris;

The fall of light on a face; Royal Collection, Windsor Castle Library

Chapter 3:

Lady with an Ermine; Czartoryski Museum, Cracow, Poland

Salvator Mundi; Louvre, Abu Dhabi

Chapter 4:

The Vitruvian Man; Galleria dell'Accademia, Venice

Studies of the Foetus in the womb; Royal Collection, Windsor Castle Library

Chapter 5:

Studies of flowing water, with notes; Royal Collection, Windsor Castle Library

The heart compared to a seed; Royal Collection, Windsor Castle Library

Chapter 6:

The Adoration of the Magi; Galleria degli Uffizi, Florence

Mona Lisa or La Gioconda; Musée du Louvre, Paris

Chapter 7:

The Virgin and Child with St Anne and John the Baptist (cartoon); Burlington House, London

St Jerome in the Wilderness; Vatican Museums, Vatican

INDEX

LEONARDO'S PAINTINGS/DRAWINGS

IDEAS

NOTABLE AUTHORS

ISBN 978-1-331-12721-5
PIBN 10000134

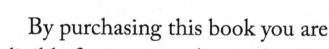

INTRODUCTION.

The traditional idea of Quakerism always carries with it a suggestion of peculiarity in dress; and this peculiarity has been so marked, that Quaker life can hardly be portrayed without an understanding of the history of the garb. The day has come, however, when the question of dress, even for the Quaker, is no longer bound up with the plan of salvation. We have him sufficiently in perspective to turn our modern camera upon him, and study the variations of this once vital question; for if it is in any degree true that "dress makes the man," certain it is that dress at one time went far to make a Quaker—at least to the world's thinking. There is a picturesque side to the story of the Quaker; he himself hardly appreciates how much of the romantic there has been in his quiet life. The trend of his thought has led him to take himself too seriously, and he has lost much of the sense of his relation to the great world around him. Quaker dress and customs have varied as the times have changed, often in a very interesting way; but perfect simplicity, uninfluenced by outside thought, is nowhere to be found in this world, short of Patagonia. The student of a philosophic turn of mind will find much light thrown upon the man in drab, if he will attentively observe his habits, manner of life and " conversation "—a word meaning in the Quaker, as in the Pauline vocabulary, his whole style of living, and intercourse with his fel-low-men.

There are three distinct periods into which the history of Quaker dress will naturally fall:—the period of persecution, when the early Friends had everything at stake, and life was to them more than meat and the body than raiment; the second, or reactionary period, when their position was established, their cause won, and prosperity, with its successes, was proving, as it always will prove, a far more dangerous foe than the perils of adversity; and the third, or modern period, when the crisis of the present brings them face to face with intricate problems, and dress again falls into its proper place in the general scheme of things. We shall see that in the face of a real issue, Quakerism disregarded the question of dress; and it is worth while to trace the growth and development of the traditional idea of Quaker costume, as it has come to be universally accepted. In other words, we shall study the Quaker in the light of a Higher Criticism, applied to the Doctrine of Clothes.

Since the great days of persecution, when, for the sake of a principle, all the minor " testimonies " gained in weight and import, bearing their share in forwarding the cause of Truth and Quakerism, many of the beliefs then peculiar to a sect are now held by multitudes of God-fearing people the world over. A total absence in the denominational schools of any proper teaching of Quaker history, has in past years made the matter of dress a veritable " cross " to many a youthful member, who has thrown off the obnoxious burden as soon as he was master of his own movements; a result that might frequently have been avoided, had he at all appreciated his inheritance. But an understanding of the spirit of Quakerism can no more come by heredity alone than can any of the other Christian virtues; and many a young soul has lived hungry for some explanation of the reason for the singularity forced upon him, quite unsatisfied by being told that the elder Friends " desired to have him encouraged." The force of example in this case has had a magnificent demonstration; but even it has failed to give the intelligent understanding of causes, without which, when the test comes, the strain must prove too great. The present crisis in the whole religious world is upon the Quaker no less than upon every other member of a sect. How many of his young people can judge, from a clear understanding of the history of their Society, whether the new problems —social, religious or moral—are counter to his own ancestors' teachings, put forth at the cost of life itself, or not? The dead bones of Quaker prophets must be made to live again in the history of their lives and all they meant, or the youth of the Society cannot be properly accounted Quakers. They will doubtless become good Christians, in the flood of modern religious teaching now surrounding them. And it is possible that this is enough, and the Quaker has done his part, and won repose. If not, then I believe that the Quakers have not sufficiently appreciated the immense chasm between seventeenth and nineteenth century needs, and that there are " crosses " far more weighty to be borne than this of the garb, which, if it be worn at all, should be regarded as a privilege. The penitential spirit of the last century Quaker, rather than combat the great evils existing in the world about him, and manfully seek to clear its political and social atmosphere, spent fruitless energy, first, in adding to the weight of this " cross " of his peculiar garb, and then in teaching his constituency how to be patient under their burden, forgetting, as Vaughan has well put it, that " there is quite as much self-will in going out of the way of a blessing to seek a misery, as in avoiding a duty for the sake of ease."

The descriptions here given have in every case had the authority of an original article of dress, or the experience of a participant in the incident quoted. Despite the lapse of time, there still exists ample material for the study of Quaker costume. Doll models still remain; the flat hat is a treasured relic in more than one family, and old silhouettes, daguerreotypes, portraits and pen drawings are to be found in many a household whose walls have never been adorned with such vanities, simply because human affection is too strong to be lightly set aside. There is no community of people among whom, as a class, family heirlooms, old plate, and the costumes of an earlier day are more highly valued or more carefully handed down from parent to child, than the Quakers. These have been called upon for their secrets of the precious past, and have been of great service in preparing the following pages, thanks to their generous owners. My acknowledgments are also especially due to Mr. Sidney Colvin, of the British Museum, for his kind permission to reproduce certain prints, and to Charles Roberts, of Philadelphia, for the use of his unique collection of Quakeriana.   A. M. G.

Haverford, Pa., 1901.

CONTENTS.

ILLUSTRATIONS.

FULL-PAGE PLATES.

ILLUSTRATIONS.

IN TEXT MATTER.

CHAPTER I.

THE COAT.

And that Friends take care to keep to Truth and plainness, in language, habit, deportment and behaviour; that the simplicity of Truth in these things may not wear out nor be lost in our days, nor in our posterity's; and be exemplary to their children in each, and train them up therein; that modesty and sobriety may be countenanced, and the fear of the Lord take place and increase among them; and to avoid pride and immodesty in apparel, and extravagant wigs, and all other vain and superfluous fashions of the world; and in God's holy fear watch against and keep out the spirit and corrupt friendship of the world; and that no fellowship may be held or had with the unfruitful works of darkness, nor therein with the workers thereof. BENJAMIN BEALING, Clerk.

Epistle of London Yearly Meeting, 4th mo. 1, 1691.

CHAPTER I.

AN entire generation has passed since the distinction of plain dress, as understood by the Quakers, became obsolete in Great Britain. The singular conservatism often shown by a democratic people manifests itself in this matter, touching the social and religious life of the same body in America, by the survival in one Quaker community of the " plain " dress of a time and occasion long since gone by. The Philosopher, whose Carlylean glance comprehends the close relationship existing between man's conscience and his clothes, realizes that so far as the Society of Friends is concerned, their peculiarities of dress belong to past history. He sees also, that whether the Quakers, having accomplished a mission than which few things are more remarkable in the social and religious history of the past, are now quietly awaiting extinction, or whether they are standing in the pause for breath before they cast aside their encumbrances to plunge into the new socialism which should be their natural inheritance in the struggles of the new century,—in any case the " pride of potential martyrdom," as a recent writer puts it, has been one of the strongest elements in the old Quakerism.

In the burning moment of the first inspiration and
enthusiasm, when the watchword was, " Come out from
among them and be ye separate," the emphasis of that
separateness was sought in the minor " testimonies " of
an earnest people. Chief among those " testimonies "
was plainness of garb. But the world has counted two
centuries and a half of progress since that day, and its
myriads of Socialists, Roman Catholics, Salvation Army
soldiers, and the wide circles of a uniformed official
class, have overtaken and swept past the Quaker. His
neat garb and his honest broad-brimmed hat are no
longer conspicuous in the moderation that has followed
the periwigged days of King Charles the Second. The
Quaker has now chosen to lay aside his distinctive garb,
there being no longer the same occasion for its existence. It marks, where it still survives, the formalism
of a caste, and the day of its inspiration is over. Since
the modifications inevitable for continuance involve
the disappearance of the distinguishing outward garb of
Quakerism, it may not be amiss to seek among its
records the history of that idea of dress which, in the
early days of persecution, so strongly fortified the mar-
tyr-spirit of the Quaker. He who has the seeing eye
must know that already the beautiful garments of our
stately grandmothers, the type of Elizabeth Fry, have
gone forever. Yet let us honor the motives of high
courage and strong principle which led a whole sect to
face one of the hardest tests of the human spirit, the
world's ridicule; the sincerity of their principles is nowhere better voiced than in the " Advices " given forth
to its members by Philadelphia Yearly Meeting in
1726: " If any who may conceive the Appearance of

Plainness to be a temporal Advantage to them do put it on with unsanctified Hearts and Minds filled with Deceit. . . . Such as they are an Abomination to God and to good. Men."

The *Tatler*, indeed, with its inimitable satire, shows us how clothes and religion get intermingled. It makes Pasquin of Rome write Isaac Bickerstaff:

There is one thing in which I desire you would be very particular. What I mean is an exact list of all the religions in Great Britain, as likewise the habits, which are said here to be the great points of conscience in England, whether they are made of serge or broadcloth, of silk or linen. I should be glad to see a model of the most conscientious dress amongst you, and desire you will send me a hat of each religion; and likewise, if it be not too much trouble, a cravat.*

There has been no attempt in the following pages to enlarge upon the doctrines of the Quakers. That has been sufficiently done elsewhere. The peculiarities of Quakerism " as to the outward," as Fox would have said, have been so marked, and its church polity for the past seventy-five years has been so much one of repression, that the outside world has known little of the Quaker; when it has perceived his presence, it has not troubled itself to understand him, nor to penetrate the atmosphere of exclusiveness that has surrounded him.

---

* Tatler, *No.* 129.—" The Old Cloak," which has been attributed to Swift, also points the same moral, although his satire is in this instance, not directed particularly against the Quakers. It begins thus :

" This cloak, it was made in old Oliver's days,
When zeal and religion were lost in a maze.
'Twas made by an elder of Lucifer's club,
Who botch'd on a shop-board and whined in a tub.
'Twas vampt out of patches, unseemly to name,
'Twas hem'd with sedition, & lin'd with the same.
This cloak to no party was yet ever true,
The inside was black, and the Outside was blue ;
'Twas smooth all without and rough all within,
A shew of religion, a mantle to sin."

His dress has had much to do with this. No one has portrayed the Quaker with a worldly hand, and at the same time been just to his principles, sympathetic with his sufferings, mindful of his foibles; and it is a fact that so far no attempt has been made from within the pale to handle his garb in the light of other people's opinions and experience, to treat him just like another man, and to attempt to understand why his costume differs. The outsider has regarded the matter as little worth his time; while to the Quaker himself, the subject has been too sacred to be lightly entered upon. Its importance has been so over-emphasized, that his young people have often failed to distinguish between the doctrine of oaths and the doctrine of the coat-collar.

The present essay, then, is an attempt to trace the development of Quaker costume. It has been approached like the history of any other costume, with no detriment, we trust, to its dignity. The Quaker's interpretation of " Truth " has generally been regarded as the cause of his peculiarities in dress. And so far as the essential doctrine of simplicity as taught by Fox may go, this is eminently true. It is true, also, of some of his customs, as, for instance, the refusal to doff the hat. The following pages, however, attempt to show that the typical Quaker dress has been, in the case of the men, a survival—a crystallization, in essential elements—of the original dress of Charles the Second; while that of the women has been an evolution, having its culmination one hundred and fifty years later in the costume of Elizabeth Fry. Both have been influenced to an unappreciated degree by the fashions of a changing world; for while the Quaker walks this " vale of tears," try as he may to withdraw, he cannot part company with his fellow-citizens. His past mistake has sprung from his effort to be a " peculiar people," as well as to be " zealous of good works." Very little excites ridicule in these modern faddist days: certainly no distinctive dress of any sort. The wide philanthropy once the inheritance of Quakerism, now belongs to the world in general. Religious toleration, for which the Quakers died, bids fair to-day if not to extinguish the Society, at least to break down its hedges and boundaries. The Athenian wore his flowing robe with the wish to be plucked on the sleeve with a " what ho ! Philosopher." The Quaker donned his garb from the opposite desire to be let alone. This, of course, was the Quaker position at a time when details served to emphasize the doctrines of their sect. In the two hundred and more years that have passed since the days of Fox, the occasion for such emphasis has largely disappeared. Not only among Friends, but everywhere, the different denominations are tending toward greater uniformity. This very fact makes people look leniently upon the peculiarities of the Quakers, who had the best of reasons at the time of their rise, for their various " testimonies." The anecdote may here be recalled of Penn and the King, when, to the sovereign's question wherein their religious beliefs really differed, the Quaker replied, " The difference is the same as between thy hat and mine; mine has no ornaments." The plain coat bears upon it the marks of an historical development. Warfare and politics are recorded in the cut of its collar and the sweep of its tail. Foreign influence, civil strife, diplomatic relations and political intrigue all have power to alter fashion and to impress

upon a certain generation a particular style of dress.
The "Steenkirk" tie, the Sedan chair, the farthingale
and the "tête de mouton" are striking importations
connected with foreign warfare and politics. But religious upheavals stir depths and work changes with a
rapidity that nothing else can equal. Let a man's conscience once become involved in his garb, and the garb
is capable of the most radical changes. The Reformation introduced simplicity at one bound into the gor-
geousness of the mediæval church. Miss Hill points out
that after Cranmer " it took us three hundred years to
reach the simplicity of the Victorian era, while the
Church accomplished the change in one generation."

There is a parallelism between clerical and Quaker
garb, both in its conservatism and its simplicity of result, as well as the profound importance attached to it
by its adherents. Dean Stanley tells us that the dress
of the clergy had no distinct intention at the start,
"symbolical, sacerdotal, sacrificial, or mystical, but
originated simply in the fashion common to the whole
community of the Roman empire during the first three
centuries." * In the earliest times in England the ton-
sure was the only distinguishing mark of the clergy.
Yet we all know to what elaborate proportions clerical
dress had run in England by the time of Cardinal
Wolsey; and the list of a few of the ordinary garments
of a country parson under Henry VIII. would make an
outfit sufficient for a modern theatrical show. "A
gown of violet cloth, lined with red, jerkin of tawny
camlet, tipped with sarcanet, two hoods of violet cloth

---

* Arthur Penrhyn Stanley, " Christian Institutions."

that Father ~~Greaton, the Jesuit~~ priest who w

~~in 1732 from Baltimore to build~~ and sett

sh Church in the Quaker City (which later b

lined with green sarcanet, a black cloth gown trimmed with lamb."* Over against this set the reforming Cranmer, in his dark cassock and leathern girdle. As the Quaker rebelled in spirit against extravagance in dress, his impulse was not to devise a new costume, but to eliminate from that he wore, the offending elements. Hence, retaining the early cut, he evolved in the passing years a costume of his own, just as the church evolved its own distinctive dress. The clerical habit as at present worn in England dates from the time of Charles II., as did the William Penn type of dress. It is striking to note that the coat of a prominent minister among Friends in New York was given upon his death, in 1856, to a clergyman of the Episcopal Church, who wore it without requiring any change whatever! We are told that Father Greaton, the Jesuit priest who was first sent, in 1732, from Baltimore to build and settle a Romish Church in the Quaker City (which later became Saint Joseph's) was wily enough on arriving to put on the Quaker habit. He soon donned his own black clerical garb; but he was careful not to offend the Quakers in dress or speech, and his first church building might easily have been a meeting-house for plainness. The dress of the bishops of the Church of England at the present day more nearly resembles that of Penn and his colleagues than any garb of modern times; vastly more, in fact, than the " plain " dress of their spiritual descendants. This includes the linen bands, as shown in portraits of Fox and Nayler.† The clerical

---

* Georgiana Hill, " History of English Dress." Vol. I., p. 236.

† The original of the latter is in the library of Peter's Court Meeting-house, London.

dress-suit of the present is a correct model of the court coat of Charles II., in cut and general style.

The most picturesque period in the whole history of English dress was that of the princely Stuarts, as Van Dyck has long been telling us. It was an age of swift change and vivid contrast, of luxury and unbridled license, when extravagance ran riot in the English court, and wonderful tales of splendor at Versailles set all St. James wild with envy. Great events crowded fast upon each other; King Charles lost his royal head, after which, for a time, the Protector and the Puritans had things their own way. Then followed the Restoration, with churchly prestige, and debauchery and extravagance striving together. A feeble attempt at popery came next under James II., and finally an established church and prosperity under Queen Anne—all this in the lifetime of one man! Into this scene, with its vivid lights and its shadows unfathomable, where Cavalier and Roundhead are eyeing each other, hand on sword and hate in heart, steps the striking figure of the early Quaker; and from the moment of his entrance on the stage, a purer faith and liberty of conscience become possible in dogma-ridden England. His true part in English history is yet to be written. Keen to denounce alike luxury in the court, and crime in the slums, loyal always to his sovereign Prince, even if refusing to doff the hat, or swear allegiance, and true always to the impartial enlightenment of every man, the Quaker is chiefly to be thanked for many of our cherished religious privileges.

Could George Fox have looked ahead to this day, we cannot doubt that he would have been perfectly satisfied with the simplicity of male costume in the world at large; and that the modification must have come without George Fox, we may be equally sure. Material progress such as ours was not possible when men had to guard blue satin coats and costly lace from soil. Fancy Mr. Edison at work in lace ruffles! Even Benjamin Franklin had to roll up his sleeves. George Fox and his contemporaries did not intend to establish a precedent of any sort when they demanded, rather arbitrarily, that their followers should discard all adornment in their dress. The Mennonites, who antedate them by a few years, and to whom the Quakers are indebted for many of their practices, had adopted simplicity of attire as one of their cardinal principles; and Independents, Presbyterians and others had been emphasizing plainness to an extreme point. The first dissension in the Leyden community of Separatists came from the lace on the sleeve of Mrs. Francis Johnson, which furnished a subject for eleven years of strife. Bradford says they were so rigid that some of them were offended at the whalebone in a dress or sleeve, or the starch in a collar. The Mennonites disapproved of ornaments even more than the Friends did at a later date, condemning buttons, buckles, and everything not absolutely necessary. The Baptist Brethren in Holland (a sect that arose in Germany about 1521), were called " Heftler " or " Knöpfler," because they excluded buttons, substituting hooks, like the Mennonite branch in Pennsylvania, known locally as " hookers." In some parts of the continent, rows of silver and metal buttons were used as ornaments on coats and waistcoats; and it was chiefly against these that the Baptist

movement was directed.   The use of hooks and eyes on
male garb instead of buttons, was confined to such lo-
calities as had made the adornment of their clothes
with a quantity of buttons an almost national custom.
The plain dress of the Quakers will be found to have
much more in common with the Baptists, than with the
Puritans, unless we include, as is often erroneously
done, most of the dissenting sects of England under the
latter head.   In the United States, certainly, the many
Puritan laws as to the dress of both sexes, and the
elaborate detail of rules regarding every minor item,
with the frequent enumeration of costly and extravagant fashions, lead us inevitably to the conclusion that
the New England Puritan was far from the plain and
meek person our fancy has been taught to draw; but
rather that he was gorgeous in his highly colored raiment, his wigs and velvet; that his wife was a positively
appalling person in her finery, so soon as prosperity had
come to the thrifty pair in their adopted land.

We can respect the feelings of the first Quakers as
to ornaments, for their " testimony " had a distinct object to accomplish; many felt with Ellwood about
" those Fruits and Effects of Pride, that discover themselves in the Vanity and Superfluity of Apparell which
I, so far as my Ability would extend to, took alas! too
much delight in.   This evil of my doings I was required to put away and cease from; and Judgment lay
upon me till I did so.   Wherefore, . . . I took off from
my apparel those unnecessary Trimmings of Lace and
Ribbands and useless Buttons which had no real service, but were set only for that which was by Mistake
called Ornament, and I ceased to wear Rings." *

---

* Journal of Thomas Ellwood.

England, Puritanly a ... fast ... the plain and
meek person our fancy has been taught   draw; but
rather   He was ... in his highly colored raiment, his wigs and velvet; that his wife was a positively
appalling person ... finery ... as prosperity had
the thrifty ... in their adopted land.

Illustrations for "War with ye Devil, or The Young Man's Conflict with ye Powers of Darkness." 1676. By K. P. Benjamin

I. The Youth before Conversion.

II. The Youth after Conversion.

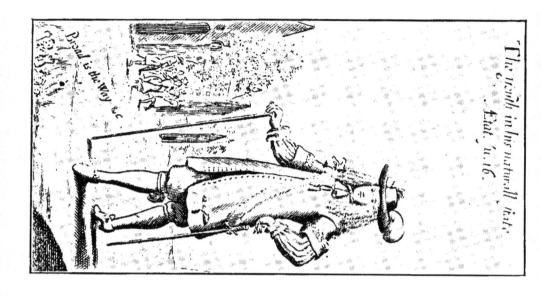

The youth in his naturall state.
Ætat. su 16.

Broad is the Way &c.

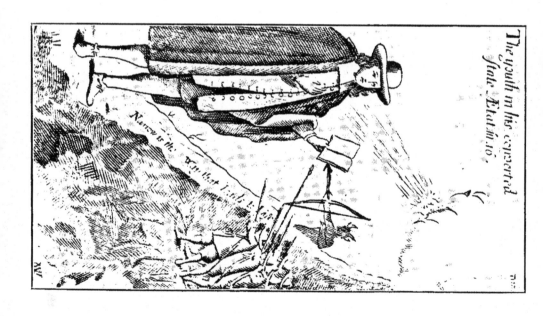

The youth in his converted
State. Ætat. su 16.

Narrow is the Way that leadeth &c.

By a very similar line of spiritual experience, Thomas Story was led to a point where the vanity of human wishes was forcibly presented to him; for even before learning of the peculiar tenets of the Friends, he had adopted some of their outward characteristics, in discarding sword and ornaments of dress. He did not meet the man whose influence led him to become a Quaker until 1691; yet in 1689, to use his own words:

I put off my usual Airs, my jovial Actions and Address, and laid aside my Sword, which I had wore, not thro' design of Injury, or Fear of any, but as a modish and manly Ornament. I burnt also my Instruments of Musick, and divested myself of the superfluous Parts of my Apparel, retaining only that which was necessary or deem'd decent. The Lust of the Flesh, the Lust of the Eye and the Pride of Life, had their Objects and Subjects presented; The Airs of Youth were many and potent; Strength, Activity and Comeliness of person were not a-wanting, and had their share; nor were natural Endowments of Mind or Competent Acquirements afar off, and the Glory, Advancements and Preferments of the World, spread as Nets in my View, and the Friendship thereof beginning to address me with flattering Courtship. I wore a sword, which I well understood, and had foil'd several Masters of that Science, in the North and at London; and rode with firearms also, of which I knew the Use; and yet I was not quarrelsome; for though I emulated, I was not envious; But this rule I formed as a Man to myself, never to offend or affront any wilfully, or with Design; and if, inadvertently, I should happen to disoblige any, rather to acknowledge, than to maintain or vindicate a wrong thing; and rather to take ill Behaviour from others by the best Handle, than be offended where no offence was wilfully designed. But then I was determined to resent, and punish an Affront or personal Injury, when it was done in Contempt or with Design; and yet I never met with any, save once; and then I kept to my own Maxims with Success; and yet so as neither to wound nor be wounded; the good Providence of Almighty being ever over me; and on my side, as ever knowing my Meaning in all my Conduct.*

---

* Thomas Story, Journal, Folio cd., p. 15.

The Quakers, in fact, will be found to have held a middle ground between the austerities of the old-line Cromwellian Puritans and Roundheads, and the extravagances of the Cavaliers. The peculiarities to which in later days they so closely adhered, were the outgrowth natural to a body which clung to practices that were once established, with the tenacity of larger but no less strongly organized religious bodies, like the Roman Catholics, the Mohammedans, or even the Chinese. A distinctive form of dress was at no time adopted by the Quakers with " malice prepense." The fact that in the second century of their existence a peculiar garb came to be .regarded as so essential, goes to prove, not vitality, but rather a period of decadence in their religious principles. The marked changes that Quaker costume has undergone, while they have not kept pace with the outside world as regards frequency of modification, are yet important as an element in studying the history of the sect. A cause is often greatly strengthened by the moral support of a distinctive and conspicuous style of dress, as for instance, that of the Salvation Army. John Wesley regretted that he had not made a regulation about dress. He wrote in his Journal: " I might have been firm (and I now see it would have been far better) as either the people called Quakers or the Moravians; I might have said, this is our manner of dress, which we know is both scriptural and rational. If you join with us, you are to dress as we do, but you need not join us unless you please; but, alas! the time is now past."

George Fox, however, did not dream of such measures among his own people. The simple, unadorned

costume of the men of his generation was all that Fox
aspired to. Along with his admonitions as to all ways of
living, he included in his denunciations every extravagance of dress. This alone meant a revolution difficult
for us to realize. The extremest form of Paris fashion
to-day would be simplicity itself compared with the
dress of an English aristocrat in the time of the first
Charles. Until the early part of the eighteenth century, there appears to have been no really distinctive
cut in Quaker costume. It is to be described in nega-
tions, was like that of every one else, and was only conspicuous for what it lacked of the popular extravagances
of the day. When men wore even more elaborate costumes than women, as in the days of the " merry monarch," anything plain was noted at once. Cromwell's
dress was so much more simple than that of the kings
before and after him, that Quaker simplicity was in his
time less conspicuous. The Protector was very frugal
in attire. He wore black cloth or velvet, sword-scarf,
trunk-hose, long boots, grey hat and silver clasp; varied
at times with doublet, cloak and hose of coarse cloth
turned up with velvet, and stockings of grey worsted
reaching over the knee to meet the hose. His hair
was simply arranged, without curls, and was somewhat
long behind. His moustache was so small as to be
quite inconspicuous. At fifty-eight he looks like a
Quaker himself, with his muslin collar and long hair.
In his portrait, by Walker, in the National Gallery, a
page ties his sash. Quakers and Puritans under the
Protector were more distinguished for differences of
opinion than differences of garb. An old author declares that " short cloaks, short hair, short bands and

long visages " were the rule. What we understand as
the typical Quaker garb, worn by William Penn, was a
survival of that of Charles the Second, when the distinctive outward marks of Quakerism were burned into
the sect, so to speak, by the rigors of persecution. The
dress of Fox was more nearly that of Charles the First.
This was to be expected of the plain countryman, who
would naturally cling to the more old-fashioned garb;
he never discarded the doublet, and always wore his
own hair long; whereas Penn, the diplomat and
courtier, followed the fashions in the cut and style of
his dress, adopting the full-skirted coat of the sovereign,
and wearing as many as four wigs in one year.

To test the correctness of this comparison, let us take
the costume of Charles the First as we have him in the
great portrait by Van Dyck in the Louvre. The King
wears a hunting dress consisting of white satin coat,
knee breeches in red, long boots with square toes, flat
lace collar, long hair, a pearl drop in the left ear (which
he even wore to his execution), and carries an enormously long cane. Divest him now of all his superfluities. Remove the enormous feather in his hat, and
Fox's own broadbrim stands revealed. Both King and
subject wear the hair " banged " on the forehead, falling in long locks on the shoulder—only the curls and
perfume are wanting in the Quaker. The lace worn by
the King at throat and wrists is missing altogether
with Fox, plain bands only being visible over his drab
coat, which buttons to the throat, and takes the place
of the King's satin doublet and rich cloak. But every
other man of plain origin wears a doublet of similar
cut to that of Fox, the drab in his case being for the

Charles the First 1624-1695. we have him in the
portrait by Van Dyck in the Louvre. The King

sake of economy, and hence simplicity in not dyeing the cloth. Leathern breeches and jerkins were universal among the "plainer sort," as George Fox called them, and were also worn from motives of economy. Trousers were not to be invented for another century. The style of knee-breeches, stockings and low shoes is identical with Fox and his King. The only difference is one of ornament. Fox's breeches have no "points," as the elaborate bows of jewelled ribbon at the knee were called; the stockings are of homespun, not silk, like the King's; and the heavy, square-toed shoes are minus the elaborate ribbons on the instep. Even the long cane is common to both. Samuel Smith, of Philadelphia, who kept a Journal, and who died in 1817, aged eighty-one, says of his travels in England: "At Samuel Lythall's, where we lodged, I saw the staff, it is said, George Fox used to travel with—a large cane stick about four feet in length and ivory head—looked as though it might have belonged to a country squire, and probably had been Judge Fell's." *And this is all.* The dress of the Quaker, when he first arose, was in cut and fashion simply the dress of everybody, with all extravagances left off; and since costume was then so elaborate, his perfect simplicity was quite enough to draw attention and render him conspicuous, even had he held his peace.

> O transmutation!
> Of satin changed to kersey hose I sing.*

But this he could not do, and many were his testimonies. In 1654, Fox wrote:

---

* Newcut, in "The City Match," I, 4. By Jasper Mayne, 1639.

My spirit was greatly burthened to see the pride that was got up in the nation, even among professors; in the sense whereof I was moved to give forth a paper directed

" TO SUCH AS FOLLOW THE WORLD'S FASHIONS.

"What a world is this! how doth the devil garnish himself! how obedient are people to do his will and mind! They are altogether carried away with fooleries and vanities, both men and women. They have lost the hidden man of the heart, the meek and quiet spirit; which with the Lord is of great price. They have lost the adorning of Sarah; they are putting on gold and gay apparel, women plaiting the hair, men and women powdering it; making their backs look like bags of meal. . . . They must be in the fashion of the world, else they are not in esteem; nay, they shall not be respected, if they have not gold or silver upon their backs, or if the hair be not powdered. But if one have store of ribands hanging about his waist at his knees, and in his hat, of divers colours, red white black or yellow, and his hair powdered, then he is a brave man, then he is accepted, then he is no Quaker. He hath ribands on his back, belly, and knees, and his hair powdered: this is the array of the world. . . . Likewise, the women having their gold, their patches on their faces, noses, cheeks, foreheads, their rings on their fingers, wearing gold, their cuffs double under and above, like a butcher with his white sleeves; their ribands tied about their hands, and three or four gold laces about their cloaths; this is no Quaker, say they. . . . Are not these, that have got ribands hanging about their arms, hands, back, waists, knees, hats, like fiddler's boys? And further, if one get a pair of breeches like a coat, and hang them about with points and up almost to the middle, a pair of double cuffs upon his hands, and a feather in his cap, here's a gentleman; bow before him, put off your hats, get a company of fiddlers, a set of music, and women to dance. . . . They are not in the adorning of the Lord, which is a meek and quiet spirit, and is with the Lord of great price."

Late in life, in Second month, 1690, he issued from the home of his stepson-in-law, William Meade, at Gooseyes, whither he had retired in feeble and broken health, a note of warning directed " To such as follow the fashions of the world."

Thomas Ellwood, whose Journal is one of the most graphic pictures of the day, but who, it is to be hoped, was a better tutor than poet, thus bewailed the prevalent extravagance:

> But Oh! the Luxury and great Excess
> Which by this wanton Age is us'd in Dress!
> What Pains do Men & Women take, alas!
> To make themselves for arrant Bedlam's pass!
> The Fool's py'd Coat, which all wise Men detest,
> Is grown a Garment now in great Request.
> More Colours now in one Waist-Coat they wear
> Than in the Rainbow ever did appear.
>
> .   .   .   .
>
> And he that in a modest Garb is drest,
> Is made the Laughing-stock of all the rest.
> Nor are they with their Baubles satisfy'd,
> But sex-distinctions too are laid aside;
> The Women wear the Trowsies and the Vest,
> While Men in Muffs, Fans, Petticoats are drest.

He warns Friends of the danger of the modes, and says:

> It hath come to pass that there is scarce a new Fashion come up, or a fantastick Cut invented, but some one or other that professes Truth, is ready with the foremost to run into it. . . . Assuredly, Friends, if Truth be kept to, none will need to learn of the World what to wear, what to put on, how to shape or fashion their Garments, but Truth will teach all how best to answer the end of clothing. . . . Let every one examine himself that this Achan, with his Babylonish Garment, may be found out and cast out, for indeed, he is a Troubler of Israel.*

" Babylonish garments " sorely troubled the Friends, and it was with those of them who were tailors by trade much as it was with John Mulliner and

---

* Thomas Ellwood, Journal, p. 343.

his musical instruments.* Gilbert Latey, a very interesting character of that early day, was a master tailor, whose attention to business, combined with his natural tact and uprightness, had won for him a very lucrative trade among the worldly, so that he was patronized by the gentlemen of fortune about the court. Becoming one of the " Children of the Light," he was no longer able to make the gay clothing that the fops of the day required, and he imperilled his fortune by declining to take any more such orders, although eventually a steady plain trade remained to him as his reward of faithfulness. King Charles the Second, while out hunting one day, met him upon the road, and the merry monarch called out to the Quaker tailor to step up to his horse's side for a chat, after which, with words of cheer, the King rode to his hounds, while the Quaker pursued his way to meeting.†

But the question of dress became more and more important as the cessation of active persecution gave the Friends time to devote more attention to its details. Dress was every day growing more and more extravagant; there seemed no limit to the extremes which it might reach. A cursory glance at the old fashion plates of this period, or an examination of Hogarth's works of a satirical character, will show us in a moment the reason for the emphasis laid on dress by the early Quakers—not the earliest, however, for these had been occupied with a struggle that involved life itself, and had no time for attention to clothes. Between

---

* See chapter on Wigs.

† Beck and Ball, " History of London Friends' Meetings," p. 250.

1660 and 1680, men's dress underwent many more changes than that of women. A large portion of a gentleman's time was given over to his elaborate toilette, and fortunes were squandered on lace and wigs by the fops and ladies of fashion. To these evils the Quakers very naturally directed their condemnation, and the subject became a prominent one in the care and instruction of their youth. How to guard a young man from the dangerous fascinations of a periwig that measured some three or four feet in length, or a young woman from a spreading farthingale, or a tight bodice in which she could barely draw the breath of life, may not seem to us now so very difficult; but we may be assured that the struggle was a hard one. No matter into what eccentricity Dame Fashion led her followers, they were willing to be guided by any blind extravagance; and the youthful Quaker cast longing eyes in her direction, even if she masqueraded in wig or farthingale, petticoat-breeches or wide hoop. More and more stringent became the laws of the Quakers on the subject; and while Aberdeen seems to have breathed in the atmosphere of the Scotch Covenanters a spirit more rigid than is to be found anywhere else in the limits of the Society, London and Dublin were not far behind. It is instructive to notice that drab tape was just as bad as red tape.

In 1686 the Meeting in Dublin seems to have shown very high order of talent in dealing with the question of dress, and went to the root of the matter when it attempted to purify the source of supply. The General Meeting appointed meetings of tailors " to see that none did exceed the bounds of truth in making of ap-

parel according to the vain and changeable fashions of
the world ; " and these meetings of " merchant tailors and clothiers " reported to the church. They very
judiciously advised Friends to " wear plain stuffs and
to sell plain things, and tailors to make clothes plain."
And also to ensure their wishes, " Friends would do
well to employ Friends that are tailors, for the en-
couragement of those Friends of that trade that cannot
answer the world's fashions." This may be the reason, as Barclay * suggests, that Dublin Friends were
spared the details of Christian simplicity that appear
on the books of their Scotch brethren, and from which
we may get an insight into the drastic measures of
Aberdeen and Edinburgh. The trade plan, we are told,
worked so well, that in 1693 they invoked the aid of
joiners, ship-carpenters, brass-founders, saddlers and
shoe-makers, to give their judgment to the meeting " in
the matter of the furniture of houses, etc., etc."; " fine,
shining, glittering tables, stands, chests of drawers and
dressing-boxes; " " large looking-glasses and painting
of rooms," as well as " painted or printed hangings."
Where these latter were needful, they would do well to
advise with concerned Elders of their meetings before
they put them up.

The Overseers of the church traveled over the country. They inspected the shops to see if " needless
things were sold," such as " lace and ribbons." They
inspected the houses with ornamental " eaves," and of
superfluous size, from the drawing-room curtains, with
other " Babylonish adornings " which were declared to

---

* Robert Barclay, " Inner Life of the Religious Societies of the Commonwealth."

be " needless," to the kitchens whose array of " shining, needless " pewter and brass pots, pans and candlesticks were evidently for ornament, and therefore contrary to the " simplicity of truth." Figured, striped or flowered stuffs, cloths or silks were, about 1693, generally condemned. As Barclay, from whom we have already quoted, says: " The whole life of man, from the cradle to the grave, was legislated upon; the ornaments on his cradle were to be dispensed with. Mothers were to suckle their children. It hath also been recommended to our Women's Meeting causing [concerning?] their child-bed dressings and superfluities of that nature that things may answer the plainness of Truth's principles both in themselves and their children from their births upwards. Coffins ought to be made plain, without covering of cloth or needless plates." In 1717 they order that chaises, except when absolutely necessary, are a needless luxury. The food, dress and even the gait of the children come under the care of the officers of the meeting, as well as the deportment of the nursemaids! In 1719 " floor-cloth," or the new fashion of carpets, was denounced, grateful to the feet of young and old on the cold, chilly floors in an English winter, but savoring of other vanities then being introduced with the growth of the Eastern trade under the care of the new East India Company. The question was, how far can one go before a comfort becomes a snare or a vanity. A vast amount of time was wasted in searching for the line of demarcation. Just before this, " the fashionable using of tea " (another Eastern importation, now become as national as the Union Jack), was ordered to be avoided; tea-tables to be laid aside, " as formerly advised "; and snuff, snuff-boxes, and the chewing and smoking of tobacco, "*except when needful,*" are reprobated! Tobacco, in the early days, was more universally used among the plain Friends than now. William Penn is said to have enjoyed his pipe, as did many another worthy. An unlocated minute of Ninth month, 1691, runs:

> It being discovered that the common excess of smoaking tobacco is inconsistent with our Holy Profession, this meeting adviseth that such as have occation to make use of it, *take it privately,* neither in their Labour nor employment nor by the highway, nor alehouses or elsewhere, too publicly.*

The climax, however, is reached, when we are told that a lowly mind would rather " admire the wonderful hand of Providence " in contemplating the necessary than the beautiful in nature, and the eye is not to be indulged in " great superfluity and too great nicety in gardens." In other words, turnips and cabbages tend to keep the mind humble, but the rose and the lily may prove a snare! And this, in the land of gardening and wall-fruit, where even the gooseberry is idealized! It surely is a wonder that all artistic sense has not been crushed out of the sect in two hundred years of such arbitrary dictation to the consciences of people, as may be found through the greater part of the eighteenth century among the Quakers, when they were a prosperous, not a persecuted, body. But the elasticity of human nature, and the eternal demand for some outlet to his pent-up artistic enthusiasm, is being manifested today in the reaction of the modern young Quaker in favor of music and the arts generally.

---

* Manuscript copy of old English Minutes, in possession of the author, made by Henry Hull, of New York, 1850.

The plain Quaker administered a silent reproof to all extravagance wherever he appeared, and the lampoons and broadsides of the day began their scurrilous attacks almost as soon as church and state combined to persecute him in earnest. One reason that we have heard so little of the anti-Quaker literature of 1655 to 1700 is because of its indecency. At a time when nobody was nice in speech or manners, it can hardly be imagined to what depths the popular lampoon sank; so that we are forced to leave these bits of Quaker history where we find them—buried in musty collections in the public libraries of England, or on the shelves of American antiquarians. It is necessary, however, to note their existence, since they show how the world regarded the Quaker. Those quoted are among the most decent. The Quakers were derided and pursued by every one. Their simplicity was said to be for purposes of deception; their frugality and consequent thrift were mocked at as penuriousness; their marriages without the priest were declared illegal, and their children were scoffed at as illegitimate. No stone was left unturned to render their lives a burden. This was a popular description:

A Quaker is an everlasting Argument; For like Afrique, he is daily teeming with some new Wonder; he that can describe him fully may boast he hath squared the circle. . . . His looks and habit cry "Pray observe me", and his whole deportment is starched and affected; you may take his face for a new-fashioned Sun-Dyal, where the forced wrinkles represent Hower lines, and his Tunable nose the gnomen. If he wants money, he need only say to one of his gang "The Lord hath sent me to borrow of thee 40 shillings." . . . These new seers ramble about to establish certain little Fopperies, as if the Salvation of the World depended on the Preaching down of Points, Cuffs, Tyth-Pigs and Pulpit-Hour-glasses; he is a kind of spiritual Gypsy that describes Grace and Piety by the Lines of the Physiognomy, and confines Christianity to such a Complexion or habit, being confident that cannot be a wedding garment that hath any trimming. . . . But 'tis no small attempt to encounter a Party whose Impious PENN hath presumed to duel the sacred Trinity.

" A candle of himself can't stand upright;—
The reason is, because his head is light." *

An anti-Quaker tract of 1679 † says: " The Quakers cry out against all external ornaments, whilst themselves at the same time doat most wickedly upon a Quirp-cravat, copied from a Chitterling original."

The Quaker was universally known as " Aminadab." Says Misson:

The Quakers are great Fanaticks; there seems to be something laudable in their outward Appearance—they are mild, simple in all respects, sober, modest, peaceable—nay, and they have the reputation of being honest; and they often are so. But you must have a Care of being Bit by this Appearance, which very often is only outward.‡

Such universal dislike was the logical result of their contrast to the exaggerated verbiage and ornate dress of the time. It is natural to expect less difference between the early Quakers and the " world's people " in cut and style of dress than in the society even seventy-five years after the death of Fox, for the very good

---

*" Plus Ultra, Or the Second Part of the Character of a Quaker, etc." 1672.

†" Work for a Cooper. Being an answer to a Libel." 1679.
Printed by J. C. for S. C. Prince of Wales Arms.

‡ " Les Quacres sont de grands fanatiques. Il parvit en eux quelque chose de louable : il semble qu'il soient doux, simples à tous égards, sobres, modestes, paisables : ils ont même la réputation d'être fidèles, et cela est souvent vrai. Mais il ne faut pas s'y tromper, car il y a souvent aussi bien du fard dans tout cet extérieur."

" Memoires et Observations faites par un Voyageur en Angleterre, 1698." Quoted by Repton, in an article On the Development of Hats and Bonnets, from the Time of Henry VIII., to the Present Day. Published in Archæologia, Vol. XXIV., p. 174.

reason that when persecution was following them, and they were being scourged, imprisoned and beaten to death, dress was a subject little dwelt upon. Simplicity only was taught; no distinctiveness other than that induced by its practice. A few years later matters are very different,* and the cut of the coat has become almost an essential in the plan of salvation. The process of adoption of a Quaker fashion has thus been described by an anonymous English writer † :

A novelty in dress is at first regarded as objectionable; then it is admitted and not considered inconsistent; and lastly, when the rest of men have passed from it, it is clung to with all the devotion which our society entertains for its peculiar customs. Where are now the cocked hats that were at first a vanity and afterward the outward visible signs of Quakerism, and have now . . . disappeared? Where are the green aprons that became us as a people? Where is the testimony against trousers, that, if one may trust tradition, once agitated the Society, and was the theme of discourses that claimed to be the utterances of eternal wisdom?

Our author concludes by saying that if we wear to-day George Fox's coat, we cannot retain the principle; if we retain the principle, we cannot retain the coat.

" A Pious Gentleman that had been thirteen years among the Separatists to make observations," wrote warningly in a Broadside to his countrymen in 1657:

---

* William Penn, Jr., to James Logan :

" Worminghurst, Aug. 18, 1702.

" My dress is all they can complain of, and that but decently genteel, without extravagance; and as for the poking iron (sword), I never had courage enough to wear one by my side."
Howard M. Jenkins, " The Family of William Penn," p. 109.

Soon after, his father, the Founder, thus writes of him to James Logan in Pennsylvania : " Pray Friends to bear all they can, and melt toward him at least civilly, if not religiously." Ibid., p. 111.

† " Nehushtan ; A Letter addressed to the Members of the Society of Friends on their Peculiarities of Dress and Language." London, 1859.

The Puritan Spirit was the spirit of Quakerism in the first degree,—which thing wise men know full well. . . . For 1 know, countrymen, what I say, that three parts of you that are religiously affected at this day are possessed with that humour that will make you Quakers if you take not great heed.*

Banbury was a great stronghold of dissenters, chiefly Presbyterians; but many Quakers were yearly tried at the Banbury Assizes, from the neighborhood of Oxfordshire. Castor, in " The Ordinary," an old play by Cartwright, 1651, says:

> I'll build a cathedral next in Banbury;
> Give organs to each parish in the Kingdom,
> And so root out the unmusical sect.†

The cant of the Presbyterians laid them open to an equal amount of ridicule with the Quakers. Little Wit in " Bartholomew Fair," is made to say: " Our mother is a most elect hypocrite, and has maintained us all this seven year like gentlefolks."

An old play, " The City Match," makes Aurelia thus remonstrate against the preaching tendencies of her Presbyterian maid:

> "Oh, Mr. Banswright, are you come? My woman
> Was in her preaching fit; She only wanted
> A table's end."
> Banswright. "Why, what's the matter ?"
> Aurelia.   " Never
> Poor lady had so much unbred holiness
> About her person: I am never drest
> Without a sermon: but am forced to prove
> The lawfulness of curling-irons before
> She'll crisp me in the morning. I must show
> Text for the fashions of my gowns. She'll ask
> Where jewels are commanded? Or what lady
> I'th primitive times, wore ropes of pearl or rubies?

---

* " Anti-Quakerism, or The Character of the Quaker Spirit." London, 1659.
† Act II., Sc. 3.

> She will urge councils for her little ruffs
> Call'd in *N*orthamptonshire, and her whole service
> Is but a confutation of my clothes.*

The long grace of the Presbyterian was another of his characteristics often ridiculed. We read of

> One that cools a feast
> With his long grace, and sooner eats a capon
> Than blesses it.

or this:

Dost thou ever think to bring thy ears or stomach to the patience of a dry grace as long as thy tablecloth; and droned out by thy son here till all the meat on thy board has forgot it was that day in the kitchen, or to brook the noise made in a question of predestination by the good laborers and painful eaters assembled together, put to them by the matron, your spouse, who moderates with a cup of wine ever and anon, and a sentence out of Knox between ? †

The Quakers were thus derided in a similar way:

Water us young Shrubs, with the Dew of Thy blessing; that we may grow up into Tall *O*aks, and may live to be saw'd out into Deal Boards, to wainscot Thy New Jerusalem! ‡

The Puritans, as we have seen, emphasized plainness of garb, but evaded the spirit of the law when they wrought embroidered texts upon their garments with a view to "moralize" them. The old play, previously quoted, has the following:

> Nay, Sir, she is a Puritan at her needle, too:
> She works religious petticoats; for flowers
> She'll make church histories; besides,
> My smock-sleeves have such holy embroideries,
> And are so learned, that I fear in time
> All my apparel will be quoted by

---

* Jasper Mayne, "The City Match." 1639.

† "Quarlous," in "Bartholomew Fair," Act I., Sc. 1.

‡ "The Quaker's Grace." Thomas Brown, "Works, Serious and Comical." London, 1720.

Some pure instructor. Yesterday I went
To see a lady that has a parrot; my woman,
While I was in discourse, converted the fowl;
And now it can speak but Knox's Works;—
So there's a parrot lost.*

The Puritan ladies showed great ingenuity in the
choice and execution of some of the sacred themes that
appeared upon the garments of members of their families. The custom lived but a short life, because of its
elaborate and expensive development. The texts and
sacred scenes that were thus worked upon clothing in
lace and embroidery, remind us of the fourteenth century fashion of emblazoning armorial bearings upon the
dress. This custom became general in France during
the reign of Charles V. A general sumptuary law in
the time of the Roses, applied to all classes, forbade cutting the edges of sleeves or borders of gowns into the
form of letters or other devices; and the tailor who
made such gown was subject to imprisonment.† The
extravagant display of gold lace and thread grew among
the Puritans to an abuse that rapidly put an end to this
sort of "moralizing," which was in every way opposed
to the professed simplicity of Puritanism. We read in
Beaumont and Fletcher:

Having a mistress, sure you should not be
Without a neat historical shirt? ‡

The range of color in Quaker clothing seems to have
been early limited to the browns and grays. Thomas
Ellwood says that there was a man in the Monthly
Meeting at Isaac Pennington's who "had his eye often

---

* Jasper Mayne, "The City Match." 1639.
† Georgiana Hill, "History of English Dress." Vol. I., p. 137.
‡ "Custom of the Country." Act II., Sc. 1.

upon me, for I was a young Man and had at that time a black Suit on." This was, of course, very early in the period of Ellwood's convincement. The women had a rather wider scope at first, but after the opening of the eighteenth century plain colors were universal among the Quakers. In the neighborhood of Oxford, indeed, brown was under a ban for a short time. "Heretofore Friends chose to wear grey clothing out of a dislike to brown, because it bore the name of a certain man of Abingdon that had stuck close upon the skirts of Friends thereabouts." * All wearing apparel was treated seriously, and was bequeathed to relatives and friends, and great minuteness was shown in disposing of it. The laborer in Queen Anne's day wore the broad brim, flat, felt hat that had been discarded by the man of fashion; a jerkin or short coat, knee breeches and heavy yarn stockings. The breeches were often of leather, adding to the neutral coloring in the matter of dress. The man of the world, on the other hand, was correspondingly gay. Even Robespierre, a century later, as Carlyle tells us, wore a sky blue coat, a white silk waistcoat, embroidered with silver, black silk breeches, white stockings, and gold shoe buckles. The doublet in Charles the Second's time was cut; it then became longer than before, and was adorned with the new buttons, just introduced, down the front. There was one royal attempt at reformation in dress, but it did not succeed.†

---

* See "Quaker's Art of Courtship," by the author of "Teague-Land Jests—Calculated for the Meridian of the Bull and Mouth." Abingdon had long been famous for its woolens, even then.

† For the new costume of the King, see Pepys' Diary, Vol. VI., p. 29. "A long cassock close to the body, of black cloth pinked with white silke under it, and a coat over it, and the legs ruffled with black riband like a pigeon's leg." Oct. 15, 1666.

By the end of this reign the picturesque old doublet had vanished and the King's coat was almost of the eighteenth century cut. The dragoons of this and the succeeding reign wore their brilliant red coats in the new square fashion, with ample sleeves, and skirts turned back with two buttons. This was the coat worn by everybody for the next hundred years, Quakers as well as others, with slight modifications. It was not until the end of the century that coats became short and grew a tail. William Penn's skirts were full—and why? Because the Stuart reign demanded a sword under the coat—quite as a mere matter of decency; and when William renounced the sword it did not strike him as at all necessary to curtail his ample skirts in anticipation of what, one hundred years later, came to be known as the " shad-belly " of his Pennsylvania successor. Yet skirts could be too full, even then.

20th. of 9 mo. 1688. It is concluded that the Friends appointed in every particular meeting shall give notice publicly in the meeting that cross-pockets before men's coats, side slopes, broad hems on cravats, and overfull skirted coats are not allowed by Friends.*

The American Friends were not behind their English cousins in this matter of plainness, and earlier even than this period had been warning their constituency of the dangers of conformity to worldliness.

In 1695 Philadelphia Yearly Meeting advised:

That all that profess the Truth and their Children, whether young or grown up, keep to Plainess in Apparel as becomes the Truth and that none wear long-lapped Sleeves, or Coats gathered at the Sides, or Superfluous Buttons, or broad Ribbons about their Hats, or long curled Periwiggs, and that no Women, their Children or Servants dress their heads immodestly or wear their

---

*MS. of Henry Hull.

Garments indecently as is too common; nor wear long Scarves; and that all be careful about making, buying or wearing (as much as they can) strip'd or flower'd Stuffs, or other useless & superfluous Things, and in order Thereunto, that all Taylors professing Truth be dealt with and advised Accordingly.

Also advised, " That all Superfluity & Excess in Buildings and Furniture be avoided for time to come."

Change had to come among the Quakers, however, as it had in the world. By the middle of the eighteenth century the country folk were following more closely in the wake of the town. " Fifty years ago," says a writer in 1761, " the dress of people in distant counties was no more like those in town than Turkish or Chinese. But now in the course of a tour you will not meet with a high crowned hat, or a pair of red stockings." Miss Hill goes on to say:

The high crowned hat was pretty well confined to the Quakers, who were as noticeable for the neatness as for the old-fashioned cut of their garments. Their linen was always fine and clean, and the quality of their sober colored coats and gowns was of the best. The most rigid discarded all additions which could in any be described as ornaments, even to the buttons with which it was the fashion to loop up the hats. The men's hats were lower and wider brimmed than the women's, which were of the regular steeple shape. Quakers, of course, did not wear wigs.*

Upon the matter of wigs we must correct Miss Hill. Many Quakers wore them, including William Penn.

In August, 1787, the London " Chronicle " published a satirical paragraph of advice to a man of fashion relative to correct costume for seaside wear:

For the morning, provide yourself with a very large round hat. This will preserve your face from the sun and wind, both of which are very prejudicial to the complexion. Let your hair

---

* Hill, " History of English Dress." Vol. II., p. 167.

be well filled with pomatum, powder and bear's grease, and tuck it under your hat.   Have an enormous chitterling * to your shirt, the broader the better, and pull it up to look as like the pouter pigeon as you possibly can.   A white waistcoat without skirts, and a coat with a collar up to your ears will do for an early hour; and if they say your head looks like that of John the Baptist on a charger, tell them you are not ashamed to look like an Apostle, what ever they are!   Your first appearance must be in red morocco slippers with yellow heels; your second in shoes with the Vandyke tie; your third in Cordovan boots, with very long rowelled spurs, which are very useful to walk in; for if you tear a lady's apron, it gives you a good opportunity of showing how gracefully you can ask pardon.   Your fourth dress must be the three cornered hat, the Paris pump, and the Artois buckle.†

The foregoing is valuable as showing how far dress had become modern in 1787.

Red heels were worn under Louis XIV., and in the time of Louis XV. these were made of wood in bright red at Court, and were considered a great mark of gentility.‡   Shoe buckles adorn the shoes of Louis XIV. in his portrait by Rigaud in the Louvre, painted in 1701; they came into England in the reign of William III., and by the end of the eighteenth century were enormous.   Then came the French Revolution, which affected even shoe buckles, and they were supplanted by ribbons or strings.   The American Quaker sea-captain, John M. Whitall, who visited England in 1819, relates that he wanted to go to meeting in Liverpool, and had a struggle in mind over putting leather strings in his shoes, instead of the worldly ribbons he would have had to buy.   But he did not "gratify pride" to that extent !§

---

* A ruffled front, falling from the neck.
† Hill, " History of English Dress."   Vol. II., p. 128.
‡ Quicherat, " Histoire de Costume en France," p. 562.
§ Hannah W. Smith, " Diary of John M. Whitall," p. 107.

Men in 1786 carried enormous muffs. These had a ribbon attached to suspend them from the neck, with a bow of ribbon tied in the center. The beau went about encumbered with this, a sword and a very long cane, no doubt with the *" very jantee "* air that the old books refer to as the *sine quâ non* of the modish gentleman of two hundred years ago. Muffs had come to America as early as 1638. Dr. Thomas Prence, in Boston, in 1725, lost his " black bear-skin muff "; and several muffs were left by will in New York in 1783.* An old French print shows a " Quaquer d' Amsterdam " in the dress of William Penn, carrying an enormous muff. Buttons of great size adorned everything possible under Charles the Second, and paint and " patches " prevailed. The riding-coats of this period were red, but in 1786 we find them green, with enormous mother-of-pearl buttons. It was about this time that a Frenchman in Philadelphia wrote that on a certain day in September the Quakers in that town " put on worsted stockings to a man ! " †

1818.
(After Martin.)

In the first years of the nineteenth century the worldly coat took on the cut-away effect seen in portraits of Jeffersonian times; and here we have the origin of the modern " plain coat," which is in reality a nondescript affair, being, as to its collar, a survival of the coat of Penn, who, however,

---

*Alice Morse Earle, " Costume of Colonial Days," p. 164.
† Elizabeth Drinker, Journal.

would have been horrified at its height; and as to
its tail, an early nineteenth century mode.   Something in its shape appealed to an American wag
long ago, who, struck by its resemblance to the fish
familiar to our shores, dubbed it the "shad!"
Had it been possible, the Quakers would doubtless still have clung to the early style of dress, but
their bravest efforts were of no avail.   The coat of William Penn had no collar whatever, as we have seen.
There came a time when the worldly coat rose straight
up to a line behind the ears, and the neckcloth passed in
many folds about the choked and gasping neck, tilting
the chin, for air and ease, to a point which carried the
nose upward and gave the beaux of the period a most
supercilious air.   The familiar portrait of Robespierre
will illustrate this, when all the gentlemen of England
were aping the fashions of the Directoire.   Presently,
because it could rise no higher, the worldly coat-collar
dropped over in a roll, and the neck was released from
all its swaddling bands of cambric.   The Quaker stopped
at this point; he had followed the fashion a quarter of
a century behind, it is true, but still followed, his coat
collar creeping up by imperceptible degrees until the
middle of the nineteenth century.   At the present time
only a faithful few are left to struggle against the inevitable roll, and these few are in America, Friends in
the mother country having ceased to observe an obsolete convention.   It took the coat collar a full two hundred years to rise to its greatest height and fall in the
snare of a worldly roll—what more natural than that
the Quaker collar should be as long in rolling?

Seventy-five years ago trousers were among the

things viewed by conservative Quakers with very grave suspicion. The evolution of the " pantalon," its rise, name, origin and effect are described by Quicherat.* The garment seems to have come from Venice in the sixteenth century. The Venetians were called " Pantaloni " in upper Italy, and the Italian comedians introduced the garment in France, in fantasy and ballets. The court of Louis XIII. danced " en pantalon," as did Richelieu himself, for the edification of Anne of Austria. The breeches were first lengthened to the calf, meeting the reversed boot-top, but trousers did not become popular at that time for stout wear, because the supreme hour had not yet come in which to discard the boot. Without attempting to dwell on the history of the most modern garment worn, it may be as well to remind ourselves that trunk hose had just been succeeded in Fox's time by breeches to the knee, adorned with fringe and ribbon; " petticoat breeches," frilled and voluminous, having been a short-lived mode. What George Fox would have done with trunk hose it would be interesting to know! At their height a law was necessary forbidding a man to carry " bags stuffed in his sacks "—a mild form of smuggling. A person before a court justice, when charged by the judges with being habited contrary to the statute, convinced them that the stuffing was not composed of any prohibited article, inasmuch as it " contained merely a pair of sheets, two tablecloths, ten napkins, four shirts, a brush, a comb and a nightcap ! " †

By the end of the eighteenth century there was a growing plainness in men's dress, and Charles James

---

* Quicherat, " Histoire de Costume en France," p. 480.
† " The Book of Costume. By a Lady of Quality." London, 1846.

Fox and his friends in the House of Commons aided its coming. 13 May, 1807, one Hamilton, at Balliol College, Oxford, wrote: "No boots are allowed to be worn here, or trousers or pantaloons. In the morning we wear white stockings, and before dinner, regularly dress in silk stockings," etc. In 1808 the "trousered beau" was present. He had before this worn silk stockings, velvet knee breeches, powdered wig, cocked hat and sword.* All through the eighteenth century Quakers wore knee breeches, with silk or yarn stockings, according to their circumstances in life, and low shoes or riding boots. It is interesting to learn from Miss Hill that knit stockings were only worn some fifty years before Fox was born. They had before been of cloth or continuous with the clothing, as in the days of trunk hose. Pepys' stockings were of silk and wool. When the "pantalon" arrived from Italy, the first were of plain light cloth, fitting very tightly. By 1830 they were much as they have since remained, the "cossack" shape being the transition, reminding us of Dr. Holmes' lines:

> They have a certain dignity that frequently appals,
> Those mediæval gentlemen, in semi-lunar smalls.

"French Pantaloons" are advertised in a Philadelphia newspaper of 1828.

In 1798 Mrs. Lloyd wrote to her son Robert, who had gone up to London to visit his friend Charles Lamb:

I was grieved to hear of thy appearing in those fantastical trousers in London. I am clear such eccentricities of dress would only make thee laughed at by the world, whilst thy sincere friends would be deeply hurt. . . . Neither thy mind nor person are formed for eccentricities of dress or conduct.†

---

* Hill, "History of English Dress." Vol. II., p. 233.
† E. V. Lucas, "Charles Lamb and the Lloyds," p. 97.

Robert Lloyd, in 1809, wrote to his wife:

Pray dispatch me from the Dog Inn at seven o'clock in the evening, 2 pair of White Silk stockings. 1 must go smart to the Opera. I have ordered a pair of dress-clothes in London.

His brother Charles inquires of him about the same time:

If Hessian boots would do to wear with pantaloons or small clothes indiscriminately, I should prefer them, but not without.*

The Lloyds were of Quaker stock, and a charmingly cultivated family, to whom the friendship of Charles Lamb was sure testimony of wit and culture. They did not remain in the circle of Quakers, but intermarried with the Wordsworths, and from them sprang three Bishops and an Archbishop of the Established Church!

The English Quakers, however, were not alone in their dread of the new fashion.

When Mr. Jefferson discarded his short breeches, silk stockings and low shoes with silver buckles, and concealed his well-formed legs in pantaloons, the Federalists were prone to regard it as the trick of a demagogue to secure favor with the mob. A gentleman in trousers and short hair! But what better could be thought or expected of a Democrat and an atheist?

In 1867, folks forty years old could remember the high stock, cruel shirt collar, ruthless coat-collar, the prodigious bonnet and general severity of costume before Channing, Dickens, Beecher, and the New York "Tribune" had begun to emancipate the American understanding from its tight fitting armor of opinion.†

Mrs. Earle tells us that the colonists of Massachusetts Bay landed, some in doublet and hose, and some in coat and breeches. The fact is interesting to the student of Quaker dress, for it is another evidence that there must have been great variety of costume among the

---

* Ibid., p. 268.
† James Parton, " The Clothes Mania."

different classes of society in England in the seventeenth century. The first mention of trousers in this
country was in 1776, although they are possibly the
" tongs " or " tushes " of 1638. The garment was at
first put to the use of what we now call overalls. The
Pilgrim men wore buff breeches, red waistcoats, and
green or sad-colored " *mandillions.*" * The indignant
Stubbes was also moved to inveigh against " mandillions " in a passage that gives a perfect picture of the
coat and jerkins of the late sixteenth and early seventeenth centuries. He says:

Their coates and ierkis, as they be diners in colours, so be
they diners in fashions; for some be made with collors, some
without, some close to the body, some loose, which they cal
mandilians, couering the whole body down to the thigh, like
bags or sacks, that were drawne ouer them, hiding the dimensions and lineaments of the body; some are buttoned down the
breast, some vnder the arme, and some down the backe, some
with flaps ouer the brest, some without; some with great sleeues,
some with small, some with none at all; some pleated and
crested behinde and curiously gathered, some not; and how many
dayes (I might saye honres or minutes of honres in the yeare)
so many sortes of apparell some one man will haue, and think-
eth it good prouision in fayre weather to lay vp agaynst a
storme.†

Doublet and hose were worn more in the Southern
colonies than in New England, and were richer in material. In the list of " apparel for 100 men," of the
Massachusetts Bay Company, Mrs. Earle tells us that
doublet and hose may be found in 1628, but they had
disappeared in New England by 1635. The doublet
was worn in England also by women in 1666, to the

* " ' Mandillions,' a sort of doublet, fastened with hooks and eyes,
and lined with cotton."—Alice Morse Earle, " Costume of Colonial Times,"
p. 218.

† Philip Stubbes, " Anatomie of Abuses." Ed. 1586, p. 49.

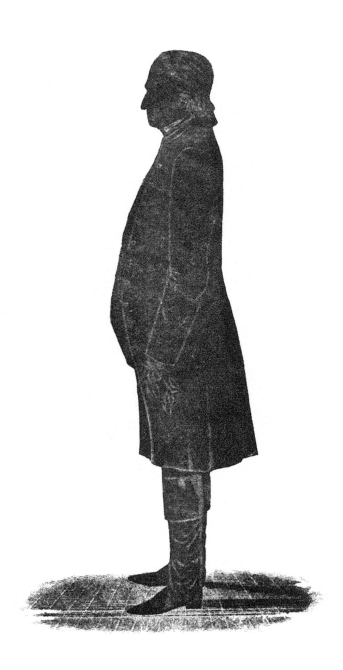

scandal of our friend, Mr. Pepys. As has been noted, George Fox wore the doublet all his life. What was known as " hair camlet " seems to have been a fashionable material among the plainer Friends for coats, while the gayer, or, as the phrase went, " the finer sort," wore velvet of various colors. John Smith, of Burlington, New Jersey, going to " pass meeting " for the first time previous to his marriage with Hannah, the daughter of James Logan, of Pennsylvania, 28th of Eighth month, 1748, wrote in his diary, " I put on a new suit of hair camlet." *

The dress of Jonathan Kirkbride, of Pennsylvania, born in 1739, is thus described by a descendant, and the description may be taken as that of many Quakers of the middle of the last century. Its cut is much like that of Elias Hicks.

During his preaching expeditions, he went out mounted on a pacing horse, a pair of leather saddle-bags, containing his wardrobe, hung behind the saddle, a silk oil-cloth cover for his hat, and an oilcloth cape over the shoulders, which came down nearly to the saddle, as a protection from storms. Stout corduroy overalls, with rows of buttons down the outside to close them on, protected the breeches and stockings. A light walking stick did double duty, as a cane when on foot, and a riding whip when mounted. . . .

He wore a black beaver hat, with a broad brim turned up at the sides so as to form a point in front and rolled up behind; a drab coat, with broad skirts reaching to the knee, with a low standing collar; a collarless waistcoat, bound at the neck, reaching beyond the hips, with broad pockets, and pocket flaps over them; a white cravat served for a collar; breeches with an opening a few inches above and below the knee, closed with a row of buttons and a silver buckle at the bottom; ample silver buckles to fasten the shoes with; fine yarn stockings. . . .

In winter, shoes gave place to high boots, reaching to the knee in front, and cut lower behind to accommodate the limb.

---

* "The Burlington Smiths," by R. Morris Smith, p. 153.

When he adopted pantaloons, with great reluctance, just before his death, at an advanced age, he complained of their feeling " so ' *slawny*,' flapping about the ankles ! " *

The men Friends of the early nineteenth century wore for an overcoat a long collarless garment of heavy cloth, like Gay's

> True Witney broadcloth, with its shag unshorn,

which was usually known among them as a " surtout," worldly French name though it was !

> That garment best the winter's rage defends
> Whose ample form without one plait depends;
> By various names, in various countries known
> Yet held in all the true surtout alone.
> Be thine of kersey firm, though small the cost;
> Then brave unwet the rain, unchill'd the frost.†

Possibly none clung to knee breeches longer than some of the Quakers in America, and the last instance that I have found is that of Richard Mott, who for forty years was clerk of New York Yearly Meeting, and who died in 1856. His daughter-in-law writes, in a letter preserved among old family papers:

> Mother Mott is better again. She is making [him] a pair of pantaloons, and I am helping her. The men have nearly all got to wearing them now, and he looks and feels so singular in his " smalls," that he could not stand it any longer, but bought some beautiful cloth in New York for the purpose.‡

Sometimes it is not clear what particular point in the costume was criticized, as at Dartmouth, Massachusetts, whose Records say:

---

* Mahlon S. Kirkbride, " Domestic Portraiture of our Ancestors Kirkbride; 1650–1824."

† Gay, " Trivia."

‡ Hannah B. Mott to her mother, Hannah Smith, from Mamaroneck, N. Y., 8 mo. 23, 1828.

Stephen Girard

27th. 1 mo. 1722; 'The visitors give account that they have been with B. S. who is gone from ye order of Friends into ye fashion of ye world in his apparel, who signified that he is resolved to have his own way.

Benjamin, we learn, was disowned; but the minutes are silent as to what he wore, which we should very much like to know. A rather more serious case was that of C. G., Jr., who on the 15th of Third month, 1756, " made an attempt to lay his intentions of marriage before the Preparative Meeting at Acoaxet & was not admitted by reason of his wearing fashionable clothes." He was labored with by the Friends, but refused to change his worldly apparel, married " out of the order," and was eventually disowned.

At Nantucket, Massachusetts, 1801, L—— H—— was disowned for " deviating from our principles in dress and address." We find that he persisted in wearing buckles, and refused to use " thee " and " thou." In 1803, at the same meeting, it is recorded that H—— C—— " had deviated in dress and address from the plainness of our Profession." *

The inventory of the household goods and clothing of Benjamin Lay, the extraordinary Anti-Slavery Quaker of Pennsylvania, is still in existence; and this curious and unique account is sufficiently instructive to warrant its partial reproduction. It will be noted that the list includes " britches " and trousers, the former of leather in several cases,† as well as a " skin coat," and jacket of the same leather as the " britches." Various cloaks and riding hoods, and seven or eight other

---

* Worth, " *N*antucket Friends' Meetings."

† William Strypers in 1685, had " two pair of leather breeches, two leather doublets, handkerchiefs, stockings, and a new hat." This constituted the outfit of the Dutchman, when he settled in Germantown, Pa., at that date. " Settlement of Germantown," by Judge Pennypacker, p. 128.

hoods in white or black, had evidently belonged to his wife, whose death took place some years before that of her husband, in 1742. Sarah Lay was also a little hunchback, an English woman, and an acknowledged minister in the Society of Friends, who accompanied her husband when he first came to America in 1731. She evidently had not been ensnared by so worldly a fashion as the bonnet, which was far from the thoughts of the good Quakeress of that date. The few items that follow are selected from the original manuscript with an eye to the style of garments worn by the Lays. Benjamin Lay died Second month 3d, 1759, aged 82. The sale (or " vendue," as the document reads) occurred the next month, and fills fifteen folio pages of description. £68 17s. 1d. were realized. The list includes one hundred and twenty-five books, mostly Friends', a copy of Plutarch's Lives, etc. His home was near Abington, Pa. The last rather startling item in this list evidently refers to a piece of damaged goods!

INVENTORY OF CLOTHING
OF
BENJAMIN LAY, OF PENNSYLVANIA,
DIED 2 MO. 3RD. 1759.

	s	d
Coat and Jacket	2	6
Buckrim Coat	0	4
2 Jackets and a frok	1	2
Plush coat	9	7
Pare of Leather Britches	3	11
Leather Jacket	5	0
" "	4	1
"	1	8
Skin Coat	0	3
Pare of Shoos	6	6
Coat and Hat	1	1
Bag and pare of Cloth boots	2	5

	s	d
Leather Jacot	10	3
Coat .	1	6
Pare of Britches	11	6
" "	4	0
Trunk .	2	0
Cloke .	1	6
A Hide and cloke	1	6
2 flanell petty cote	3	3
Clock [cloak] and riding-hood	2	4
Petecoat .	3	1
Crap gound [crêpe gown]	3	1
Calleminco gound	4	6
Camblit "	1	1
Quilted petecoat	10	1
Winder curtius	1	11

		s	d
Black silk scarf	1	18	0
Ditto	1	17	1
Black silk scarf	0	18	0

	s	d
Black hood	11	0
Whit silk "	3	9
A " " "	5	0
Ditto .	4	1
A silk handkerchief	7	0
Ditto .	2	9
A silk handkerchief	7	0
pare of silk gloves	5	0
" " gloves .	1	10
A whit hood	2	3
" linen "	1	4
Ditto .	2	0
2 muslin handkerchiefs	4	1
A whit hood	3	1
" "	4	1
3 " aprons	5	11
Pocket handkerchief	5	1
6 caps	4	9
" "	4	8
10 "	5	3
3 cambric handkerchiefs	4	4
8 pinners	7	0
A checkard apron	2	3

	s	d
20 neck cloths	4	3
sundry mittens	2	3
a green apron	2	0
Ditto	2	4
a pare of pockets	1	0
3 pare worsted stocks	4	7
1 dimity wastecoat & 2 shifts	18	0
12 diaper napkins & 2 table-cloths 3	10	0

Besides shirts, stockings, gloves, " 17 shifts," 12 table-cloths, towels, napkins, sheets, pillow-cases, "curtins," "a hammack," quilts, "vallians," etc., "to numerous to mention."

Also, a variety of dry-goods in the piece, 40 lbs. whalebone, thimbles, needles, buttons, 12,000 pins, stay-tape, 1 doz. flints; and finally, " 8 yards of damnified ozonbriggs! "*

The dress of Nicholas Biddle is described by the Frenchman, M. de Bacourt, so late as 1840, as " a blue coat with brass buttons, yellow nankeen pantaloons, canary colored gloves, and a glossy beaver." The same M. de Bacourt is said to have made the *mot*, that the "world is ruled by three boxes—the ballot-box, the cartridge-box, and the band-box! "

The only title of honor recognized by Friends seems to have been that of Doctor. The ills of the flesh were so heavy in the days before the use of modern methods of healing, that the physician who could in any way alleviate suffering was made welcome for his kindly services, and his title was generally given him. England was far behind Holland in the healing art, and Friends went to the Netherlands, where Leyden was famous in science and learning, to study medicine. A flourishing body of Quakers already existed in Amsterdam. Anatomy and physiology were taught with

---

*Ozonbrigg—One of the many materials with Eastern or other curious names, so much in use in the sixteenth and seventeenth centuries. Spelt also Oznaburg, Ozenbridge, etc.; originally made at Osnabrück, Hanover. Linen. (Alice Morse Earle.)

Dutch thoroughness, and Rembrandt's great painting, "The Anatomist," was a correct representation of the scientific training which that nation was giving to the whole world. The Doctor, in the seventeenth century, was a great social personage. His power and his presence were only second to that of a great church dignitary. No one ever questioned his authority on any point, and to his utterances the people paid great heed. He had but just stepped over that mysterious borderland lying between mystery and science, and to the unlettered of his day, his knowledge was hardly to be attained without supernatural means. Both on the continent and in England he wore a distinctive dress. The black cloth garb was quite clerical in effect, and the great bush wig was invariably accompanied by a gold-headed cane. Portraits of Doctors Fothergill and Lettsom, both very eminent men, and both Quakers, show them in clothing of rather lighter hue, but with the adjuncts of cocked hat, wig and cane. The Quaker profession in England maintained the courtesy and the garb without, however, any of its exaggerations; and respect for their calling led them to wear the wig throughout the period of its history—a motive which did them honor, although, at this date, we may not be able to recognize any added sentiment of beauty or dignity in that adornment.

In America, democratic as it was—and yet most conservative, so far as adhering to a style of dress is concerned—the wig was not considered *de rigueur* among Friends, where its adoption, with Doctors, as with other mortals, was entirely a matter of taste. We can therefore the better understand Ann Warder's astonishment at the appearance of a Doctor in Philadelphia, wearing none of the insignia of his profession. She writes, in 1786, " We dined at Nicholas Waln's in company with there sisters and two public Friends." (A usual term for minister among the Quakers.) " One, I understood, was a country Physician, but how would he look by the side of ours, instead of a great Bush Wig, and everything answerable, his Dress was as humble as possible." At meeting, the next day: " The Doctor I mentioned yesterday appeared beautifully "; that is, he preached or prayed acceptably to his audience. The Doctor of Divinity also shared in a professional costume as he does now, and this lends meaning to the note of Thomas Story, who in 1717, at Radnor, Pennsylvania, in describing meetings he had held at that place, says: " We heard also of a Doctor of Divinity in one of our meetings, disguised in a blue coat; but not of any objections made." *

The new thing, whatever it might be, was viewed askance by Quakerism, which, in America, at least, was never more fearful of innovations than during the period immediately succeeding the departure of the Quakers from the Pennsylvania Assembly in 1756. They withdrew from active life, and paid more attention to the limitations of dress and custom among their membership, and this grew upon them with the passing years. Richard Talbot, of Ohio, was visited by Friends of his Yearly Meeting for putting on *suspenders;* and umbrellas caused many anxious moments when they were introduced among the Friends. The first umbrella carried in Edinburgh was borne by Alexander

---

* Thomas Story, Journal, p. 573. (Folio.)

Wood, a surgeon, in 1782. It was a huge gingham apparatus, clumsy and awkward to a degree. It was also a surgeon who the following year carried a yellow glazed linen umbrella down Glasgow streets, justly proud of the new importation from Paris. Before this, huge green paper fans were employed as a protection from the sun, while the rainy-day devices were many. Jonas Hanway, however, although he has the credit of carrying the first umbrella in London, in 1756, must now give way to a Philadelphia Quaker, for on February 20, 1738, an "umberella" was imported to Philadelphia in the good ship " Constantine," as shown by the invoice, for the " proper account and risque " of Edward Shippen, who, indeed, for aught we know, may have worn out that nine shilling umbrella long before Jonas Hanway carried his.* Nathaniel Newlin carried the first umbrella to Chester (Pa.) Meeting, and to this evidence of a worldly spirit Friends took great exception, and made remonstrance, although Nathaniel was a person of weight, and had sat six times in the Pennsylvania Assembly.

As for the women, they had long been used to following the advice of Gay:

> Good housewives all the winter's rage despise,
> Defended by the riding hood's disguise;

but it was considered a very feminine and unmanly performance at first to be seen carrying an umbrella, and only women might

> Underneath the umbrella's oily shed,
> Safe through the wet on clinking patten tread.
> Let Persian dames the umbrella's ribs display,
> To guard their beauties from the sunny ray;

---

* " Pennsylvania Magazine of History and Biography." Jan., 1901.

> Or sweating slaves support the shady load,
> When Eastern monarchs show their state abroad.
> Britain in winter only knows its aid,
> To guard from chilling showers the walking maid.*

The grandmother of the Philadelphia lady who vouches for the following had a no less thrilling experience in the attempt to be in the mode than had Nathaniel Newlin. During her girlhood her father brought her an umbrella. She carried the novel gift with great pleasure and delight, but so new and unknown was the article that the meeting to which she belonged became alarmed and the Overseers dealt with the worldly-minded father. During the controversy one woman Friend said to the young girl, "Miriam, would thee want that held over thee when thee was a-dyin'?" That of course settled the matter, and the offending umbrella was relegated to seclusion. Many present necessities of the toilet were unknown luxuries in the early days. We are told that in 1650 Sir Ralph Verney sent to a friend a present of "teeth-brushes and boxes," which were new-fangled Parisian articles, called by him, "inconsiderable toyes." †

There are few more sensitive souls than that of sweet and tender John Woolman, to read whom in these sordid days is like a breath from the Elysian Fields. We could not all find it possible, or even our duty, to live so near his ideal; for to few human beings is it given to so completely sever their connection with the world, and the things of the world. Nevertheless, there is no more salutary reading for these strenuous days than the small but precious contribution made by John

---

* "Trivia."
† Georgiana Hill, "Women in English Life." Vol. I., p. 158.

Woolman to the body of English literature. He is here named because of the travail of soul that he endured over his clothes; for to him, poor dear, the dye in his garments was as great an object of uneasiness of spirit as the lack of it would have been to William Penn! He tells us in his Journal, that amazing record of a soul's experience, that " the thought of wearing hats and garments dyed with a dye hurtful to them, had made a lasting impression on me." This was in the year 1760, when the Quaker tailor was just forty years old, and his calling had led him to see the vanities of men rather intimately.

This, and the wearing more clothes in summer than are needful, grew weary to me, believing them to be customs which have not their foundation in pure wisdom. The apprehension of being singular from my beloved friends was a strait upon me; and thus I continued in the use of some things contrary to my judgment.

But our Journalist fell ill and in the depths he records his mind brought into a state of perfect submission to the will of God, as he interpreted it. For nine months he continued to wear out the garments he had already in use, and then his first move in the direction of the new reform was to buy an undyed hat.

I thought of getting a hat the natural color of the fur, but the apprehension of being looked upon as one affecting singularity felt uneasy to me. Here I had occasion to consider that things, though small in themselves, being clearly enjoined by Divine authority, become great things to us; and I trusted that the Lord would support me in the trials that might attend singularity, so long as singularity was only for His sake. On this account I was under close exercise of mind in the time of our General Spring Meeting, 1762, greatly desiring to be rightly directed; when, being deeply bowed in spirit before the Lord, I was made willing to submit to what I apprehended was required of me, and when I returned home got a hat the natural color of the fur.

No portrait, alas, exists of John Woolman, but this lets us know that his hat was a beaver of the natural color. Doubtless he would never have consented to have his " counterfeit presentment " taken. He had some mental stress because of this step, for he adds that after this,

In attending meetings, this singularity was a trial to me, and more especially at this time, as white hats were used by some who were fond of following the changeable modes of dress, and as some Friends who knew not from what motives I wore it grew shy of me, I felt my way for a time shut up in the exercise of the ministry. . . . My heart was often tender in meetings, and I felt an inward consolation which to me was very precious under these difficulties. Some Friends were afraid that my wearing such a hat savored of an affected singularity; those who spoke with me in a friendly way, I generally informed, in a few words, that I believed my wearing it was not in my own will. I had at times been sensible that a superficial friendship had been dangerous to me; and many Friends being now uneasy with me, I had an inclination to acquaint some with the manner of my being led into these things; yet upon a deeper thought I was for a time most easy to omit it, believing the present dispensation was profitable, and trusting that if I kept my place, the Lord in His own time would open the hearts of Friends toward me. I have since had cause to admire His goodness and loving kindness in leading about and instructing me, and in opening and enlarging my heart in some of our meetings.

Surely nothing could be more beautiful than the spirit here shown, although a practical mind might find some criticisms possible. But if all the Friends to-day bought their hats and bonnets in the same spirit, it would surely not be long before the Society of Friends again became a power in the world. Shall any one hereafter say that there is nothing of philosophy in clothes? The Quaker custom of self-examination and comparison with the ideal life, and a disparagement of native gifts and talent, made the humility in which the Quaker was " clothed as with a garment," and which he seldom ceased in the last century to recommend, take on sometimes a melancholy hue.

Aggressive as the Quaker garb would seem to have been upon a superficial glance at the situation, it will be found that the sect made no effort to force their peculiarities upon the public, nor have they ever done so. They and their hats became conspicuous by force of circumstances, and of course were at once in the public eye. They did not preach Quaker, but only plain dressing; and they would at first have denied their public position on the subject had they been given the choice. The Quakers have always had the good sense to hold quite in the background their views on dress, when they have gone out as missionaries to what we are pleased to call " the heathen." And herein they have been wise in their generation. How much good would they have accomplished, for instance, by insisting that a Hindu woman should at once put on the plain bonnet? It is quite as reasonable to expect the Quakers to adopt the Chinese dress, as, indeed, more than one has done. There is a beauty of line in certain forms that Quaker dress has taken, that is pleasing to the artist, and possesses still more attraction for the moralist or historian. It is hardly perceptible to him who is unfamiliar with Quaker history. The modern idea of beauty in dress is no longer one of personal adornment, but there is a moral quality that enters into it, which is quite the product of the last three hundred years. The merely decorative element is one that has always appealed to the savage on the plains, or in Central Africa.

The purely æsthetic side of dress was present to the Greek as never before or since; and to the Knight in armor came a sense of protection together with the appeal to his prowess. But it is only of late years that we have had a conscience in our clothes; and what is beautiful must now stimulate our feeling for the best and truest. We do not object to the peculiarities of the Quaker garb as did the public in Oliver Cromwell's day, to whom it was offensive because an implied reproach. But we see in it the memory of martyr and saint and hero, and we suffer it, because to us it stands as a symbol of some of the qualities for which the human soul has greatest need. A feeling of sadness creeps over our mind that its history has become altogether that of the past.

Sunshade. 1760.

CHAPTER II.

THE SPIRIT OF THE HAT.

> Any Cappe, whate'er it be,
> Is still the signe of some Degre.
> "*Ballad of the Caps*," 1656.

> Ne dit-on pas qu'il ne faut pas penser avoir toutes ses aises en ce monde?
> *Lois de la Galanterie.*

CHAPTER II.

THE SPIRIT OF THE HAT.

TWO hats in the history of the church stand forth conspicuous from the mass. In shape they are not unlike. The oldest has a round crown, and plain wide brim, and is unadorned save for cord and tassel. Gorgeous in brilliant red, it typifies churchly prestige and power; and the cardinal who wears it is a functionary of what has been the most powerful church organization on the face of the earth. To but one other hat has ever attached so much religious significance. That is the drab broad-brim of the early Quaker. How many controversies have been waged, how many hard words flung over the apparently simple matter of the hat! On this futile subject we have had countless tracts, pamphlets and sermons; while lawsuits, loss of property and loss of life are all on record. The spiritual welfare of an entire sect has at one time seemed to depend on the manner of wearing the covering for the head. The whole "testimony" of the early Quaker against the frivolities of his day was concentrated in his hat.

It is important to remember that the period was but just past when this had been a part of the costume, no more to be removed when entering the house or seated at table than the shoes or doublet. Hats were worn in

church, and the clergy preached in them. The elegant
courtiers at the French and English courts were now
beginning to greet the ladies and their superiors in rank
with the new sweeping bow—" making a leg," as it was
termed—with consummate grace and art, the hat's
long, graceful feather sweeping the floor in the action.

This is not a Parisian fashion book, nor yet a history
of worldly costume; nevertheless, we must seek the
origin of the Quaker hat among the abodes of fashion.
This part of the costume has a very interesting history,
and might in itself fill a good-sized volume. The felt
hat with which we are chiefly concerned goes back to
the time of the early Greeks. There is a felt hat on a
statue of Endymion in the British Museum. The Nor-
mans at the conquest wore hats of the same durable
material, and we love the " flaundrish bever hat " of the
Merchant, in the Canterbury Tales. Among the
peasantry of the seventeenth century, the old English
and Scotch " bonnets " were worn, usually of cloth or
other heavy stuff, low and broad in shape; while at all
times in the early history of England some variety of
the hood was to be found among both sexes alike.
Chaucer's Reve was rewarded by his master with
" thanks, a cote and hood "; and the Monk—

> " For to fasten his hood under his chinne,
> He had of gold ywrought, a curious pinne."

At the coronation of Anne Boleyn, the Aldermen
" toke their hoddes from their necks, and cast them
about their shoulders." * The old time-honored bonnet
had been superseded by the hat in the early sixteenth
century; and in the reign of Henry VIII., we find certain old prints that give us the jaunty hat always asso-

---

* Archæologia, Vol. XXIV., p. 172.

ciated with that monarch, showing the hood still worn
underneath it, or thrown over the shoulder. Felt hats
had been found most durable for soldiers' wear, and
their lasting qualities made them popular with the common people. Ashton tells us that a new-fashioned
beaver hat, sometimes called felt and made by the
Dutch, came in about 1559.
They were afterward made in
England by the Dutch refu-
gees at Wandsworth, and were
a luxury only to be afforded by
fine gentlemen. A good hat
was very expensive, and important enough to be left
among bequests in a will.
They were borrowed and hired
for many years, and even down
to the time of Queen Anne, we
find the rent of a *subscription
hat* to be two pounds six shil-

Douglas, Earl of Morton.
1553.
(After Repton.)

lings per annum! There must have been great peace
and harmony in the wearing of that hat, one would
think! In the time of Elizabeth beaver hats were an extravagant luxury, and "were fetched from beyond the
seas, where a great sort of other varieties do come beside." The hats were small at first, and one old writer
says:

> "So propre cappes,
> So lytle hattes,
> And so false hartes
> Saw y never." *

The "hattes" soon grew as broad as that of the Wife
of Bath, and were known as "castors." The print of a

---

* "Maner of the World Now-a-Days."

fashionable man of 1652 has the hat-brim extending horizontally, with a long drooping feather, threatening

Hat of Charles I.
(After Martin.)

to fall. This was the hat of Charles the First, which has since come down to us as the Quaker broad-brim. The steeple - crowned hat of James I. still exists in beaver in Wales, worn by both men and women, the latter placing it over the hood or cap in the manner of the first Quaker women. Nothing has ever destroyed the hold of the felt hat upon the affections of the English nation.

> "The Turk in linen wraps his head,
>   The Persian his in lawn too;
> The Russ with sables furs his cap,
>   And change will not be drawn to;
> The Spaniard's constant to his block,
>   The French inconstant ever;
> But of all felts that can be felt,
>   Give me your English beaver." *

Old Philip Stubbes, in 1585, wrote of

HATS OF SUNDRIE FATIONS.†

Sometymes they vse them sharpe on the croune, pearking vp like the spere, or shaft of a steeple, standyng a quarter of a yarde aboue the crowne of their beades, some more, some lesse, as please the phantasies of their inconstant mindes. Othersome be flat and broad on the crowne, like the battlemetes of a house. An other sorte haue rounde crownes, sometymes with one kinde of band, sometymes with another, now blacke, now white, nowe russed, now redde, now grene, nowe yellowe, now this, now that, neuer content with one colour or fashion two daies to an ende. And thus in vanitie they spend the Lorde his treasure, consuming their golden yeres and siluer daies in wickednesse and sinne. And as the fashions bee rare and strange,

---

* "English Mutability in Dress."
† Philip Stubbes, "Anatomie of Abuses," 1586.

A   Party

so is the stuffe whereof their hattes be made diners also; for some are of silke, some of ueluet, some of taffatie, some of sarce-net, some of wooll, and, whiche is more curious, some of a certaine kinde of fine haire; these they call beuer hattes, of xx. xxx. or xl. shillinges price, fetched from beyonde the seas, from whence a greate sorte of other vanities doe come besides. And so common a thing it is, that euery seruyng man, countrieman, and other, euen all indefferently, dooe weare of these hattes. For he is of no account or estimation amongst men if he haue not a ueluet or taffatie hatte, and that must be pincked, and cunnyngly carued of the beste fashion. And good profitable hattes be these, for the longer you weare them the fewer holes they haue. Besides this, of late there is a new fashion of wearyng their hattes sprong vp amongst them, which they father vpon a Frenchman, namely, to weare them with bandes, but how vnsemely (I will not saie how assie) a fashion that is let the wise judge; notwithstanding, howeuer it be, if it please them, it shall not displease me.

And another sort (as phantasticall as the rest) are content with no kinde of hat without a greate bunche of feathers of diners and sondrie colours, peakyng on top of their heades, not vnlike (I dare not saie) cockescombes, but as sternes of pride, and ensignes of vanity. And yet, notwithstanding these flut-terying sailes, and feathered flagges of defiaunce of vertue (for so they be) are so advanced in Ailgna [England], that euery child hath them in his hat or cap: many get good liuing by dying and selling of them, and not a few proue theselues more than fooles in wearyng of them.

Bright, in " Bartholomew Fair " (Act I., Sc. 4), says:

> By this two-handed beaver, which is so thin
> And light, a butterfly's wings put to 't would make it
> A Mercury's flying hat, and soar aloft.

And Edgeworth, in the same play:

See him steal pears in exchange for his beaver hat and his cloak, thus.

Gay afterward wrote:

> The Broker here his spacious beaver wears;
> Upon his brow sit jealousies and cares.*

---

* " Trivia."

A list of clothing for Prince Henry, eldest son of James I., in a bill rendered by Alexander Wilson, tailor, September 28, 1607, contains "a side hunting coat camblett wrought alle thicke with silke galowne in 2 together [double ?] with a whoode [hood] of same camblett," etc. Also, "Beavers of divers colours, lined with satin or taffeta," at sixty shillings each, and "new dying and lining three beavers with taffeta or sateen," five shillings.* Plumes on the broad hat came in at the end of the sixteenth century, and continued to the time of Queen Anne. The Spanish Dons on the streets of London were familiar figures in their flat-crowned hats and short cloaks, taking snuff prodigiously and smelling of garlic. Plain broad-brim hats of shovel shape were worn a good deal in the country and by poorer Londoners for many years after this, when the cocked hat had begun its long and eventful reign. Samuel Pepys, to whose invaluable diary we must often turn, tells us, under date of November 30, 1663: "Put on my new beaver"; and the next year he says: "Caught cold by flinging off my hat at dinner." In a note to this passage in Lord Clarendon's "Essay on Decay of Respect due to Old Age," the author says that in his younger days he never kept his hat on before his elders "except at dinner"! This custom lasted into the next century. Pepys says again (February 22, 1666-7): "All of us to Sir W. Pen's house, where some other company. It is instead of a wedding dinner for his daughter. . . . We had favors given us all, and we put them in our hats, I against my will, but that my Lord [Brouncker] and the rest did." This was doubt-

---

* Archæologia. Vol. XXIV. 1793.

less at table. Planché says that the absence of hats in the print of the banquet for Charles II. can only be accounted for by the presence of the sovereign.

The gentleman of fashion in 1695 wore his hair long under a broad plumed hat. The jeweled sword at his side dangled from an embroidered scarf; enormous coat cuffs concealed his hands, when they were not thrust into a huge muff. The large bordered hat was turned up at three sides, and until 1710 kept the adornment of plumes. After that the cord and ribbon seem to have been adopted.* These flapping brims grew so broad as to necessitate looping up, and hence the origin of the cocked hat, which had a long and honored career. The absence of cocking denoted the sloven.†

"Take out your snuff-box, cock, and look smart, hah," says Carlos, in Cibber's "Love makes a Man." Their numerous shapes are alluded to by Budgell ‡: "I observed afterwards that the variety of Cock in which he moulded his Hat, had not a little contributed to his Impositions upon me." That man was to be guarded against "who had a sly look in his eye, and wore the button of his hat in front." Both sexes wore small looking-glasses. Men even wore them in their hats. In

---

* " Le bas de milan, le castor,
  Orné d'un riche cordon d'or."
  —Quicherat, " Histoire de Costume en France," p. 474.

An early poem, " The Mercer," belonging to the thirteenth century, (Percy Soc., Vol. XXVII., p. 9,) says: " J'ai beax laz à chapeax de fentre." (" I have beautiful lace for beaver hats "). The cable hat-band was introduced about 1599; and in the speech of Fastidio in " Every Man Out of His Humour," we find him saying: "I had a gold cable hat-band, then new come up, of massie goldsmith's work."

† " My mother . . . had rather follow me to the grave than see me tear my clothes, and hang down my head and sneak about with dirty shoes and blotted fingers, hair unpowdered and a hat uncocked." (Rambler, 109.) See also, Ashton, " Social Life in the Reign of Queen Anne," p. 107.

‡ Spectator, 319.

" Cynthia's Revels " we read: " Where is your page?
Call for your casting bottle, and place your mirror in
your hat, as I told you." This, however, was the height
of affectation. Ladies wore mirrors in their girdles,
and on their breasts; and Lovelace says:

> " My lively shade thou ever shalt retaine,
> In thy enclosèd, feather-framèd glasse." *

The cocked hat was universal, and was worn by boys
as well as men—the " tri-corne " of the French. The
varying cocks † were well known; there were, for instance, the " military cock," the " mercantile cock,"
the " Denmark cock "; they were ridiculed occasionally
as the " Egham, Staines and Windsor," from the three-
cornered sign post of that name. During this period
all hats were black, with a gold or silver band.

The London *Chronicle* (Vol. XL, p. 167, for the year
1762) has the following:

Hats are now worn upon an average, six inches and three-
fifths broad in the brim, and cocked between Quaker and Kevenhuller. Some have their hats open before, like a church-spout,
or the tin scales they weigh flower in; some wear them rather
sharper, like the nose of a greyhound; and we can distinguish
by the taste of the hat, the mode of the wearer's mind. There
is the military cock, and the mercantile cock; and while the
beaux of St. James wear their hats under their arms, the beaux
of Morefield 'Mall wear theirs diagonally over the left or right
eye. Sailors wear the sides of their hats uniformly tucked down
to the crown, and look as if they carried a triangular apple-
pasty upon their heads. . . . With Quakers it is a point of their
faith not to wear a button or a loop tight up; their hats spread
over their heads like a pent-house, and darken the outward man,
to signify that they have the inward light.

---

*Thistleton-Dyer, " Domestic Folk Lore," p. 115.

† In the two-cocked hat originated our naval and military cocked hats
of modern uniform.

The " Kevenhuller " would seem to have been an exaggerated form of cock, for one writ-
ing in *The Connoisseur*, in 1754 (No.
36), had said of the women's hats in
that year: " They are more bold and
impudent than the broad-brimmed,
staring *Kevenhullers* worn a few years
ago by the men."

The " Kevenhuller."
(After Hogarth.)

The " Ladie's Advice to A Painter," in the *London
Magazine* for August, 1755, ran thus:

> Painter, once more shew thy art;
> Draw the idol of my heart;
> Draw him as he sports away,
> Softly smiling, sweetly gay;
> Carefully each mode express,
> For man's judgment is his dress.
> Cock his beaver neat and well,
> (Beaver size of cockleshell);
> Cast around a silver cord,
> Glittering like the polish'd sword.
> Let his wig be thin of hairs,
> (Wig that covers half his ears).

Toward the end of the century there were signs of a
change. In 1770 hats became round; in 1772 they rose
behind and fell before, as in the portraits of some of
the old worthies well known. The round hat that again
appeared after 1789, with highish crown and wide
brim, was the ancestor of the top hat of the nineteenth
century. In 1776, the period of the American Revolution, the popular hat in Paris was that " à la Suisse,"
known later as the " Alpine " hat. Parisian anglo-
maniacs preferred the " jockey," small and round.
Then there were hats " à la Hollandais,"and " à la
Quaker," both the latter round in form, with large

brim, usually worn in preference by the more old-
fashioned. The French Revolution put a period to
wigs, and hence also to the " chapeau bras "; for as a
protection these enormous powdered periwigs rendered
hats superfluous, beside the necessity for displaying
what had been come at with such expenditure of time
and money!

> " His pretty black beaver tucked under his arm,
> If placed on his head, might keep it too warm ! "

After the great periwig disappeared, the " tie " wig
followed, and then the " queue " of natural hair, with its
neat ribbon bow, so familiar to us in the portraits of
Washington and the men of the succeeding generation.
The hat again became a necessity rather than a luxury,
and resumed its place on the head. The beaver hat had
a long life of two hundred years. Its weight was doubtless an element in its loss of popularity. For several
years the " filled beaver " (a silk finish on a felt body,
now obsolete), was worn; and by the early nineteenth
century was leaving the cocked hat solely to conservative men of the older generation for full dress.

1810 saw the manufacture of the first all-silk hat.
It did not become popular in Paris, and consequently
anywhere else, until 1830. At that period the soft hat
for purposes of dress was rejected, and the top hat
came, and has never gone. At first it was the " Wel-
lington," with " yeoman " crown; then the "Anglesea,"
with bell-shaped crown; then the D'Orsay, with ribbed
silk binding and large bow on the band.* The American, like the Frenchman, has been largely released from

* Georgiana Hill, " History of English Dress. Vol. II., p. 254.

the dominion of the stiff hat for ordinary occasions; and this freedom is traceable to the influence respectively of the first Mexican war, when we made the acquaintance of the soft and picturesque Spanish hat; the rush of the " '49ers," who were again introduced to it, in California three years later; and the wild enthusiasm that greeted Kossuth when he first came to our shores wearing the " Alpine " hat and feather.* We drew the line at the feather, but his hat is with us still.

Such, briefly, is the history of the worldly hat, during two hundred years of Quakerism. Let us see what the Quaker did with his. The hat worn by Fox and ever since associated in our minds with the Quakers, was that of the cavalier, without the feather, worn less jauntily, but still the same. William Penn's more familiar figure will occur to us. Now it is easy to perceive that in a community where the people had been accustomed to see their older members retaining the hat much of the time while indoors, and had regarded the rapidly prevailing custom of removing it on entering the house as an affectation of the " smart set," that the moment any notion was suggested of the conscience being involved in the retention of that article, there would be a prompt response. Not only did the Quakers decline to greet their neighbors by doffing the hat, but they were equally stiff in the presence of the sovereign. Swift writes to Stella: " My friend Penn came here—

---

* This hat was much like the Welsh hat still worn, and the Tyrolese steeple hat. There was an old legend on the other side of the mountains, that the Tyrolese were men who wore such high-pointed hats that they could not walk about on the mountains without knocking down the stars. So the Lord God drew down the clouds every night to keep the stars in Heaven! The Spanish hat was somewhat the same. " Upon his head was a hat with a high peak, somewhat of the kind which the Spaniards call *calané*, so much in favor with the bravos of Seville and Madrid." George Borrow, " Romany Rye," p. 34.

Will Penn, the Quaker—at the head of his brethren,
to thank the Duke for his kindness to their people in
Ireland. To see a dozen scoundrels with their hats on,
and the Duke complimenting with his off, was a good
sight enough." *   Charles II. once granted an audience
to the courtly Quaker, William Penn, who, as was his
custom, entered the royal presence with his hat on. The
humorous sovereign quietly laid aside his own, which
occasioned Penn's inquiry, " Friend Charles, why dost
thou remove thy hat ? " " It is the custom," he replied,
" in this place, for one person only to remain covered."

Apropos of Barclay's dictum in the Apology, " It is
not lawful for Christians to kneel or prostrate themselves to any man," an observer of the English who
traveled among them from the Continent in 1698, thus
wrote, noting a slight improvement in the manners of
the stricter Quakers at that date:

Plusieurs d'entre eux, depuis quelques années, s'humanisent
un peu, a l'égard de la salutation; ils n'ôtent pas le chapeau,
Dieu les garde de commetre cet horrible pêche: mais ils com-
mencent à baiser un peu le menton, à faire une espèce de petite
inclination de tête.

Old Tom Brown wrote:

These are more just than the other dissenters, because, as they
pull not off their hats to God, so they pull them not off to men,
whereas, the others shall cringe and bow to any man they may
get sixpence by, but ne'er vail the bonnet to God, by whom they
may get Heaven.†

Fox says:

Moreover, when the Lord sent me into the world, he forbade
me to put off my hat to any, high or low, and I was required to
thee and thou all men and women, without any respect to rich
or poor, great or small. And as I travelled up and down, I was

---

not to bid people Good-morrow or Good-evening, neither might I bow or scrape with my leg to any one; this made the sects and professions rage.

At the Launceston assizes, in 1656, Fox was brought into court wearing his hat, with his companion, Edward Pyot. He says:

We stood a pretty while with our hats on, and all was quiet. I was moved to say, "Peace be amongst you." Judge Glyn, a Welshman, then Chief Justice of England, said to the gaoler, "What be these you have brought here into court?" "Prisoners, my Lord," says he. "Why do you not put off your hats?" said the judge to us. We said nothing. "Put off your hats," said the Judge again. Still we said nothing. Then said the Judge, "The court commands you to put off your hats." Then I queried, "Where did ever any magistrate, king or judge, from Moses to Daniel, command any to put off their hats, when they came before them in their courts, either among the Jews, (the people of God), or the heathen? and if the law of England doth command any such thing, shew me that law, either written or printed." The Judge grew very angry, and said, "I do not carry my law-books on my back." . . . So they took us away, and put us among the thieves. Presently after he said to the gaoler, "Bring them up again." "Come," said he, "where had they hats, from Moses to Daniel? Come, answer me, I have you now." I replied, "Thou mayest read in the third of Daniel, that the three children were cast into the fiery furnace by Nebuchadnezzar's command, with their coats, their hose and their hats on." This plain instance stopped him; so that not having any thing else to the point, he cried again, "Take him away, gaoler."

In October, 1657, at Edinburgh, Fox was obliged to appear before the Royal Council, and upon his entrance into the Council Chamber the doorkeeper removed his hat. "I asked him," says Fox, "why he did so, and who was there, that I might not go in with my hat on? I told him I had been before the Protector with my hat on. But he hung up my hat and had me in before them."

At Basingstoke, which Fox calls " a very rude town," he had a meeting, at the close of which he says: " I was moved to put off my hat and pray to the Lord to open their understandings; upon which they raised a report that I put off my hat to them, and bid them goodnight, which was never in my heart." At Reading, 1658, he adds: " We had much to do with them about our hats, and saying Thou and Thee to them. They turned their profession of patience and moderation into rage and madness; many of them were like distracted men for this hat-honour." At the Exon assizes Friends were fined for not putting off their hats. At Tenby, John-ap-John was imprisoned for wearing his hat in what Fox calls " the steeple-house," which he entered after leaving the meeting which Fox was at the time conducting. Next day, in a conversation with the Governor, Fox says:

I asked him, " Why he cast my friend into prison ? " He said, " For standing with his hat on in the church." I said, " Had not the priest two caps on his head, a black one and a white one? Cut off the brims of the hat, and then my friend would have but one; and the brims of the hat were but to defend him from the weather." " These are frivolous things," said the Governor. " Why, then," said I, " dost thou cast my friend into prison for such frivolous things ? "

In London, before Sir Henry Vane, Friends were finally admitted to court with their hats on, chiefly through the mediation of others.

That so serious results should have followed so apparently innocent a peculiarity as the refusal to remove the hat, or give what the Quakers termed " hat-honor," seems almost incredible to us now. And doubtless there were many in the position of Johnson's " pious

gentleman," who, though " he never entered a church, never passed one without taking off his hat." Robert Barclay sums up the whole matter when he says:

Kneeling, bowing and uncovering of the head is the alone outward signification of our adoration towards God, and therefore it is not lawful to give it unto man. He that kneeleth or prostrateth himself to man, what doeth he more to God? He that boweth and uncovereth his head to the Creature, what hath he reserved to the Creator ? *

It has been the mistake of writers upon costume not only to assert that the shape of the hat has never materially altered among the Quakers, but that they never wore cocked hats at all. That cocked hats accompanied the wigs, and were the usual form of head-dress at one time, even in the minister's gallery, is a perfectly established fact. George Dillwyn, who died in 1820, wears the transition hat, from the cock, to the broad-brim revived and modified. The broad-brim and the cock are the two forms of the Quaker hat. The common sense of the cock early appealed to the practical Quaker mind, and we have many portraits of prominent Quakers in hats of varying cock—Dr. Fothergill, Dr. Lettsom, William Cookworthy in England; and in America, Robert Proud, the Pembertons, Owen Jones, and many others. The Americans were always more strict in dress than the English, largely because his proximity to the continent familiarized the Englishman with more cosmopolitan ideas. However, the kind of cock was vastly important. Hannah Callowhill Penn, William Penn's second wife, in writing to her son Thomas Penn, in London, December, 1717, says:

---

* " Apology." Proposition XV.

I wish thou could have shifted till nearer Spring for a hatt, for I doubt to buy a good one now 'twill be near spoyled before the Hight of summer. . . . However, consider and act for the best Husbandry, and then please thyselfe; but be sure wch. ever 'tis, that 'tis packed up in a very Frd. like way, for the fantastical cocks in thine and thy brother Johne's hats has burthened my Spiritt much, and Indeed more than most of your Dress besides; therefore, as thou Vallues my Comfort, Regulate it more for the future. I have a Multitude of Toyls and Cares, but they would be greatly Mitigated if I may but behold thee and thy Brother, persuing hard after Vertue and leaving as behind your backs the Toyish allurements and snares of this uncertain world.*

In spite of himself, the Quaker was carried along on the tide of fashion; indeed, he might to this day be

Owen Jones.
Colonial Treasurer of Penna.
Nat. 1711.   Obiit 1793.
Ae. 82.

wearing his heavy beaver hat, had it not, like the mammoth, become extinct! Certain of the " plainer sort " (not in the sense in which George Fox used the term, but meaning the more strict in guise) for many years refused to dye the beaver of their hats. The last white beaver hat did not disappear from Philadelphia until 1876, when what we know as the modern

silk hat appeared.† A modification of it was adopted by the cosmopolitan Quaker, and has ever since been retained. To the initiated, however, the silk hat goes a long way to mark the man; and the decree of King Edward VII. in favor of that adornment, keeps it *de rigueur* in England

---

* Howard M. Jenkins, " The Family of William Penn," p. 99.

† John Hetherington wore the first silk top hat on the Strand, in London, in 1797. The style was his own invention, and he was mobbed in consequence.

Four Old-Time Pennsylvania Workhouse

John Pemberton, 1727-1795
Henry Drinker, 1734-1809 sense   which
James Pemberton, 1724-1809 the term, but
John Parrish, 1730-1807 in use)

JOHN PEMBERTON.

HENRY DRINKER.

JAMES PEMBERTON.

JOHN PARRISH.

and America. As the silk hat of the cabinet minister is not the mercantile silk hat, nor yet that of
the cleric, so the Quaker hat also retains its individuality; and in its shiny perfection and its amplitude
of dimensions, when mounted above the occasional
straight coat collar, more nearly resembles the dress
of the American Roman Catholic priest than any other.
The modern young Quaker has now freed himself
from the conventions of the early nineteenth century, and is often ignorant of the true reasons for the
peculiarities of his forefathers. When the court gallants of James II. lowered their crowns and widened

Puritan.   1653.

their brims, the Puritans kept their crowns high.
Charles II. escaped in a " very greasy old grey steeple-
crowned hat, with the brim turned up, without lining
or hat-band." The high-crowned hat was beginning to
be old-fashioned before his time; hence its choice as a
means of disguise. So tall a hat had had its inconveniences, as we read: " I pray, what were our sugar-loofe
hats, so mightily affected of late, both by men and
women, so incommodious for us, that every puffe of
winde deprived us of them, requiring the employment

of one hand to keep them on." * The tall hat came to America on our Pilgrim Fathers, where its shape underwent a slight alteration. The brim became more narrow, and the top rather less pointed. Difficulty in finishing the beaver quite so finely also left the fur more fluffy. We are told that this hat lasted in New England until the time came for Benjamin Franklin to go to France, when, as we know, he went to Paris in a New England chimney-pot hat. This was at once adopted by the ardent Parisians, who almost worshiped the American envoy, as " anti-English," the symbol of Liberty, etc. For some years the French had a monopoly of it; then it came to England, and eventually to America again, transformed and modified into the modern top hat. It may be noted that the Quakers adopted the court style of James II., and not the Puritan hat, when they first wore the beaver, illustrating in the hat, as has elsewhere been shown in their long hair, the loyalty to the crown that was a part of their conservatism. One of these early Quaker hats, once the property of Reuben Macy, may now be seen in the museum at Nantucket, Massachusetts.†

The attitude of the Quakers at once led to endless controversies, whose repetition here is unnecessary.

---

* Bulwer, " Artificial Changeling." Quoted by Repton, in Archæologia. Vol. XXIV., p. 181.

† A French Canadian Journal of recent date (Montreal " Presse," ed. hebdomadaire, May 18th, 1899), thus describes with mild surprise and courteously expressed admiration, a nineteenth century Friend who has retained the plain garb of the latest form evolved. He is called " un ministre Quaker," " d'une taille gigantesque." " Pour ne parler que de sa coiffure, disons de suite qu'il portait un chapeau de castor de dix-huit pouces de hauteur avec des bords droits d'égales dimensions. . . . Il ne parle qu'à la seconde personne, et n'ôte son fameux couvre-chef que *pour dormir !* En dehors de sa toquade réligieuse, dont il vous entretient a l'exclusion de tout autre sujet, c'est un gentilhomme d'une intelligence remarquable."

Much literature appeared on the subject, which furnished a fruitful source to the writer of satirical tracts. Such things were published as " Wickham Wakened: or The Quakers Madrigal, in Rime Dogrell," beginning:

> The Quaker and his brats
> Are born with their hats,
> Which a point with two Taggs
> Ties fast to their Craggs.*

Certain Friends warned their members that the removal of the hat was a dangerous formality. During worship, however, Fox had given instructions that the

Nantucket Beaver Hat.

head should be uncovered at time of prayer, and Friends should either reverently kneel, as among the Episcopalians, or stand, as did the Presbyterians. The latter custom eventually became adopted.

The " Canons and Institutions " of Fox, in Article Seventh, condemn " those who wear their Hattes when

---

* By Martin Llewellyn, of Christ Church, Oxford.

Friends pray." Fox was originally in the habit of attending the Church of England. When welcome doctrine was expounded, he removed his hat; if, however, the preacher uttered unwelcome sentiments, he solemnly put it on as a protest; and if the matter continued to offend him, he rose and silently left. It was for purposes of habitual protest that Quakers first learned to sit in places of worship with their hats on. The protest was a decorous and inoffensive one, compared with much of the rough dealing then prevalent. There was no proper attitude of reverence in the London churches up to, and during the time of Queen Anne; lolling, rising, or sitting at will being the rule, even among the Episcopalians.* The Presbyterian minister's example in the pulpit was so far followed, that often in country neighborhoods, one might see the louts of the congregation fling on their hats in sermon time. In Scotland, in 1740, a traveler condemns "a custom which I see is getting pretty general among the lower sort, of cocking on the hat when the sermon began." William Mucklow, who, in his "Spirit of the Hat," had said that "the removal of the hat in worship and during prayer is the beginning of a formal worship," was eventually "recovered to a better mind," and brought to agree with Fox and to be more in charity with Friends. George Whitehead says,† "All preaching cannot be that entire and peculiar prophesying, which, when one is immediately called to, I grant it is most seemly to stand up with the hat off." Some others beside the Independents preached with the hat on. Lady Montague

---

* See Spectator, *No.* 455, and Tatler, *No.* 241.
† "The Apostate Incendiary Rebuked," p. 30.

wrote from Nimeguen, in the Netherlands, in 1716 [Letters]: " I was yesterday at the French church, and stared very much at the manner of the service. The parson clapped on a broad brimmed hat in the first place, which gave him the air of What d'ye call him, in Bartholomew Fair." Up to the middle of the eighteenth century, the hat was a prominent object in their pulpits. At a parish in Clydesdale (Scotland), the patron said to a new candidate for the incumbency, " Sir, there are two nails in the pulpit, on one of which the late worthy minister used to hang his hat. If you put your hat on the right one, it will please; none of the others have hit upon it." He did so, and got the place !* The clergy in the earliest days in England had worn woollen caps, which in some form long prevailed. The Scotch minister of 1700 was not so different from his congregation in dress as one hundred years later, when an official clerical uniform had been evolved and received general recognition. The cleric of the earlier date wore gray homespun, like his next neighbor, with a colored cravat; while in 1800, he appeared on Edinburgh streets, wearing a brown wig, or possibly powdered hair in a pigtail, a cocked hat, black single-breasted coat, frills and ruffles, knee-breeches and silver-buckled shoes, and bore himself with a general air of dignity that his predecessor would have regarded as savoring of worldliness to the last degree. Culture and religion, in those early days in Scotland, could never go hand in hand.

Martin Mason, of Lincoln, who was one of John Perot's schism in regard to taking off the hat in time

---

* H. G. Graham, " Social Life in Scotland in the Eighteenth Century." Vol. II., p. 104.

of prayer,* and who wrote verses to the memory of
Perot, says, in a letter to a friend, "What matter
whether Hat on or Hat off, so long as the Heart is
right?" †

The majesty of the law demanded recognition in the
removal of the hat; and it was in the courts that Friends
suffered most severely because they could not conscien-
tiously observe the conventionalities. The famous case
of William Penn and William Meade, the son-in-law of
Margaret Fox, may be cited as an early instance. After
their discharge by the jury at the trial, September 1-5,
1670, they were re-committed to Newgate in default
of payment of fines for "contempt of court" in declining to remove their hats during the trial. Admiral
Penn paid their fines two days later, without their
knowledge, and they were released. Thousands of
similar cases are to be found in England. The feeling
was the same in New England. But the presence of
Penn at the head of the administration of affairs in
Pennsylvania gave the Quakers in that colony a distinct
advantage in regard to some of their scruples. After
his death, the traditions of his proprietaryship are well
exemplified in the following petition and the resulting
order of the Chancellor. Sir William Keith, who filled
that office, instituted in 1720 a Court of Chancery,
and it was before that court that the eminent Chief Justice Kinsey appeared with his hat on. John Kinsey
was prominent both as lawyer and Quaker, and when he

---

* Ellwood refers to Perot's "peculiar error of keeping on the Hatte
in Time of Prayer, as well publick as private, unless they had an immediate motion at that time to put it off."

† Joseph Smith, Catalogue of Friends' Books. Vol. II., p. 153. See
also, by Richard Richardson, of London, "Of adoration in general, & in
particular, of Hat-Honour—their rise, etc." 8vo, 1680.

followed the usual custom of his sect in retaining his hat, the President promptly ordered it taken off, which was accordingly done.* This arbitrary proceeding called forth

The humble address of the people called Quakers, by appointment of their Quarterly Meeting, held in Philadelphia, for the city and county, 2nd. of second month, 1725,—

May it please the Governor: Having maturely considered the inconveniences and hardships which, we are apprehensive, all those of our community may be laid under who shall be obliged or required to attend the respective courts of judicature in this province, if they may not be admitted without first having their hats taken off from their heads by an officer, as we understand was the case of our friend John Kinsey, when the Governor was pleased to command his to be taken off, before he could be admitted to speak in a case depending in a Court of Chancery, after that he had declared that he could not, for conscience, comply with the Governor's order to himself to the same purpose; which, being altogether new and unprecedented in this province, was the more surprising to the spectators, and as we conceive (however slight some may account it) has a tendency to the subversion of our religious liberties.

This province, with the powers of government, was granted by King Charles the Second to our proprietor, who, at the time of the said grant, was known to dissent from the national way of worship in divers points, and particularly in that of outward behavior, of refusing to pay unto man the honors that he, with all others of the same profession, believe only to be due to the Supreme Being; and they have, on occasions, supported their testimony, so far as to be frequently subjected to the insults of such as require that homage.

That the principal part of those who accompanied our said proprietor in his first settlement of this colony with others of the same profession, who have since retired into it, justly conceived that by virtue of said powers granted to our proprietor, they should have a free and unquestioned right to the exercise of their religious principles, and their persuasion in the aforementioned points and all others, by which they were distinguished from those of all other professions. And it seems

---

* Proud. Vol. II., p. 197.

not unreasonable to conceive an indulgence intended by the crown, in graciously leaving the government to him and them in such manner as may best suit their circumstances which appears to have been an early care in the first legislators, by several acts, as that of Liberty of Conscience, and more particularly by a law of the province, passed in the thirteenth year of King William, Chapter xcii, now in force. It is provided, " That in all courts, all persons, of all persuasions, may freely appear in their own way, and according to their own manner, and there personally plead their own cause, or, if unable, by their friends," which provision appears to be directly intended to guard against all exceptions to any person appearing in their own way, as our friend at the aforesaid court.

Now, though no people can be more ready and willing, in all things essential, to pay due regard to superiors, and honor the courts of justice, and those who administer them, yet, in such points as interfere with our conscientious persuasion, we have openly and firmly borne our testimony in all countries and places where our lot has fallen.

We must therefore, crave leave to hope, from the reasons here humbly offered, that the Governor, when he fully considers them, will be of opinion with us, that we may justly and modestly claim it as a right, that we and our friends should, at all times, be excused in the government from any compliances against our conscientious persuasions; and humbly request that he would, in future, account it so to us, thy assured, well-wishing friends.

Signed by appointment of the said meeting,

John Goodson,	Samuel Preston,	Morris Morris,
Rowland Ellis,	William Hudson,	Anthony Morris,
Reece Thomas,	Richard Hill, ˙	Evan Evans.
Richard Hayes,		

On consideration had of the humble address presented, this day read in open court, from the Quarterly Meeting of the people called Quakers for the city and county of Philadelphia; it is ordered, that the address be filed with the Register, and that it be made a standing rule of the Court of Chancery for the Province of Pennsylvania for all time to come, that any practitioner of the law, or other officer or person, whatsoever, professing himself to be one of the people called Quakers, may, and shall be admitted, if they so think fit, to speak or otherwise officiate or apply themselves decently unto the said court without being obliged to observe the usual ceremony of uncovering their heads, by having their hats taken off. And such privilege, hereby ordered and granted to the people called Quakers, shall at no time hereafter be understood or interpreted as any contempt or neglect of said Court; and shall be taken only as an act of conscientious liberty, of right appertaining to the religious persuasion of the said people, and agreeable to their practice in all civil affairs of life.

BY SIR WILLIAM KEITH, Chancellor.*

The refusal of Fox and his contemporaries to remove their hats before Justices, etc., had not been a new thing in England. In Bishop Aylmer's time "there were a sort of people who counted it idolatry to pull off their hat or give reverence, even to princes." † These were probably a sect of the Anabaptists. Aylmer was Bishop of London between 1578 and 1594. The German Baptists refused the customary greetings.

This method of protest had been in use among other dissenters also, as the following instance from New England will serve to illustrate:

William Witter, of Lynn, Massachusetts, was an aged Baptist, who had already been prosecuted by the Puritans; but in 1651, being blind and infirm, he asked the Newport church to send some of the brethren to him, to administer the communion, for he found himself alone in Massachusetts. Accordingly, John Clark (the pastor) undertook the mission, accompanied by Obadiah Holmes and John Crandall.

They reached Lynn on Saturday, July 19, 1651, and on Sunday staid within doors, in order not to disturb the congregation. A few friends were present, and Clark was in the midst of a sermon, when the house was entered by two constables with a warrant signed by Robert Bridges, commanding them to arrest certain "erroneous persons being strangers." The travellers were at once seized and carried to the tavern, and after dinner they were told that they must go to church. . . . The unfortunate

---

* Michener, "Retrospect of Early Quakerism," p. 368.

† Robert Barclay, "Inner Life of the Religious Societies of the Commonwealth," p. 501.

Baptists remonstrated, saying that were they forced into the meeting house, they should be obliged to dissent from the service, but this the constable said, was nothing to him, and so he carried them away. On entering, during the prayer, the prisoners took off their hats, but presently put them on again and began reading in their seats. Whereupon Bridges ordered the officers to uncover their heads, which was done, and the service was then quietly finished. When all was over, Clark asked leave to speak, which, after some hesitation, was granted, on condition he would not discuss what he had heard. He began to explain how he had put on his hat because he could not judge that they were gathered according to the visible order of the Lord; but here he was silenced, and the three committed to custody for the night.*

After a violent struggle, the ministers under John Norton's lead succeeded, on the 19th of October, 1658, in forcing the capital act through the Legislature, which contained a clause making the denial of reverence to Superiors, or in other words, wearing the hat, evidence of Quakerism.†

This was at the time of the famous trial of the Southwicks.

We are told of four Quakers, who, on the 27th of Eighth month, 1658, at Boston, were brought before the General Court. They were Samuel Shattuck, N. Phelps, Joshua Buffum, and Ann Needham. George Bishop's account of their case as he addressed that Court is as follows:

They answered that they intended no Offense to you in coming thither (for they must come to you in their clothes, if they come decently, of which the hat is part) for it was not their Manner to have to do with Courts. And as for withdrawing from the Meetings, or keeping on their Hats, or doing anything in Contempt of them or their Laws, they said, the Lord was their Witness (as he is) that they did it not. So ye rose up and bid the Jaylor take them away.‡

The Puritan minister, John Wilson, at the hanging of the

---

* Brooks Adams, "The Emancipation of Massachusetts," p. 111.
† Ibid., p. 170.
‡ George Bishop, "New England Judged," p. 85.

Quaker, William Robinson, on Boston Common, in 1659, said to the Quakers present, "Shall such Jacks as you come in before Authority with your Hats on ?" To which Robinson replied, "Mind you, mind you, it is for not putting off the Hat we are put to Death.*

Later on, the usual fine for keeping on the hat seems to have been twenty shillings.

The long hair of the Quakers was an offence to the Puritans of Massachusetts, as well as to those on the other side of the Atlantic. Edward Wharton was a "turbulent Quaker," whose persecutions were related by George Bishop,† in reply to his inquiry of the Boston judges:

"Wherefore have I been fetch'd from my Habitation, where I was following my honest Calling, and here laid up as an Evil-Doer ?" "Your Hair is too long (reply'd you), and you are disobedient to that Commandment which saith, 'Honour thy Father and Mother.'" To which said Edward, "Wherein ?" "In that you will not put off your Hat, (said you) before the Magistrates."

The same Wharton, with four other Quakers, was brought before the General Court, Boston, 3 mo., 1665.

Their hats, (the great offence), were commanded to be taken off, and thrown on the Ground; which, being done, Mary Tomkins set her foot upon one of the Hats, and calling to you said, "See, I have your Honour under my Feet." Whereupon you demanded of her where her habitation was? She answered, "My Habitation is in the Lord." ‡

A feeling of irritation is hardly to be wondered at on the part of any judge who got no more direct reply from a prisoner than that of Mary Tomkins. But this was a trifling matter; for to bluff and confound the Jus-

---

* George Bishop, " New England Judged," p. 124.
  † Ibid., p. 304. See also Brooks Adams, " The Emancipation of Massachusetts," p. 151.
  ‡ Ibid., p. 460.

tice was the proper method employed by all men in the
English Courts of Law in that day, when literature
shared in the involved style of intercourse and address,
then universal. "Turbulent" was a term applied to
these early Quakers by their contemporaries, and, indeed, by some of those contemporaries' descendants,
who inherit still the old persecuting spirit.

Thomas Ellwood in 1660, when, as a youth, he was
undergoing much for the sake of his hat, gives us a
description of his costume that is most interesting to us
now. He says:

While I was in London, I went to a little meeting of Friends,
which was then held in the House of one Humphrey Bache, a
Goldsmith, at the Sign of the Snail, in Tower Street. It was
then a very troublesome time, not from the Government, but
from the Rabble of Boys and Rude People, who, upon the turn
of the Times, (upon the return of the King) took Liberty to be
very abusive.

When the Meeting ended, a pretty Number of these unruly
Folk were got together at the Door, ready to receive the Friends
as they came forth not only with evil Words, but with Blows.
. . . But quite contrary to my Expectation, when I came out,
they said one to another, "Let him alone; don't meddle with
him; he is no Quaker, I'll warrant you."

I was troubled to think what the Matter was, or what these
rude People saw in me, that made them not take me for a
Quaker. And upon a close examination of myself, with respect
to my Habit and Deportment, I could not find anything to place
it on, but that I had then on my Head a large Mountier Cap of
black Velvet, the Skirt of which being turned up in Folds, looked
(it seems), somewhat above the common Garb of a Quaker; and
this put me out of Conceit of my Cap.

Not long after this he writes:

When a young Priest, who, as I understood, was Chaplain in (a certain) family, took upon him pragmatically to reprove me for standing with my Hat on before the Magistrates,
and snatch'd my Cap from off my Head, Knowles (the Deputy-

Lieutenant) in a pleasant manner corrected him, telling him he mistook himself in taking a Cap for a Hat (for mine was a Mountier-Cap) and bid him give it me again; which he (though unwillingly) doing, I forthwith put it on my Head again, and thenceforward none meddled with me about it.

Again, he adds:

I had in my hand a little Walking-Stick with a Head on it. which he took out of my Hand to look on it; but I saw his Intention was to search it, whether it had a Tuck in it [sword] for he tried to have drawn the Head; but when he found it was Fast, he returned it to me.

The violent antipathy of Thomas Ellwood's father to any Quaker who refused to remove his hat in his presence, caused his son many painful scenes with the worthy squire, and an alienation that was a grief to both. One of these occasions is thus described by Ellwood:

The sight of my hat upon my head . . . (made) . . . his passion of grief turn to anger; he could not contain himself; but running upon me with both hands, first violently snatcht off my Hat and threw it away; and then giving me some buffets on the head he said, "Sirrah, get you up to your chamber." . . . I had now lost one of my hats, and I had but one more. That therefore, I put on, but did not keep it long; for the next Time my Father saw it on my Head, he tore it violently from me, and laid it up with the other, I knew not where. Wherefore I put on my Mountier-Cap, which was all I had left to wear on my head, and it was but a very little while that I had that to wear, for as soon as my Father came where I was, I lost that also. And now I was forced to go bareheaded wherever I had Occasion to go, within Doors and without.* . . .

The day that I came home I did not see my Father, nor until noon the next Day, when I went into the Parlour where he was, to take my usual Place at Dinner. As soon as I came in, I observed by my Father's Countenance, that my Hat was still an Offence to him; but when I was sitten down, and before I had

---

* " The History of the Life of Thomas Ellwood," by Himself; pp. 50–2, 3d ed. 1765.

eaten anything, he made me understand it more fully, by saying to me, but in a milder Tone than he had formerly used to
speak to me in, " If you cannot content yourself to come to Dinner without your Hive upon your Head [so he called my Hat],
pray rise and go take your Dinner some where else." Upon
those words, I arose from the Table, and leaving the Room, went
into the Kitchen, where I staid till the Servants went to Dinner, and then sate down very contentedly with them. . . . And
from this time he rather chose, as I thought, to avoid seeing me,
than to renew the Quarrel about the Hat.*

It appears that many wore caps and other varieties
of head dress at first among the Friends, for the broad-
brim was only just becoming sufficiently popular to be
safely adopted by them without any risk of seeming
too much in the mode.   Moreover, they were all too
much engaged in preaching and in ministering to their
brethren who were in suffering from present or past
imprisonments, to devote much time to dress, and each
wore what best suited his purse and convenience.   This
is fully demonstrated in a charming little incident related by Ellwood, who met the great young missionary,
Edward Burrough, on his way to Oxford.   Burrough
was one of the early Quaker martyrs, dying in a foul
prison at the age of twenty-eight.

When I was come within a mile or so of the city (Oxford),
whom should I meet upon the way, coming from thence, but Edward Burrough! I rode in a Mountier (montero) cap (a dress
more used then than now), and so did he; and because the
weather was exceeding sharp, we both had drawn our caps down,
to shelter our Faces from the Cold, and by that means neither
of us knew the other, but passed by without taking notice one
of the other till a few Days after, meeting again, and observing each other's dress, we recollected where we had so lately
met.†

---

* "The History of the Life of Thomas Ellwood," by Himself; p. 68.
† Ibid., p. 31.

This was in the year 1659. The Century Dictionary defines a montero cap as derived from the Spanish " Montero, a hunter," and describes it as " a horseman's or huntsman's cap, having a round crown with flaps which could be drawn down over the sides of the face." *

But the cap, as time went on, had to be given up, for it was not very long before the broad-brim became unfashionable, and then it grew to be the distinctive mark of the Quaker. His following was so large that the hat became the badge of Quakerism wherever he went.

Thomas Story, the famous Quaker traveler and preacher, who became a member of Penn's Council of State, Master of the Rolls, and Commissioner of Claims in Pennsylvania, describes graphically in his Journal the sufferings he endured as a young man on the subject of the hat; his treatment by his father was quite similar to that of Penn and Ellwood. All three were brought up as refined young men, carefully instructed by solicitous parents in all the airs and graces of polite society when it demanded far more formality and elaboration of manner than these busy, telephonic times will now permit their descendants. He tells us that in 1691 he was invited to meet some gentlemen at a tavern, and says:

I was not hasty to go, looking for the Countenance of the Lord therein, neither did I refuse; but my Father & some others, being impatient to have me among them, came likewise to me. I arose from my seat when they came in, but did not move my

---

* " His hat was like a Helmet, or Spanish *Montero,*" (Bacon). Evelyn's " Tyrannas" calls the Montero " light and serviceable when the sun is hot, and at other times ornamental."

Hat to them as they to me. Upon which my Father fell a weep-
ing and said, I did not use to behave so to him. I intreated
him not to resent it as a Fault, for Tho' I now thought fit to
decline that Ceremony, it was not in Disobedience, or Disrespect
to him or them; for I honoured him as much as ever, and desired he would please to think so, notwithstanding exterior
Alteration.*

Of course it is possible to multiply indefinitely incidents that show the struggles of the spirit in terms of
the hat. This affected even political questions, as well
as those social and religious; yet no more innocent body
of people ever walked the earth than they under the
broad-brims. In 1801 Richard Jordan, a well-known
American minister of the Society, was traveling on the
Continent with Abraham Barker, a Friend from New
Bedford, Massachusetts, and the party arrived in Paris.
Richard Jordan mentions the following incident in his
Journal:

It may not perhaps be amiss to mention how we were treated
at the municipality, where we attended to present our passports.
We were stopped by the guards, who had strict orders, it seems,
not to suffer any man to pass unless he had what is called a
cockade in his hat, but on our desiring our guide to step forward and inform the Officers that we were of the people called
Quakers, and that our not observing those signs of the times
was not in contempt of authority, or disrespect to any office,
but from a religious scruple in our minds,—it being the same
with us in our own country—they readily accepted our reasons;
and one of the officers came and took us by the guards, and so
up into the chamber, where we were suffered to remain quietly
with our hats on, until our passports were examined by two
officers, and again endorsed under the seal of the republic, permitting us to go to Calvisson, in Languedoc. Thus it often appears to me that we make our way better in the minds of the

---

*Thomas Story, Journal, p. 40. (Folio ed.)

people when we keep strictly to our religious profession, in all countries and among all sorts of persons.*

Joseph John Gurney relates his own experience upon the first occasion that his Quakerism affected his hat. The step was very marked for one who had not previously been a pronounced Friend, and ، who was so much in the midst of worldly interests as were all the Gurneys.   He says:

I was engaged long beforehand to a dinner party. For three weeks before I was in agitation from the knowledge that I must enter the drawing-room with my hat on. From this sacrifice, strange and unaccountable as it may seem, I could not escape. In a Friend's attire and with my hat on, I entered the drawing-room at the dreaded moment, shook hands with the mistress of the house, went back into the hall, deposited my hat, and returned home in some degree of peace. I had afterward the same thing to do at the Bishop's. The result was that I found myself a decided Quaker, was perfectly understood to have assumed that character, and to dinner parties, except in the family circle, I was asked no more.

This was in 1810, when the Quaker " testimony " had become but an eccentricity to the world, which chose to laugh rather than make it a cause for persecution.   Samuel Gurney and his brother Joseph John possessed in a remarkable degree the physical beauty that so distinguished the family, and the black velvet cap worn in later life by the latter over his beautiful hair, then growing gray, gave him the air of a fine old Roman Catholic Archbishop.

It was no easy matter for the Quakers at any period thus to mortify the flesh, and Barclay says for himself and all his brethren:

---

*Richard Jordan, Journal, p. 106.

This I can say boldly in the sight of God, from my own experience & that of many thousands more, that however small or foolish this may seem, yet we behooved to suffer death rather than do it, [i.e., remove the hat] and that *for conscience' sake;* and that, in its being so contrary to our natural spirits, there are many of us to whom the forsaking of these bowings and ceremonies was as death itself; which we could never have left if we could have enjoyed our peace with God in the use of them.

Royalist Hat, time of Commonwealth.
(After Martin.)

CHAPTER III.

BEARDS, WIGS AND BANDS.

Now a beard is a thing that commands in a King
  Be his sceptres never so fair ;
Where the beard bears the sway, the people obey,
  And are subject to a hair.
     .   .   .   .
Now of the beards there be such a company,
  And fashions such a throng,
That it is very hard to handle a beard,
  Tho' it be never so long.

Ballad of the Beard, Temp. Ch. I.

CHAPTER III.

BEARS, WIGS AND BANDS.

IT happened that Quaker customs began to crystallize at a time when smooth faces were universal; and to this accident is due their later "testimony" against beards, which would have been quite as strong against the practice of shaving off a natural adornment had the sect arisen a century earlier. It was noted by the early historian Sewel, as one of John Perot's "extravagant steps," that he had allowed his beard to grow! Portraits of James Nayler, the "Apostate," show him in a full pointed beard; and there are also prints of the early Quaker preachers with flowing beards, but they are conspicuous exceptions. The full beard of Henry IV. had by 1628 become the pointed beard. Quicherat states as the origin of the smooth face the sportive order of Louis XIII. to his courtiers to cut off all the beard, leaving only a small tuft on the chin.* The Russians were conspicuous exceptions to this fashion; and Evelyn, under date 24 October, 1681, writes of the Russian Ambassador at the court of St. James: " 'Twas reported of him he condemned his sonn to lose his head

---

* The following verse celebrates this :
"Helas ! Ma pauvre barbe,
Qu'est-ce qui t'a faite ainsi ?
C'est le grand roy Louis,
Treizième de se nom,
Qui toute a ésbarbé sa maison."

for shaving off his beard and putting himselfe in ye French fashion at Paris, and that he would have executed it had not the French King interceded."

The beard disappeared when the ruff went out, and smooth faces are associated with the time of the early Quakers, and the reign of the Stuarts. The moustache was not then fashionable, hence that military appendage did not have occasion to meet the disapproval of the Quakers until long after; and I have nowhere found any notice taken of the moustache in any meeting so far. Early in the present century an English fashion book remarks: "Young bucks have mounted the 'Jewish mustachio' on the upper lip." Parton says: "It is hard to believe in the soundness of a person's judgment who turns his collar down, when every one turns it up, or who allows his hair to grow long, when the rest of mankind wear theirs short." * Even more attention has been paid to the morality, so to speak, of the hair, than to that of the beard. Political opinions expressed themselves with the revolutionary party in England in the short hair of the Roundheads. The Puritans, therefore, are to be found with short locks, making religious capital out of what were really their political sympathies. The early Quakers, always conservative, and never, like the Irish, "agin the Government," wore the long hair of the Royalists (as did the French) for some years for fear of resemblance to the rebels. A notice published in 1698 mentions a delinquent Quaker "wearing his own hair straight and lank." The Germans wore unkempt beards and moustaches. The clergy, like the Quakers,

---

* James Parton, "The Clothes Mania."

have always been rigid in their ideas of dress, and even in the time of Stephen did not wear long hair or beards. Wigs, also, which appeared for a short time then, were later condemned, along with flowing locks. By 1487 they were wearing long beards, as in earlier times, but they were condemned for wearing long hair, and charged to cut it " short enough to show the ears." Carefully curled and powdered hair was the forerunner of the periwig. The clergy held out longest against adopting it, and were the last to discard it, except professors of the law. The first cleric to wear an official wig was Archbishop Tillotson, in the reign of James II. Once introduced, the wig was worn until the time of the French Revolution, just before which a fine wig cost thirty to forty guineas. Bishop Blomfield first set the example of wearing his own hair. Archbishop Sumner wore a wig so late as 1858, at the wedding of the Princess Royal. The church has now discarded the wig entirely, while the law is the only profession that retains it. The Speaker of the House of Commons is most imposing in a full-bottomed wig, while short wigs are worn by judges and barristers. The court coachmen and some of the servants of the nobility still wear the wig as a part of the livery.

King Charles the Second, lax as he was in his own person and costume, and wearing perhaps the heaviest periwig in the realm, had, nevertheless, certain notions of what was befitting the clergy. We read:

A letter was written by [him] to the University of Cambridge, forbidding its members to wear periwigs, smoke tobacco, or read their sermons; and when he was at *Newmarket, Nathaniel Vincent, Doctor of Divinity, Fellow of Clare Hall, and Chaplain to his Majesty, preached before him in a long periwig and Holland sleeves, according to the fashion in use among gentlemen at that time. This foppery displeased the King, who commanded the Duke of Monmouth, then Chancellor of the University, to cause the statutes concerning decency of apparel to be put in execution, which was accordingly done.*

Thomas Story, the well-known Quaker preacher and traveler, relates † the following that was told him of Peter the Great, after that monarch had attended a Meeting of the Quakers at Friedrichstadt (Holstein) in 1712. The Czar was at one time attending a meeting held in a Dutch market place:

Being rainy Weather, when they were at it, the Czar wearing his own Hair, pulled off the great Wigg from one of his Dukes, and put it on himself, to Cover him from the Rain, making the owner stand bareheaded the while, for it seems he is so absolute, that there must be no grumbling at what he does, Life and Estate being wholly at his Discretion.

The portraits of George Fox show him with long locks, reaching to the shoulder, but he never wore a wig; while on the contrary, William Penn wore as many as four in one year. On the subject of his own long hair, Fox speaks occasionally in his Journal. In 1655, when before Major Ceely, during a journey into Cornwall, he says of the Major:

He had with him a silly young priest, who asked us many frivolous questions; amongst the rest, he desired to cut my hair which was then pretty long; but I was not to cut it, though many were offended at it. I told them I had no pride in it, and it was not of my own putting on.

A few months later, at Bristol, when Fox stood in the orchard that seems to have been a favorite meeting place for both Baptists and Quakers, addressing some thousands of people from the great stone that did duty

---

* " The Book of Costume, By A Lady of Quality." London, 1846.
† Thomas Story, Journal, p. 496. (Folio.)

as a pulpit, a certain " rude, jangling Baptist " began to find fault with Fox's long hair; but, he adds, " I said nothing to him." The following year, in Wales (1657), Fox's Journal records:

Next morning one called a Lady sent for me, who kept a preacher in her house, but I found both her and her preacher very light and airy; too light to receive the weighty things, of God. In her lightness she came and asked me, " If she should cut my hair ? " I was moved to reprove her, and bid her cut down the corruptions in herself with the sword of the spirit of God; so after I had admonished her to be more grave and sober, we passed away. Afterward in her frothy mind, she made her boast that she " came up behind me and cut off the curl of my hair "; but she spoke falsely.

The fascinations of the wig proved too much for the other Quakers, however, and it soon became quite general among them, as the records of many old meetings testify. In 1698 periwigs on men and high headdresses on women are condemned. By 1717 so great a declension in plainness of dress had taken place, that a paper on " Pride, Plainness of Dress," etc., was issued by London Quarterly Meeting. This document inveighs against " men's extravagant Wigs and wearing the hair in a beauish manner "; it grants that " modest, decent or necessary (!) " wigs might be allowed; but prevailing modes are condemned. Some of the old Friends, in 1715, mourned, with good reason, we should think, that " some of the young people cut off good heads of hair to put on long extravagant, gay wigs." The periwig—" falbala," or " furbelow," the dress wig of the reign of Queen Anne—was the culmination of the art of dress in the life time of the second generation of Quakers. Ashton tells us that it was the invention of a French courtier to conceal a defect in the shoulders of the Duke of Burgundy. Its use spread all over Europe, and came to America. The true antiquarian holds everything worth preserving merely because it has been preserved. Hence we are blessed with the long list of the Kings' fools of old times, and among them we find that of Saxton, the Court fool of Henry VIII., who is the first person in modern England recorded to have worn a wig. In an account of the Treasurer of the King's Chambers in that reign is the entry: "Paid for Saxton, the King's fool, for a wig, 20s." *

The first official notice to be found of the wig among the early Quakers is in 1691, when London Six Weeks Meeting issued a "testimony" against "those that have imitated the world, whether it be men, in their extravagant periwigs, or modes in their apparel; or whether it be women in their high towering (head) dress, gold chains, or gaudy attire; or whether it be parents, like old Ely, not sufficiently restraining their children therefrom; . . . or whether it be in voluptuous feasting without fear, or costly furnitures, and too rich adorning of houses," etc.†

The "Wigges" may well have been called extravagant. An advertisement of Queen Anne's time, not many years before this, appeared in London, to the effect that on a certain public coach, " Dancing shoes not exceeding four inches in height, *and periwigs not exceeding three feet* (!) *in length,* are carried in the coach box gratis ! " ‡ One of the dangers of London streets in that uncomfortable period of their history has been noticed by the poet Gay:

---

* Walpole, " Anecdotes of Painting " ; 3d ed., Vol. I., p. 135.
† Beck and Ball, " History of London Friends' Meetings," p. 117.
‡ Ashton, " Social Life in the Reign of Queen Anne," p. 109.

You'll sometimes meet a fop of nicest tread,
Whose mantling peruke veils his empty head.

. . . .

Him, like the miller, pass with caution by,
Lest from his shoulder clouds of powder fly.

. . . .

Nor is the flaxen wig with safety worn;
High on the shoulder, in a basket borne,
Lurks the sly boy, whose hand to rapine bred,
Plucks off the curling honors of the head.*

The wearing of wigs among the Quakers must have been much more common than has been supposed, particularly with those somewhat fashionably inclined, if we may judge from the large number of minutes and other papers against that vanity, as well as the many allusions to them in letters of an early date. William Cookworthy and Doctors Fothergill and Lettsom have already been instanced in describing their cocked hats. William Dillwyn, in both America and England, wears a rather smaller wig than theirs.

William Dillwyn.
1805.

The care of the wig was a serious matter, and in every way its use was in direct opposition to Quaker principles of moderation and economy. It is therefore the more striking to discover how uni-

---

* "Trivia." The "Ladies' Answer" to a ballad ridiculing black hats and capuchins (published by Percy Soc., Vol. XXVII., p. 205), thus remonstrated with the men :

"I wonder what these men can mean
To trouble their heads with our capuchins?
Let 'em mind their ruffs and mufetees :
Pray, what harm in our black hats is found,
To make them so much with scandal abound?
Why can they not let the women alone,
When idle fashions they have of their own ?
With ramelie wigs and muffetees."

versally it was worn by the Friends, completely refuting Miss Hill's statement that the Quakers never wore wigs. For a time it was not considered decent or respectable to appear in public without one; and the Quakers were really less conspicuous by yielding to public opinion, than if they had opposed it more strenuously. As in the case of the adoption of pantaloons, the pressure of circumstances was too much for them; although we find them slow to adopt the wig, and, contrary to their usual custom in matters of dress, among the first to discard it. The wig was expensive, demanding a great deal of time and money in its proper care; it was heavy and awkward, and very messy and dirty, particularly when powdered; and the periwig in the hands of a careless person became a positive source of danger. What would a modern Board of Health have said to Pepys' entry in his Diary, under date September 3d, 1665?

Put on my coloured silk suit very fine and my new periwigg, bought a good while since but durst not wear, because the plague was in Westminster when I bought it. It is a wonder what will be the fashion after the plague is done, as to periwiggs, for nobody will dare to buy any haire, for fear of the infection, that it had been cut off of the heads of people dead of the plague.

Foulis, of Ravelston, Scotland, in 1704, pays " for a new long periwig, 7 guineas and a halfe." His dress wig costs " 14, 6s." Scots, or a guinea; a new hat, 7 Scots; a bob-wig, a guinea.* Allan Ramsay, the poet, was a Jack-of-all-trades as well, and among other things, he made wigs and " barberized " customers in his night-cap. A friend of his, who was a Scotch judge, put his wig in a sedan-chair to keep it dry from the

* H. G. Graham, " Social Life in Scotland in the Eighteenth Century."

rain, and himself quietly walked home. The umbrella was still in the future; and a powdered periwig in a hard rain meant a ruined pocket book, and a head weighed down with a load of paste, drying into a mould of plastered hair! Therefore Gay's timely advice:

> When suffocating mists obscure the morn,
> Let thy worst wig, long used to storms be worn;
> This knows the powdered footman, and with care
> Beneath his flapping hat secures his hair.*

The "wigge," however, had come to stay. Through the whole of the eighteenth century it prevailed. The "Ranelagh Tail" was the beginning of the end, so to speak, toward the period of the American Revolution, as is seen in the portraits of some of the English officers of that time; the Americans, like Washington, usually preferring to wear their own hair tied with a ribbon in a knot behind, and occasionally powdered; the fashionable use of powder disappeared about 1794. Napoleon wore his queue and "cadenettes" in the campaign in Italy, sacrificing both in Egypt, where he prided himself on being unique among his Generals, who flattered his fancied resemblance, with short hair, to Titus. The "cadenette" † was worn well over the left ear, to which the gallants attached a large jewel.

---

* "Trivia."

† "Cadenette." So called from Maréchal Cadenet, of France, in the seventeenth century. The Century Dictionary defines it as "a lovelock, or tress of hair worn longer than the others."

> "L'ondoyant et venteux pennache
> Donnant du galbe à ce bravache,
> Un long flocon de poil natte
> En petits anneaux frisottes
> Pris au bout de tresse vermeille
> Descendoit de sa gauche oreille." *

---

* Quoted by Quicherat, "Histoire de Costume en France," p. 475.

This may be seen in the portrait of Charles I. in the Louvre, who wears a large pearl.

The English ladies wore the wig devotedly, probably for the same good reason that moved Mrs. Pepys. Her husband says (March 13, 1665): "My wife began to wear light locks, white almost, which, though it made her look very pretty, yet not being natural, vexes me, that I will not have her wear them." After the Brighton races, the bellman once gave notice to the inhabitants of that place that a lady had lost a wig coming from Broadwater. A reward offered brought no evidence of it. A great while after a bird's nest was discovered in a tree by some boys, who, climbing to seize the treasure, were surprised to find the lost wig, containing a few sticks, and the maker's name intact. We are also told of the discovery of a hedgehog's nest in the lost scratch wig of a toper, who dropped it along the roadside! Thomas Ellwood had his opinion of the women who wore wigs, and did not hesitate to express it in most forcible, if not melodious, strains. The friend of Milton really waxed indignant:

> "Some Women (Oh the Shame!) like ramping Rigs,
> Ride flaunting in their powder'd Perriwigs;
> Astride they sit (and not ashamed neither)
> Drest up like men in Jacket, Cap and Feather!" *

Lady Suffolk (Letters; 1728) says:

Mrs. Berkeley drives herself in a chair in a morning gown, with a white apron, a white handkerchief pinned under her head like a nun, a black silk over that, and another white one over the hat!

Nugent (Travels; 1766) describes the Duchess of Mechlenburg-Schwerin in " a riding-habit, with a bag-

---

* Thos. Ellwood, "Speculum Seculi; or a Looking Glass for the Times."

wig, and a cocked hat and a feather." He several times tells us: "The ladies do wear hats and bag-wigs."

The "Life and Actions of John Everett" (1729-30), tells us that "The Precisions" (as he calls the Quakers), "for the most part, though they are plain in their dress, wear the best of commodities, and though a smart toupie is an abomination, yet a bob or a natural of six or seven guineas' price, is a modest covering allowed of by the saints."

It is probable that the Quakers affected the "bob" wig chiefly. This style of wig was not intended for full dress, and the following instance, mentioned by Swift,* will well illustrate the distinctions in wig-wearing:

As Prince Eugene was going with Mr. Secretary to Court, he told the Secretary that Hoffman, the Emperor's resident, said to his Highness that it was not proper to go to Court without a long wig, and his was only a tied up one. "Now," says the Prince, "I know not what to do, for I never had a long periwig in my life; and I have sent to all my valets and footmen to see whether any of them have one, that I might borrow it, but none of them has any." But the Secretary said it was a thing of no consequence, and only observed by gentlemen ushers.

John Byrom, on the appearance of the President of a Club in a "black bob-wig" wrote:

"A phrensy? or a periwigmanee,
That overruns his pericranie?" †

The father of Stephen Grellet, an officer in the court of Louis XVI., wears a "cauliflower" wig, as shown in his silhouette.

---

* Swift, "Journal to Stella," January 1, 1712.

† Leslie Stephen, "Studies of a Biographer," p. 91.

The American Puritans in the time of Charles I., issued a manifesto against long hair in their colony, calling it " an impious custom and a shameful practice for any man who has the least care for his soul to wear long hair." They enact that it shall be cropped and not worn in churches so that those persons who persist in this custom " shall have both God and man at the same time against them." * The Puritans permitted their people to wear out the clothes they brought with them, after which the sumptuary laws of Massachusetts went into force. These ordered that no slashed clothes were to be worn, but that one slash in each sleeve might be permitted! Beaver hats were prohibited. " Immoderate great shoes " were condemned, and four years later short shoes are also condemned as leading to " the nourishing of pride and exhausting men's estate." In 1651 the Government was solicitous to preserve the distinctions of rank; men must not be too richly dressed, nor wear " points " (ribbons with jeweled ends to tie up the clothing, often very gay) at the knee. Women with an income under two hundred pounds were not to wear silk or tiffany hoods. Long hair was condemned by the Legislature, and by the Grand Jury; while with a curious disregard for consistency, the women were condemned who cut and curled theirs. Evidently the modern prejudice against long-haired men and short-haired women is not so new. Wigs also fell under condemnation, but they prevailed by the end of the seventeenth century, despite the Fathers.

The sumptuary laws of the early Massachusetts col-

---

* See also " Dialogue between Captain Long-Haire and Captain Short-Haire." Brit. Mus. Harleian MSS. Pub. by Percy Soc. Vol. XXVII., p. 170.

onists are much like the orders of the Quakers to their constituency a little later. What must be emphasized all through this study of the Quaker idea of dress is the fact that their attention to plainness, and to all the details of every day life, was a natural reaction from dogmatism, royal prerogative and worldly extravagance. It was by no means a characteristic of the Quakers alone, but was even more pronounced among the Separatists, the Mennonites, and the Puritans; and of the latter body, none were so arbitrary or narrow as those who sought religious freedom in America. This is not the place for large quotations from the laws of the Massachusetts Colony. But it was the temper of the times which led Puritan and Quaker alike, whether in England, Holland or America, to attempt to rule the consciences of the people in minor matters of daily life, and thus to narrow the spiritual outlook of a whole sect. The other bodies threw off these small peculiarities, as the exigencies of the time in New England, for instance, demanded an active participation in the life— political and social—of the growing commonwealth. The Quakers in Pennsylvania, on the contrary, after 1756, the period of their withdrawal from the public arena, no longer participated in the political and social developments of the most rapid period of growth in that colony; they thereby preserved many little peculiarities of their most conservative sect, which peculiarities would necessarily have been rubbed off in contact with men of other minds. This must be borne in mind regarding the Quakers; for the same method of treatment would have preserved Puritan customs to us as interesting religious fossils to the present day.

Wigs were denounced in the Massachusettts legislature as early as 1675. John Eliot said that the wars and disturbances in the Puritan Meeting House were a judgment on the people for wearing wigs; * and he reluctantly acknowledged that " the lust for wigs is become insuperable! " We know that John Wilson and Cotton Mather wore them. A young woman of Rhode Island, named Hetty Shepard, when visiting Boston, in 1676, wrote in her diary:

I could not help laughing at the periwig of Elder Jones, which had gone awry. The periwig has been greatly censured as encouraging worldly fashions not suitable to the wearing of a minister of the Gospel, and it has been preached about by Mr. Mather, and many think he is not severe enough in the matter, but rather doth find excuse for it on account of health.†

Pepys records the first time he put on his wig, which was in 1663. By 1716 they were universal, although in 1722 the Puritans declared at Hampton that " ye wearing of extravagant, superfluous wigges is altogether contrary to Truth." The New York Assembly taxed every wig of human or horse hair mixed. The early Colonists, both Baptists and Friends, in 1689-1698, unitedly attacked the wearing of periwigs in men and high headdresses in women, the former holding that the anticipated appearance of the Fifth Monarchy made such frivolity both unnecessary and inappropriate. Portraits of Endicott, Judge Sewall, and others who abjured the wig, show them in small black skullcaps. The Judge, who wore a hood, probably did so to afford his neck the protection that the wearers of wigs

---

* W. R. Bliss, " Side Glimpses from the Colonial Meeting-house," p. 97.

† Ibid. P. 136.

enjoyed with that vanity, and which in the bleak New England climate gave the custom more semblance of sense than anywhere else. The portrait of Moses Brown, the well-known Quaker of Providence, shows him in a similar substitute for the wig.

One of the earliest Quaker minutes in New England relating to the subject of wigs, occurs at Dartmouth, Massachusetts, whose Monthly Meeting records, under date First month 21, 1719: " A concern lying on this meeting Concerning of Friends Wearing of Wigs is referred to be proposed to the next Quarterly Meeting." Soon after, at the suggestion of the Yearly Meeting at Philadelphia, New England Yearly Meeting advised (1721) that the important subject of wigs be taken up. As a consequence of this action, in Sixth month of that year, Dartmouth Monthly Meeting appointed John Tucker and Thomas Taber, Jr., " to draw up something relating to wigges "; and Sandwich Quarterly Meeting, on First month 19, 1722, saw fit to elaborate its views as follows:

The Sense and Judgment of Sandwich Quarterly Meeting in Relation to Wigs is that if any friend by reason of Age or Sickness have lost their Hair, may wear a small decent Wig as much like their owne Hair as may be—but for any friend to cut of their Hair on purpose to wear a Wig seems to be more pride than Profit and when any professing truth with us go into the same, they ought to be proceeded against as disorderly walkers.

There is evidence of many who became so far " disorderly walkers " as to be quite unable to resist the fascinations of an artificial superstructure. The same meeting records some years later:

1 mo. 1791: R—— D—— hath given way to the Lust of the Eye and the Pride of Life in following some of the vain Fations and Customs of the times and Continues Therein; Especially that

of waring his Hair long which is a shame according to the Apostles Declaration; also tied with a string [doubtless the worldly black ribbon worn by the Father of his Country, an example for all loyal citizens to follow] and some other modes that we have not unity with; also attended a marriage out of the order of Friends; for all which we have Labored with him.

This case shows the period of transition from the wig to the natural hair worn long, tied and powdered. Nantucket Records, dated Seventh month 6, 1803, also relate that F. H. " has deviated from our principles in dress, particularly in tying the hair."

Dartmouth Meeting, in 1733 (Tenth month 17) showed its sorrow for one of its members " going from education " in the following minute:

Whereas, H—— T——   . .. hath had his Education among Friends but for want of keeping the Spirit of Truth and ye good order Established among Friends, hath gone from Education & let himself into a Liberty that is not agreeable to our Holy Profession, by wearing Divers sorts of Periwigs and his Hat set up on three sides like ye Vain Custom of ye World, and also Speaking of Words not agreeable to our Profession, & for these his outgoings he has been Labored with and Advised to forsake the same, but he hath not done it to ye Satisfaction of ye Monthly Meeting, but still goes on with his vain conversation, to the grief of (the) sincere-hearted among us. Therefore for the clearing of Truth of Such Reproachful things we are concerned to give Forth this as a Public Condemnation.

Philadelphia, now the most conservative, was at that period the most fashionable town in the new country, and we find its Quaker Meeting struggling with the wig-mania some time before there is any record of its appearance among that body in New England. Such minutes as the following are not uncommon:

It being spoken to at this Meeting as a grief upon some friends, That many comes out of England with fashionable Cloathes and great Perriwigs, which, if care be not taken may (its feared) tend to Corrupt the Youth of this place. This Meeting recommends the same [to the next Quarterly Meeting.] —Philadelphia Monthly Meeting, 26 of 2 mo. 1700.

The friends appointed by the preparative Meeting to bring in the testimony of Ancient Friends concerning fashionable cloathing and Long Perriwigs, have done it, and they are desired to recommend the same to the next Quarterly Meeting.—Do., 30 of 3 mo. 1701.

Likewise the Friends appointed to Enquire into the Conversation and Clearness of Abraham Scott, Report that they cannot find but that he is clear in relation to marriage and debts, but as to his orderly walking amongst Friends, they cannot say much for him on that account. Yet upon his appearance before this meeting, making some acknowledgment of *Extraordinary Powdering of his Periwig*, which is the chief (thing) Friends had against him, and hoping to take more care for the future, Samuel Carpenter and Anthony Morris are desired to write him a Certificate and sign the same on behalf of this Meeting.—Do., 25 of 5 mo. 1701.

Under the same date we find:

Some course might be taken with the Taylors that make profession of Truth, and are found in the practice of making such fashionable cloathing as Tends to the Corruption of Youth.

They do not seem, however, to have gone the lengths of Dublin Meeting:

28 of 6 mo. 1702; Philadelphia Monthly Meeting desires that the proposition of the last Preparative meeting about cutting of hair & wearing of perriwigs, may be laid before the next Quarterly Meeting. . . . 17th. of 6 mo. 1703; Ordered that friends in their particular meetings make inquiry if there be any in the use of perriwigs extravagantly or unnecessary.

We also find the following, in an Epistle of Philadelphia Yearly Meeting to the Quarterly and Monthly Meetings, dated Seventh month 18, 1723, " on third day as usual ":

As to such young people who have been educated in the way of Truth, or make profession with us, if they do not continue in well doing, but frequent scandalous or tipling houses, and delight in vain and evil company and communications or shall use gaming, or drink to excess, or behave rudely or such like enormities or shall decline our plain manner of speech or imitate the vain antick modes and customs of the times—the men with their extravagant wigges, and hattes set up with three corners; and the women in their immodest dresses, and other indecencies. It is our advice and earnest desire that parents and guardians, whilst such youth are under their tuition, do restrain them, and not indulge or maintain them in such pride or extravagances. But if they will not be otherwise reformed, then the *Overseers* or other Frd's shall use their endeavours to restrain them, and if that cannot prevail, let the offenders (after dealing and admonitions), have notice to be at the next succeeding monthly meeting, in order to be further dealt withall in the Wisdom of Truth, according to the Discipline.

It is a curious fact that wigs were discarded with more apparent reluctance in democratic America than in England. To appear on the streets of New York, about 1800, without a wig was scarcely decent, and Parton tells us that " many men surrendered the pigtail only with life." In 1786, Ann Warder's Philadelphia nephews wore their hair still in the queue, a fashion quite gone out at that date in London. She says: " I threatened the Execution of these Pig-Tails before I will submit to introduce them as my nephews in our country, which they both acknowledge will be cheerfully resigned." *

In the year 1795, Martha Routh, the English Friend who wore the first " plain bonnet " in America, attended a meeting of the settlers in the Alleghany mountains, " to which," she says, " came many Menonists and Dunkers. Some of the Elders wear their beards, as they say, according to ancient custom, but do

---

* Ann Warder, MS. Journal.

not enjoin it as a part of their religion." * These same German Baptists argued that Adam came into being fully equipped with a luxuriant beard; and that Aaron's reached to the hem of his garment. They also quoted Leviticus 19: 27. In respect to Adam, they were hardly behind the Rev. George Wickes, the Puritan divine, who lived during the fashions in dress of the Hogarth period. He died in 1744. A sermon that he preached at Harwichtown has been preserved to us, and is quoted by Bliss. The following extracts seem appropriate:

Adam, so long as he continued in innocency, did wear his own hair and not a Perriwig. Indeed, I do not see how it was possible that Adam should dislike his own hair, and therefore cut it off, so that he might wear a Perriwig, and yet have continued innocent. . . . The children of God will not wear Perriwigs after the Resurrection. . . . Elisha did not cover his head with a Perriwig, altho' it was bald. To see the greater part of Men in some congregations wearing Perriwigs is a matter of deep lamentation. For either all these men had a necessity to cut off their Hair, or else not. If they had a necessity to cut off their Hair, then we have reason to take up a lamentation over the sin of our first Parents which hath occasioned so many Persons in one Congregation to be sickly, weakly crazy Persons. Oh, Adam, what hast thou done! †

Elizabeth Drinker was a Quaker lady of the last century, in Philadelphia, to whose keen powers of observation we are greatly indebted for much valuable information. She writes, in 1794: "Two bearded men drank tea here," recording the fact in much the same way that she had noted the passing by of an elephant, then a rare sight, a short time before.‡ The Puritan was

---

* Martha Routh, Journal, p. 139.

† W. R. Bliss, "Side Glimpses from the Colonial Meeting-house," p. 142.

‡ Elizabeth Drinker, Journal.

everywhere more numerous than the Quaker; and for
this reason, his peculiarities occupy a more conspicuous
place in literature than those of the latter.   His long
hair has been noted by no less a hand than that of Ben
Jonson.   Brother Zeal-of-the-Land Busy, the Puritan in
" Bartholomew Fair," is made by the dramatist to say:

For long hair, it is an ensign of Pride, a banner; and the
world is full of these banners, very full of banners.*

The famous picture of King Charles L, at St. John's
College, Oxford, written in the Psalms, in the smallest
possible handwriting that can be deciphered, was thus
apostrophized by one Jeremiah Wells:

The Presbyterian maxim holds not here
That calls locks impious if below the ear;
When every fatall clip lops off a prayer,
And he's accurs'd, that dare but cut thy hair.

There are a few rare Quaker pamphlets against wigs.
The following extracts from two of the most unique
will serve to illustrate the kind of literature devoted to
the subject.   As usual, in such cases, it is more attractive to the antiquarian than the scholar:

A TESTIMONY AGAINST PERIWIGS AND PERI-WIG MAKING AND
PLAYING ON INSTRUMENTS OF MUSIC AMONG CHRISTIANS, OR
ANY OTHER IN THE DAYS OF THE GOSPEL.   BEING SEVERAL
REASONS AGAINST THOSE THINGS.   BY ONE WHO FOR GOOD
CONSCIENCE SAKE HATH DENYED AND FORSAKEN THEM.
JOHN MULLINER.   1677.

This curious pamphlet relates the suffering of mind
undergone by Mulliner, who was at one time a barber
of Northampton, in regard to making " borders," wigs
and periwigs for his trade.   He says:

As to my Employment of Periwig making, it is more than
twelve years since I began to make them, and much might be

---

* Act III., Sc. 1.

said for the making of them by some, yet much questioning and reasoning have I had within myself for some time—so that at some times I have been troubled when I have been making of them.

He had apparently argued to himself:

There is hardly any man but is desirous of a good head of Hair, and if Nature doth not afford it, if there be an art to make a Decent Wig or Border, what harm is that? As for those whose hair is wasted, fallen and gone off their Heads through infirmity of Body, and for want of it do find that their health is impaired, or lessened, if such do wear short Borders for their health sake, and for no other End or Cause Whatsoever, I judge them not; but let none make a pretense that they wear Borders or Wigs for their Health, when in Reality, another thing is the Cause.

.   .   .   .

And let all those who have Hair growing upon their heads, sufficient to serve them, I mean what is really needful or useful, be content therewith, and not find fault with their own hair and cut it off, and lust after and put on others Hair.

.   .   .   .

As I had been a publick Professor of this Employment for some time, I must bear my Testimony against them; and that was, I should send for my two men, as I had instructed in that way, and tell them how I was troubled and take a Wig and burn it before them, as a Testimony for God against them. . . . So, according to the pain and sorrow that lay hard upon me, I gave up to do it, and I thank God I have much ease and comfort of mind since I have done it.

.   .   .   .

I was a great lover of Musick, and many times as I have been thinking of God and of the condition I was in, it would have brought trouble upon me; so that many times I have took my Cittern or Treble Viol or any instrument as I had most delight in, thinking to drive away these Thoughts, and I have been so troubled, as I have been playing, that I have laid my instrument down and have reasoned with myself, . . . and fell a crying to God, and my music began to be a burden. . . . I would fain have sold my Instruments, but that I had not freedom in my mind to do; for if I did, those who bought them would have made use of them as I did, and I thought I could not be the cause of it; so

I took as many as I suppose cost forty shilling, and *Burned Them*, and had great Peace in my mind in doing of it, which is more to me than all the pleasures in this world.*

A Declaration against Wigs and Periwigs.

By Richard Richardson.

Jer. 22 : 24. Phil. 3 : 3

Several Testimonies having been given by Friends against Pride in Apparel relating to Women; 'tis considerable whether Women being reflected on, may not reasonably reflect on Men, their artificial frizzled Hair; for Women's Hairs on Men's Heads swarm like one of Egypt's Plagues, and creep in too much upon and among Christians. And a Nehemiah is desirable, that might pluck off this strange Hair of strange Women lusted after. (Nehem. 13: 25.) And the Heathen may rise up against us, for an Ambassador coming before a Senate with false Hair, a Grave Senator said, What credit is to be had to him whose very Locks do lye? And if, upon necessity the Locks of any amongst us do lye, 'tis fit they should lye to purpose, viz., so as not to be discovered from native Locks! For to seek to deceive so as to be perceived, argues as much want of Wit as of Sincerity; and a want of an Endeavor in it not to be perceived, argues a want of Humility and Moderation!

.   .   .   .   .

If Heat causes Headach, sure a Wig under a Hat is not a means to cure it. The Prophet Elisha likely had neither, when Bethel Boys cried, A Bald Head!

.   .   .   .   .

John Mulliner, A Friend about Northamton, a Wig-maker, left off his trade and was made to burn one in his Prentices sight and Print against it. John Hall, a Gentleman of Northumberland, being Convinced, sitting in a meeting, was shaken by the Lord's Power, pluck'd off and threw down his Wig; so 'tis considerable whether care may not be taken, that conceited conterfit [counterfeit] Calvinists may not continue amongst us, nor that any of the people of God make themselves Bald for Pride now, as they did of old for Sorrow. (Levit. 21. 5.)

.   .   .   .   .

The Apostles Peter and Paul forbad ornament of Plaited Hair (as ours translate; Crisp'd or Curl'd, as others) and the An-

---

* This was reprinted in 1708.

cients write, that they both had Bald-Heads, and if they should have covered them with Women's Hair, would they not have re. torted Was that the cause, Peter and Paul, that you had us leave off our Locks, that you and such like might get them yourselves to make Peri-wigs of?

And then Friend Richard's feelings overcame him entirely, and he says:

Who can refrain to fall into a Poetical Vein, and Paint out in such sad Colours, that it may look as ugly as it doth. For a glorying in a Shame as an Ornament, Sharppens a Pen to describe it to make it appear as it is. Difficile et Satyram non scribere!

METAMORPHOSES.

The manner of this Age unmannerly
Is, Man unmanning, Women's Hair to buy.
Dub Poles and Joles Dame Venus' knights to be,
Smock-coat and Petticoat-Breech their Livery;
Scarce man-like fac'd, though Woman-like in Hair,
As sting-tail'd Locusts in the Vision were;

.   .   .   .   .

And like unto the Phrygian Ganymede,
Or as Tiresias Femaliz'd indeed;
Or one that (sith he would a Woman be)
Put Period to Assyrian Monarchy.
Hair in a Night turn'd Hew, of old 'tis said,
An old man young, a Boy a Girl was made;
Elders so now transform'd to Girls appear,
And Girls to Boys by their short curtail'd Hair.
By bulls, some seem 'ith twilight turn'd to owls,
As antique Harpyes, or some new Night Fowles.
As charming Sirens (bate their ugly Hair)
Having their Arms, Necks, Brests, Backs, Shoulders bare,
Nay, for their Knights rich Garters some prepare.

While long hair was the fashion for men, the collar was unpretending, and an inch or two its utmost height. Henry VIII., who introduced short hair, kept up a simple band of this sort; and no lace was worn. Bands for the neck were of Italian cut-work, costing as

much as £60. "Partelets" were of velvet or lawn,
larger than bands, and worn like the earlier "gorgets"
of embroidered lawn, velvet or Venetian work.*
French gentlemen began to wear collarettes or frilled
ruffles about 1540.† The shirts of this period were of
very fine holland, with no neckband, but a neckcloth,
the most stylish being the "Steenkirk," after the battle of that name. Starch reached the extreme of its use
or abuse in the enormous ruffs of Queen Elizabeth's
reign.‡ Small ruffs were still worn in the early Quaker
times, but they were less starched. Aurelia, in Jasper
Mayne's play, "The City Match," when her Puritan
maid has become worldly, and enters her presence in
fashionable attire, exclaims:

> O, miracle! out of
> Your little ruff, Dorcas, and in the fashion—
> Dost thou hope to be saved? §

and again:

> Ere I'll be tortured thus, I'll get dry palms
> With starching, and put on my smocks myself. ‖

Quarlous, in "Bartholomew Fair," says of an acquaintance:

> Ay, there was a blue-starch woman of the name;

and Nightingale, in the same play, sells "A Ballad of
Goose-green starch and the Devil, i.e, a Goodly ballad
against Pride, showing how a Devil appeared to
a lady which was starching her ruff by night." Yellow starch was most in vogue in England. Old Stubbes

---

* Georgiana Hill, "History of English Dress," Vol. I., p. 187.

† Quicherat, "Histoire de Costume en France," p. 175.

‡ One Mrs. Turner introduced yellow starch from France with great
success. By a dreadful irony of fate she was hanged for the murder of
Sir Thomas Overbury in a starched ruff!

§ Act IV., Sc. 3.

‖ Act II., Sc. 1.

scoffs at " the liquor which they call starch, wherein the devil hath willed them to dye their ruffs! " *   He says of their " great ruffes and supportasses " :

They haue great and monstrous ruffes, made either of cambrike, holland, lawne, or els of some other the finest cloth that can be got for money, whereof some be a quarter of a yarde deepe, yea, some more, very few lesse, so that they stande a full quarter of a yearde (and more) from their necks hanging ouer their shoulder points in steade of a vaile. But if Æolus with his blasts, or Neptune with his storms, chaunce to hit vpon the crasie barke of their brused ruffes, then they goe flip flap in the winde like ragges that flew abroade lying vpon their shoulders like the dish cloute of a slut. But wot you what? the deuill, as he, in the fulnesse of his malice, first inuented these great ruffes, so hath he now found out also two great pillers to beare vp and maintaine this his kingdome of pride withal (for the deuill is kyng and prince ouer al the children of pride) The one arch or piller, whereby his kyngdome of great ruffes is vnderpropped, is a certaine kind of liquid matter, whiche they call starch, wherein the deuill hath willed them to washe and diue their ruffes well, whiche, beeying drie, will then stande stiff and inflexible about their necks. The other piller is a certaine denice made of wiers crested for the purpose whipped ouer either with gold thred, silner, or silke, and this he calleth a supportasse or vnderpropper; this is to bee applied round about their neckes vnder the ruffe, vpon the out side of the bande, to beare vp the whole frame and bodie of the ruffe, from fallying and hangying doune.

Ruffs gradually went out, clergymen and judges being the last to abandon them, and embroidered muslin or lace collars in Van Dyck style came in. These were worn with no coat collar whatever, in order that they might lie flat on the shoulders; and this is the collar of the time of Penn, whose coat, as we have seen, was collarless. His sovereign's coat was ornamented with a deep lace collar, reaching to the point of the shoul-

---

* " Anatomie of Abuses," 1586.

der, under which any collar of cloth had been impossible. Therefore, when William Penn cast off his laces, he laid bare his collarless state, and it required one hundred and fifty years to develop the straight coat cut of his successors.

But the form of neckwear known as " bands " was no sooner introduced than it commended itself at once to the Quaker, and was forthwith adopted. Bands are the only item of civil dress that the clergy still retain to-day, surviving in the gown and bands of the Presbyterian Church, as those who know Dr. Parkhurst's familiar figure will recall. Without entering into the question of its authenticity as a portrait, Sir Peter Lely's painting of George Fox in bands is rather striking in connection with our present association of that portion of the costume with the clergy. The Bevan portrait of Penn shows him in bands, as does that of Milton at the age of eighteen. The latter wears the " falling-band." The bands, worn very soon by most Quakers, gave them another peculiarity among the fashionable lace and embroidered collars; and the public was quick to make a hit. An anti-Quaker tract of 1671 * says: " A Quaker is a vessel of Phanaticism drawn off to the Lees; a common shore [sewer] of Heresie, into which most extravagant opinions at last disembogue and enter; the fag end of Reformation marked with a sullen meagre look and this characteristic ' Thou.' . . . [He] decries superstition, yet idolizes Garbs and phrases. You may know him by his diminutive *Band* that looks like the forlorn hope of his shirt

---

* " Character of a Quaker in His True and Proper Colors ; or, The Clownish Hypocrite Anatomized." London, 1671.

crawling out at his collar, for his purity consists only in his dress, and his religion is not to speak like his neighbors."

Bands were worn by the less fashionable, and by literary and professional men, after they ceased to be universally popular. The Dutch were very partial to them; and the portrait of the painter Le Febvre, with his pupil, in the Louvre, shows both in bands.

Walpole, in his " Anecdotes of Painting," thus describes the Quakers:

A long vest and cloke of black or some other grave colour, with a collar of plain linen called a turnover, and a broad band, with the hair closely cropped, distinguished the men of every rank, and the ladies equally excluded lace, jewels and braided locks.

At one time bands had a certain political significance, and on their introduction into Ireland, in 1728, the following " Answer to the Band Ballad, by a Man Milliner," declared:

The town is alarm'd and seems at a stand,
As if both the Pope and the Devil would land
To doom this whole Isle in the shape of a band—
Which nobody can deny, deny; which nobody can deny.

The bands and lace tie following it were succeeded by the white stock; then came the muslin cravat, which was always a favorite with the Quaker, and a graceful dress at all times; to this succeeded the modern rule of the starched shirt collar, almost as uncompromising in some of its forms as anything worn in the days of Queen Elizabeth. Stiff linen bands, or soft cambric ones, were worn by all Puritans. We find four plain bands and three falling ones supplied to each settler of Massachusetts Bay. Sumptuary laws forbade embroid-

ery. The Judges of the Supreme Court wore bands
when on the bench until this century. The linen collar, turned down over the doublet, was known as the
" falling band."

GABRIEL-MARC-ANTOINE DE GRELLET,
father of Stephen Grellet. 1789.

CHAPTER IV.

THE QUAKERESS.

Mistress Anne Lovely. — "Isn't it monstrously rediculous that they should desire to impose their quaking dress upon me at these years? When I was a child, no matter what they made me wear; but now — "

Betty.—"I would resolve against it, madam; I'd see 'em hanged before I'd put on the pinch'd cap again."

. . . .

Mistress Lovely.—"Are the pinch'd cap and formal hood the emblems of sanctity? Does your virtue consist in your dress, Mrs. Prim?"

Mrs. Centlivre: "A Bold Stroke for a Wife."

When she to silent meeting comes,
　With apron green before her,
She simpers so like muffle plums,
　'Twould make a Jew adore her.

Old Verse.

CHAPTER IV.

THE QUAKERESS.

 NONCONFORMITY has nowhere expressed itself more fully than in Quaker dress. There is unconscious satire in the old Quaker plea that no change has crept into their institutions; in regard to their dress, at least, this is all a mistake. But one creature exists in which no change, which is the other name for growth, has been going on, and that is the fossil. On the contrary, an instance of adaptability in dress on the part of the Quakers is their prompt acceptance of the shawl, which, at its introduction, near Revolutionary times, was at once seized upon as eminently adapted to Quaker needs. Possibly the most notable instance of adherence to a style is that of Mrs. Noah, in the famous toy ark. It will be remembered that she wears high stays, with a very waspish waist, and her petticoats are extended by what are evidently padded hips. The headdress crowning her rather conventional features—so far as she has any lineaments at all—is a most frivolous "Tam o' Shanter,"—or is it a flat hat, rather circumscribed in extent? At any rate, here is a lady who has dressed just the same for several hundred years, and we should weep to see her change now.

It would be very valuable to us to learn what was the exact costume worn by Margaret Fell (afterward Margaret Fox) and her talented and interesting daughters. We only know how her contemporaries dressed, and have a few details of the family wardrobe in those Swarthmoor account books which still exist. That they wore the popular style of dress, without adornments, is altogether likely, for she has left on record her disapproval of anything tending to *uniformity* among the Friends. We shall not be far wrong, I think, if we imagine George Fox's wife in a hood of black wadded silk, a short, full skirt, standing well out from the hips, and held in position by an array of petticoats (for she would never have worn the false hips then in vogue); a kerchief of muslin, over a low bodice, stiff and long in the waist, and laced with many eyelets, its cord of blue or white or black, depending upon whether her gown were red or blue; her shoes heavy, low and square-toed, with heels that may have been another color from the shoe itself, but not the fashionable red, and higher than we should now care to wear upon the street. Her cloak, whose color we dare not speculate upon, was of substantial cloth, with a hood for ornament when not in use, as it often was, particularly in her long journeys on horseback from county to county attending public meetings. She may have called it a " capuchin," for that was the form of cloak then coming into wear. But we are not privileged to possess descriptions of her personal appearance nor of her style of dress, as is the case with both of her distinguished husbands. We learn from one or two references to old letters of ancient worthies, that she was fair and comely, and

Maria Webb says that she had a "beaming countenance," and a "most sweet, harmonious voice." But with these slight references we are fain to be content. A few items of clothing touched upon in the family letters give us our only clue to the style of dress worn by the women of the Swarthmoor circle. John Rous, the son-in-law of Margaret Fell Fox, writes her from London in 1670:

> Yesterday, by John Scott, the Preston carrier, I sent a small box of sugar for present use, directed for Thomas Green. The hasp was sealed as this letter is, and in it was a white mantle, and a white sarsanet hood for thee, and some playthings for the children.*

The following items from a portion of the old Swarthmoor Account Book of 1673, which is quoted from at length in "The Fells of Swarthmoor Hall," are very interesting for the light they throw upon the style of dress in the Fell family. The precious old book is in Sarah Fell's handwriting. Sarah was the eldest daughter of the household, and the head of affairs and its business manager, to whom, after her marriage with William Meade, the whole family, including her mother, repeatedly appealed in despair to clear up the confusion into which Swarthmoor affairs immediately fell after she left the home. In some cases the cost of the articles given is illegible:

By money pd. Thos. Benson for dying 2 pr. stockings sky colour, of mine, and a petticoat red, of mine . . . . (Defaced)
By money pd. for a hat for little Mary Lower I gave her 0 0 6
For 20 yds. Cumberland cloth 2 0 9
Paid for a vizard mask for myself & a hat . . . . . . (Defaced)

---

* Maria Webb, " The Fells of Swarthmoor Hall," p. 231.

By money pd. for 1 yd. and nail of black paragon for apron for self	0	2	0
Paid for leading strings for little Margaret Lower	0	0	2
By money paid for a blue apron and strings for myself	0	1	3
By money pd. for a black hood for sister Susan....	0	4	0
By money pd. for a black alamode whiske* for sister Rachel	0	2	0
By money paid for a round whiske for sister Susanna	0	4	4
Do. for a little black whiske for myself	0	1	10
1678.			
By money pd. for clogging a pair of clogs and for nailes to mend shoes for my boy, Tom Harrison, (own account)	0	0	5½

Sarah (Fell) Meade wrote to her sister, Rachel Abraham, from London, under date "The 19th. of 10th. [December] 1683"

I have endeavoured to fit my dear Mother with black cloth for a gown, which is very good and fine, and as much as Jno. Richards saith is enough to the full, 5 yards and half, and what materials as he thought was needful to send down, vizt. silk, both sewing and stitching, gallowne ribbon, and laces, and I was very glad to know what she wanted, for it has been in my mind a pretty while to send her and you something, and I could not tell what she might need or might be most serviceable to her was the reason of my thus long forbearance, and so I desire her acceptance of it, and yours of the small things underwritten:

3 pair doe skin gloves such as are worn in winter, for mother, sister Lower and thyself; the thickest pair for mother if they fit her, but that I leave to you to agree on as you please.

1 pair same sort of gloves for brother Abraham.

4 ells of Holland, for sister Lower and thyself, each two ells.

2 pots of balsam, one for my mother, the other for sister Yeamans.

3 pocket almanacs, for sister Yeamans, sister Lower and thyself.

---

*Whisk, " A neckerchief worn by women in the seventeenth century. Also called 'falling-whisk,' apparently to distinguish it from the ruff." —" The Century Dictionary."

1 muslin nightrail for sister Yeamans, which she sent for.

100 needles, of which half for sister Yeamans, which she sent for, the other half hundred for sister Lower and thyself.

There is (in the box) for sister Lower, which she sent to sister Susanna to buy her, a colored stuff manteo, cost 14s., and 11 yards and half of black worsted stuff, at 2s. per yard, cost 22s. Sister Susanna exchanged the old 20s. piece of gold as she desired, which yielded 23s. 6d., so she is out of purse for her 12s. 6d. Black stuff was worse to get than colored, which is now mostly worn; but she hath done as well as she can, and hopes it will please her; its a strong, serviceable stuff.

Mary Frith presents her service to (sister Yeamans), and takes it kindly that she should send her her fillet.

I am thy affectionate sister,   S. M.

(P. S.)

We advise you to make my mother's cloth gown without a skirt, which is very civil, and usually so worn, both by young and old, in stiffened snits.*

These were all women of cultivation and good taste, and the sister in London kept them posted as to the correct mode of dress, with an evident desire that their mother should not be allowed to appear singular in her garb, although no time was wasted by any of them on the frivolities of dress. The simple, homely view of the family life presented in these and other letters of the Fells, allows us to clothe them with a personality that gives them a living charm when we meet them again in the larger arena of public life, in court or prison. Making " my mother's gown without a skirt " is probably making it without an overdress of any sort, the full, stiffened petticoats that were then the mode requiring none. The Quaker women had been

---

* Maria Webb, " The Fells of Swarthmoor Hall," p. 92.

wearing the short overskirt represented in the Quaker-ess Tub-Preacher,* and it was evidently to this that the reference was made. The " whisk " above referred to is the forerunner of the handkerchief worn by Eliza-beth Fry and her successors ever since.

Sometimes the modest dress of the Quakers was sad-ly misrepresented, and when the course of true love in the case of Thomas Lower and Mary, daughter of Judge Fell and Margaret (afterward Fox), did not at first run quite smoothly, certain persons at Plymouth circulated a description of her and her sister that Thomas hastened to deny. He writes Mary:

> At Plymouth both thou and sister Yeamans were painted with naked necks, and in costly array, until T. S. [Thomas Salt-house] and I deciphered you, and quite defaced the former coun-terfeit by representing you in a more commendable dress. The authors of these unsavory belchings I cannot fully discover, but that which brings report will also carry.

The Fells lived in days of more extravagance of taste than we, although a recent writer on modern dress asserts that women to-day appear " one season like wriggling worms in lampshades, and the next, fes-tooned and befringed in the upholstery of a four-post bedstead." †

No wonder that Fox, to whom it must have been as gall and wormwood to be obliged to touch upon the subject at all, cried out, in a moment of wrath and in-dignation, to the women of his day, " Away with your long slit peaks behind in the skirts of your waistcoats," " your skimming-dish hats," " unnecessary buttons,"

---

* See illustration, " The Quaker Meeting."

† Lady Gwendolen Ramsden, " The Nineteenth Century," for Novem-ber, 1900, " On Extravagance in Dress."

" short sleeves," " short black aprons," " vizzards,"
" your great needless flying scarfs, like colours [flags]
on your backs." But they went on, the world's people;
and the Quakers of Queen Anne's time saw fashions
come and go that beside the beautiful costumes of the
great days of Van Dyck and Bol, seem the very embodi-
ment of grotesqueness—the hoop, the periwig, and the
tight stays. Finally, in 1770, an Act was passed by
Parliament to the effect that

All women, of whatever age, rank, profession, degree, whether virgins, maids or widows, that shall from and after such Act
impose upon seduce or betray into matrimony, any of his Majesty's male subjects by the scents, paints, cosmetics, washes,
artificial teeth, false hair, Spanish wool, iron-stays, hoops, high-
heeled shoes, etc., shall incur the penalty of the law now in force
against *witchcraft,* and like misdemeanors, and that the marriage
upon conviction shall be null and void!*

Of the two wives of William Penn we possess a fine
portrait of the first—the fair Gulielma Springett,
whose life and love are one of the sweet romances of
Quakerism. She is represented in the silk hood worn
by the mother and the wife of Cromwell, and by most
of the nobility and gentry of England in her day, with
the border of a dainty muslin cap showing beneath.
Her brocaded gown is short and very full at the hips;
the pointed laced bodice cut low in the neck, and filled
in with a kerchief; the elbow sleeves turned back in a
large loose cuff, beneath which fine muslin under-
sleeves appear. It is probable that her dress does not
represent the costume of the plainest Friends of her
day, any more than did that of her distinguished husband. But the dress of contemporary modish ladies

---

* Georgiana Hill, " Women in English Life," Vol. I., p. 317.

with which we are able to compare it is so vastly more elaborate than " Guli's," that we at once recognize the presence of Quaker moderation, combined with taste and good sense, such as we should expect in the daughter of Lady Springett. Hannah Callowhill, the second wife of William Penn, brought up in the rather austere community of Friends in Bristol, whose mercantile atmosphere did not foster the arts or the graces of life among her immediate family or associates, represents an older woman, in sober attire, whose gowns and aprons were of a plainer hue, and whose whole mien was one of seriousness and sobriety. The portrait that we have of her is also taken in the hood, and there is no evidence of any cap underneath.*

The Quakeresses were not unfamiliar in their modest garb to the lords and ladies about the Court. Seven of them, in 1765, went together to wait upon Queen Charlotte, " when her Majesty ordered her lady-in-waiting to compliment each of them, which they returned in a sensible and modest manner." † Margaret Fell, both before and after her marriage to George Fox, made various visits to the Court, usually accompanied by another woman Friend.

Aberdeen and Dublin seem to have been from the

---

* The original of the portrait of Gulielma Penn is a painting on glass in the possession of the descendants of Henry Swan, of Holmwood, Dorking, England, who died in 1796. The copy from which this present example is taken, forms the frontispiece to the " Penns and Penningtons of the Seventeenth Century," by Maria Webb.

The portrait of Hannah ·Penn is from a painting in the Banqueting Room of Independence Hall, Philadelphia. This is a copy in its turn of a crayon drawing in possession of a descendant of Francis Place, the artist, who lived near Darlington. Place is said to have taken the portrait during one of the frequent visits of the Penns to their sister, who lived near him.

† British Museum " Scrap Book " (4152, H, 5).

evidence of any ca

The Quakeresses were not unfamiliar in their modest
garb   the lords and ladies about the Court.   Seven
o upon Queen
Charlotte, wh

first the meetings most anxious to keep their membership as plain as possible. The former issued an early "Testimony" to the effect that "no colored plaids be worn any more, but either mantles or low hoods." An order prohibiting plaids, in the land of the Scotch, did violence to long-cherished traditions of patriotism and clan-feeling, and the Aberdeen Friends wasted many years in trying to enforce arbitrary laws of dress. The Friends give gaiety as the ground of their objection to plaids, and herein show their want of tact, for this garment had fallen under condemnation for another reason than its fashion among the Scotch in the town of Glasgow, where the Kirk Session Books say: * "Great disorder hath been in the Kirk by reason of women sitting with their heads covered in time of sermon, sleeping." This led to condemnation of hoods, under whose friendly protection the Scotch women could indulge in a refreshing nap during the interminable sermons of the Scotch clergy. Thirty years later, in 1637, the plaids worn by the plain folk over the head were condemned for the same reason, and not, as has been thought, for the gay coloring.

The clothing of the common people, as well as of the more well-to-do, was spun by the women of the family, and woven by the village "wabster." The spinning-wheel was in use in England in the time of the first Friends, but in many of the country districts, and almost everywhere in Scotland, the old "rock and reel" were still employed. The "rock" was the hand distaff, referred to by Spenser in the "Faery Queen" (IV., iii. 48):

---

* Planché, "Dictionnaire de Costume," p. 244.

Sad Clotho held the rocke, the whiles the thrid
By griesly Lachesis was spun with paine.

Burns also makes Bess, in "Bess and her Spinning-Wheel," say:

Oh, lecze me on my spinning wheel,
Oh, lecze me on my rock and reel.

1730 saw the wheel introduced into Scotland, before which " rockings," somewhat corresponding to our old quilting parties, were great social events. The cloth thus prepared was made up into garments at home, or by traveling tailors, for a milliner was only known in the large cities, where her business was not only to clothe the living, but to " dress dead corpses," and sell " dead flannels." The peripatetic tailor was paid two or three pence a day and his food, or " diet." The traveling weaver was also an institution, and bought the thrifty housewife's yarn, giving or selling in exchange new and tempting webs of cloth. The " dead flannels " referred to were the wool garments in which, according to the law of England, in 1678, enacted in order to encourage the wool trade, all corpses were required to be buried, heavy fines being imposed for its evasion. Friends were usually careful to comply with these requirements, as instances on record in minutes of various meetings abundantly show.

Many of the first Quaker women were of the peasant class, as would be natural with the converts of a race of open air preachers. A very short time saw ladies of wealth and position, like Lady Springett, taking their places in the meetings; but the women of the fields were wearers of homespun gowns, and not until the next century were these confined to any special color. Red was

very popular in the early half of the seventeenth century; and scarlet was common among the Quaker
women, as it always has been among the peasants of
other countries besides England, both for its apparent
warmth, and for its lasting qualities.   Among the
household accounts of Margaret Fell we find charges
for scarlet cloth, after the manner of the good housekeeper in the Book of Proverbs, who " clothed her
household in scarlet."   When she became the wife of
George Fox he bought her scarlet cloth for a mantle.
He writes his wife, about 1678, that with the money she
had sent him to buy clothes for himself he purchased of
Richard Smith a piece of " red cloth for a mantle, believing she needed that more than he needed the coat."
Again, from Worcester prison, he wrote to her that he
had got a friend to purchase " as much black Spanish
cloth as would make her a gown," with what she had
given him, adding, " It cost a great deal of money, but
I will save." *

It is to be hoped that she did not wear with her gay
wrap one of the green aprons that the Friends were
then regarding as almost the badge of Quakerism, and
which were so identified with the Quaker women that
the satires then plentiful in the shape of broadsides and
pamphlets, all made playful allusions to the green
aprons.

This garment happened to be in high favor at the
time the Quakers arose, and to this accident is due many
an entry in minutes of Dublin, Aberdeen and London
meetings, advising their young women with great detail
as to the style and color of their aprons.   The fashion

---

* Maria Webb, " The Fells of Swarthmoor Hall," p. 259.

held for many years, and this important article of costume was worn by court lady and little scullery maid alike. The favorite color with everybody was green at first; long afterward we find Swift writing to Stella:

You shall have your aprons; and I'll put all your commissions as they come in a paper together; and don't think I'll forget (your) orders because they are friend's; I'll be as careful as if they were stranger's.[*]

The apron is described as of green silk, in a letter of April 24th. Later (October 30th, 1711):

Who'll pay me for this green apron? I will have the money; it cost ten shillings and six pence. I think it plaguey dear for a cheap thing, but they said that English silk would cockle, and I know not what.

In the following year Swift has several more commissions from Stella for green aprons from the metropolis.

In 1698, Aberdeen Meeting said:

Let none want aprons at all, and that either green or blue, or other grave colors, and not white upon the street or in public at all, nor any spangled or speckled silk or cloth or any silk aprons at all. And dear Friends, we being persuaded that none of a right spirit will be so stiff or so willful as to prefer their own lusts or wills to our tender sense or advice, and labor of love in these things.[†]

The Women's Quarterly Meeting of Lincolnshire, 21st of Fourth month, 1721, says:

We think green aprons are very decent and becoming us as a people.

In 1735, a young woman Friend named May Drummond, of Edinburgh, who appears to have been a per-

---

[*] Journal to Stella, April 5th, 1711.
[†] Aberdeen, " A Testimony," 5 mo. 28th, 1698.

son of attractive appearance, and much real ability, was given an audience with Queen Caroline. An original letter of that date, from which the following is an extract, gives an interesting description of her ministry and personal appearance, and emphasizes the green apron. She is described as preaching to audiences of more than three thousand people. The writer then goes on:

> She hath also been to wait on the Queen, and was more than an hour in her presence. Att her first coming in the Queen soon began and asked her many questions which May was not very forward to answer, but after some little pawce she began and had a good opportunity for near half an hour (with little interruption) To speake to the Queen the Princesses and some Ladys of honour (so called) which she and those three friends who accompanied her had good reason to think was very much to all their satisfaction ffor she spoke in such a tender handsome and moving manner that pretty much affected all present so that I believe that her visit was not onely acceptable but of very good service. The Queen seemed much pleased with her plain dress, and *green apron,* and often said she thought it exceedingly neat and becoming.

The French country women in the reign of Louis XI. wore white aprons at work, or in demi-toilette, when going to the town to market. The negligée of 1672 consisted of a black dress with a white apron, and we are told by Boursault (" Mots à la Mode ") the name of this apron:

> L'homme le plus grossier et l'esprit le plus lourd,
> Sait qu'un " Laisse-tout-faire " est un tablier court.

After the regency the apron, having had a period of disfavor, reappeared in France on young people, and was a part of ordinary costume, the overdress being abandoned and the apron worn with a jacket ("caraco") and a flounced skirt. The apron descended to the bor-

der of the gown, had pockets, and was trimmed on the
edge. It was without ends ("bavettes"), a style confined to chambermaids.* Miss Hill describes a lady of
Queen Anne's day thus:

She wore a black silk petticoat with red and white calico
border, cherry-colored stays, trimmed with blue and silver, red
and dove-colored damask gown flowered with large trees, a yellow
satin apron trimmed with white Persian, muslin head-cloth with
crowfoot edging, double ruffles with fine edging, a black silk fur-
belowed scarf and a spotted hood! †

A bride in the middle of the eighteenth century wore
a sprigged muslin apron trimmed with lace, over a silver muslin "night-gown"—(an elegant affair, probably
so called because *not* worn at night). Nollekin's wife
also wore on her wedding day "an elegant lace apron."
The opening of the nineteenth century saw the Parisians adoring simplicity, and they took back into favor
again the discarded white apron, which soon became a
part of full dress. The rustic straw hat à la shepherdess
was in favor as also in England, and the gipsy hat tied
down with a ribbon or a silk handkerchief. Straw was
worn only with morning dress; the time of year mattered little.

During the latter half of the eighteenth century the
plainest women among the Friends wore aprons of what
now seem very gay colors—blue, green, etc. The reason for this is that the white apron was in the height
of fashion. Watson, the Annalist, says, in writing of a
period about 1770:

The plainest women among the Friends (now so averse to fancy
colours), wore their coloured silk aprons, say of green or blue,

---

* Quicherat, "Histoire de Costume en France," pp. 328, 520, 574.
† Georgiana Hill, "History of English Dress," Vol. II., p. 73.

etc. This was at a time when the " gay " wore white aprons. In time, white aprons were disused (by the latter), and then the Friends left off their colored ones and used white.

A letter of Richard Shackleton's * dated Ballitore, 14th Third month, 1776, shows that the green apron, even, had its dangers, in its tendency to become a special costume for wear on occasions of public meetings, or during the time of religious worship:

What shall I say about these green aprons? I think we are of one mind about them. I believe it is the Master's mind that His disciples and followers should be distinguished from the world by a singularity of external appearance. I suppose it is also His will that a certain peculiarity of habit should distinguish them on the solemn occasion of assembling for Divine worship, or other religious performances.

When Sarah, the wife of George Dillwyn, was in London, in 1784, she wrote to a member of her family:

I think the women here far before the men—they dress extremely neat and exact, a few of the plainest with black hoods and green aprons. Some go to meeting without aprons, but generally carry fine muslin or cambric ones in their pockets, to put on when they get in the house; if we don't bring one, they always offer.

This also shows us the time of transition from the green to the white apron, which did not lose its hold among the plainer Quakeresses for nearly a hundred years.

The skirt of the dress was worn with very full gathers, soon followed by false hips, and the natural successor to this was of course the famous hooped petticoat of history and song, which made its appearance in 1709. The crinoline, or hoop, was invented by one Mrs. Selby, remaining through a longer period than the

---

* Quoted by R. Morris Smith, " The Burlington Smiths," p. 157.

old farthingale, and was eventually banished by George IV.* The following appeared at Bath in 1711:

The Farthingale Revived: or

MORE WORK FOR THE COOPER. A PANEGYRICK ON THE LATE, BUT MOST ADMIRABLE INVENTION OF THE HOOPED PETTICOAT.

> There's scarce a bard that writ in former time
> Had e'er so great, so bright a theme for rhyme.
> The Mantua swain, if living, would confess
> Ours more surprising than his Tyrian dress;
> And *Ovid's* mistress, in her loose attire,
> Would cease to charm his eyes, or fan Love's fire.
> Were he in Bath, and had these coats in view,
> He'd write his metamorphosis anew.
> Delia, fresh hooped, would o'er his heart prevail
> To leave Corinna and her tawdry Veil.

1835.

The hoop-petticoat was, no doubt, thought very fine in the country. It had the merit, which many fashions did not possess, of bestowing importance upon the wearer. " Insignificant-looking women, to whom before nobody had paid any attention, now came into notice; and portly women became positively awful in their majesty ! " †

The style had a great revival 1850-1865, both with gay and plain.

---

* The stomacher was an earlier garment, introduced in the fifteenth century. It was worn by both sexes, and by King Edward IV.

† A POPULAR BALLAD OF 1733.

> What a fine thing have I seen to-day,
>   Oh Mother, a hoop !
> I must have one, you cannot say nay—
>   Oh Mother, a hoop !
> For husbands are gotten this way, to be sure,
> Men's eyes and Men's hearts they so neatly allure.
>   Oh Mother, a hoop, a hoop ; Oh Mother, a hoop !
>   —Percy Soc., Vol. xxvii., p. 220.

There are no doubt to be found in the archives of many old Quaker families certain queer and very ugly long jackets of a shapeless sort of pattern, known in their day and generation as a "short-gown." The "short-gown and petticoat" may be met with in literature occasionally still, or in the letters of our great-grandmothers. It is difficult to understand the early enthusiasms over such a thoroughly inartistic garment; perhaps feminine ingenuity found an outlet in its decoration rather than its outline. At all events, the muse became thus inspired:

THE SHORT-BODY'D GOWN. (1801.)

Last midsummer day Sally went to the fair,
For to sell her yarn. Oh, how she did stare!
Both wives, maids and widows, in every shop round,
They all were dressed up in a short-body'd gown!

So home in the evening Miss Sally she hies,
And tells it her mother with greatest surprise;
Saying, "Two hanks a day will I spin the week round
Until I can purchase a short-body'd gown.*

When Ann Warder landed in New York, in 1786, she wrote to her sister in London:

The women all wear short gowns, a custom so truly ugly that I am mistaken if I ever fall into it. Notwithstanding they say I shall soon be glad to do it on account of the heat.

Thomas Chalkley was sufficiently moved by the horrors of the hoop to say:

If Almighty God should make a woman in the same shape her hoop makes her, Everybody would say truly it was monstrous. So according to this real truth they make themselves monstrous by art.

---

* Percy Society, Vol. XXVII., p. 264.

The bodices worn at the time that dress begins to be a subject for official notice in meetings were laced, and opened in front, exposing the tight stays in gay colors worn beneath them. The bodice was cut very low, the

1787.

bosom being covered with a "tucker" or "modesty piece" worn across the top of the bodice in front. In 1713 we find the *Guardian* growling at the ladies who are beginning to discard the latter in order to follow the fashion. The year 1800 finds the court ladies wearing a becoming broad muslin collar of very "sheer" quality, and the Quakeresses adopted the style quite generally, as may be seen by comparing the two illustrations of that date. In 1644, when gowns were very décolleté, Quicherat tells us that the ladies wore, en negligée, a white fichu or handkerchief, known as the "whisk," and a linen or fine lace scarf for dress. This simplicity was encouraged by Anne of Austria. The handkerchief seems to have been the one portion of the Quakeress dress that has come down unchanged to modern times.

Thus it was with the "world's people," and as Quaker persecution ceased, vanity in dress arose, alas! even among them; poor Susan Ponder was disowned for "conforming to the fashions of this wicked world." Aberdeen Meeting has an elaborate description of what is and is not to be suffered in men's and women's dress. In 1703 the young women came to York Quar-

Miss Fitzgerald, Lady in Waiting to Queen Caroline, especi-
rally, After the painting by Sir Thomas Lawrence ill
...ns of that date. In 1844, when gowns we...
Margaret Morris, Wife of Isaac Collins, jr., 1792-1832.
décolleté. Cuthbert tells ... hat the ladies
From the drawing on stone by J. Newsam, after
...with the original painting...hief, known as t

II.

terly ·Meeting in long cloaks and the new Paris importation called the "bonnet." They were therefore not only ordered to take the advice of their elders before coming to "these great meetings here in York," but one subordinate meeting actually ordered the young women of its own meeting to appear before it "in those clothes that they intend to have on at York." *
However, neither this, nor the strict oversight of Aberdeen, was sufficient in the early years to exclude all worldliness; for in 1720 we find all these vanities noted in the minutes of the latter as existing among the young Quakeresses: "Quilted petticoats, set out in imitation of hoops; cloth shoes of a light color, with heels white and red; scarlet and purple stockings, and petticoats made short to expose them." In that year, York Quarterly Meeting sent the following letter to the monthly meetings composing its constituency, which was in its turn sent to each particular meeting of women. The original from which this is copied was directed to "the Women Friends of Rilston Meeting, These." †

Att our Quarterly Meeting held att York, ye 22 & 23 4th. Mon. 1720 The Monthly Meets. were called & there was thatt answered for all, either by Representatives or papers & most gave account thatt things were pretty well amongst them notwithstanding there are severall things remains amongst us wch are very Burthensome to the honest-hearted & have been weightily spoken against wch its Desired the Representatives would Deliver in the Wisdom of Truth (viz.) the imitating the Fashions of the World in their Headclothes some haveing four pinner ends hang-

---

* Robert Barclay, "Inner Life of the Religious Societies of the Commonwealth," p. 491.

† Devonshire House Collection, London.

ing Down* and handkerchiefs being too thin some haveing them hollowed out & putt on farr of their necks also their gown sleeves & short capps wth a great Deal to pinn up in the Skirt also their Quilted petticoats sett out in imitation of hoops some wearing two together also cloth Shoes of light Colors bound wth Differing colours and heels White or Red wth White Bands and fine Coloured Clogs & strings also Scarlet or Purple Stockings & petticoats made Short to Expose ym. Friends are also Desired to keep out of the fashion of wearing black hats or shaving [chip] or straw ones with crowns too little or two large wth wch else the Judgment of Truth is gone out agst.

Signed in behalf of the meeting by

> MARY WHITE,
> SARAH ELAM,
> HANNAH ARMITSTEAD,
> TAMER FIELDING,
> MARY SLATER.

The early Quaker women wore their hair, like that of the men, cut low and straight on the forehead, and braided or put in a knot on the top of the head. It was the era when the great commode was approaching, reaching its height in the reign of Queen Anne. This perilous structure consisted of " a frame of wire two or three stories high, fitted to the head and covered with tiffany or rather thin silk now completed into a head-dress." † The word " commode " was never used for this head dress in America.

> Nor holy church is safe, they say,
> Where decent veil was wont to hide
> The modest sex' religious pride;
> Lest these yet prove too great a load,

---

* Pinners appear to have been the pendant ends, streamers, or lappets, hanging down at the sides of the face, or occasionally behind—like "liripipes," which were longer, and always at the back. These were all quite distinct from cap *strings*.

† " The Book of Costume. By a Lady of Quality." London, 1846.

'Tis all compris'd in the commode;
Pins tipt with diamond, point and head,
By which the curls are fastened,
In radiant firmament set out,
And over all the hood sur-tout.
Thus, face that e'rst near head was plac'd
Imagine now about the wast,
For tour on tour, and tire on tire,
Like steeple Bow, or Grantham spire,
Or Septizonium, once at Rome,
(But does not half so well become
Fair ladies' head) you here behold
Beauty by tyrant mode controll'd.*

The articles required in a lady's toilet bore many and curious names; they were so incomprehensible to the uninitiated, that the following anecdote is most amusing:

A raw lass, being entertained in service, and hearing her mistress one day call for some of them, she was so far from bringing any, that she verily took her to be conjuring, and hastily ran out of the house, for fear she should raise the devil! †

The contrast to the Quakeress may be imagined. A French style in favor at this time also consisted of a bandeau of jewels worn over flowing locks in negligent fashion on the shoulders, to match the "love-lock" of the men. The "love-lock" was introduced by Charles I., and consisted of a curl of greater length than the rest of the hair, worn on the left side. This soon became the rage. A corresponding lock with the ladies

---

*From "Mundus Mulieribus, or, The Ladies Dressing-Room unlocked, and Her Toilet spread," 1670. Anonymous. This is an elaborate description of women's costume. It is given in the publications of the Percy Society. Vol. XXVII., p. 190.

† Quoted by Repton, "Archæologia." Vol. XXVII., p. 56.

was the " heart-breaker." *   The high headdress lasted
much later than the love-lock.   In 1698 we find
Jonathan Edwards rebuking its appearance in Puritan
New England.   The Puritan women are often represented with " banged " hair.   The " high head " had a
period of decadence, and was revived again in 1715,
and Addison writes soon after: " There is not so
variable a thing in nature as a Lady's headdress; within my memory I have known it rise and fall above
thirty degrees."   " I pretend not to draw the quill
against that immense crop of plumes."   The " commode " killed itself by its own extravagance, the time
and expense required to put up one's hair becoming so
great that the hair-dresser could not make his rounds
to any but the most wealthy oftener than once in three
weeks or a month, leading one satirical writer of the
period to remark:

I consent also to the present style of curling the hair so that
it may stay a month without combing, tho' I must confess that
I think 3 weeks or a fortnight might be sufficient time!

The tremendous " crop," or turban, that all lovers of
" Cranford " will remember, was a favorite of the ladies
later on.   The moment a woman became a Quaker, the
fact was proclaimed to all the world by her discarding
all extravagant headdresses.   The early Methodists
were quite as pronounced.   An old Norfolk journal
has the following:

Several fine ladies who used to wear French silks, French
hoops, 4 yards wide, tête de mouton heads, and white satin
smock petticoats, are now turned Methodists, and followers of

---

* Another "heart-breaker" is described as "False Locks set on
Wyers to make them stand at a distance," about 1670.   They resembled
butterfly wings over the ears.

Mr. Whitefield, whose doctrine of the new birth has so prevailed over them, that they now wear plain stuff gowns, no hoops, common night mobs, and old plain bags!

Stubbes, from whom we have before quoted, describes the elaborate coiffure of an elegant dame:

Then followeth the trimming and tricking of their beades, in laying out their haire to the shewe, whiche of force must be curled, fristed, and crisped, laid out (a world to see) on wreathes and borders, from one care to another. And least it should fall down, it is vnder propped with forks, wiers, and I cannot tell what, like grim sterne monsters, rather than chaste Christian matrones. Then on the edges of their boulstered hair (for it standeth crested rounde their frontiers, and hanging ouer their faces like pendices or uailes, with glasse windowes on euery side) there is laide great wreathes of golde and siluer curiously wrought, and cunningly applied to the temples of their beades. And for feare of lacking anything to set forthe their pride withall, at their haire, thus wreathed and creasted, are hanged bugles (I dare not say bables), ouches, ringes, gold, siluer, glasses, and suche other childish gewgaws, and foolish trinkets besides, whiche, for they are innumerable, and I vnskilfull in women's termes I cannot easily expresse. But God giue them grace to giue ouer their vanities, and studie to adorn their heades with the incorruptible ornaments of vertue and true godlinesse.

The ancient London graveyard of the Friends, in Lower Redcross Street, Southwark, was removed a few years since, not having had any interment made in it since 1799. One of the graves was found to be that of a young woman who wore on her head a pad quite perfect, such as was customary at the time to keep the hair high on the crown; and in the mass of auburn hair, long and fine, was a handsome tortoise shell comb.* This would indicate the tendency, before alluded to, for the Quakers to follow the dictates of fashion, even at a safe distance. It was a passing fancy in the early

---

* Beck and Ball, " The London Friends' Meetings," p. 238.

days to draw up the petticoat through the pocket hole
and other openings, thereby displaying the gaiety of
that garment. We may note the case of the maid,
who being required by John Bolton, on an order from
George Fox, to sew up the slit in her waist-coat skirt
behind, answered that she "saw no evil in it; and
James Claypoole thought it suitable to their principle
that she should first see the evil in it herself before she
judged it, and not (saith he) because we say it." *
Wherein James showed great discrimination. The
Quakeresses who wore the hair low were really more
in the French mode, the artistic sense of that nation
rebelling sooner against the rule of the "commode,"
which seems after the law of contraries to have won its
name from its inconvenience, much as the "night-
gown" and "night-cap" were elegant constructions,
never worn at night!

February 15th, 1765, the Duchess of Devonshire
wrote to her mother:

I was too tired to write. My sister and I were very smart for
Carlton House. Our gowns were night-gowns of my invention.
The body and sleeves black velvet bound with pink, and the
skirt, apron and handkerchie crape, bound with light pink, and
large chip hats with feathers and pinks. My sister looked vastly
pretty.

Of course all the Germans of the last century were
devotees of the "schlafrock," which, however, was
emphatically a lounging garment, a purpose with
which is instinctively associated all our ideas of the
old-time German "Herr Professor," who never made
his toilet until the working hours of the day were

---

* "Tyranny and Hypocrisy Detected." — Answer to a pamphlet,
"The Spirit of the Hat." London, 1673.

over, and not always then. Macbeth dons a "night-gown," and so does Julius Cæsar, both being loose robes.

Henrietta Maria, Queen of Charles I., in her well-known portrait in the National Gallery, wears her hair curled, and is seen in a simple yellow satin gown, with broad lace at the low neck, and at the elbow sleeves. She wears a pearl necklace and chain.   Catherine, Duchess of Queensbury (1700-1777), the daughter of Lord Clarendon, and the patroness of Gay, Prior and others, called by Walpole, "Prior's Kitty, ever young," wears in her por-trait in the National Gallery a cos-tume almost Quaker-like in its sim-plicity, with a simple coiffure, and a

1756.

kerchief thrown over the shoulders. Even Nell Gwynn (1650-1687) is simple in short sleeves, low neck, and short curly hair.

Thomas Story, whose wide acquaintance took him among the "world's people," tells us of an attempt he made to convert the Countess of Kildare to Quaker dress:

It being the Time of the Assizes, many of the higher Rank were in Town on that Occasion, and divers of our Friends being ac-quainted with several of them, one Day came to my Friend John Pike's to Dinner, the young Countess of Kildare, and her Maiden Sister, and three more of lesser Quality of the Gentry. Upon this occasion we had some free and open Conversation to-gether, in which this Lady and the rest commended the plain Dress of our Women, as the most decent and comely, wishing it were in Fashion among them. Upon this I told her "That she and the rest of her Quality, standing in Places of Eminence, were the fittest to begin it, especially as they saw a Beauty in it; and they would be sooner followed than those of lower Degree." To this she replied, "If we should Dress ourselves Plain, People would gaze at us, call us Quakers, and make us the Subject of their Discourse and Town-talk; and we cannot bear to be made so particular."

I answered, "The Cause is so good, being that of Truth and Virtue, if you will espouse it heartily upon its just Foundation, a few of you would dash out of Countenance, with a steady and fixed Gravity, Abundance of the other Side, who have no Bottom but the Vain Customs of The Times; and you will find a Satisfaction in it, an Overbalance to all you can lose, since the Works of Virtue and Modesty carry in them an immediate and perpetual Reward to the Worker." This seemed not unpleasant, being said in an open Freedom; But then, alas! all was quenched at last by this; they all of them alledged, "That our own young Women of any Note, about London and Bristol, went as fine as they with the finest of Silk and Laced Shoes; and when they went to Bath, made as great a Show as any." Not knowing but some Particulars might give too much occasion for this Allegation, it was a little quenching; but, with some Presence of Mind, I replied, "I have been lately at London and Bristol, and also at the Bath, and have not observed any such; but at all these three Places generally indifferent plain, and many of them, even of the younger sort, very well on that Account; But such among us who take such Liberties, go beside their Profession, and are no Examples of Virtue, but a dishonour and Reproach to our Profession, and a daily and perpetual Exercise to us; and I hope you will not look at the Worst, since, among us everywhere, you may find better and more general Examples of Virtue and Plainness." This they did not deny; and so that Part ended.*

London Quarterly Meeting, in 1717, issued a paper in which the women are exhorted not to deck themselves with " gaudy and costly apparel," nor to wear " gold chains, lockets, necklaces and gold watches exposed to open view." The " immodest fashion of hooped petticoats " is condemned; the wearing of mourning, and worldly conversation. " Likewise there is a declension crept in among us of unbecoming ges-

---

* Thomas Story, Journal. Folio edition, p. 533. 1716.

tures in cringing and bowing of the body by way of
salutation, which ought not to be taught or countenanced in our schools or families." The document
then asks:

How shall any persons reputed Quakers wearing extravagant
wigs, open breasts, their hats and clothes after a beauish fashion, gold chains with lockets and gold watches openly exposed,
like the lofty dames, or hooped petticoats, like the wanton women, be distinguished from the loose, proud people of the world?[*]

Stubbes had declared[†] that the perfumes so prevalent
at this time were " engines of pride, allurements to
sinne, and provocations to vice ! " If cleanliness is
next to godliness, old Stubbes may indeed have been
right; for the heavy odors in use covered up a multitude of sins. The prevalent use of snuff made the silk
handkerchief a necessity. A few dainty folk used
those of cambric. An old advertisement calls attention to " handkerchiefs that will wash in a weak lather
of soap without prejudice." [‡] The custom of ladies
smoking was a fad with the " smart set " of that day as
well as our own. They still painted, a custom which
Evelyn (11th of May, 1654) had noticed beginning:
" I now observed how the women began to paint themselves, formerly a most ignominious thing."

As for patching, it was universal, and evidently only
another " snare " for the feminine Quaker mind! We
learn from Pepys (May 1, 1667) of the patching of one
maid:

That which I did see and wonder at with reason, was to find
Pegg Pen in a new coach, with only her husband's pretty sister

---

* Beck and Ball, " London Friends' Meetings," p. 77.
† "Anatomie of Abuses," p. 200.
‡ Ashton, " Social Life in Reign of Queen Anne," p. 118.

[Margaret Lowther] with her, both patched and very fine, and in much the finest coach in the park. . . . When we had spent half an hour in the park, we went out again, . . . and so home, where we find the two young ladies come home and their patches off. I suppose Sir W. Pen do not allow of them in his sight!

The "stay-maker" was the companion of the wig-maker; there are several Quakers whose names appear in the old London records as "stay-makers," or "bodice-makers." They advertised "both wooden and whalebone corset-busks." When the wig-makers ceased to be found among the Quakers, the bodice-makers pursued their way alone, that trade not being under condemnation, which only served to ruin the health, and was less conspicuous than the wig. "Fashion babies" have been alluded to; these merit more than a passing notice. They were models of costume, originally sent by Paris modistes to London and other cities of large population, displaying the very latest ideas in dress. The fashion plate was then far in the future, and even the Quakers employed this method of communicating their ideas as to the "proper thing" in drab to their country friends, or, as in the case of the doll model that was given to Stephen Grellet, to other communities of their own sect.

Several of these dolls have been kindly loaned me for examination. Just as Mademoiselle Martin, a famous modiste of the time of Marie Antoinette, was in the habit of sending doll models of the latest style, called "babies," to the most distant parts of Europe, so these quaint little Quaker dolls served to show the distant friend what was worn at the metropolis. There were, as we have seen, many changes of style in Quaker dress. The difference between them and the "world's

people " lay in the magnitude and profundity of the
question, relatively speaking; for quite as much
thought and expenditure of time and money went
into the alteration of a pleat in the Quaker bonnet, or
a flap on the Quaker coat, as ever entered into the construction of a Paris " confection." Of these models—
for it is a mistake to call them dolls, since they were
anything but toys—one, for instance, is in the exact
dress of Rebecca Jones, a well-known Philadelphia
Friend, who lived from 1739 to 1818. She wears the
bonnet with soft crown and a very large cape spreading
in three points down the back and to the tip of each
shoulder. The crown of another bonnet made about
1790, still extant, has a double box-pleat at top in center and four pleats down the side, clearly showing the
coming stiff pleats in the " coal-scuttle " of later development. " Patty Rutter " is also a doll with a serious purpose, dressed in 1782 by Miss Sarah Rutter, of
Philadelphia, and sent to Mrs. Samuel Adams, of
Quincy, Massachusetts. It was presented to the
Museum in Independence Hall in 1845. The doll is
in Quaker dress, consisting of white silk bonnet and
shawl, and drab silk gown. At her side hangs a chate-
laine, with watch and pencil. The doll and her costume are still intact. The most interesting of all these
models, however, is that of the Grellet family. Stephen Grellet was a famous French Quaker, who, as
Etienne de Grellet du Mabillier, escaped from Limoges,
his patrician father's home, at the time of the French
revolution, and with a brother took refuge in America.
Meeting with the Quakers, he became convinced of
their principles, and at the time of his death was one

of their most famous preachers. He was in England
in the year 1816, intending to visit the French at Con-
génies in France, where was a little community re-
markably in sympathy with the Friends, although having had no communication with them originally. English Friends desired to aid his efforts to build up their
small meeting. The Quaker women of London, therefore, made and dressed for them a model in wax of a
properly gowned woman Friend. Some untoward
event recalled the preacher to his American home before he succeeded in the accomplishment of his original
purpose. Upon his arrival, the doll was discovered,
to his astonishment, in one of his trunks. When
he wrote to ask how to dispose of the doll, the
reply was: " Give her to thy little daughter." That
" little daughter," living in New Jersey until July,
1901, to the great age of ninety years, was herself the
authority for this story of " Rachel," as the beautiful
doll has always been called. The fine rolled hem of the
cap-border bears witness to the exquisite needle-work
of the last century.

An increasing manifestation of the love of dress was
marked throughout the colonies. The Friends from
England noted this with an anxious eye, and in nearly
all the meetings in America may be found records dealing with that tendency. Finally, Friends of Philadelphia Yearly Meeting, then held at Burlington, New
Jersey, issued the following note of warning:

From Women ffriends at the Yearly Meeting held at Burlington, The 21st. of the 7th. Month, 1726.

To Women ffriends at the Several Quarterly & Monthly Meetings belonging to the same,—Greeting.

Dear and Well-beloved Sisters:

        A Weighty Concern coming upon many ffaithful ffriends at this Meeting, In Relation to divers undue Liberties that are too frequently taken by some yt. walck among us, & are Accounted of us, We are Willing in the pure Love of Truth wch. hath Mercifully Visited our Souls, Tenderly to Caution & Advise ffriends against those things which we think Inconsistent with our Ancient Christian Testimony of Plainness in Apparel &c., Some of which we think it proper to Particularize.

As first, That Immodest ffashion of hooped Pettycoats, or ye. imitation of them, Either by Something put into their Pettycoats to make ym sett full, or Wearing more than is Necessary, or any other Imitation Whatsoever, Which we take to be but a Branch Springing from ye. same Corrupt root of Pride.

And also That None of Sd ffriends Accustom themselves to wear their Gowns with Superfluous ffolds behind, but plain and Decent. Nor to go without Aprons, Nor to wear Superfluous Gathers or Pleats in their Capps or Pinners, Nor to wear their heads drest high behind, Neither to Cut or Lay their hair on ye fforehead or Temples.

And that ffriends are careful to avoid Wearing of Stript Shoos, or Red or White heel'd Shoos, or Clogs, or Shoos trimmed wh. Gawdy Colours.

Likewise, That all ffriends be Careful to Avoid Superfluity of Furniture in their Houses, And as much as may be to refrain Using Gawdy floured or Stript Callicos and Stuffs.

And also that no ffriends Use ye Irreverent practice of taking Snuff, or handing Snuff boxes one to Another in Meetings.

Also That ffriends Avoid ye Unnecessary use of ffans* in Meetings, least it Divert ye mind from ye more Inward & Spiritual Exercise wch. all ought to be Concern'd in.

And also That ffriends do not Accustom themselves to go in bare Breasts or bare Necks.

There is Likewise a Tender Concern upon or minds to recommend unto all ffriends, the Constant use of ye plain Language It being a Branch of our Ancient Christian Testimony, for wch. many of or Worthy Elders underwent deep Sufferings in their Day As they Likewise Did because they could not give ye Com-

---

    * "Ffaus" first came to New England in 1714, so were not new in Pennsylvania and New Jersey at this time, although they were not in common use before 1750, and the Friends considered them very gay.

mon Salutation by Bowing and Cringing of ye Body wch. we
Earnestly desire ffriends may be Careful to Avoid.

And we farther Tenderly Advise and Exhort That all ffriends
be careful to Maintain Love and Unity and to Watch against
Whispering and Evil Surmisings One against Another, and to keep
in Humility, That Nothing be done through Strife or Vainglory,
and yt. those who are Concerned to take an oversight over the
fflock, Do it not as Lords over God's heritage, but as Servants
to ye Churches.

Dear Sisters, These Things we Solidly recommend to yor Care
and Notice In a Degree of yt. Divine Love wch hath previously
Manifested Itself for ye Redemption of a [MS. illegible] ye Vain
Conversations, Customs, & Fashions yt. are in ye World, That
we might be unto ye Lord, A Chosen Generation, A Royal Priest-
hood, An Holy Nation, A Peculair People, Shewing forth ye
Praises of him who hath called us out of Darkness into his Mar-
vellons Light, that We may all walck as Children of the Light
& of ye Day, Is ye Earnest Desire of our Souls.

We Conclude wth. ye Salutation of Unfeigned Love, yor ffriends
and Sisters.

Signed on behalf & by ordr. of ye sd. Meeting By
                              HANNAH HILL.

The " surprise " fan was made with an unexpected
joint, like the early parasols. Ann Warder notes the
constant and needless use of fans, and with some com-
placency, remarks upon her own forbearance in the matter, " lest it should prove a disturbance to others."
Only two days after her arrival from England, under
date 9th of June, 1786, she wrote, " Such a general use
of fans my eyes never beheld. You scarcely see a
woman without one. And in winter, I am told, they
visit with them as a plaything." She noticed a
child with a dirty face playing in the street. The
mother " did not wash its face in the daytime for fear
of spoiling its complexion !" " Their mode of dressing children in Philadelphia," she regards, as " not so
becoming as with us. I have scarcely seen a White

worn over the ordinary dress, the skirt
often protected by original photograph."   M

Frock since my arrival. Not a woman has visited me but was elegant enough for any Bride, indeed we could almost persuade ourselves that was the case from so much saluting."

No costume was more important for the Quaker woman of the seventeenth and eighteenth centuries than that designed for use on horseback. This was even more the case in the colonies than in England, where, in London, at least, the sedan chair and the coach were cosmopolitan luxuries enjoyed very early. Country Friends, however, had to ride everywhere, and a woman, and especially a woman minister, if she traveled at all, must of necessity be a good horsewoman. The riding hood, with cape or long cloak attached— called a " Nithesdale " or " Capuchin," respectively— was worn over the ordinary dress, the skirt of which was often protected by a " safeguard." Mrs. Earle defines a " safeguard " as an " outside petticoat of heavy linen or woollen stuff, worn over other skirts to protect them from mud in riding on horseback." Ann Warder wrote of the Quaker women of Pennsylvania, in 1786, " They are very shiftable. They ride by themselves with a safeguard, which, when done with, is tied to the saddle, and the horse hooked to a rail, standing all meeting time as still as their riders sit." The " safeguard " seems to have disappeared in New England after 1750, indicating the introduction of the riding habit, which was appearing in England, and exciting the ridicule of the cynical Dean of St. Patrick's,[*]

---

[*] " I did not like [Miss Forester], although she be a toast and was dressed like a man." Swift, Journal to Stella, August 11th, 1711. The riding habit, which was the dress Swift alluded to, had just come in. Pepys, 1666, had also described the ladies in the galleries at Whitehall, in doublets, with periwigs and hats.

and others. The flat beaver hat, with very broad brim, and crown not two inches in height, was much worn for riding, and its contemporary cloak is of heavy grey stuff, the originals from which the illustration was taken being known to be over one hundred and fifty years old.

An accompaniment of the riding costume was the riding-mask, vizor, or, as usually written, " vizzard."

Lady's Riding Hat.

It was of this that Fox wrote, "Away with your unnecessary buttons," " your skimming-dish hats," " *vizzards*," etc. He is probably referring also to the " vizzard " which was used as well in walking, and at one time worn hanging by a ribbon or cord at the side. In 1645, we are told, the Puritans of Plymouth, Mass., for " some unaccountable reason," forbade them to their people. We should think that the reason of extravagance might have proved as sufficient with them as with the Quakers. For old Stubbes, not long before this, had been making his ultra-Puritanical

strictures on almost all varieties of English dress, and
he thus scores the visors:

When they vse to ride abroad, they haue visors made of veluet
(or in my iudgment they may rather be called inuisories) where-
with they couer all their faces, hauing holes made in them
agaynst their eies, whereout they looke. So that if a man
that knew not their guise before, shoulde chaunce to meete one
of theme, he would thinke he mette a monster or a deuill: for
face he can see none, but two broad holes against their eyes
with glasses in them. Thus they prophane the name of God, and
line in all kinde of voluptuousnesse and pleasure, worse than
euer did the heathen.*

The mystery of their attachment while riding, with
possibly both hands occupied with a restless horse, is
solved by learning that the article had a silver mouth-
piece, by which the teeth of the wearer held it in place,
leaving her free to grasp the reins or the pillion, as
the case might be. There was no protection from rain
or sleet in those days before the umbrella, and a rainy-
day costume was imperative. All sorts of devices were
permissible.

> Good housewives all the winter's rage despise,
> Defended by the riding-hood's disguise.
>
> . . . . . .
>
> Why should I teach the maid, when torrents pour
> Her head to shelter from the sudden shower?
> Nature will best her ready hand inform
> With her spread petticoat to fence the storm.
>
> Gay. " Trivia."

Reference has elsewhere been made to the gay coloring of the clothing among the early Puritans in New
England, but by the middle of the eighteenth century
their garb was generally as " sad " in color as their ordinary life was in tone. A pleasant contrast to them

---

* Philip Stubbes, "Anatomie of Abuses," p. 76. Ed. 1586.

are the homely Dutch Vrouws of New Amsterdam, who wore gowns of the gayest tints, as they went clinking along the streets in their heavy footgear. The Quaker women of the colonies seem to have more in common with the latter than with the Puritans, despite their sobriety of living.   Scarlet cloaks found their way to America very early in the history of Penn's colony, and there seems to have been much latitude in dress.   The wealthy women Friends in Pennsylvania in the days of the Founder, dressed far more expensively and elaborately than they ever did at a later date; they flourished about in "white satin petticoats, worked in flowers, pearl satin gowns, or peach-colored satin cloaks; their white necks were covered with delicate lawn, and they wore gold chains and seals, engraven with their arms." Miss Repplier tells us that Sarah Logan Norris, the wife of Isaac Norris, of Fairhill, wore a gown of deep blue.   Mary, the daughter of Thomas Lloyd, who married Isaac Norris, the elder, wore blue and crimson; while her granddaughter, Mary Dickinson, wore deep red.   All these women were Quakers of the best families in the country.   It is worth while to note that the daughter of Mary Dickinson, Maria Logan, was far more plain than her mother or grandmother had been, showing a growing tendency of the Quakers to emphasize plainness, and an increasing attention to uniformity of garb among their members.   The presence of the Founder seems to have had much the effect of the residence of the sovereign in a small estate.   His courtly dress and manners had their inevitable effect upon the Quakers, whether in London or Philadelphia; and had it been possible to prolong his life through the next century, his people might have been spared much of their narrow policy, political as well as social, by the aid of his sane and experienced advice. There is universal testimony to the beauty and picturesqueness of the young Quakeresses of the aristocracy in the early days. The portrait of " The Fair Quaker," Hannah Middleton Gurney, whose costume was identical with that of Gulielma Springett, William Penn's first wife,* is that of a surpassingly handsome woman; and the Frenchman, Brissot, wrote of the Philadelphia Quakeresses many years after at the time of the Revolution, when dress was plainer among them:

These youthful creatures whom nature has so well endowed, whose charm has so little need of art, wear the finest muslins and silks. Oriental luxury would not disdain the exquisite textures in which they take delight.

The Frenchman did not fail to admire anything so artistic, and the Duc de la Rochefoucauld is the next to express himself, adding, " Ribbons please the young Quakeresses, and are the greatest enemies of the sect." †

Many agreed with the writer who not long before had said:

Behold the smart Quaker that looks in the glass,
Her hair doth all other companions surpass;
You deform your sweet faces, I vow and declare;
You should cut off your lappets and burn your false hair.‡

---

*See explanatory note regarding this portrait in Maria Webb's " Penns and Penningtons of the Seventeenth Century," to which the engraving of " Guli " Penn forms the frontispiece. It is quite distinct from the engraving with the same title, here reproduced.

†Agnes Repplier, " Philadelphia; The Place and the People," p. 286.

‡" The Mountain of Hair," 1760. Percy Soc. Vol. XXVII., p. 245.

Our great-grandmothers, if we may judge by the clothes that have come down to us, were, as a rule, smaller women than the average in these days of their tall and athletic descendants.

The private Diary of Ann, wife of James Whitall, of Red Bank, New Jersey, under date, 21st 12 mo., 1760, has the following:

Oh, will there ever be a Nehemiah raised at our meeting to mourn and grieve! Oh, the fashions and running into them! The young men wearing their hats set up behind, and next it's likely will be a ribbon to tie their hair up behind; the girls in Pennsylvania have their necks set off with a black ribbon; a sorrowful sight indeed! . . . There is this day Josiah Albertson's son, all the son he has, and his hat is close up behind!

A little later, 3 mo. 18, 1762:

Oh, I think, could my eyes run down with tears always for the abomination of the times. So much excess of tobacco; and tea is as bad, so much of it, and they will pretend they can't do without it; and there is the calico—Oh, the calico! . . . I think tobacco and tea and calico may all be set down with the negroes, one as bad as the other.*

The mournful strain in which the above is written was somewhat characteristic of the more sober plain folk among the Quakers of the last century. Many old letters exist in which are recorded prolonged wails and groanings in spirit over bonnet strings, hat-bands, shoe-buckles, and such momentous matters, all treated with the utmost gravity. Great interests were at stake in both England and America at these periods; but the Friends withdrew themselves from contact with outside interests of all sorts; and this, in addition to the greater isolation of each little community than in modern times, due to the difficulty of travel, tended

---

* Hannah Whitall Smith, "The Life of John M. Whitall."

to cultivate a feeling of their own importance in the world, and to the exaggeration of details in their little neighborhoods; so that the appearance of a man on the street with a new cock to his hat, or of a young woman with a black ribbon at her neck, shook the community to its foundations! It is amusing to read, in the editor's comments on the above diary, that at the very time the writer was so bewailing the worldliness of a black ribbon, she herself sat under the gallery of Woodbury meeting, arrayed in a straw bonnet lined with pink silk! After all, there is no standard of perfect plainness. The matter is entirely a relative one.

In the month of May, 1771, Isaac Collins, of Burlington, N. J., married Rachel Budd, of Philadelphia, at the "Bank Meeting," in that city. His wedding dress was a coat of peach blossom cloth, the great skirts of which had outside pockets; it was lined throughout with quilted white silk. The large waistcoat was of the same material. He wore small clothes, knee buckles, silk stockings and pumps—a cocked hat surmounted the whole. The bride, who is described as "lovely in mind and person," wore a light blue brocade, shoes of the same material, with very high heels —not larger at the sole than a gold dollar—and sharply pointed at the toes. Her dress was in the fashion of the day, consisting of a robe, long in the back, with a large hoop. A short blue bodice with a white satin stomacher embroidered in colors, had a blue cord laced from side to side. On her head she wore a black mode hood lined with white silk, the large cape extending over the shoulders. Upon her return from meeting after the ceremony, she put on a thin white apron of ample dimensions, tied in front with a large blue bow. The gaiety of this display positively takes our breath, particularly when we reflect that the bride had once belonged in John Woolman's own meeting. And yet, it only serves to show that the entire question of dress is relative, custom and precedent usually dictating what is unlawful, the whole matter being arbitrary to a startling degree. Our heart goes out to this beautifully picturesque Quaker couple, of whom the groom was already making a name for himself in the printer's art, and who shortly after issued the colonial currency of New Jersey in connection with the greater Franklin.* Apparently, the plain Friends were so accustomed to brilliant dressing in the neighborhood of Philadelphia, a very gay town in that day, that they did not take alarm at the colors introduced on this occasion, despite all they had said and written on the subject of dress in their official character.

That the younger Quakers followed the changes of Dame Fashion has been, we think, fully demonstrated. The wedding of Isaac Collins and Rachel Budd carried out the styles then prevailing. The ideal painting by Percy Bigland, "A Quaker Wedding," historically correct in its representation, shows a dress plainly influenced by the times, as the "empire" gown of the bride indicates. The "Two Friends," belongs to the years between 1835 and 1840, and since that time the present generation can refer to the costumes of their own parents. Older people have worn the modern plain bonnet and shawl for fifty or sixty

---

* I am indebted to the great-granddaughter of this picturesque couple for the description, which is authentic.

A Quaker Wedding, 1820.

After the original painting by Percy Bigland in possession of
Isaac H. Clothier, Wynnewood, Pennsylvania.

years. Before that time, the same bonnet had a soft crown; and a long hooded cloak—cloth in winter and silk in summer—was substituted for the shawl. The Quakers have always shown their exquisite taste in choice of materials, and have instinctively realized that nothing but the best stuffs would lend themselves with dignity to the severe simplicity of their garb. This could have been better realized some thirty years ago, when each of our great cities supported at least one large shop where Quaker goods exclusively were sold. The fact that the Quakers can now be served at any shop speaks volumes for either their deterioration or their progress—depending upon one's point of view.

By the time of the Revolution, Philadelphia far surpassed all other towns in the colonies with its extravagance and luxury of living, winding up with the "Meschianza"—that pageant whose tradition is still rehearsed in the ears of modern townsfolk, sounding more like a page from the fairy tales of the Middle Ages than actual happenings in the city of Penn. A Hessian officer, writing of the ladies of America at that time, says,[*]

They are great admirers of cleanliness, and keep themselves well shod. They friz their hair every day and gather it up on the back of the head into a chignon, at the same time puffing it up in front. They generally walk about with their heads uncovered, and sometimes but not often wear some light fabric on their hair. Now and then some country nymph has her hair flowing down behind her, braided with a piece of ribbon. Should they go out, even though they be living in a hut, they throw a silk wrap about themselves and put on gloves. They also put on some well made and stylish little sunbonnet, from which their roguish eyes have a most fascinating way of meeting yours. In

---

[*] Alice Morse Earle, "Costume of Colonial Times," p. 31.

the English colonies the beauties have fallen in love with red silk or woolen wraps.

A letter of Miss Rebecca Franks, a Philadelphia belle visiting in New York in 1778, speaks thus of society there in that year:

1776.
(After Martin.)

You can have no idea of the life of continued amusement I live in. I can scarce have a moment to myself. I have stole this while everybody is retired to dress for dinner. I am but just come from under Mr. J. Black's hands, and most elegantly dressed am I for a ball this evening at Smith's, where we have one every Thursday. . . . The dress is more rediculous and pretty than anything I ever saw—a great quantity of different coloured feathers on the head at a time beside a thousand other things. The hair dressed very high, in the shape Miss Vining's was the night we returned from Smith's—the Hat we found in your Mother's closet wou'd be of a proper size. I have an afternoon cap with one wing, tho' I assure you I go less in the fashion than most of the ladies—no being dressed without a hoop.

The Journal of Elizabeth Drinker, of Philadelphia, under date " December 15, 1777," says:

Peggy York called this morning. . . . She had on the highest and most rediculous headdress that I have yet seen.

A little later, July 4, 1778:

A very high headdress was exhibited thro' ye streets this afternoon, on a very dirty woman, with a mob after her with drums etc. by way of ridiculing that very foolish fashion.

The Two Friends.
After the engraving by Bowyer, London, about 1855.

In 1786 Ann Warder's Journal describes similar extravagance:

"Came to call"—a fine girl called the perfection of America but her being drest fantastical to the greatest degree and painted like a doll destroyed every pretension to Beauty, in my mind.

Such extravagance recalls the old poem:

THE LADIES' HEAD-DRESS.

Give Chloe a bushel of horse-hair and wool,
  Of paste and pomatum a pound,
Ten yards of gay ribbon to deck her sweet skull,
  And gauze to encompass it round.

Of all the bright colours the rainbow displays
  Be those ribbons which hang on her head,
Be her flounces adapted to make the folks gaze,
  And about the whole work be they spread.

Let her flaps fly behind, for a yard at the least;
  Let her curls meet just under her chin;
Let these curls be supported, to keep up the jest,
  With an hundred, instead of one, pin.

Let her gown be tuck'd up to the hip on each side;
  Shoes too high for to walk, or to jump;
And, to deck the sweet creature complete for a bride,
  Let the cork-cutter make her a rump.

Thus finish'd in taste, while on Chloe you gaze,
  You may take the dear charmer for life;
But never undress her—for, out of her stays
  You'll find you have lost half your wife.*

An American in London at the end of the last century, whether Quaker or not, was bound to have some surprises in contrasting the styles at home and abroad.

---

* From Publications of Percy Society, Vol. XXVII., p. 259. Printed first in "London Magazine" for 1777, and very popular.

In 1781, Lady Cathcart, an American by birth, wrote of London fashions:

They wear for morning a white poloneze or a dress they call a Levete [Levite] which is a kind of gown and Peticote with long sleeves made with scarcely any pique in the back, and worn with a sash tyed on the left side. They make these in winter of white dimity, and in summer of muslin with chintz borders.

We are told that the " robe-levite " imitated this garment, and that the " monkey-tailed levite " had a curiously twisted train, and was a French fashion.* Our " Fair Quaker " of this date wears what is no doubt a " Levite." Did its name help to make it seem less worldly?

George and Sarah (Hill) Dillwyn, very plain Friends from Philadelphia, went over to visit their English relatives in London soon after the peace was signed. Her letters to her family at home in New Jersey are the observations of an alert, lively woman, to whose philosophical mind the gay capital served as an amusement, but not in the least a temptation. Her opportunities for observation were of the best. She writes to her sister, M. Morris, dating her letter, " London, 4 12th. 1785 ":

I find it in vain to keep pace here with the nice dames, so don't care a fig about it; let us be dressed as we will, I find the best of them take a great deal more notice of us than either of us desires.†

They mention their reticules—spelt preferably by all, apparently, " ridicule; " these side pockets must match the gown, with tassel and strings.

" When writing of women," said Diderot, " we should dip our pen in the rainbow, and throw over each

---

* Mrs. Earle, " Costume of Colonial Times," p. 152.
† " Letters of the Hill Family," edited by J. J. Smith, p. 256.

She comes, like some bright Angel from the ...   **THE**   *...*
In every Grace, Beauty and Love ...   **FAIR QUAKER**   *...*

line the powder of the butterfly's wing, instead of sand ! " No such ethereal notion is left of woman in these athletic days of the golfing girl, but it is not so long since exercise was a disgrace, and to seem to live on anything more substantial than air, a crime against good taste. Gowns, of course, partook of the general æsthetic tendency, and the period of classicism in dress left its imprint on the garb even of the Quaker ladies of the early part of this century. Fashions as a rule change gradually, but at the French Revolution they made a sudden revolt, and down came the "high heads" and the "poufs au sentiment," the latter a pleasing structure some four feet high, representing at the wearer's whim, gardens and trees, and ships under full sail in billowy seas of gauze, or models of their nursery and babies and all their pet animals. The reaction went to the other extreme, when Paris sought to reproduce Greek simplicity; the "statuesque" effects that resulted might have caused even a Greek statue to blush. The desired effect was attained by discarding to the limit of decency, and even beyond it, all possible undergarments. None too many, according to our hygienic ideas in this day, had ever been worn. But a scanty cambric petticoat in the last days of the last century was quite the heaviest undergarment possible. The clinging draperies that resulted displayed a curious commingling of classical names; and one fine lady is quoted as wearing at the same time in 1809, "a robe à la Didon, a Carthage Cymar, and a Spartan Diadem." Tito, Daphne, Ariadne, Calypso, Diana and the whole Greek array were levied upon to distinguish different styles; and even Medusa lent her

name to a coiffure! The only thing to be said in favor
of this riot of classicism was that it put an abrupt end
to cocked hats, wigs, pigtails and hair powder. Hoops
became past horrors, as did expanded petticoats; but
while the less enthusiastic English refused to be quite
so unrestrained in dress as their neighbors across the
channel, they followed sufficiently far to attain a high
disdain for any underclothing that interfered with
statuesque effects, and perilous indeed must have been
the results in the unfriendly English climate. Gauze
and silks and tiffanys and taffetas, India muslins and
delicate gossamers were considered heavy enough for
winter wear by our English grandmothers, who, poor
things, killed themselves off before their time and trans-
mitted many an ill to their descendants as a tribute to
Dame Fashion. Shoes came from France, and were of
finest kid, for by some unaccountable mental bias it
was no more possible then than it is now for the English to make a graceful shoe. Rouge was described as
an " animating appendage " to the toilette, and cold
water was regarded as an enemy to good looks—" the
natural enemy to a smooth skin ! " Prince Jerome
Bonaparte married Miss Elizabeth Patterson on Christ-
mas eve, 1803. A gentleman who was present wrote:

All the clothes worn by the bride might have been put in my
pocket. Her dress was of muslin richly embroidered, of extremely fine texture. Beneath her dress she wore but a single garment.*

The classical craze wore itself out, as crazes will.
The only reason that it has here been referred to is because the scanty supply of underclothing which it per-

---

* Mrs. Hunt, " Our Grandmothers' Gowns," p. 15.

mitted caused our Quaker grandmothers many an ill, in the tradition left them that true refinement demanded an attire too airy to be compatible with the sharp changes of an English or American winter. Nobody wore woollen garments in the early nineteenth century, and for a long time cloth was regarded as very unfeminine even for an outside wrap. Linen was universal, and silk stockings with the thinnest lasting, or " prunella " shoes and slippers, with soles of paper-like thickness, were the usual foot-covering in houses full of draughts caused by open fires. Carpet or " list " shoes were donned by old ladies for snow and ice, and clogs and pattens were worn by the belles of the day. To be sure, heavy fur pelisses were worn in bitter weather, but were at once thrown aside on entering the house.

We find that calicoes with gay and fanciful designs became very fashionable after the Revolution in America; and it is no doubt to this mode that the Diary of Ann Whitall refers. An old newspaper says, " Since the peace, calico has become the general fashion of our country women, and is worn by females of all conditions at all seasons of the year, both in town and country." The French calicoes were delicate in texture and color, and were said to have been so popular that they were even worn in the freezing cold churches and meeting houses in the dead of a New England winter. There was nothing modest about some of the designs, if we may believe the old advertisements, which describe patterns called " liberty peak," "Covent Garden crossbar," " Ranelagh half-moon," and a " fine check inclosing Four Lions Rampant and three flours de Luce." Some were adorned with the portraits of political heroes, like Washington and Franklin. We are further told that these designs were stamped by blocks for the hand, which are still in existence.* The New England mantua-maker of 1668 charged eight shillings per day —a fair comparison with a modern seamstress—and the dressmaker who made up the calicoes a hundred years later got no more. A young married woman, who was a Friend, wrote to her sister from Washington, Dutchess County, New York, Seventh month 13th, 1828:

Yesterday was Preparative Meeting. The clerk was a young girl, I think not twenty years of age, dressed in a painted muslin, with a very large figure, almost white, a cape with a small transparent handkerchief round the neck, and a bonnet of white silk in the real English fashion, gathered very full, and altogether the most showy looking clerk I ever saw. . . .

I went over to the store yesterday and bought a real calico gown, a dress one,—light, to put on afternoons, when it is too cold for gingham, as it mostly is in this elevated region. I find it necessary to be pretty much dressed all the time if one is to keep up with the custom of the house. Even Mother made up a white apron, as she says she did not bring one, thinking they w'd not be worn here, but she finds her mistake.

The large figures became more modest later on. On the back of an old letter, dated 1833, in my grandmother's handwriting, I find the following memorandum: " Very small figures are the fashion here now for waistcoats and for gowns too."

Just before this she had written:

I can't bear to wear anything but crepe handkerchiefs this hot weather. . . . Short sleeves only are wearable either. I have not yet ventur'd to cut off more than one pair, but think I shall.

---

*Alice Morse Earle, " Costume of Colonial Times," p. 74.

These calicoes and figured stuffs were so famous for their large design that what to-day would seem to us a very conspicuous figure, was considered proper for Rebecca Jones to wear in Philadelphia on the occasion of her first appearance in the ministry. The original material is really a printed brown linen; the name of calico seems to have been of general application to stuffs of this sort. The early Friends had borne their testimony against these flights of fancy,* but "flour'd and figur'd things" have seemed to recur in feminine costume in some form ever since the days of Mother Eve.

It is hard to imagine the Quaker woman without her shawl; yet that article of dress was not worn in this country until 1784, when "a rich assortment of shawls" was advertised in Salem, Mass. The garment was the result of the East India trade, just beginning at this time, and was not worn in Europe much before the opening of the present century. An observant attender of Quaker meetings must have noted the manner in which the plain Quakeress sometimes takes her seat, as, with a hand behind her, palm outward, she gives an indescribable little "*flip*" to the corner of her shawl, to turn it up behind at the moment of seating herself to avoid wrinkles in the tail! The air with which that "*flip*" is sometimes given by a quick-motioned young woman, is levity itself. And none but the initiated can know of the art involved in donning the plain shawl

---

* "1st of 5 mo., 1693, Minute 7th. Before a minute offered to the Quarterly Meeting, concerning Fr'ds making, ordering, or selling striped cloths silks, or stuffs, or any sort of flour'd, figur'd things of different colours. It is the judgment of the Quarterly Meet'g that Friends ought to stand clear of such things." Unlocated. Copy by H. Hull, New York, 1850.

properly; the depth of the three folds exactly in the center of the back of the neck, and the size of the pin that holds them; the pin on the tip of each shoulder, to hold the fullness in sufficient firmness, without pulling, and without showing that it *is* a pin; and the momentous decision whether the point of the shawl is exactly in the middle, or not—indeed, there are impressive moments in the lives of all women.

Some form of cloak, usually hooded, was universal before the simplicity of the shawl commended itself at first sight to the Quakeress of the nineteenth century. The return of the Emperor Napoleon from his campaign in Egypt, bringing to Josephine some beautiful cashmere shawls, gave that garment a great vogue in 1807. The Empress took an immense fancy to the shawl, and there was a time at which she was scarcely ever seen without one in the morning. It is said that "she had about five hundred, for many of which she had given as much as ten or twelve thousand francs. The Emperor did not like to see her wrapped in her shawls within doors, and sometimes pulled them off and threw them in the fire, but she always sent for another."

The "Belle Assemblée" discourages the shawl. It says:

It is only wonderful, that such an article of dress should ever have found its path to fashionable adoption in the various circles of British taste. In its form, nothing can be more opposed to every principle of refined taste, or carry less the appearance of that elegant simplicity at which it aims. It is calculated much more to conceal and vulgarize than to display or regulate the contour of an elegant form, and is totally destitute of every idea of ease, elegance, or dignity. Whatever charms it may have for the sickly taste of the tawny BELLES of the torrid zone, nothing but that witching beauty which occasionally veils itself in the rusticity and homeliness (like the sun, its mists and clouds) that it may dazzle anew, with the refulgent splendor of its taste and charm, could render even tolerable the introduction of an habiliment which turns any female NOT beautiful and elegant into an absolute DOWDY. IT is the very contrast to the flowing elegance of the Grecian costume, whose light and transparent draperies so admirably display the female form.*

A Quaker poet thus expressed himself later:

> Observe yon belles! behold the waspish waist!
>   See the broad bishop spreading far behind;
> The shawl immense, with uncouth figures graced,
>   And veil loose waving in the playful wind;
> Mark the huge bonnets, stuck on hills of hair,
> Like meteors streaming in the turbid air.†

The impressions of the life and manners of the seven sisters Gurney, of Norwich, England, by A. J. C. Hare,‡ show the Quaker influence at work on a set of young people to whom no privileges of culture or refinement had ever been denied. The family to which belonged Joseph John and his talented sister, Elizabeth Gurney, better known by her married name of Elizabeth Fry, may well merit a little attentive study. Harriet Martineau describes the sisters as "a set of dashing young people, dressing in gay riding habits and scarlet boots, and riding about the country to balls and gaieties of all sorts. Accomplished and charming young ladies they were, and we children used to hear whispered gossip about the effect of their charms on heart-stricken young men." The seven are said to

---

*1807, quoted by Mrs. A. W. Hunt, in " Our Grandmothers' Gowns," p. 28.

†Samuel J. Smith, of Hickory Grove, N. J.

‡Augustus J. C. Hare, "The Gurneys of Earlham."

have linked arms, and in their scarlet * riding-habits,
in which they scoured the country side on their ponies,
stopped the great mail-coach from ascending the neigh-
boring hill!   The brother Daniel states in his " Reminiscences," that his four younger sisters never wore bonnets on the Earlham grounds, but put on little red
cloaks in which they ran about as they liked.   Louisa
Gurney (afterward Mrs. Samuel Hoare) writes, June
5th, 1797, " In the evening I dressed up in Quaker
things, but I felt far too ashamed to say or act anything," so strong was the influence of the Quaker spirit.
The same seven sat in a row in front of the ministers'
gallery at Norwich Meeting.   One day Betsey (Elizabeth Fry) had on a pair of " new purple boots lined
with scarlet," which sounds amazingly gorgeous to us
at this day.   Betsey was counting upon the delights of
the shoes to console her through the tedium she anticipated.   But as it proved, this was to be a memorable
day to her.   It was the fourth of February, 1798, and
Betsey was eighteen.   William Savery, the great
American preacher, was present, and his sermon was so
forceful and appealed so to her, that she became convinced of the truth of Quaker principles and became a
Quaker from that time forth.

   That same meeting seems to have shocked Friend
Savery, for he wrote that he found it very gay for a
Friends' meeting.   " There were," he says, " about two
hundred under our name, very few middle aged.   I
thought it the gayest meeting of Friends I ever sat in,
and was quite grieved at it. . . . Marks of wealth and
grandeur are too evident in several families in this

---

* " Kutusoff " mantles of scarlet cloth were much worn later.

place." Maria Edgeworth describes Elizabeth Fry after years had passed, in her "drab-colored silk cloak and plain borderless silk cap." When Joseph Fry first determined to marry Elizabeth Gurney, if it were possible, he saw her in a brown silk gown, with a black lace veil bound around her head like a turban, the ends pendant on one side of her face, and contrasting with her beautiful light brown hair. Richenda, her sister, writes of the "troutbecks" they were all wearing at the seaside in 1803. These were hats of that year. Red cloaks are mentioned, and the fashions of the time show the brilliant colors of wraps and all outside garments of the day to have been very startling. All except the plainest Quakers made some concession to the mode. Priscilla Gurney writes to Hannah, her sister, afterward the wife of Sir T. Fowell Buxton, "Chenda and I wear our dark gowns every day, and our aprons in the evening." This was in February, 1803. In 1805, Louisa Gurney writes to her sister, Elizabeth Fry, "I often seem to see thee in thy pink acorn gown attending to all thy flock in the dining room," etc. This "pink acorn gown" was probably a pattern similar to the calicoes and printed stuffs so popular among the Friends at the time, to which reference has already been made. We are told that in May, 1807, at the marriage of the Buxtons, "The house was overrun with bridesmaids in muslin cloaks and chip hats." In 1813, Katherine Fry says, "Our Aunts Catherine and Rachel (Gurney) wore no caps, but a headdress of crêpe folded turbanwise. Both were brown in the morning; in the afternoons, Aunt Catherine's were dark red; Aunt Rachel's, white. Aunt Rachel also frequently wore white muslin dresses.   They had few or no ornaments. Aunt Catherine always wore dark or black silk, but often with a red shawl.   Aunt Priscilla, as a Friend, was dressed in a dark silk or poplin gown, exquisitely neat, finished and refined." The Aunt Catherine who was the head of the family, while never a Quaker, always regarded the preferences of those who were of that faith in her circle, and studied an elegant simplicity of dress that was the admiration of her friends, seeking to avoid any marked or startling contrasts among the very varied views of the sisters.

Their intimate friend was the author, Amelia Opie; that talented convert to the faith went into it with her customary ardor, and the change from worldly garb was made at one leap, when once she became convinced of the necessity for the sacrifice of her love of color, which, as the wife of the artist, John Opie, had been more than ordinarily cultivated.* But she seems to have seen in the simple elegance of her Quaker friends, sufficient outlet for all artistic aspirations in the realm of costume; and certainly no more stately women could have been found in the King's domain to set off the possibilities of silk and satin, when worn with grace and distinction.   As though partly in explanation of what seemed to their friends an extraordinary step, Southey wrote of Mrs. Opie:

I like her in spite of her Quakerism—nay, perhaps the better for it. It must always be remembered amongst what persons she had lived, and that religion was never presented to her in a serious form until she saw it in drab.

---

* Joseph John Gurney, in writing of her at this time, says, "Great was her agony of mind in view of changing her dress, and of addressing her numerous friends and acquaintances by their plain names, and with the humbling simplicity of thee and thou."

So remarkable a figure was that of Elizabeth Fry in the elegant simplicity of Quaker dress, whether in the prison of Newgate, or before the crowned heads of Europe, that her dress has become fixed in the public mind as the type of woman's Quaker costume. Elizabeth Fry writes to her husband from The Hague, after an audience with the King and Queen, in 1847, "I wore a dark plain satin, and a new fawn colored silk shawl." At this time, however, it was no new thing for Elizabeth Fry to wait upon royalty. Her first visit to court was made in 1818, when Queen Charlotte commanded her presence at the Mansion House, upon which occasion A. J. C. Hare says, "Royalty offered its meed of approval at the shrine of mercy and good works." The Queen's stature was diminutive; she was covered with diamonds, her countenance lighted up with an expression of the kindest benevolence. Elizabeth Fry's simple Quaker dress added to the height of her tall figure. She was slightly flushed, but kept her wonted calm. Her daughter wrote afterward:

They entered, Lady Harcourt in full court dress, on the arm of Alderman Wood in scarlet gown; and then the Bishop of Gloucester (Ryder) in lawn sleeves, leading our darling mother in her plain Friend's cap, one of the light scarf cloaks worn by plain Friends, and a dark silk gown. I see her now, her light flaxen hair, a little flush in her face from the bustle and noise she had passed through, and her sweet, lovely, placid smile.*

Ann Warder, whose interesting Journal covers three years, from 1786 to 1789, among the Friends of Philadelphia and vicinity, gives us vivid pictures of life in the young republic, and the privilege of quoting from

---

* A. J. C. Hare, "The Gurneys of Earlham."

its unpublished pages has been gladly availed of. She tells us that upon landing from the ship Edward, in New York, in 1786, they were taken at once to the home of a Friend of the family. "The woman Friend of the house came up, and as a mark of her welcome, untied my cap to help strip me." At this period, Ann Warder was twenty-eight. On being told that her appearance was singular, she explained that "countries differed; riding dresses with us were very much worn, and mine in England would be esteemed a plain one. This is a specimen of their singularity on this Island [Long Island]; scarce any had Buckles, and not a looped hat did I see." When word reached Philadelphia by messenger of the arrival of John Warder and his English wife, ten minutes sufficed to see their Brother Jeremiah and his wife on their way to New York to meet them. Haste probably accounts for the appearance of the new arrival from the South, who is thus described by the English woman, and contrasted with her husband, his brother. She allows us to see the unconventional dress of the Quaker of that day:

His dress unstudied, a Cocked Hat, Clumsy Boots, Brown cloth large Breeches, Black Velvet Waistcoat, light old Cazemar [cassimere] coat, handkerchie instead of stock which is tied on without much pains. Conceive J. W. [her husband] with his suit— Nankeen Inexpressibles and white silk stockings, much more resembling an English gentleman.

She adds:

The women I have seen at present appear Indolent, which may perhaps be a reason for Mother Warder's bearing such a high character for notability.

To be a "notable" housewife was to reach woman's summit of social ambition at that day among the Quakers.

Got B. Parker to go out shoping with me. On our way happened of Uncle Head, to whom I complained bitterly of the dirty streets, declaring if I could purchase a pair of pattens, the singularity I would not mind. Uncle soon found me up an apartment, out of which I took a pair and trotted along quite Comfortable, crossing some Streets with the greatest ease, which the idea of had troubled me. My little companion was so pleased, that she wished some also, and kept them on her feet to learn to walk in them most of the remainder of the day.

The patten and clog are often spoken of interchangeably, but the clog is of vastly greater antiquity. The patten dates from the reign of Queen Anne, and is raised on a supporting ring; an excellent example may be seen in the museum of Independence Hall. Gay's charming explanation of their origin in his " Trivia " will, of course, come in mind. The clog in the illustration is from a beautiful pair carefully preserved in New Jersey. The hollow for the heel, and the preposterous elevation on the instep, designed to fill the arch of the foot in the companion shoe or slipper, are explained, and the illustration from our originals almost duplicated, in Fairholt's " Costume in England," which may be properly regarded as the final authority on matters of historical costume.

An insane woman remarked on Ann Warder's appearance when she visited the asylum in Philadelphia, that she (A. W.) was the " most clumsy woman in the party, but she believed it was because she had on too many petticoats."

I could not help being struck with two women Minister's appearance, both having Drab Silk Gowns, and Black Pasteboard Bonnets on. To see an old man stand up with a Mulberry Coat, Nankeen Waistcoat and Breeches with white stockings would look very Singular in England. My cap is the admiration of plain and gay.

A shopping expedition is recorded to find white leather mitts. " In not less than twenty [shops] did we ask for them before we succeeded; there is no place regular for different trades, as with us."

The apron, as we have seen, had its day of popularity, and it is perhaps interesting to notice that the sleeve, which early in the seventeenth century was often a separate article of dress, after the old custom from the time of the Wars of the Roses, was apt to be of another color than the gown, and green was still the fashionable shade at this period. A famous old song of the time, in everybody's mouth, was " My Lady Greensleeves." It is mentioned by Shakespeare in the " Merry Wives of Windsor," where Falstaff says: " Let the sky rain potatoes; let it thunder to the tune of ' Green-Sleeves.' " (Act V., Scene 5.) Part of the old song is as follows: *

> Alas, my love, you do me wrong
>   To cast me off discourteously;
> And I have loved you so long,
>   Delighting in your company.
>
>   Greensleeves was all my joy,
>   Greensleeves was my delight;
>   Greensleeves was my heart of Gold,
>   And Who but Lady Greensleeves?
>
> I have been ready at your hand
>   To grant whatever you would crave;
> I have both waged life and land
>   Your goodwill for to have.
>
> Thou couldst desire no earthly thing
>   But still thou hadst it readily.
> Thy music still to play and sing;
>   And yet thou wouldst not love me.

---

* From " A Handful of Pleasant Delites," by Clement Robinson, 1584.

My men were clothèd all in green,
  And they did ever wait on thee,
All this was gallant to be seen,
  And yet thou wouldst not love me.

They set thee up, they took thee down,
  They served thee with humility,
Thy foot might not once touch the ground,
  And yet thou wouldst not love me.

Thy gown was of the grassy green,
  Thy sleeves of satin hanging by,
Which made thee be our harvest queen,
  And yet thou wouldst not love me.

Greensleeves, now farewell, adieu!
  God I pray to prosper thee!
For I am still thy lover true;
  Come once again and love me.

Walter Rutherford is quoted by Miss Wharton as objecting violently to " a late abominable fashion from London, of ladies like Washerwomen with their sleeves above their elbows." This was in 1790. Elbow sleeves were worn by all the plain Friends at one time; and long " mitts," reaching to the shoulder, elaborate and exquisitely plaited linen and fine muslin under-sleeves, with the little gold link buttons to fasten them at the ends, are now in my possession. Through the latter half of the eighteenth, and the beginning of the nineteenth century, all plain women Friends wore gowns with low neck and short sleeves. This, I think, may be taken as an universal rule. The neck was protected by a dainty muslin or lawn handkerchief, folded across the bosom and pinned at the waist on each side. Over this was worn a soft silk shawl, and the shades of delicate gray or drab were often productive of the most exquisite effects, with a fresh young face. The young girl put on her cap before she was fairly grown up; and the first little girl sent to Westtown School in Penn-

Hannah Hunt,
Westtown's First Scholar.
1799.
(Aetat 11.)

sylvania, in 1799, wore a cap of large proportions. No baby came into the world, whether of Quakerdom or of fashion, in the last century, without at once having its hairless little pate clapped into a more or less uncompromising cap, many of those still in existence being very elaborately embroidered. But we might forgive them for refusing to the little head the proper circulation of air, if they had not sinned in a far worse way when they at once enclosed the poor little ribs in the most cruel of *stays.* For a long time, I tried to persuade myself that it was only the ultra-fashionable (or the Chinese) that so treated their offspring. But, alas! the pair of stiff, diminutive stays in my own possession has never been in the hands of the " world's people "; they come straight to me from a long line of Quaker ancestry, and I am reluctantly forced to believe that it was my own great-grandmother who refused freedom to the small ribs of her children, and laced the uncompromising implement of torture on her new-born infant. There are even now certain conservative women across the border in Canada, who still put their babies in tight jackets of this kind immediately after their birth, under the impression, which I suppose animated our great-grandmothers, that the small body needed " support," forsooth, much more than freedom!

When the children got to be of a suitable age for such instruction, literature like the following was read to them, with what effect, either on manners or morals, we are not told:

COUNSEL TO FRIENDS' CHILDREN.

Written at Coggeshall, Essex,
1745, by Anthony Purver.*

Dear little Friends, not tainted yet with ill,
By Sense not biassed, nor misled by Will;

.   .   .   .   .

Dress not to please, nor imitate the *N*ice;
Be like good Friends, and follow their Advice.
The rich man, gaily cloth'd, is now in Hell,
And Dogges did eat attirèd Jezebel.

.   .   .   .   .

Speak truly still, with Thou and Thee to One
As unto God; and feed the Pride in *N*one;
Give them no flatt'ring Titles, tho' they scoff,
Lest God, provok'd, should quickly cut you off.
Him only did not the three Children fear,
And with their Hats before the King appear?

It may be set down as a safe rule, in seeking for a Quaker style or custom at any given time, to take the worldly fashion or habit of the period preceding. When the mode changes, and a style is dropped, the Quaker will be found just ready to adopt it, having by that time become habituated to its use. Of all this process he is quite unconscious; the philosophy of such matters having never been presented to him. He might, indeed, shrink from the suggestion that there is any philosophy of clothes, at all; but Carlyle has so

---

* Anthony Purver was born at Uphurstborn, near Whitechurch, in 1702, and died at Andover, Hampshire, 1777, aged 75. He was buried in the Friends' grounds at the latter place.

taught us. A very modern instance of this familiariz-
ing process and ultimate acceptance of what, on its first
appearance, is set down as a vain fashion, is the recent
adoption in one of the largest boarding-schools in the
society, and the only plain one, of the ordinary straw
sailor-hat among the girls, just as its popularity is on
the wane.

It will be noted that during the period following the
time of William Penn up to that of the summit of Elizabeth Fry's fame—an interval of nearly one hundred
and fifty years—there was no established type of
Quaker dress. No woman of the society had ever
come before the public eye in such a way as to impress
it with her personality, or stamp her character upon
the public mind. Elsewhere, I have indicated that the
witchcraft persecutions had caused the preaching
woman who was the contemporary of William Penn,
who came from the same class of society as the witch
who was hung or burned with such wanton cruelty on
both sides the Atlantic, and who wore a garb exactly
similar, to be seized upon as the type of our nursery
" witch." The most conspicuous instance was taken;
otherwise, we should have had the Quaker woman in
her cap and pointed hat, her apron and her high-heeled
shoes, standing beside William Penn upon our boxes
of Quaker oats. But during the interval that followed
the preaching of the first Quaker women, in the fields
and on upturned tubs in the halls and kitchens of the
early Quakers, no striking Quaker woman arose, until,
at Newgate, appeared Elizabeth Fry's beautiful figure
in its exquisite setting. The great movement in England toward prison reform organized by her noble

aft *Elizabeth Fry 1780-1845.* pr

whofer who painted by George Richmond, Wallis

effort, has made her the type of the Quaker woman **for** all time.

A MEDITATION ON THE PRIDE OF WOMEN'S APPAREL.

(From "A New Spring of Divine Poetry," James Day, 1637. Percy Society. Vol. XXVII, p. 143.)

See how some borrow'd off-cast vaine attire,
Can puff up pamper'd clay and dirty mire:
Tell me, whence hadst thy cloaths that make thee fine,
Was't not the silly sheep's before 'twas thine?
Doth not the silk-worm and the oxe's hide,
Serve to maintain thee in thy cheefest pride?
Do'st not thou often with those feathers vaile
Thy face, with which the ostridge hides her taile?
What art thou proud of, then? me thinks 'tis fit
Thou shouldst be humble for the wearing it:
Tell me, proud madam; thou that art so nise,
How were thy parents clad in Paradise?
At first they wore the armour of defence,
And were compleatly wrapt in innocence:
Had they not sin'd, they ne're had been dismaid,
Nor needed not the fig-tree's leavy ayde!
Whatever state, O Lord, thou place me in,
Let me not glory in th' effect of sin.

" Madam, I do as is my duty —
Honour the shadow of your shoe-tie."

—Hudibras.

CHAPTER V.

THE EVOLUTION OF THE QUAKER BONNET.

Then let Fashion exult in her rapid vagaries;
From her fascinations my favorite is free;
Be Folly's the headgear that momently varies,
But a Bonnet of Drab is the bonnet for me.

Bernard Barton.

Borrow'd guise fits not the wise—
A simple look is best;
Native grace becomes a face
Though ne'er so rudely drest.

Thomas Campion, 1612.

CHAPTER V.

THE EVOLUTION OF THE QUAKER BONNET.

TO one brought up within the fold it is no light matter to approach so awful a subject as the Quaker bonnet. There was a certain solemnity about it that was born of terror. Whether it presided at the head of the women's meeting, or ventured in winter storms, protected in its satin or oil-skin case under the Friendly umbrella, or even lay alone in splendid state upon the bed of the welcome guest—anywhere, everywhere, it was a solemn thing. Born of much meditation, constructed with care and skill and many pricks (if not of conscience, at least of fingers *); with time and money and eyesight lavished recklessly upon it, that no deviation of a pleat from the pattern, or tint from the color, or grain from the quality might be wanting— shades of our grandmothers! Can we get our bonnet sufficiently in perspective to realize that it is already a matter of history, that the next generation will know the true Quaker bonnet no more, and that if some of these matters of custom and costume of the past among the Friends are not soon preserved, valuable opportunities for future students of the Quaker will be lost? Let us try.

---

* Plain bonnet-making was a trade exceedingly hard on the fingers.

Again it becomes necessary, in order to study the Quaker headdress, to examine first the worldly bonnet and mode of dressing the hair. The clue to all the changes within the Society may be found without; and not a pleat of the bonnet as now worn by the plainest Friend; not a turn of the shawl, not a flare of the coat nor a roll of the hat-brim, but had its origin at some remote day—let us whisper it softly—in Paris! There was a time when the bonnet, which for the sake of distinction, we shall call Elizabeth Fry's—the " technical " Quaker bonnet, so to speak, known among the irreverent as the " coal-scuttle," or " sugar-scoop," or " stiff-pleat "—was a new thing in America. It came to this country on the head of an accredited English woman Friend, Martha Routh,* who was also a minister; and echoes of its coming had preceded her. A contemporary journal, still in existence, tells us:

Martha Routh, a Minister of the Gospel from Old England, was at Goshen (Pennsylvania) Meeting the 11th. day of 11th. mo. 1798; was a means (if I mistake not) of bringing bonnets in fashion for our leading Frd's, and hoods or Caps on the Cloaks in the Galleries, which of Latter time the Hoods on the Cloaks of our overseers and other active members have increased to an alarming hight or size:—how unlike the dress of their grand·mothers! †

What should we not give to behold that same " dress of their grandmothers ! " Martha Routh made a second visit to America in 1802. She writes in her Journal on her return home after her first visit that

---

*Martha Routh, born 1743, died 1817.

† From " A Memorandum Book belonging to Ennion Cook, of Birmingham, Chester county, Pennsylvania," dated 1820. Ennion Cook was the village schoolmaster, and the old memorandum book is in possession of a descendant.

oman Friend, Martha Routh, who was also
; and echoes of its coming had preceded
contemporary journal, still in existence, tells us:

they were taken by a French privateer, when a young man in the boarding party remarked to her that she and her women companions looked like the nuns in France. "I told him," she says, "that we were Friends or Quakers, and inquired if they had heard of such in their country? He replied that they had." *
But American Friends have always been more conservative in their dress than their English cousins, probably because the latter's proximity to the continent forced them into more cosmopolitan habits. At any rate, American Friends were shocked at the giddy structure. But time went on. They gazed, they admired, they stole a furtive pattern; they made the venture, and behold! When a synonym was wanted for conservatism, for stability, for all things that endure, it was found in the Quaker bonnet. How sad that it must soon be as extinct as the dodo! To understand the evolution of this bonnet, it is necessary to go back more than three hundred years, and see through what changes the worldly bonnet has passed.

The faces of fifteenth century women, declares Viollet le Duc, were of a uniform type; the prevailing style of headdress during the Wars of the Roses having a tendency to cause a superficial resemblance among persons really unlike. Individuality is obscured by the universal adoption of a distinctive effect in bonnets or gowns. This illusion of similarity is marked among the few existing portraits of that period, when the imposing "steeple headdress" was the mode. That towering structure was composed of rolls and rolls of long linen, reaching two feet above the

---

* Journal of Martha Routh, p. 280.

head, and going to a point like an extinguisher, from whose apex floated a long gauzy veil. Until the evolution of the Quaker bonnet, no headdress existed lending such uniformity of type to the faces it surmounted, the "commode" and the "high head" not excepted. The "head rail" of the Saxon period, and the "wimple" or "gorget" of Plantagenet times, came down to the early seventeenth century as the hood, with which we shall presently make closer acquaintance. The "head rail" was not shaped at all, but consisted merely of a long piece of linen or stuff drawn over the head like a hood, and loosely wrapped about the neck, the grace of the latter movement, even on the most ungainly, exceeding that of the partly shaped wimple, which was more attractive in early English poetry than in actual life! The wimple was of silk or white cloth; and when discarded by the women of the period was retained as the "gorget" by the nuns, who to-day may thus trace the origin of the white

1641.

band worn about face and throat, under the black hood.* So universal was the hood that men as well as women wore it; and it remained in general use until the time of Henry VIII.† About 1644, both in France and England, we find again the "coif," usually worn in black, and really another form of hood of crêpe or taffetas, brought forward and tied under the chin.‡ Small bonnets or hoods, with two long "pattes," behind

---

* Hill, "History of English Dress." Vol. I., p. 61.
† See chapter on Hats.
‡ Quicherat, "Histoire de Costume."

the ears, or "mouchoirs" with lace, or "toquets" of
velvet (called "bonnets de plumes" because worn with
so many plumes), were all tentatively suggesting the
coming riot of headdress.   A handkerchief of lace fastened with a pin, covered the hair in the time of Richelieu; and the "coif" of deshabille, often called the
"round bonnet" ("sans passe ?") became the bonnet
after many years seen in the accompanying engraving
of the "Fair Quaker."   French women of the lower
classes, and servants, wore the "coif" with two long
"drapeaux" or "bavolettes" streaming   down   behind—doubtless the origin of the modern "bavolet."

English women of the common-
alty in the seventeenth century
wore broad hats like the men, of
beaver, with lower crowns, and
caps beneath, tied at the chin.
The black beaver hat was also
popular for riding. It was not
a universal custom with the lower classes at this period to cover
the head at all; while shortly
after, by way of contrast, Pepys
tells us that the aristocracy did

1635.
(From Hollar.)

not remove the hat, even at table. When the wimple was
worn under the hat, the latter was fastened on with a
hat-pin; so that there is truly nothing new under the
sun, not even this modern convenience. At the end of
Queen Anne's reign, the revival of the silk trade gave
a temporary popularity again to the silk hood.   The
pointed beaver hat with the cap below, although
chiefly a middle-class costume, was in vogue among a

few of the plainer in taste of the aristocracy, as may be seen in the portrait of Hester Pooks, second wife of John Tradescant, the younger. She lived from 1608 until 1678; her portrait hangs on the stairway of the Ashmolean Museum at Oxford. She wears a costume exactly similar to the Quakeress Tub-Preacher, including cap and peaked beaver hat, the only difference in dress being the rich lace upon her gown.

This peculiar headdress has remained from the time of James I. (who is responsible for the beaver hat in this form) to the present day among the Welsh women; and almost all of the earliest prints of the Quaker women who preach, show them dressed in this cap and hat. It is impossible, in examining any of these pictures, to avoid the suggestion that here is the hat of the conventional *witch* of our childhood—the old woman, who, for so many years, has swept the cobwebs from the sky; and we are justified in the conclusion. The steeple-

From "Memoires, etc., d'Angleterre." 1698.

crowned hat was worn over the hood about the period between 1650 and 1675; it was popular with the middle and lower classes, and familiar throughout the kingdom. It will be remembered that the terrible witch trials of the Continent, England and Massachusetts in America, all culminated during the latter half of the seventeenth century, the sufferers being chiefly drawn from the class who wore this dress. What more natural and inevitable than that the woman who wore so

women who preach, show them dressed in this cap and
hat. It is impossible, examining any of these pictures, to *The Quakers' Meeting* is the hat of the
conventional witch of our childhood—the old woman,
who, for so many years, has swept the cobwebs from the
sky, and we are justified in the conclusion. The steeple-
crowned hat was worn over the
period between
it was popular
with the middle and lower
classes, and familiar throughout

striking a garb should need but a broomstick to en-
able her to set out as the typical witch, in her journey
to immortality and posterity?*   The ideal Quaker
man's garb is that of this period, as seen in the well-
known broad-brim of William Penn, immortalized even
in " Quaker Oats," and on boxes of lye. But the proper
companion for him is the *witch* of story; while, curiously enough, the type of the Quakeress did not crys-
talize until time gave us Elizabeth Fry, a century and
a half later.

Soon after this early period the " City Flat Caps "
became prominent, and were worn by both sexes in a
modified form.   The edict went forth that the three-
cornered minever caps for
women should not be worn
by the wives of those who
were not " gentlemen by
descent." † The little black
hood, in the Stuart period,
was getting to be thought
old-fashioned, but its be-
comingness retained it long
in popularity.   The large
" capuchins," of which we
read for many years after

Hood Worn by Cromwell's Wife.

this, were riding-hoods, very popular among the
young Quakeresses. It was probably this style of hood
whose strings annoyed the dear men Friends of South-

---

*The high-crowned hats and point-lace aprons in which the " Merry
Wives of Windsor " are often shown, belong properly to the seventeenth
century and not the fifteenth. The pointed hat is still the stock property
of old women to the present day.

†Georgiana Hill, " History of English Dress." Vol. I., p. 226.

wark Meeting, London, in 1707, by dangling down on
their heads when hung on the rail above. These " capuchins " were ample enough for storm garments, and, indeed, belonged properly under that head.* The meeting records say:

> It being taken notice of that several women Friends at the
> Park Meeting do usually hang their riding-hoods on the rail of
> the gallery, whereby the Friends that sit under the rail of the
> gallery are incommoded, It's left to Robert Fairman and Mary
> Fairman to take order for remedying the same.†

The " capuchin " came into this country as a fashionable hooded cloak early in the eighteenth century, and
shared its popularity with the smaller " cardinal," a
similar garment or hood, so named because the original
was of scarlet cloth, like the mozetta of a cardinal.
The capuchin (named from its resemblance to the garment distinguishing the monks of that order) was worn
by high and low, rich and poor, plain and gay; and the
Friends talked unhesitatingly about their " capuchins "
and " cardinals," when nothing would have induced
them to mention the " heathen " days of the week, or
the months of the year! Such things do even " consistent " Friends come to when they seek a literal
gospel.

The old hood came with the Pilgrims into New England, and for two centuries was worn by high and low.
The subject of covering the head had been receiving
the attention of the Puritan divines, and they exceeded

---

* Other varieties of these were, " hongrelines," " cabans," " royales,"
" balandras," " houppelandes," " mandilles," " roquets," etc. Quicherat,
" Histoire de Costume en France," p. 458.

† Beck and Ball, " History of London Friends' Meetings," p. 227.

the Quakers in their notice of such matters. It must at no time be thought that the Quakers were alone in their extreme care for the dress of their constituency. The Puritan clergymen preached more about bonnets and hats than ever the Quakers did ; and their opinions were very varied. For instance, Mr. Davenport, at New Haven, preached that the men, upon the announcement of the text, should remove their hats and stand up; Mr. Williams, un-

Cromwell's Time.
(After Repton.)

der whose care was the flock at Salem, Massachusetts, exhorted the women of his congregation to wear veils during public worship, quoting Scripture precedent, of course; while a brisk discussion took place between Cotton and Endicott, at Boston, on the 7th of March, 1633, at the " Thursday Lecture," as to whether all women should veil themselves when going abroad. Mr. Cotton argued that, as by the custom of the place, veils were not considered in New England a sign of the subjection of women, they were in this case not commanded by the Apostle. Endicott took the other side, demanding the proper covering of the head, particularly in time of worship. Soon after, at Salem, Cotton preached so effectively, that one Sabbath day sermon sufficed to convince his female hearers of the correctness of his attitude, and the veil did not become customary.*

---

* Dr. Dexter, " As to Roger Williams," p. 31.

A sumptuary law of James II., in Scotland, ordains, " That noe woman come to the kirk or mercat [market] with her face mussled, that sche may nocht be kend, under the pane of escheit of the curchie." * There were many minds.

The World, a periodical for 1753, contains a letter condemning the ladies for wearing their hats in the churches during divine service, as transgressing against the laws of decency and decorum. At the arraignment of Ann Turner before the King's Bench in 1615, for the murder of Sir Thomas Overbury:

The Lord Chief Justice told her that women must be covered in the church, but not when they are arraigned, and so caused her to put off her hat; which being done, she covered her hair with her handkerchief, being before dressed in her hair, and her hat over it.†

In 1726, an advertisement in the *Boston News Letter* of September relates the loss of a hood:

On the Sabbath, the 28th of August last, was taken away or Stole out of a Pew at the Old North Meeting House, A Cinnamon Colour'd Woman's Silk Camblet Riding-Hood, the head faced with Black Velvet.

We are tempted to hope the " cinnamon colour'd woman " got her hood back again ! ‡

The hat was a fashionable rival to the hood, and both men and women alike appeared in felt, beaver and castor hats. The earliest variety of the Puritan hat knew no difference for the two sexes. A " straw hatt " left in the will of Mary Harris, of which Mrs. Earle tells us, was a great rarity in New London in the year 1655, and would have been so equally in London itself

* Percy Soc. Vol. XXVII., p. 77.
† Archæologia. Vol. XXVII., p. 61.
‡ W. R. Bliss, " Side Glimpses from the Colonial Meeting-house."

at the same date. We should much like to know what might have been the shape of the " Ladies Newest Fashion White Beaver Riding-Hats," advertised for sale in Boston in 1773. They had been called an "affectation " by all but the ultra-fashionable. Pepys, the ever-watchful, notices one of the earliest hats with commendation. " I took boat again," he says, " being mightily struck with a woman in a hat that stood on the key." * By degrees the tall, steeple-crowned hats became relegated to the country women, and the poorer class in the towns. Ward, speaking of an assembly of " fat, motherly flat-caps," at Billingsgate, says:

Their chief Clamour was against High heads and Patches; and said it would have been a very good Law, if Queen Mary had effected her design and brought the proud Minks's to have worn High Crowned Hats instead of Top-Knots.†

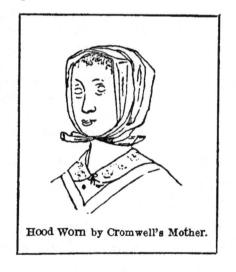

Hood Worn by Cromwell's Mother.

Elizabeth, the mother of Cromwell, sacrifices no taste to her Puritanism, but wears a handkerchief with broad point lace, and a green velvet " cardinal," the hood just described as affected by the Quaker women. A lady of rank, in Paris, in 1664, is shown in a hood of the same style. Indeed, in these stormy Puritan times, some peo-

---

* Pepys' Diary, June 11th, 1666.

† Misson, *London Spy.* Quoted by Ashton. See also letters of Mme. de Sévigné for a description of her daughter's hair, as arranged by Martin, court hair-dresser.

ple came to regard plain dress as an affectation,
put on just as the French ladies at the court of
Marie Antoinette all took to playing dairymaid.
Still another hood for riding was the "Nithesdale" of
the early eighteenth century. No garments were more
popular than this and the "cardinal" among the young
Quakeresses, as letters of the period testify.

THE RIDING-HOOD.

Let traitors against kings conspire,
Let secret spies great statesmen hire,
Nought shall be by detection got,
If women may have leave to plot;
There's nothing clos'd with bars or locks
Can hinder nightrayls, pinners, smocks,
For they will everywhere make good,
As now they've done the Riding-hood.

Oh thou, that by this sacred wife,
Hast saved thy liberty and life,
And by her wits immortal pains,
With her quick head hast sav'd thy brains:
Let all designs her worth adorn,
Sing her anthem night and morn,
And let thy fervent zeal make good,
A reverence for the Riding-hood.*

The song, of which these are the last two stanzas,
was composed after the battle of Preston, when Sir
William Maxwell, Earl of Nithesdale, and a supporter
of the house of Stewart, was taken prisoner. He was
tried and sentenced to death. By the skill of his
Countess, who disguised him in her dress and large
hood, he escaped from the Tower the evening before
the sentence was to have been executed, and died in

---

* Percy Society. Vol. XXVII., p. 207.

Rome in 1744. The pluck of the heroic Countess was celebrated throughout England, and the hood which so largely contributed to the success of the disguise, became thereafter known as the " Nithesdale."

The " mob " was a rather slovenly undress, always spoken of disparagingly. There were advertised " Women's laced Head-Cloths," commonly called " Quaker's Primers," and " Dowds." * The later turbans of the " Cranford " ladies will at once come to mind, although this formidable headdress was for elaborate and state occasions as well. A beautiful painting in the Louvre by Sir Thomas Lawrence of J. Angerstein and his wife, shows the turban at its best. From the first quarter of the eighteenth century until the period of the French Revolution, ladies' headdress underwent rapid and appalling changes. A satirical pamphlet (quoted by Quicherat) names " coiffures à la culbutte " and " à la daguine "; in 1750 we find them " en dorlette," " en papillon," " en équivoque," " en vergette," " en désespoir," " en tête de mouton." Mademoiselle Duthé is described as wearing " un bonnet de conquête assurée! " Changes were made with lightning rapidity. A despairing beau in the *London Magazine*, in April, 1762, wrote:

Then of late, you're so fickle that few people mind you;
For my part, I never can tell where to find you!
Now dressed in a cap, now naked in none,
Now loose in a mob, now close in a Joan:
Without handkerchief now, and now buried in ruff;
Now plain as a Quaker, now all of a puff.†

---

*Ashton, " Social Life in the Reign of Queen Anne," p. 134.
†From " A Repartee," *London Magazine*, April, 1762.

A "Lavinia" unbleached chip hat, trimmed with white sarsenet ribbon, was shown in 1810.   The white satin cap underneath was supplemented with an artificial rose in the front of the bonnet.   The ladies at this time all talked about the arrangement of their "hind" hair, which was often worn "à la Grecque," the other half into which the "hind" hair was divided, being down the back in fascinating ringlets!   Jane Austen, the novelist, wrote her sister Cassandra from London in 1811:

"Lavinia" chip hat for walking; trimmed with white sarsenet ribbon, 1819.

> I am sorry to tell you that I am getting very extravagant and spending all my money. . . . Miss Burton has made me a very pretty bonnet and now nothing can satisfy me but I must have a straw hat of the riding-hat shape.

Not long before she had written:

> I am quite pleased with Martha and Mrs. Lefroy for wanting the pattern of our caps; but I am not so well pleased with your giving it to them. Some wish, some prevailing wish, is necessary to the animation of everybody's mind; and in gratifying this, you leave them to form some other which will not probably be half so innocent. . . . Flowers are very much worn, and fruit is still more the thing. . . . I cannot help thinking that it is more natural to have *flowers* grow out of the head than *fruit*. What do you think on that subject?*

There were "conversation" or "cottage" bonnets, of straw or chip.   The style was really a modified coalscuttle; "the most fashionable straw bonnets for the

---

* *O. F. Adams, "The Story of Jane Austen's Life," pp. 69–151.*

promenade are the *conversation cottage,* which have
have been much distinguished for their negligent neatness!" The "mountain" hat also enjoyed large proportions. In 1808, straw hats and bonnets were only
used in walking or morning costume. In carriage or
evening dress, the hair was worn with veils, flowers,
lace handkerchiefs or similar light attire.

Ann Alexander, an English Friend, who was
in America in 1805, is said by the daughter of
the Friend who was her hostess in this country, to
have taken her bonnet to pieces in order to turn the
silk, when, to the surprise of the American, the English woman's plain bonnet was discovered to have had
a foundation of *straw.*

The "commode," already described, was a pon-
derous headdress, with such a place in history and
literature that its adventures would fill a volume.
Its banishment took a special edict on the part of
Queen Anne.* But the Quakeresses do not seem
generally to have fallen a prey to its enchant-
ments. With its departure it again became possible to dress the hair low. During its reign hats,
which began to appear, some of them in turban shape,
had had no more connection with the head than the
" chapeau bras " of the men. At one time hat *brims*
only were worn to shade the eyes, a whole hat on such
a structure being manifestly a work of supererogation!

But through it all the hood in some form still remained. A popular cap for indoors at this time was the
" fly-cap," in shape like a butterfly, edged with garnets
and brilliants. The ladies at home also wore the " cor-

---

* The name *commode* does not appear to have been used in America.

nette," a little hood with long ends made of a strong gauze called " marli," or even of baptiste. They were later the constant wear of the peasant women about and after 1730. In this class the hood negligé was without ends. The " bagnolette " was an outdoor protection,

"Cornette."

Composed of tulle, quilling of blonde around face, bunch of flowers on top. Style is French, " simply elegant and becoming " !

October, 1816.

something on this order. In France it was the " capeline sans bavolet." * It was really the old coif of Louis XIV.'s time, worn on the back of the head, and without anything at nape of neck. The old cape worn by elderly ladies became the mantelet. This was for cold weather, while the mantilla was a summer garment worn like a long fichu, thrown over the head and knotted on the breast. The mantilla and mantle must not be con- founded. The latter was often a large furred pelisse, buttoned from top to bottom in front, and affording perfect protection. There were broad-brim straw hats in the early days of Queen Anne, and for holidays the high-crowned hat of beaver still had some vogue.† The straw hat came in as early as the reign of James II. (1685 to 1688), and the hoods for a short time were dis- carded, to be revived again under French influence in 1711. Pepys says: " They had pleasure in putting on straw hats, which are much worn in this coun- try." At this time there was a feeble return to sim- plicity, and one writer says: " The ladies have been

---

* Quicherat.
† Ashton, " Social Life in the Reign of Queen Anne," p. 248.

moulting, and have cast great quantities of lace, ribbons, and cambric." Swift writes to Stella: "May 19th. 1711; There is a mighty increase of dirty wenches in straw hats since I knew London." *

It is interesting to note that in America, as long as the negro women were slaves, they were forced by their mistresses to wear the bandanna head-handkerchief as the badge of their servitude. When the Civil War set them at liberty this detested badge was cast off, and the many tails and curious knots peculiar to the true African style appeared, as Mr. Bliss says, " the real inheritance of ancestral taste in chignons, straight from Guinea!" There were many names for the varieties of hood in England, for as many years, and the old ballads and broadsides have helped to preserve these. For instance, "Fine Phillis," printed in 1745, but much older in date, has the following:

> She's a fine lady,
>   When she's got her things on;
> On the top of her head
>   Is a fine burgogon—
> A crutch there on the side
>   To show her off neat,
> And two little confidants
>   To make it compleat.

The bourgoigne was that part of the headdress nearest the head—the " crutch " (cruche) and " confidants " were curls. The hoods were " shabbarons " (chaperon) and " sorties "; the latter, a walking hood. Cardinals and capuchins have been described. " Rayonnés " were hoods pinned in a circle, like sunbeams.

---

* Journal to Stella.

The dress of Anne of Cleves, when brought to England to marry Henry the Eighth, is thus described as to the headdress:

She had on her head a kall [caul] and over it a round bonet or cappe set ful of orient pearle of a very proper fassyion, and before that she had a cornet of black velvet and about her necke she had a partlet set full of riche stones which glistered all the felde.*

The " pinched cap " seems to have been a favorite matter of allusion to characterize the Quaker women by many of the old contemporary writers. Tom Brown, who lived certainly until 1704, and who, of course, had little but derision for the Quakers, says: " What have we here? Old Mother Shipton of the second edition, with amendments; a close black hood over a pinched coif, etc." The " Querpo hood " † worn chiefly by the Puritans and plainer people, was also a Quaker peculiarity after it was discarded by the worldly. Ned Ward, in a dialogue between a termagant and her miserly husband, makes her say:

No face of mine shall by my friends be viewed
In Quaker's pinner and a Querpo hood.

The first mention that Mrs. Earle finds of bonnets in any records of New England is in the year 1725, when two were sent to England in the wardrobe of Madame Usher. By 1743 they were popular, and the middle of the century saw bonnets of many shapes—" Sattin," " Quilted," " Kitty Fisher," " Quebeck," " Garrick,"

---

*Quoted by Repton, Archæologia, XXVII., p. 37.

†" Querpo " was a corruption of the Spanish *Cuerpo,* signifying close fitting. An undress. The body " in querpo "—*i. e.,* in body-clothing—close. See Hudibras:

" Exposed in querpo to their rage
Without my arms & equipage."

" Prussian," " Ranelagh," and others. They were of " plain and masqueraded newest fashion crimson, blue, white and black." There is no hint of the shapes, unfortunately. We are told of the Puritan women in a certain congregation, that " ye women may sometimes sleepe and none know by reason of their enormous bonnets. Mr. White doth pleasantlie saye from ye pulpit hee doth seeme to be preaching to stacks of straw with men among them ! " In 1769, in Andover, it was " put to vote whether the Parish Disapprove of the Female sex sitting with their Hattes on in the Meeting House in time of Divine Service as being Indecent " (with a capital I!). The " Hattes " were ordered off, but with no more effect than if the meeting house had been a modern theatre!

The calash, invented by the Duchess of Bedford in 1765 was so much more like a buggy-top, or covering to a gig, both in form and size, that it can hardly be termed a bonnet, except that to cover the head was its sole function.

It was made of thin green silk shirred on strong lengths of rattan or whalebone placed two or three inches apart, which were drawn in at the neck; and it was sometimes, though seldom, finished with a narrow cape. It was extendible over the face like the top or hood of an old-fashioned chaise or calash, from which latter it doubtless received its name. It could be drawn out by narrow ribbons or bridles which were fastened to the edge at the top. The calash could also be pushed into a close gathered mass at the back of the head. Thus, standing well up from the head, it formed a good covering for the high-dressed and powdered coiffures of the date when they were fashionably worn—from 1765 throughout the century; and for the caps worn in the beginning of this century. They were frequently a foot and a half in diameter. . . . They were seen on the heads of old ladies in country towns in New England certainly until 1840 and possibly later. In England they were also worn until that date, as we learn from Mrs. Gaskell's "Cranford" and Thackeray's "Vanity Fair." *

The "punkin" hood was the winter mate to the calash in New England, quilted with rolls of wadding, and drawn tight between the rolls with strong cording. It was very heating to the head.

The caps of the women in this country by the middle of the eighteenth century were in great variety. "Fly caps" appear here also. "Round ear'd caps" had no strings; "strap caps" had a band passing under the chin. A little boy, aged eight years, wrote to his Quaker grandmother:

Burlington, 12 mo. 23, 1833.—Mother wears long-eared caps now, and I think they look better than the old ones. She has worn them a considerable time now, and I have got quite reconciled to the change.

His mother at this time was about thirty-five.

"Bugle fly-caps" were worn in Pennsylvania in 1760. Mob caps are described by Mrs. Earle as a "caul with two lappets," and as we may learn from many old portraits, were much worn. The "mobs" were no doubt the streamers which gave the name to the cap, and their undue length proved a source of uneasiness to the Quakers. The mob cap is most familiar to us in the portraits of Martha Washington, and it is undoubtedly the English original of her cap which furnished the pattern for the familiar type of head dress worn by Elizabeth Fry and Amelia Opie. The milkmaids of London on a May-Day were a sight, in yellow

---

* Alice Morse Earle, "Costume of Colonial Times," p. 72.

I. *Martha Washington, Silhouette.*

II. *Amelia Opie, 1769-1853*

Engraved by Lightfoot, from the medallion done in Paris by David.

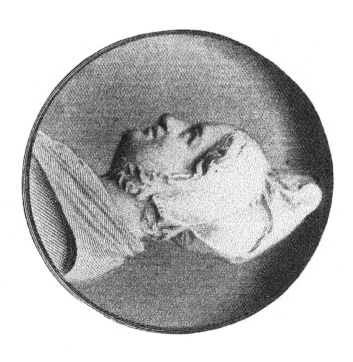

and red quilted petticoats, pink and blue gowns, mob caps with lace ends, and flat straw hats with lace lappets, named for Peg Woffington.*

From this time on we find some form of the hat always present. The wide style of hair dressing permitted a lower hat or cap; and at one time fashionable women wore countrified straw hats. Grosley (early George III.) says of Lord Byron's trial: " Many ladies had no other headdress but a riband tied to their hair, over which they wore a flat hat adorned with a variety of ornaments." This hat had a " great effect." " It affords the ladies who wear it that arch roguish air which the winged hat gives to Mercury." † Close caps, ridiculed as " night-caps," literally hoodwinking the wearer, were born in 1773, and three styles of hair dressing are quoted for that year: " A slope bag with no curls, the front toupée brought high and straight; a long bag with about six curls," or " the hair straight with about nine curls crossways." Small chip hats were added. But the universal cap, once worn by young as well as old, was going out; and by June, 1795, at the Royal Birthday festivities not a cap was to be seen. The last hood had disappeared five or six years earlier, and the hat and bonnet had the field. We are told of " bewitching straw hats with open brims tied under the chin, worn in summer; and straw hats so

1786.

---

* Hill, "History of English Dress," Vol. I., p. 182.
† Ibid., Vol. II., p. 50.

round and close as to look like caps, with which dainty
little white veils were worn half way over the face."
Bonnets had been enormous, the tremendous " poke "
having come in with French fashions after the French
war. This was the bonnet of which Moore wrote:

> That build of bonnet whose extent
> Should, like a doctrine of Dissent,
> Puzzle church-goers to let it in;—
> Nor half had reached the pitch sublime
> To which trim toques and berets climb;
> Leaving, like lofty Alps that throw
> O'er minor Alps their shadowy sway,
> Earth's humbler bonnets far below,
> To poke through life their fameless way.

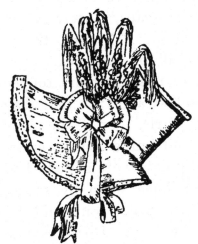

Parisian Promenade Hat. 1816.

Bonnets had fallen back to more decent dimensions
after the French revolution, and hats received a round
form that justified their Parisian name of " chapeaux
casques." *　London still remained for a time the para-

---

* " Le Cabinet des Modes " rejoicingly said, " Nos mœurs commen-
cent à s'épurer : le luxe tombe."

dise of the "high head," and ostrich feathers and plumes had yet a vogue. The bonnet, indeed, had hardly a fair chance, for the towering coiffures made it

1776.

not only unnecessary, but almost impossible. The *Times*, in 1794, says "The ladies' feathers are now generally carried in the sword-case at the back of the carriage." A little later came a paragraph as follows:

There is to be seen on Queen Street a coach on a new construction. The ladies sit in a well, and see between the spokes of the wheels. With this contrivance, the fair proprietor is able to go quite dressed to her visits, her feathers being only a *yard and a half high!*

With the entrance of the nineteenth century came a simpler coiffure, and white satin and black velvet hats were worn on the lowered hair. It was now the ladies' turn to wear hats indoors, and they danced and dined and appeared at functions in their hats, just as they car-

ried white muffs for evening dress. A silver bear muff
in 1799, in Philadelphia, cost $14.00, one of grey bear
$19.00.

Snuff-taking was not unusual among refined people.
There are plenty of references to the old-fashioned
Quaker women of the South indulging in a bed-time
pipe, and we may be sure that the more fashionable
" snuffed." In Puritan New England a clergyman
held forth against mitts, calling them " wanton, open-
worked gloves slit at ye thumbs and fingers for ye purpose of taking snuff ! " Dolly Madison, the favorite
and adored of society in America, was an ardent snuff-
taker. " You are aware that she snuffs, but in her
hands the snuff-box seems a gracious implement with
which to charm."

All Paris wore hats indoors. Then came the formidable turban, to which reference has already been
made, destined later to become the cap. At this period
even young girls wore caps; and up to 1845 " day-
caps," with ribbon ends as long as bonnet strings, and
tied under the chin, were worn. As the styles seem
always to have been calculated for elderly women, it
may be fancied what an effect they had on a young
face ! The bonnets of 1850 were round and flared wide
in front, permitting the cap below to be seen. Then a
frill was substituted for the cap, which then and there
had its death blow, for the young, at least. England is
still eminently the land of caps, so far as the older
ladies are concerned. Miss Hill describes " black lace
bonnets with a cape or curtain at the back, worn over a
hood made of white lawn tied under the chin "—a fashion surviving in the bonnets with white frilled front

worn in the middle of the nineteenth century, and still occasionally met with among old-fashioned people.

Fairholt has given us a beautiful old Scotch version of "The Garment of Gude Ladies," belonging to the fifteenth century, which describes such a lady's head-dress as might be the Quaker ideal:

> Would my gude lady lufe me best
> And wark after my will,
> I suld ane garment gudliest
> Gar mak hir body till.*
> Of hé honour suld be hir hud,†
> Upon hir heid to wear;
> Garniest ‡ with governance so good,
> Na demyng suld hir deir.§

It has seemed necessary thus to dwell upon the history of the worldly bonnet, in order the better to follow the progress of that of the Quaker. We may thus trace the succession of the latter's changes. First came the plain hood, together with the pointed high hat surmounting a similar hood; the two styles almost contemporary, and, at least with those not Quakers, often significant of class distinctions. Then came the adoption by degrees, and with many compunctions of conscience, of the hat and bonnet in varying form. The line of descent is quite evident from the time of the "capuchin" and "cardinal" or other form of hood, which among the worldly, served as an outdoor dress in the day of the "high-head," down to the end of the

---

* Cause to be made for her.

† Of high honor should be her hood.

‡ Garnished.

§ No opinion should dismay her—cause her to fear censure. Percy Society, XXVII., p. 59.

eighteenth century. The Quakers simply retained it
through all the mutations of fashion, until the introduction of the bonnet, the flat hat having kept parallel
with it until the evolution of the bonnet of Quakerism
in the last century. Why the flat hat should have
seemed more plain to the dear Friends, than the small
and modest affair at first introduced as the " bonnet,"
it would puzzle us to determine. But the real bonnet
was not accepted by the Friends without many misgiv-
ings; and the women of Aberdeen, always careful of
the letter of the law, thus cautioned their younger
members in the year 1703:

"As touching Bonnets—it is desired that a question
be moved at the Quarterly Meeting whether any should
be worn, yea or nay." And the meeting thus put itself on record on this momentous question; that
" though they might be lawful, it was not expedient to
wear them ! " *

Can anything be more delicious than this verdict?

Priscilla Hannah Gurney was one who long retained
the old-fashioned black hood, which gave much character to her appearance. So late as 1818, Katherine,
daughter of Elizabeth Fry, remembered this ancient
Quakeress relative, who had had great influence upon
her famous mother. Priscilla Gurney was the daughter of Joseph and Christiana Barclay. She is described
as slight in build, and elegant in figure and manner,
dressing in the hood, to which reference has been made,
long after it had been discarded by others. It is probable that the plain Quaker bonnet has been an evolu-

---

* Minutes of Aberdeen Monthly Meeting, 4 mo., 1703.

tion from the original flat hat of beaver of the middle
of the eighteenth cen-
tury. The bonnet one
degree less plain, with
a square crown, and
gathers, instead of
pleats, would seem to
be the lineal descend-
ant of the peculiar hat-
like bonnet worn by

18th Century Flat Hat.

the " Fair Quaker " of our engraving. It is probably that against which Aberdeen took exception
as " not expedient," and marks a transition period
in bonnets in the world, as well as in the ranks
of Quakerism. But the history of the flat hat is
of great interest. Specimens of these still exist,
and it is from one of these that our illustration
is taken. The thought of putting on the worldly
construction from Paris may have alarmed the plain

Bonnet of Martha, wife of Samuel
Allinson, of Burlington, N. J.;
died 1823. No strings, one
large box pleat in soft
crown.

Quakeress under her broad
hat a century ago. But who
could have foreseen, in the
dip of the brim that she gave
to her flat hat by tying its
strings under her chin, the
evolution of the present bonnet? The dip eventually be-
came secured by permanent strings; a soft crown or
cape was added to the resulting cylinder, and the " creation " was complete! The illustrations are from
contemporary articles, showing the evolution of the

hat into the bonnet, and the change from the first soft crown that was tentatively added to the uncompromising five stiff pleats of the Quaker bonnet in its highest development.

Watson, the annalist of Philadelphia, says: "The same old ladies whom we remember as wearers of the white aprons, wore also large white beaver hats, with scarcely the sign of a crown, and which was confined to the head by silk cords tied under the chin." A recent writer * tells the following tale, which was related to him by an aged relative, to the effect that she remembered "a distinguished female preacher sitting in the ' gallery ' of a country meeting house in summer, with one of these broad, flat, dish-like white beavers on her head, when a cock, flying in through the low, open window, behind the ' gallery,' and perhaps mistaking the hat for the head of a barrel, perched upon it and uttered a vigorous crow !"

In the year 1786, Ann Warder, who came out at that date from London to join her husband at Philadelphia, went up into the country to attend the funeral of her old friend, Robert Valentine. She was asked, very much to her consternation, to sit in the "ministers' gallery," but made her escape. "I felt so conscious of being higher than I ought to be, intirely among *Cloth Hats*," she wrote, "that I beg'd to return near the Door with the excuse it would be cooler." * Those beaver hats were to the Quaker of the eighteenth century what the plain bonnet, technically so called, has

---

* R. M. Smith, " The Burlington Smiths," p. 157.

† MS. Journal of Ann Warder, 1786–1789.

been to the nineteenth century Quaker. Yet one who should now appear in Arch Street Meeting, Philadelphia, wearing that strange garb of other days would be looked at askance, and hardly admitted into full standing, any more than a certain Irish Friend, who not long since appeared, wearing the dress of William Penn. Indeed, George Fox and William Penn would themselves find a very dubious welcome, if that welcome depended either on their dress or their methods!

A Friend in a Southern Quarterly Meeting in Carolina early in the nineteenth century sent up to Philadelphia, then the center of Quaker fashion, for a black plain bonnet, laying aside her beaver hat. For this proceeding, and its evidence of what the Friends were pleased to regard as her hopeless worldliness, she was severely " dealt with " by the officers of her meeting. There were heart burnings, we may be sure, over bonnets then, even if they were not worldly, and an old family letter written by my grandmother in 1829, says: " —— had a great deal to say on the inroads of fashion, etc., and spoke so particularly as to mention the young women having one kind of bonnet to wear in the streets, and another to meeting. This is very generally the case, I believe." We may be glad to think that the modern young Quakeress has no such temptations to hypocrisy. The same writer adds, a short time later, " A plain young man is hardly to be found anywhere now, and Susan B—— says plain hats are hardly even asked for now. I mean bonnets, for all are called hats here." This was in New York, in 1830.

A painting of Gracechurch Street Meeting, London, about 1778, shows a large assemblage in a pillared hall, whose dignity and dimensions are quite imposing. It is lighted solely from the roof. The men sit on one side, the women on the other, both in rising seats and on the main floor. Some of the women wear the newly-introduced bonnet, like that of the " Fair Quaker," and others wear the flat beaver or " skimming-dish " hat, in some cases tied down over the ears; in others, not. A few of the older women wear hoods. Many of the men are in wigs, and all wear cocked hat, skirt-coat, and knee-breeches. All wear their hats, except the preacher, whose cocked hat hangs on a peg in the wall behind him. Groups of the " world's people " look down upon the worshiping Friends from the galleries above, each group apparently accompanied by a plain Friend who sits with them. This picture is very interesting, as showing the period of transition to the plain bonnet, and fully demonstrating the extent to which the cocked hat and wig were worn among the Quakers during the height of that fashion. It is worth noting that the seats all have the luxury of backs—not a common thing by any means in the meetings of the day.

A Dutch engraving entitled, "Assemblée des Quakers à Amsterdam—Un Quaker qui prêche," shows a plain room lighted from a dome in the ceiling. The hard benches, without backs, are occupied by men in full skirted coats, wigs and cocked hats. They carry enormously long canes, fastened to the wrist by a cord. A few worldly men standing as spectators in the background, wear swords. The hat-brims of two men

A painting of Gracechurch Street Meeting, London, bout 1778, shows a large assemblage in a pillared all, whose dignity and dimensions are quite imposing. t is lighted solely from the roof. The men sit on one ide, the women on the other, both in rising seats and n the main floor. Some of the women wear the newly-ntroduced bonnet, like that of the "Fair Quaker," and others wear the flat beaver or "skimming-dish" hat, in some cases tied down over the ears; in others, not. A few of the older women wear hoods. Many of the men are in wigs, and all wear cocked hat, skirt-coat, and knee-breeches. All wear their hats, except the preacher, whose cocked hat hangs on a peg in the wall

Gracechurch Street Meeting,

London, 1776.

Original painting in Devonshire House collection, London.

the cocked hat and wig were worn among the Quakers during the height of that fashion. It is worth noting that the seats all have the luxury of backs—not a common thing by any means in the meetings of the day.

A Dutch engraving entitled, "Assemblée des Quakers à Amsterdam—Un Quaker qui prêche," shows a plain room lighted from a dome in the ceiling. The hard benches, without backs, are occupied by men in full skirted coats, wigs and cocked hats. They carry enormously long canes, fastened to the wrist by a cord. A few worldly men standing as spectators in the background, wear swords. The hat-brims of two men

stiffened in the ... Mrs. Lucock of
ont-road, Plymouth, who is 84 years of age, is
call with undiminished pride and satisfaction

From the original in the "Aurora Borealis," published

Friends are not cocked. The women, plain and gay alike, wear hoods, and many of them crinoline. The date of the picture is much earlier than the preceding.

A lovely picture of a young Quakeress, called " The Bride," published originally in the *Aurora Borealis,* a literary annual of Newcastle-upon-Tyne, in the year 1833, shows a sweet young woman in cap and handkerchief, her shawl lightly thrown over her shoulders, and her plain bonnet lying on the table beside her. The cap is an exaggeration of that of Martha Washington, and the bonnet, it will be observed, has a soft crown. That worn by the Queen, in August, 1849, on the Royal Yacht, in Kingston Harbor, has a similar shape, except that it is probable that the Queen's was somewhat stiffened in the crown. Mrs. Lucock, of Beaumont-road, Plymouth, who is 84 years of age, is able to recall with undiminished pride and satisfaction the fact that she once made a bonnet for the late Queen in an early year of her reign. Mrs. Lucock was at the time a young woman employed in a London business which had the orders for the Royal bonnets, the size and shape of which gained for them the name of " coal-scuttles." It is an impressive lesson to one who thinks that the Quakers have cut their clothes by their rule of conscience, and always worn the same style of garment, to examine the cuts and modes in a Parisian fashion journal of 1840-1849, called " Le Conseiller des Dames," from one of which our plate is taken. There our Friend may see the plain bonnet of to-day, exactly reproduced for the ladies of fashion, and worn by Queen Victoria, with only the ostrich plume to betoken any

difference existing between Quaker and worldly. **The
young Quakeresses of the middle of the nineteenth cen-**
tury were given to wearing silk and satin bonnets of
very delicate light colors, pearl gray and a rose pink
being favorites. The quilled bonnets, and those with
a plain front and gathered crown, both now adhered to
in Philadelphia, and considered plain, may here be seen
in their beginning, and that the modification for every
bonnet has had its inspiration in Paris, there seems no
possible doubt. It has been with the Quaker bonnet, as
with every other garment the Quaker has ever worn:—
the cut has originated in that center of all ideas of fashion, and the abode of taste, Paris; while the expression
of Quakerism lay simply in the absence of any superfluous adornments. In this one idea lies the secret of
Quaker dress. Anything that has tended to pervert
this into a uniform, unchanging and arbitrary, has been
directly counter to the true spirit of simplicity and
meekness which characterized the early Friends.

Sarah Dillwyn, the wife of the well-known Quaker
preacher, George Dillwyn, wrote to her sisters in
America, upon her arrival in London, early in the year
1784:

My G. D. said he did not wish me to look singular, and my
bonnet was much so ... so out she went and bought some nice thin
"mode" such as they wear, and made it presently herself; she
would have me wear a cloak of hers with a hood, as the plainest
of them do. . . . She had on a quilled round hat of gauze, white
shade, and I think, a cream-coloured dress, but not so bedizened
as I've seen some;—and a little round hoop. The girls did not
look tawdry; ... Neither of them answers George Fox's description; *he paints high!**

---

* J. J. Smith, " Letters of the Hill Family," p. 247.

r dress. *Anything that has* tended to per
to a uniform, unchanging and arbitrary, has b

After an engraving by Freeman. London, 1837.

y, as our exacts are scarcely ...

r word, and although the ...

the great ... Conseiller des Dames, Paris.

Fashion Plate, about 1840.

Mary Holgate was a plain bonnet maker in Philadelphia two generations ago. Her finger became injured through making the hard pleats in the bonnet crowns, and she lost the use of her hand. This incident, together with the retirement of the popular bonnet-maker, caused in that city a much greater use of bonnets with the more easily made gathered crowns, since which period these bonnets have received the sanction of the plainest wearers. This style of bonnet has been referred to as the "shun-the-cross." An aged Friend of the latter half of the eighteenth century, when a young girl, promised her father on his death-bed that she would never put on the stiff-pleated plain bonnet, then beginning to be worn, and considered very gay, as our extracts have abundantly shown. She kept her word, and although she was a plain Friend and lived to the great age of ninety-four, she never flinched in her determination to keep her promise, although the flat bat that was the substitute made her very conspicuous, at a period when the stiff-pleat had become correct for the most severe. Finally, after having made a solitary appearance at a certain western meeting for many years, wearing that conspicuous headdress, she determined that she could still keep her promise to her father, and be less conspicuous, by wearing an unconventional bonnet of her own invention. A green lining which she put in it when well advanced in years rather surprised her friends; but she informed them that it was a "relief to her eyes in the sunshine." Her granddaughter had a green wool gown which she feared her grandmother might regard as too gay. When

questioned about it, her grandmother said, " No harm
in wearing green and blue; the grass is green, and the
sky is blue ! "   She died in 1857, having moved from
the South to Ohio, then called " Northwest Territory,"
about 1803. Some interesting old Quaker bonnets may
be seen in the collection of ancient garments at the
Museum in Nantucket, Massachusetts.   A Quaker bon-

ENGLISH BONNET.

net of black silk, of the date 1728, has small stiff pleats
in the crown; while one of drab, dating from the Revolution, has much larger stiff pleats, showing the development of the present Philadelphia " plain " bonnet,
known in New England as the " Wilburite " bonnet.
There is also in the same collection, one labeled " English " bonnet, distinguished chiefly by a wider flare to

the front. The English bonnets seem always to have had a shorter front, and a wider flare at the face; in fact, to have had a much more sensible shape, if comfort was to be considered at all, as it evidently was not in America! Nothing more dangerous could have been devised for an elderly person whose sight or hearing was somewhat defective than the long tunnel sides of the pasteboard front of a plain bonnet of the nineteenth century.

Ann Warder, whose journal has already been quoted, was remonstrated with by an intimate friend for wearing a "whalebone" bonnet, because of its greater worldliness than one of pasteboard, as the early plain bonnets were always called. We should be glad to know what the condemned bonnet was like. Quite probably the lining was of some bright color, and the "casing" or "drawn" bonnet is no doubt its natural successor. Apropos of the "pasteboard" bonnets, we may read in *Poulson's Daily American Advertiser* for Saturday, August 23d, 1828, among the Philadelphia advertisements, the following notice: "Bonnet-boards—50 groce of good quality at a low price, and a few groce of fine quality." They were for sale by James Y. Humphreys, at 86 South Front Street. Doubtless these were the foundations, for the fronts of both worldly and plain bonnets consisted of pasteboard forms, over which the silk or other covering was stretched, resulting in the "poke" or the "coal-scuttle" as might happen. The same interesting Warder Journal, which went in instalments to an English sister in London, has the following entry:

September, 1788. [Ann Warder had no dread of the "heath-en" names of the months.] I put no cloak on this forenoon, but was obliged to afterward, not to look singular, for some had long ones lined with Baize down to there toes, but no hoods, instead of which a lay-down coular [collar] which would look very dis-agreeable to me but for the Cape to there Bonnets, hiding the neck. Black are worn more here than with us;—no Brown ex-cept Cloth.

This was at Yearly Meeting time, then in the au-tumu, to prepare for which she had written just before:

9mo. 22.—This forenoon I sat pretty close to my needle, in some degree preparing for Yearly Meeting, wishing to want noth-ing in the Cap or Apron way that week.

The thieves that she mentions as having broken into the house during the previous week, made off, among other things, with " a new white Myrtle gown, a petti-coat, apron, boots, J's new white hat and two old ones." The " Cape to there Bonnets, hiding the neck," was that of the " wagon " bonnet, so called from its resem-blance to the top of a " Jersey " wagon; they were usually of black silk, and had a pendant piece of the same from the back of the bonnet, covering the shoul-ders. The " wagon " bonnet antedated the " coal-scuttle," still lingering among us. It was the style worn by Rebecca Jones, of Philadelphia, the friend of John Woolman.

But the plain bonnet had its intricacies, and it is not for the stranger to learn them in a day. Like the stars, one bonnet differeth from another in glory. Eventually, modifications of the extreme conservative crept in; and we have the popular close bonnet, with fine gathers rather than pleats, and a shorter front, which allows itself a furtive bow under the square crown, and which is found in the more modern shades of blacks and browns, rather than the original drabs and grays, called long ago by an irreverent young Friend, the "shun-the-cross" bonnet. It daily grows harder to discern social differences in congregations by means of the once infallible test of hats and bonnets. Even among the worldly, the distinction of class dress

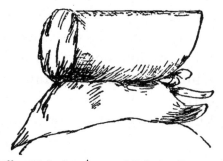

Bonnet from doll model of costume of Rebecca Jones, of Philadelphia; died 1817. Dressed by "Sally Smith," of Burlington, N. J. Soft gathered crown, large cape with three points—one on each shoulder and one in center of back.

is nearly or quite obliterated. It is therefore a surprise to find a sect in Pennsylvania who "disown" at the present day for gaiety of attire—a thing not known now among Friends for many years.*

The plain bonnet, too, has had its romance. In the

---

* *The Public Ledger* for November 1, 1899, had the following remarkable notice:

"BARRED FROM CHURCH BY HAT

"Miss May Oller, of Waynesboro, . . . who lately returned from a trip to the Holy Land, has been expelled from the Antietam German Baptist Dunkard Church for discarding the plain bonnet for a pretty creation of the milliner's art. At a meeting of the church authorities in July, Miss Oller was notified that she must return to the wearing of the bonnet, and that she would be given until October to put away her hat. . . . Although the defence was set up that the annual meeting had made the wearing of a hat or bonnet discretionary, Miss Oller's expulsion was ordered by a large majority. . . . Miss Oller is the daughter of the late Bishop Jacob F. Oller."

days when it concealed youth and beauty, and the broad-brim had to bend, in order to see within its depths, hearts were warm and faces gay, even in sober garb; and the old story was whispered just the same in the long tunnel of the bonnet. The little street urchins were once said to have chased a beautiful Quakeress some distance down the street of one of our great cities, in order to run around in front and peep up at the lovely laughing eyes that met their admiring glances. One young bride is said to have threatened to cut a slit in the side of her bonnet, in order to be able to see her new husband when driving beside him on their way to meeting! Are we not to suppose that his sentiments might have been those of the Quaker friend of Wendell Phillips, as he sat quietly thinking to himself:

> My love's like a red, red rose
> That's newly blown in—*the Sixth Month!*

Then, too, the crashing kiss of two full-fledged Quaker bonnets is something awe-inspiring to contemplate. The bonnets collide at top speed; occasionally they have been known to telescope, when the rescue is effected by a third party. The usual result, however, is to send each bonnet far back on the head of the wearer, since the front projects some inches beyond the face —when a necessary pause for readjustment follows, infinitely funny to a spectator blest with a sense of humor.

Now the Quaker philosophy of costume is essentially in the direction of plainness and moderation. But the study we have been making shows us how contrary to the true spirit of Quakerism the technical bonnet, for instance, really is. Adopted in the days of decadence of spirituality, when life was easy, and time permitted infinite attention to details, the bonnet became literally a snare, a fetish, a sort of class distinction, at one time almost as exclusive in its work as the mark on the forehead of the high caste Brahmin. That day is effectually past; the modern Quakeress has now but the tradition to preserve of the outward shell, and must address herself to far greater moral problems. She must, nevertheless, like Charles Lamb, who loved the Quakers, endeavor to " live up to that bonnet."

Politics and religion have alternately determined the style of women's headdress. In the days of Charles James Fox, the women of his way of thinking wore a fox tail in the hat or bonnet. To-day, as we pass along the street, the nun, the Quaker, the Dunkard, and the Salvation Army girl are the only types left where the doctrine of the wearer may be read at a glance. To the initiated, the Quaker bonnet once spoke volumes; a glance sufficed to distinguish Beaconite, Wilburite, Maulite, Gurneyite, or Hicksite, and the dwellers in the Mesopotamia of the East. But time has leveled distinctions here as elsewhere ; and manifestations of doctrinal difference are sought to-day, with more regard for truth, in the heart rather than on the head.

The venerable Margaret (Fell) Fox, eight years after her husband's death, raised her voice in warning against legal conformity, seeing in the society for which she had done and suffered so much a tendency

altogether contrary to the spirituality of the Gospel.
From her published epistles we extract the following:

Legal ceremonies are far from Gospel freedom; let us beware of
being guilty or having a hand in ordering or contriving what is
contrary to Gospel freedom; for the Apostles would not have
dominion over their faith, but be helpers of their faith. It is a
dangerous thing to lead young Friends much into the observation
of outward things, which may easily be done, for they can soon
get into an outward garb to be all alike outwardly, but this will
not make them true Christians.

Epistle from M. Fox to Friends, 4 mo., 1698.

"Wilburite."   1856.   "Gurneyite."

INDEX.